Fodor's 93 Cape Cod, Martha's Vineyard, Nantucket

Candice Gianetti

Fodor's Travel Publications, Inc.
New York•Toronto•London•Sydney•Auckland

Fodor's Cape Cod, Martha's Vineyard, Nantucket

Editor: Jillian L. Magalaner
Editorial Contributors: Phil Joseph, Marcy Pritchard, Malcolm Wilson
Creative Director: Fabrizio La Rocca
Cartographer: David Lindroth
Illustrator: Karl Tanner
Cover Photograph: Catherine Karnow/Woodfin Camp

Design: Vignelli Associates

About the Author

Candice Gianetti is a freelance writer and editor who lives on Martha's Vineyard.

Special Sales

Contents

2 Portraits of Cape Cod, Martha's Vineyard, and Nantucket

Foreword

For their help in putting together this guide, the author wishes especially to thank Michael Frucci at the Cape Cod Chamber of Commerce, Frank Ackerman at the Cape Cod National Seashore, Randi Vega at the Martha's Vineyard Chamber of Commerce, and Maurene Stepp at the Nantucket Chamber of Commerce.

While every care has been taken to ensure the accuracy of the information in this guide, the passage of time will always bring change, and consequently the publisher cannot accept responsibility for errors that may occur.

All prices and opening times quoted here are based on information supplied to us at press time. Hours and admission fees may change, however, and the prudent traveler will avoid inconvenience by calling ahead.

Fodor's wants to hear about your travel experiences, both pleasant and unpleasant. When a hotel or restaurant fails to live up to its billing, let us know and we will investigate the complaint and revise our entries where the facts warrant it. Send your letters to the editors of Fodor's Travel Publications, 201 E. 50th Street, New York, NY 10022.

Highlights '93 and Fodor's Choice

Highlights '93

Two months after August 1991's Hurricane Bob wreaked havoc on the Cape and islands, an unnamed **October nor'easter** caused even more damage. Whereas the hurricane got the south side of the Cape, the storm caused wholesale shoreline erosion on the eastern, Atlantic side, as well as the loss of National Seashore stairways and Race Point's bathhouse (all since replaced) and much of Nauset Light Beach's parking lot. (In many cases, the 15- to 20-foot tidal surges have actually created wider beaches by leveling the dunes and carrying the sand out.) Also lost was about 40% of the as-yet unexcavated sections of the archaeological dig at Coast Guard Beach.

On Nantucket, the October storm cut a quarter-mile breach through a section of dunes and beach called the Galls, and the 8-foot-deep channel cut off Great Point, including the lighthouse, for months; more than 3 miles of primary dune were devastated. Martha's Vineyard and the Army Corps of Engineers continue to struggle with the massive erosion of Oak Bluffs's Beach Road, between Sengekontacket Pond and the ocean, intensified by the August and October storms. On Chappaquiddick, dune loss will be repaired through snow fencing, though the process will take years.

Like the weather, air travel to the Cape and islands has always been unpredictable, and in these difficult times it is not less so. A bright spot is the expanded operations of a local airline, **Cape Air.** In late 1991 it absorbed **Edgartown Air,** and since then it has been busily becoming indispensable to the area. Joint fares and ticketing-and-baggage agreements with many major airlines help ease travel preparations and bridge the gap in winter service left by the pullout in 1991 of Continental from year-round service.

In other transportation news, Hyannis will be getting a new **Steamship Authority terminal.** The structures are expected to cost about $4 million; the land, $4.5 million. Work is set to begin when all the permitting is completed, around 1994, and be finished the next year.

In Hyannis, an exhibit of **photographs from John F. Kennedy's Cape Cod years** was installed in the old town hall on Main Street as an intermediate step while fundraising continues toward a local JFK Museum. The photographs, which span the years 1934 to 1963, have been culled largely from the collection of the John Fitzgerald Kennedy Library in Boston. Two of the Cape's longtime tourist attractions have been closed as a result of the deaths of their owners: the **Seth Nickerson House,** Provincetown's oldest structure, and Brewster's **Drummer Boy Museum,** dedicated to bringing the history of the American Revolution to life.

Some historic Nantucket buildings got a boost in 1992. At the 1845–6 **Hadwen House,** a two-year project to restore the interior to its look at the height of the whaling era is under way. The c. 1740 **Macy-Christian House,** closed for years, was reopened to the public. Boston's Museum of Afro-American History is spearheading a fundraising effort to turn the 19th-century **African Meeting House,** at the intersection of York, Pleasant, and Atlantic avenues, into a staffed exhibit space documenting the African-American experience on the island.

On Martha's Vineyard, the Agricultural Society acquired 21 acres at the West Tisbury Panhandle in 1992, planning at some point in the near future to build a **new agricultural hall** to replace the current 133-year-old structure — a local landmark — and expand the fairgrounds in which the county fair is traditionally held. Meanwhile, the venerable **Alley's General Store,** next door, was closed after the summer of 1992 for a major overhaul before reopening in summer 1993. Oak Bluffs and Edgartown both got new, much needed **visitor centers** in 1992 — Oak Bluffs' in a Victorian gazebo near the Flying Horses carousel, Edgartown's in the old police station on Church Street. In April 1992 the old **Seamen's Bethel** was moved from its location near the Steamship Authority wharf in Vineyard Haven to the grounds of the hospital, ending a century of service at the waterfront location. Another departure in 1992 was the **Windfarm Museum,** which closed after 14 years of teaching alternative agricultural technologies to visitors and summer interns.

On Cape Cod, lots of restaurant-industry news: The **Cranberry Moose** in Yarmouth Port has metamorphosed into **Abbicci,** under the same management but with a new, modern look and a contemporary Italian menu. **La Cipollina** in Yarmouth Port folded its tent after many years of popularity; its building was quickly snapped up by **Inaho,** formerly in a little storefront in Hyannis. Chatham's **Queen Anne Inn** has entered into a five-year arrangement with Brewster's renowned Chillingsworth, which now operates the inn's restaurant as well as its own, though along quite different lines. **East Bay Lodge** in Osterville was bought out of receivership by new owners, who have totally revamped both restaurant (now first class, with an excellent wine cellar) and accommodations. New owners at the **Sea Crest** resort in Falmouth took the October 1991 storm damage to its beachfront restaurant and accommodations as an opportunity to revamp and refresh its facilities, includings its ocean-view restaurant.

Other new Cape Cod tourist facilities include **New Seabury** resort's health club, a café at **Heritage Plantation** in Sandwich, and two exciting developments in summer entertainment: the opening of the **Coconuts Comedy Club** in Hyannis, with comics from the cable channels, and an ambitious concert series by Provincetown's **Club Euro,** featuring major international world-music bands. **First Night Cape Cod,** a New Year's arts festival and celebration embracing the towns of Falmouth, Hyannis, Orleans, and Provincetown, was inaugurated in 1991–2; daytime activities along historic Route 6A were added for 1992–3.

The passage of the 1992 **Americans with Disabilities federal law** meant that the already above-average accessibility levels on the Cape and islands have been further improved; the focus of work here is on telecommunications. Yarmouth has a new **disabled-accessible pier** at the end of Bass River on Nantucket Sound.

Some final developments of interest to tourists: What are seen as **American Express's** exorbitant charges to retailers lost the company many outlets, while the **Discover** card seemed to conquer the Cape and islands. New regulations further limit **vehicle access to Nantucket's beaches,** including a year-round ban at Dionis Beach; a summer ban at Jetties; and a daytime ban in summer at Cisco, Madaket, Surfside, and 'Sconset. And on Martha's Vineyard, a new **Elderhostel** live-in program began in 1992, including quilting weekends, two-week poetry workshops, and a week for chamber musicians, as well as programs on the culture, environment, and history of the Vineyard.

Fodor's Choice

No two people will agree on what makes a perfect vacation, but it's fun and helpful to know what others think. We hope you'll have a chance to experience some of Fodor's Choices yourself on Cape Cod, Martha's Vineyard, and Nantucket. For detailed information about each entry, refer to the appropriate chapter.

Special Moments

Sunset Jeep rides through the Provincetown dunes

Watching fireworks from the Oak Bluffs green, Martha's Vineyard

A community sing at the Oak Bluffs Camp Ground, Martha's Vineyard

Glimpsing Nantucket town as you approach by ferry

Lunch in the rose garden of Chanticleer, Nantucket

Stargazing from Nantucket's Loines Observatory

Sights

Bright purple cranberries floating on the flooded bogs just before harvest, Cape Cod and Nantucket

The old New England scene of the waterwheel-powered Dexter Gristmill on Shawme Pond in Sandwich

Hallet's Store, a century-old drugstore in Yarmouth Port

The marsh life at Bass Hole Boardwalk, Yarmouth Port

Harbor seals off Race Point in winter, Provincetown

Whales breaching alongside your whale-watch boat

The candy-colored Victorian cottages of the Oak Bluffs Camp Ground, Martha's Vineyard

Nantucket's cobblestone streets and historic architecture

The moors of Nantucket in fall

Museums

Heritage Plantation, Sandwich

Julia Wood House, Falmouth

Old Atwood House and Museums, Chatham

Dukes County Historical Society, Edgartown, Martha's Vineyard

Whaling Museum, Nantucket

Viewpoints

From the Pilgrim Monument, Provincetown, of the town and surrounding waters

From the Province Lands Visitor Center observation deck, for a 360° panorama of duneland and ocean

From Nobska Light, Woods Hole, of the Elizabeth Islands and Martha's Vineyard across the sound

From Chatham Light, of the "Chatham Break"

From Scargo Hill, Dennis, of the lake and town below and of ocean and bay beyond

From Gay Head Cliffs, Martha's Vineyard, of the cliff striations and the Elizabeth Islands across the sound

From First Congregational Church, Nantucket, for the best view of Nantucket's moors, ponds, streets, and lighthouses

Nature Areas

Cape Cod National Seashore

Monomoy Wildlife Refuge, off Chatham

Nickerson State Park, Brewster

Wellfleet Bay Wildlife Sanctuary, South Wellfleet

Felix Neck, Martha's Vineyard

Long Point, Martha's Vineyard

Coatue–Coskata–Great Point, Nantucket

Eel Point, Nantucket

Beaches

Nauset Light, Coast Guard, and Race Point beaches on the Cape Cod National Seashore

Sandy Neck Beach, West Barnstable

Old Silver Beach, North Falmouth

Lucy Vincent Beach, Chilmark, Martha's Vineyard

South Beach, Martha's Vineyard

Surfside Beach, Nantucket

Eel Point, Nantucket

Shopping

The weekly flea market at the Wellfleet Drive-In Theatre

Farmer's markets on Martha's Vineyard

Farm stands everywhere

Route 6A on Cape Cod for crafts and antiques

Provincetown, Wellfleet, and Nantucket for art

Cape Cod Mall, Hyannis

Eldred's auction house, East Dennis

Rafael Osona auction house, Nantucket

Tree's Place, Orleans, for crafts and art

Scargo Pottery, Dennis

Janis Aldridge, Nantucket, for beautifully framed antique prints

Lightship baskets on Nantucket

Nantucket-theme rugs by Claire Murray, Nantucket

Art Galleries

Long Point, Provincetown

Provincetown Art Association and Museum

Blue Heron Gallery, Wellfleet

Granary Gallery, West Tisbury, Martha's Vineyard

Robert Wilson Galleries, Nantucket

Taste Treats

Clam chowder at The Flume, Mashpee

Fried clams at Baxter's, Hyannis

Cioppino at Roadhouse Cafe, Hyannis

Portuguese kale soup at Land Ho!, Orleans, or The Moors, Provincetown

Ice cream at Four Seas, Centerville

Fresh, sweet bay scallops in fall and winter

Dining

Chillingsworth, Brewster (*Very Expensive*)

Regatta of Falmouth-by-the-Sea (*Expensive*)

The Paddock, Hyannis (*Moderate–Expensive*)

Nauset Beach Club, Orleans (*Moderate*)

Up the Creek, Hyannis (*Inexpensive–Moderate*)

L'étoile, Edgartown, Martha's Vineyard (*Very Expensive*)

Lambert's Cove Country Inn, West Tisbury, Martha's Vineyard (*Expensive*)

Zapotec, Oak Bluffs, Martha's Vineyard (*Moderate*)

Topper's, Nantucket (*Very Expensive*)

Club Car, Nantucket (*Expensive*)

The Hearth at the Harbor House, Nantucket (*Moderate*)

Le Languedoc bistro, Nantucket (*Inexpensive–Moderate*)

Lodging

Chatham Bars Inn, Chatham (*Very Expensive*)

Captain's House Inn, Chatham (*Expensive*)

Wedgewood Inn, Yarmouth Port (*Expensive*)

Mostly Hall, Falmouth (*Moderate*)

Old Sea Pines Inn, Brewster (*Inexpensive–Moderate*)

Charlotte Inn, Edgartown, Martha's Vineyard (*Very Expensive*)

Lambert's Cove Country Inn, West Tisbury, Martha's Vineyard (*Expensive*)

Sea Spray Inn, Oak Bluffs, Martha's Vineyard (*Inexpensive*)

Wauwinet, Nantucket (*Very Expensive*)

White Elephant, Nantucket (*Very Expensive*)

Harbor House, Nantucket (*Expensive*)

Cliff Lodge, Nantucket (*Moderate*)

Corner House, Nantucket (*Inexpensive–Moderate*)

Children's Activities

Aqua Circus of Cape Cod, West Yarmouth

Pirate's Cove minigolf, South Yarmouth

Water Wizz Water Park, Wareham

Vineyard Playhouse and Actors Theater of Nantucket children's events

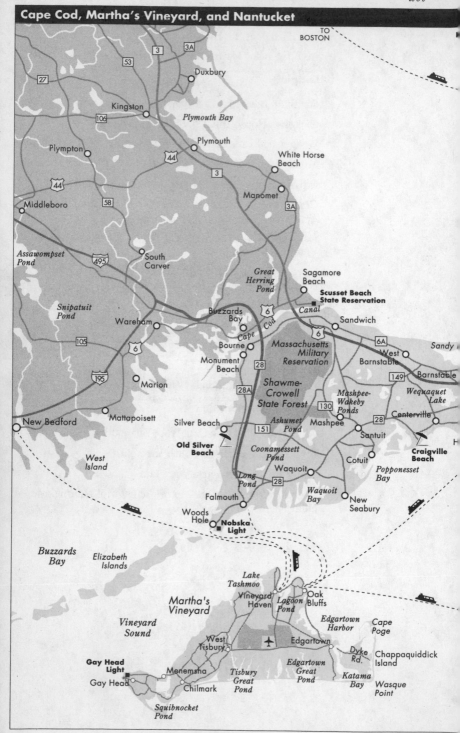

Cape Cod, Martha's Vineyard, and Nantucket

TO BOSTON

Duxbury

53

3

3A

27

Kingston

Plymouth Bay

106

Plympton

Plymouth

White Horse Beach

44

3

Middleboro

58

Manomet

3A

Assawompset Pond

495

South Carver

Great Herring Pond

Sagamore Beach

Scusset Beach State Reservation

Snipatuit Pond

Wareham

Buzzards Bay

Cape Cod

Canal

6

Sandwich

6

6A

West Barnstable

Sandy

105

6

Bourne

Cape

28

Massachusetts Military Reservation

149

195

Monument Beach

28A

Shawme-Crowell State Forest

Mashpee-Wakeby Ponds

130

Barnstable

Wequaquet Lake

Marion

Centerville

Mattapoisett

Silver Beach

Ashumet Pond

151

Mashpee

28

Santuit

Old Silver Beach

Craigville Beach

New Bedford

West Island

Coonamessett Pond

Waquoit

Cotuit

Popponesset Bay

Long Pond

28

Waquoit Bay

New Seabury

Falmouth

Woods Hole

Nobska Light

Buzzards Bay

Elizabeth Islands

Lake Tashmoo

Vineyard Haven

Lagoon Pond

Oak Bluffs

Martha's Vineyard

Vineyard Sound

West Tisbury

Edgartown Harbor

Cape Poge

Edgartown

Dyke Rd.

Chappaquiddick Island

Gay Head Light

Menemsha

Tisbury Great Pond

Edgartown Great Pond

Katama Bay

Wasque Point

Gay Head

Chilmark

Squibnocket Pond

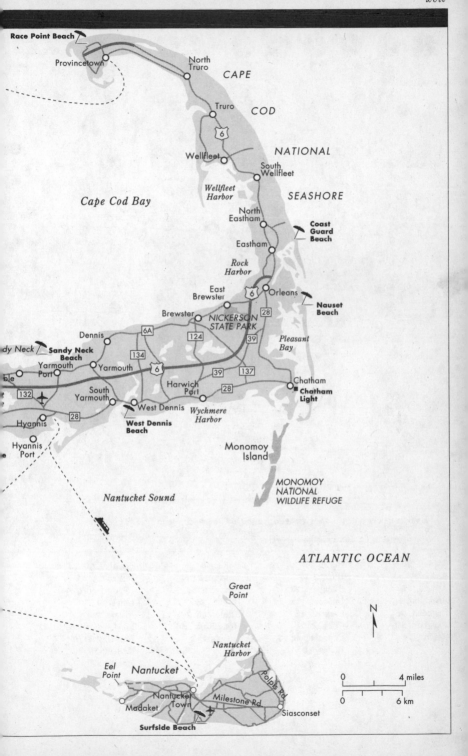

Race Point Beach

Provincetown

North
Truro

CAPE

Truro

6

COD

Wellfleet

South
Wellfleet

NATIONAL

Cape Cod Bay

*Wellfleet
Harbor*

SEASHORE

North
Eastham

**Coast
Guard
Beach**

Eastham

*Rock
Harbor*

East
Brewster

6

Orleans

**Nauset
Beach**

Brewster

*NICKERSON
STATE PARK*

28

Dennis

6A

124

39

*Pleasant
Bay*

dy Neck

**Sandy Neck
Beach**

134

Yarmouth
Port

Yarmouth

6

ble

132

South
Yarmouth

Harwich
Port

39

137

Chatham

**Chatham
Light**

28

Hyannis

28

West Dennis

**West Dennis
Beach**

*Wychmere
Harbor*

Hyannis
Port

Monomoy
Island

Nantucket Sound

MONOMOY
NATIONAL
WILDLIFE REFUGE

ATLANTIC OCEAN

Great
Point

N

*Nantucket
Harbor*

*Eel
Point*

Nantucket

Madaket

Nantucket
Town

Milestone Rd

Polpis Rd

Siasconset

0   4 miles

0   6 km

Surfside Beach

World Time Zones

MONDAY
SUNDAY

International Date Line

+12 +13   -9

+11   +12

Numbers below vertical bands relate each zone to Greenwich Mean Time (0 hrs.).
Local times frequently differ from these general indications,
as indicated by light-face numbers on map.

| +11 | +12 | -11 | -10 | -9 | -8 | -7 | -6 | -5 | -4 | -3 | -2 |

Algiers, **29**
Anchorage, **3**
Athens, **41**
Auckland, **1**
Baghdad, **46**
Bangkok, **50**
Beijing, **54**

Berlin, **34**
Bogotá, **19**
Budapest, **37**
Buenos Aires, **24**
Caracas, **22**
Chicago, **9**
Copenhagen, **33**
Dallas, **10**

Delhi, **48**
Denver, **8**
Djakarta, **53**
Dublin, **26**
Edmonton, **7**
Hong Kong, **56**
Honolulu, **2**

Istanbul, **40**
Jerusalem, **42**
Johannesburg, **44**
Lima, **20**
Lisbon, **28**
London (Greenwich), **27**
Los Angeles, **6**
Madrid, **38**
Manila, **57**

xix

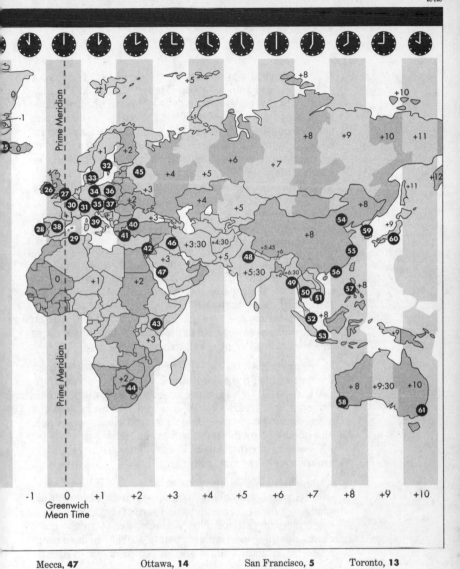

-1   0   +1   +2   +3   +4   +5   +6   +7   +8   +9   +10

Greenwich
Mean Time

Mecca, **47**	Ottawa, **14**	San Francisco, **5**	Toronto, **13**
Mexico City, **12**	Paris, **30**	Santiago, **21**	Vancouver, **4**
Miami, **18**	Perth, **58**	Seoul, **59**	Vienna, **35**
Montréal, **15**	Reykjavík, **25**	Shanghai, **55**	Warsaw, **36**
Moscow, **45**	Rio de Janeiro, **23**	Singapore, **52**	Washington, D.C., **17**
Nairobi, **43**	Rome, **39**	Stockholm, **32**	Yangon, **49**
New Orleans, **11**	Saigon (Ho Chi Minh	Sydney, **61**	Zürich, **31**
New York City, **16**	City), **51**	Tokyo, **60**	

Introduction

The world to-day is sick to its thin blood for lack of elemental things," wrote Henry Beston in his 1928 Cape Cod classic *The Outermost House,* "for fire before the hands, for water welling from the earth, for air, for the dear earth itself underfoot." It is this that the Cape and its neighboring islands most have to offer an increasingly complex and artificial world: the chance to reconnect with elemental things. Walking along the shore, poking among the washed-up sea life or watching birds fish in the surf, listening to the rhythm of the waves, experiencing the mystery and tranquillity of night on the beach or the power of a storm on water — all this is somehow strengthening and life-affirming and utterly, satisfyingly real.

Cape Cod — a craggy arm of a peninsula 50 miles southeast of Boston — and the islands of Martha's Vineyard and Nantucket share their geologic origins as debris deposited by a retreating glacier in the last ice age. They also share a moderate coastal climate and a diversity of terrain that foster an equally diverse assortment of plant and animal life, some of which exist nowhere else in northern climes.

Barrier beaches (sandbars that protect an inner harbor from the battering of the ocean), such as Monomoy on the Cape and Coatue on Nantucket, are breeding and resting grounds for a stunning variety of shore and sea birds, and the marshes and ponds are rich in waterfowl. Stellwagen Bank, just north of Provincetown, is a prime feeding grounds for whales and dolphins, and shallow sandbars are favorite playgrounds for harbor and gray seals.

Among the flotsam and jetsam along the shores beachcombers find horseshoe crabs, starfish, sea urchins, sponges, jellyfish, coral, and a plethora of shells: white quahogs, elegant scallops, blue mussels, long straight razor clams, spiraling periwinkles, pointy turret shells, smooth round moon snails, conical whelks, rough-ridged oysters.

Much of the land, including a third of Nantucket's acreage and a quarter of the Vineyard's, is protected from development. Nature preserves encompassing pine forests, marshes, swamps, cranberry bogs, and many other varieties of terrain are laced with well-marked walking and bicycling trails. On Nantucket, acres of moorland are spread with a rough tapestry of gnarled scrub oaks, low-lying blueberry bushes, fragrant bayberry, bearberry, and heather (the last originally brought to Nantucket from Scotland by accident in a shipment of pine trees).

Thanks to the establishment of the Cape Cod National Seashore in 1961, one can walk for almost 30 miles along the

Atlantic beach virtually without seeing a trace of human habitation — besides a few historic shacks in the dunes of Provincetown, or the lighthouses that stand watch over the Cape's dangerous shoals. Across dunes anchored by hearty poverty grass sprawl beach plums, pink salt-spray roses, and purple beach peas.

Through the creation of many National Historic Districts — in which change is kept to a minimum to preserve the historical integrity of the area — similar protection has been extended to the Cape and islands' oldest and loveliest manmade landscapes. One of the most important, as well as most visually harmonious, is along the Old King's Highway, where the Cape's first towns — Sandwich, Barnstable, and Yarmouth — were incorporated in 1639. Lining this tree-shaded country road are simple saltboxes from the earliest days, fancier houses built later by prosperous sea captains, and the traditional Cape cottages, shingles weathered to a silvery gray, with soft pink roses spilling across them or massed over low split-rail fences. Here, too, are the white-steepled churches, taverns, and village greens that savor of old New England, as well as some of the Cape's many windmills.

Practically the entire island of Nantucket is part of its historic district. A rigid enforcement of district guidelines has created a town architecturally almost frozen in time, and one of the world's great treasures. Among the neat clapboard and weathered-shingle houses that line its cobblestone streets and narrow lanes are former warehouses, factories, and mansions dating back to the golden age of whaling.

Most recently, Provincetown was designated a historic district, preserving for posterity its cheerful mix of tiny waterfront shops (former fish shacks) and everything from a 1746 Cape house to a mansarded French Second Empire to an octagonal house.

Besides the districts, the Cape and islands preserve their past in a wealth of small museums — nearly every town has one — that document local history, often back to Indian days. (In 1620, when the Pilgrims first anchored at Provincetown, exploring the Cape before heading on to Plymouth, an estimated 30,000 Wampanoags lived on Cape Cod.) Often set in houses that are themselves historic, these museums provide a visual history of the lives of the English settlers and their descendants, including their economic pursuits: from farming, to the harvesting of salt, salt hay, and cranberries (still an important local crop), to fishing and whaling, to tourism, which began as far back as the late 19th century.

The importance of whaling to the area — Nantucket was the world's premier whaling port in the early to mid-19th century, and it was a Yarmouth man who taught Nantucketers how — is reflected in the historical museums. The travels of the area's whaling and packet-schooner seamen and captains are illustrated with such items as antique nautical equipment, harpoons, charts, maps, journals, scrimshaw created during the often years-long whaling voyages, and gifts brought back from exotic ports for wives who had waited so patiently (those who *had* waited, that is — some women chose to go along with their husbands for the ride).

A number of museums have a specific focus — for example, Nantucket has a wonderful one dedicated to whaling. The area's first documented trading post has been re-created in Bourne on its original site. Provincetown and Nantucket have museums on the U.S. Life Saving Service. Brewster has a whole complex of exhibits on firefighting and apothecaries. Chatham has a train museum, Sandwich doll and car museums, Mashpee an Indian museum.

The economies of the Cape and the islands are extremely dependent on tourism, and most options in tourist facilities can be found. Lodgings range from no-frills guest houses and motels to antiques-and-lace bed-and- breakfasts to full-service resort hotels on the beach; families can opt for waterfront condominiums, minimalist cottages in the woods, or ultraluxurious summer homes with breathtaking ocean views. Restaurants include rustic, nautical-motif fish houses as well as elegant gourmet restaurants (a specialty of Nantucket) and everything in between. Dining can be a romantic experience, with views of dramatic sunsets over water, or a gathering of family and friends at wharfside picnic tables to devour fried clams.

All three areas are noted for interesting shopping (for crafts, art, and antiques especially); for lots of theater, both small community groups and professional summer stock; and for plenty of recreational offerings that take advantage of the marine environment, including water sports, fishing charters, and even Jeep safaris to isolated beaches for surfcasting. All are also family oriented — especially the Cape, which has endless amusements to offer children beyond the ever-beckoning beach. There are also such typical New England entertainments as chowder suppers and clambakes.

Cape Cod is the area most suffering from overdevelopment. Massive growth in tourism in years past led to construction of tacky roadside motels, nightmare stretches of wall-to-wall tourist magnets along Route 28, and the megabuildup of Hyannis. Also, getting over the bridges that join the Cape to the mainland can be misery at peak weekend times in summer. But wise planners can avoid that problem, as they can avoid the built-up areas and stick to the many still-charming areas if they choose. Within its 70-mile span, the Cape offers a broad spectrum of vacation experiences: picturesque old New England towns, an extraordinary scientific community at Woods Hole, the frenetic shopping and people-watching former art colony of Provincetown, the tamer art-gallery town of Wellfleet, and quiet cottage communities with little more than a clam shack and a general store to divert one's attention from the beach.

Nantucket, about 12 miles by 3, is reached by plane or a two-hour ferry ride, and its remoteness appeals to those seeking escape. It has just the one town, plus a small beachside village of rose-covered cottages that once housed an actors' colony. Large tracts of undeveloped moorland and nature preserves give the island an open, breezy feel. It has long been a summer bastion of the quietly wealthy, who are likely to be seen dressed down to the hilt and tooling around on beat-up bicycles.

Martha's Vineyard, on the other hand, is known as the celebrity island, for its star summer residents in the arts and entertainment who participate in the annual Celebrity Hat Auction and other high-visibility charitable events. Nantucketers tend to think of their sister island as glitzy, which it could be called only in comparison. About 20 miles by 10, the Vineyard offers more variety than Nantucket: Its six towns range from a young and rowdy seaside town of Victorian cottages to a rural New England village to an elegant, well-manicured town of sea captains' homes and flower gardens. The landscape, too, is more varied, including a 4,000-acre pine forest, rolling farmland enclosed by dry stone walls, and dramatic clay cliffs.

Both islands are ringed with beautiful wide, sandy beaches, some backed with high or low dunes, others with moorland, others bordering marshes. Either Martha's Vineyard or Nantucket can be profitably visited in a day trip from a Cape Cod base but will well repay a longer stay.

The season" used to be strictly from Memorial Day to Labor Day, but the boundaries have blurred; many places now open in April or earlier and close as late as November, and a core remain open year-round. Unfortunately, most of the historic sites and museums, largely staffed by volunteers, still adhere to the traditional dates and so are inaccessible in the off-season.

Each of the seasons invites a different kind of visit. In summer, you have your choice of plunking down somewhere near a beach and never moving, filling your schedule with museums and activities, or combining the two in whatever mix suits you. In fall, the water may be warm enough for swimming as late as October, crowds are gone, and prices are lower. Turning foliage, though nothing like the dramatic displays found elsewhere in New England, is still an enjoyable addition to a fall visit; it reaches its peak around the end of October. Moors turn purple and gold and rust; burning bush along roadsides flames a brilliant red. Cranberries ripen to a bright burgundy color and are harvested by a method fascinating to watch. Trees around freshwater marshes, ponds, and swamps tend to color earlier and brighter; the red maple swamps, Beech Forest in Provincetown, and

Route 6A from Sandwich to Orleans are particularly colorful spots.

Fall and winter are oyster and scallop season, and the restaurants that remain open feature a wide selection of dishes made with the freshly caught delicacies. Winter is a quiet time, when many tourist-oriented activities and facilities shut down, but prices are low and you can walk the beaches in often total solitude. For a quiet or romantic weekend getaway, country inns offer cozy rooms with canopy beds, where you can curl up before the fireplace after returning from a leisurely, candlelit dinner. The Chatham Bars Inn in Chatham offers theme weekends, such as wine tasting or swing dancing, that can make for a festive winter break. On Martha's Vineyard, the Harbor View Hotel also offers winter mystery and other theme weekends in attractive transportation-plus packages.

As for spring, it gets a bit wet, and on Nantucket expect a good dose of fog. Still, the daffodils come bursting up from roadsides, especially on Nantucket, and everything begins to turn green. By April, seasonal shops and restaurants begin to open, and locals prepare for yet another summer.

1 Essential Information

Before You Go

Visitor Information

Cape Cod Chamber of Commerce (junction of Rtes. 6 and 132, Hyannis 02601, tel. 508/362–3225) will send free general information and a directory of accommodations. Let them know if you're interested in a particular town or activity; they will provide more detailed information or pass your request on to the local chambers, which also provide brochures. (For a list of local chambers, *see* Essential Information in Chapter 3, Cape Cod.)

The **Martha's Vineyard Chamber of Commerce** (Box 1698, Vineyard Haven 02568, tel. 508/693–0085) and the **Nantucket Chamber of Commerce** (Main St., Nantucket 02554, tel. 508/228–1700) each charge $3 for a guidebook that includes a directory of member services, a listing of events, and lots of ads. The more comprehensive *Nantucket Guide* (Box 1018, Nantucket 02554, tel. 508/228–3866) costs $5 by mail.

The following offer free information on all of Massachusetts, including the Cape and islands:

Department of Environmental Management (Division of Forests and Parks, 100 Cambridge St., Boston 02202, tel. and TDD 617/727–3180) has brochures and maps on state forests and parks, including a leaflet on camping.
Department of Food and Agriculture (100 Cambridge St., 21st floor, Boston 02202, tel. 617/727–3018) has information on agricultural fairs, farmer's markets, and pick-your-own apple, strawberry, and vegetable farms.
Division of Fisheries and Wildlife (Field Headquarters, Westboro 01581, tel. 508/792–7270) offers free information on fish and wildlife laws (supply a stamped, self-addressed business-size envelope) and a list of other publications, including pond maps of the Cape and the islands.
Massachusetts Office of Travel & Tourism (100 Cambridge St., 13th floor, Boston 02202, tel. 617/727–3201 or 800/447–MASS in MA) puts out a guidebook, a calendar of events, a skiing brochure, a bed-and-breakfast guide, campgrounds listings, and a road map.

Tour Groups

If you want to see as much of Cape Cod and the islands as possible in a short time, then you might want to consider an escorted motorcoach tour. Group tours generally pack a lot of sightseeing into a relatively short time span, traversing the entire area in less than a week. This way, you're sure to hit all the traditional tourist spots and perhaps a few out-of-the-way places you might not be able to get to on your own. Keep in mind, though, that you can only spend as much time in one place as the tour itinerary allows. If freedom and flexibility are more important to you, pick up a map, decide where you want to go, plot a route, and experience the region on your own at a leisurely pace. Most major rental-car companies offer weekly rates.

When evaluating a tour, be sure to find out exactly which expenses are included (particularly tips, taxes, service charges, side trips, additional meals, and entertainment); ratings of all hotels on the itinerary and the facilities they offer; cancellation policies for both you and the tour operator; and, if you are traveling alone, the cost for a single supplement.

The following sampling of operators and packages should give you an idea of what is available. For additional resources, contact your travel agent or the sources listed in Visitor Information, above. Most tour operators request that bookings be made through a travel agent — there is no additional charge for doing so.

Brush Hill Tours (439 High St., Randolph, MA 02368, tel. 617/986–6100) runs day trips to the Cape from Boston mid-May–October, with stops in Provincetown, Sandwich, and Hyannis.

Cosmos Tourama, the budget affiliate of **Globus-Gateway** (95–25 Queens Blvd., Rego Park, NY 11374, tel. 718/268–7000 or 800/221–0090), offers a five-day tour of Boston and Cape Cod, with stops in New York, Plymouth, and Newport, June–October. Its nine-day New England Fall Foliage tour includes stops in Hyannis and Plymouth.

Country Squire Tours (668 Main St., Hyannis, MA 02601, tel. 508/771–6441 or 800/225–8051) offers eight-day New England tours including the Cape and islands, year-round.

Domenico Tours (751 Broadway, Bayonne, NJ 07002, tel. 201/823–8687 or 800/554–8687) offers three- to 11-day escorted Cape tours April–October, including visits to Falmouth, Hyannis, the National Seashore, and Provincetown. Different packages add Plymouth, a whale watch, Boston, Nantucket, Martha's Vineyard, and/or Newport.

Gadabout Tours (700 E. Tahquitz-Canyon Way, Palm Springs, CA 92262, tel. 619/325–5556 or 800/952–5068) has an 11-day tour of New England with several days on the Cape.

Maupintour (Box 807, Lawrence, KS 66044, tel. 913/843–1211 or 800/255–4266) offers six-day tours out of Boston June–September, stopping in Lexington, Concord, Sandwich, Provincetown, Martha's Vineyard, and Nantucket.

Mayflower Tours (Box 490, Downers Grove, IL 60515, tel. 708/960–3430 or 800/323–7604 outside IL) offers an eight-day New England tour out of Boston, including visits to Martha's Vineyard, Plymouth, and Hyannis.

Talmage Tours (1223 Walnut St., Philadelphia, PA 19107, tel. 215/923–7100) gives you five days on Cape Cod and Martha's Vineyard spring through fall.

Tauck Tours (Box 5027, Westport, CT 06880, tel. 203/226–6911 or 800/468–2825 outside CT) gives you one week on the Cape, Martha's Vineyard, and Nantucket June–October.

Package Deals for Independent Travelers

Amtrak (tel. 800/321–8684) offers a summer Great American Vacations package that includes train fare and Hyannis hotels.

Tips for British Travelers

Visitor Information The U.S. **Travel and Tourism Administration** (Box 1EN, London W1A 1EN, tel. 071/495–4466) has information and brochures.

Passports and Visas You need a valid 10-year passport to enter the United States (cost: £15 for a standard 32-page passport, £30 for a 94-page passport). Application forms are available from most travel agents and major post offices and from the Passport Office (Clive House, 70 Petty France, London SW1H 9HD, tel. 071/279–3434 for recorded information or 071/279–4000). You do not need a visa if you are staying 90 days or less, have a return ticket, are traveling with a major airline (in effect, any airline that flies from the United Kingdom to the United States), and complete visa waiver form I-94W, which is supplied either at the airport of departure or on the plane. If you fail to comply with any one of these requirements, you will need a visa. Apply to a travel agent or the **United States Embassy** (Visa and Immigration Department, 5 Upper Grosvenor St., London W1A 2JB, tel. 071/499–3443 for a recorded message or 071/499–7010). Visa applications to the U.S. Embassy must be made by mail, not in person. Visas can be given only to holders of 10-year passports, although visas in expired passports remain valid.

Customs Entering the United States, a visitor age 21 or older can bring in 200 cigarettes or 50 cigars or 2 kilograms of tobacco; one liter of alcohol; and duty-free gifts to a value of $100. You may not bring in meat or meat products, seeds, plants, or fruit.

Returning to the United Kingdom, a traveler age 17 or older can take home: (1) 200 cigarettes or 100 cigarillos or 50 cigars or 250 grams of tobacco (if you live outside Europe these allowances are doubled); (2) two liters of still table wine; (3) one liter of alcoholic drink over 22% volume *or* two liters of alcoholic drink under 22% volume (fortified or sparkling wine); *or* two more liters of still table wine; (4) 60 ml of perfume and 250 ml of toilet water; and (5) other goods to the value of £32 but not more than 50 liters of beer or 25 cigarette lighters.

Airports and Airlines There are no transatlantic flights directly to Cape Cod or the islands. Boston is the nearest city with an airport that handles international flights. To get from Boston to the Cape and the islands, *see* Arriving and Departing, *below.*

Flying time to Boston from all British airports is more than six hours on most flights, about four hours on the Concorde.

Three airlines fly to Boston from London Heathrow: **British Airways** (tel. 081/897–4000), **Northwest** (tel. 0345/747800), and **TWA** (tel. 071/439–0707). Northwest also has four flights a week to Boston from Prestwick, near Glasgow in Scotland. There are no flights to Boston from London's Gatwick airport.

British travelers combining a trip to New England with a visit to New York should consider flying into New York's JFK airport or the Newark airport, both of which offer more flights from Britain than Boston does. Four airlines fly to New York from London Heathrow: British Airways, TWA, American (tel. 0800/010151), and United (tel. 0800/888555). British Airways has as many as six flights a day, two on the Concorde. Three airlines fly to New York from London Gatwick: **British Airways, Continental** (tel. 0293/776464), and **Virgin Atlantic** (tel. 0293/562000); British Airways also flies to New York from Manchester, England.

Airfares vary enormously, depending on the type of ticket you buy and the time of year you travel. All of the major airlines offer APEX tickets, which must be booked in advance and have certain restrictions. Even cheaper are the cut-price tickets offered by various agencies; check out the small ads in the daily and Sunday newspapers. Ticket agencies such as Trail Finders, STA, and Travel Cuts offer good deals.

Insurance We recommend that you take out insurance to guard against health problems, motoring mishaps, theft, flight cancellation, and loss of luggage. Most major tour operators offer holiday insurance, and details are given in brochures. For free general advice on all aspects of holiday insurance, contact the **Association of British Insurers** (51 Gresham St., London EC2V 7HQ, tel. 071/600–3333). A proven leader in the holiday insurance field is **Europ Assistance** (252 High St., Croyden, Surrey CRO 1NF, tel. 081/680–1234).

Tour Operators The following is a selection of companies that offer tour packages to Cape Cod. For details of these and other resources, consult a travel agent.

British Airways Holidays (Atlantic House, Hazelwick Avenue, Three Bridges, Crawley, West Sussex RH10 1NP, tel. 0293/518022) also has a Grand New England tour that visits Cape Cod.

Cosmosair (Ground Floor, Dale House, Tiviot Dale, Stockport, Cheshire SK1 1TB, tel. 061/480–5799) features Cape Cod in a 13-day escorted coach tour of the highlights of New England.

Jetsave Travel Ltd. (Sussex House, London Rd., East Grinstead, W. Sussex RH19 1LD, tel. 0342/312033) includes four days at Cape Cod in its 15-day, self-drive holiday on the New England Trail. Cape Cod is also visited for a whale watch cruise on the 10-day Autumn Gold coach tour.

Kuoni Travel (Kuoni House, Dorking, Surrey RH5 4AZ, tel. 0306/742222) has a Grand New England coach tour with two nights on Cape Cod, and New England fly/drive tours with longer stays on Cape Cod.

North American Vacations (Acorn House, 172/174 Albert Road, Jarrow, Tyne & Wear NE32 5JA, tel. 091/483–6226) offers a 5-day coach tour of the sights on Cape Cod and Martha's Vineyard, and also has self-drive tours.

When to Go

Memorial Day through Labor Day (in some cases, Columbus Day) is high season on Cape Cod, Martha's Vineyard, and Nantucket; then you'll find good beach weather (swimming from about mid-June sometimes into October) and everything open, but also high prices, crowds, and traffic.

Spring and fall are the times to enjoy more peaceful bird walks, nature hikes, and country drives, along with lower inn and restaurant prices. Evergreens and scrub make up a good part of the area's ground cover, so the display of autumn colors is not like that in other parts of New England; still, under crisp blue skies in the clear autumn light, the Lower Cape and islands' cover of heather, gorse, blueberry, bayberry, boxberry, and beach plum resembles, in Thoreau's words, "the richest rug imaginable spread over an uneven surface." Spring, too, is beautiful, bursting with wildflowers and greening grasses, though it does arrive late and is unpredictable — on Nantucket especially, spring is often damp and foggy.

In winter, many museums, shops, restaurants, and lodging places close, especially on the islands. Many golf courses, however, remain open year-round, except when it snows (some then open their courses to cross-country skiers), and the Cape's strong community theater network continues throughout the year, as do a core of other activities. A number of intimate bed-and-breakfasts and inns — some with fireplaces, canopy beds, and well-stocked libraries and board-game collections — also remain open, and for as much as 50% off high-season rates, they make romantic retreats after a day of ice fishing, pond skating, or otherwise enjoying winter in the country. On the islands especially, though, don't come in winter looking for action.

Many towns on the Cape and islands celebrate Christmas in an old-fashioned way, with wandering carolers and bands, theatrical performances, crafts sales, and holiday house tours. Nantucket's Christmas (or Shopper's) Stroll is the best-known event (*see* Festivals and Seasonal Events, *below*). The Cape extends the season to six weeks, from Thanksgiving to New Year's, offering special packages, inn and restaurant discounts, and a full program of activities (including First Night celebrations in many towns) to promote the area as a year-round destination.

Lodging reservations are tight in summer in the whole area. The most intense tourist time is the last two weeks in July and most of August; if you come then without a hotel or inn reservation, you'll still find accommodations, but be prepared to settle for less than your first choice. Also book well in advance (several months) for a visit to Nantucket during the Daffodil Weekend, in late April, or the Christmas Stroll, the first weekend in December; many people return every year for these events, which are worth planning a trip around.

Climate Remember that though its beaches rival the best the Caribbean has to offer, the Cape is not the Caribbean and does not come with its near-guarantee of sun-filled days. Certainly there are plenty of idyllic beach days to go around, but rain or fog is not an uncommon part of even an August vacation on the Cape. Visitors who do not learn to appreciate the beauty of the land and sea in mist and rain may find themselves mighty cranky.

Temperatures in winter and summer are milder on the Cape and islands than on the mainland, due in part to the warming influence of the Gulf Stream and the moderating ocean breezes. As a rule (and there have been dramatically anomalous years), the Cape gets much less snow than the mainland, and what falls generally does not last. Still, winter can bring bone-chilling dampness, especially on the windswept islands.

The following are average daily maximum and minimum temperatures for Hyannis; it's likely to be two to three degrees cooler on the coast and on the islands.

Jan.	40F	4C	May	62F	17C	Sept.	70F	21C
	25	– 4		48	9		56	13
Feb.	41F	5C	June	71F	22C	Oct.	59F	15C
	26	– 3		56	13		47	8
Mar.	42F	6C	July	78F	26C	Nov.	49F	9C
	28	– 2		63	17		37	3
Apr.	53F	12C	Aug.	76F	24C	Dec.	40F	4C
	40	4		61	16		26	– 3

For tide information and weather and coastal marine forecasts, call 508/771–5522 or 508/255–8500.

Festivals and Seasonal Events

The Massachusetts Office of Travel & Tourism (*see* Visitor Information, *above*) offers events listings and a whale-watch guide for the entire state. Each year the June/July issue of *Cape Cod Life* magazine (*see* Further Reading, *below*) includes a Summer Leisure Guide, with a calendar of activities.

Late Apr.: Nantucket's five-day **Daffodil Weekend** (tel. 508/228–1700) celebrates spring with a flower show, shop-window displays, and a procession of antique cars adorned with daffodils that ends in picnics at Siasconset. For about five weeks from mid-April to mid-May, 2 million daffodils bloom along Nantucket roadsides and in private gardens.

Summer: From June through August, the area is busy with **summer theater, town band concerts,** and **arts and crafts fairs.**

Early June: Hyannis Harbor Festival (tel. 508/775–2201) is a free two-day celebration that includes the blessing of the fleet, boat races, entertainment, and food. **Cape Cod An-**

tique Dealers Association Annual Antiques Show at the Heritage Plantation (tel. 508/888–3300) is attended by dealers in fine 18th- and 19th-century English and American furniture, folk art, Sandwich glass, jewelry, and more.

Late June: In Edgartown's **A Taste of the Vineyard** (tel. 508/627–4440), a benefit for the Historical Preservation Society, ticket holders wander among tents set up downtown as they sample treats provided by local restaurants, caterers, and wine sellers. It's a formal evening, with dancing and an auction.

Last Sun. in June: The Blessing of the Fleet (tel. 508/487–3424) in Provincetown is the culmination of a weekend of festivities, including a quahog feed, a public dance, and a crafts show. On Sunday, a parade ends at the wharf, where fishermen and their families and friends pile onto their boats and form a procession. The bishop stands on the dock and blesses the boats with holy water as they pass by.

July: Falmouth Festival (tel. 508/385–8689) displays the work of 200 artists and craftsmen and has live music, jugglers, and food.

July 4 weekend: The Mashpee Powwow (tel. 508/477–0208) brings together Wampanoag Indians from North and South America — and welcomes visitors — for three days of dance contests, drumming, a fireball game, a road race, and a clambake, plus the crowning of the Mashpee Wampanoag Indian princess on the final night. Native American foods and crafts are sold, and many tribe members dress in traditional or ceremonial garb. **Fireworks displays** are still a part of Fourth of July celebrations in several Cape towns and on Nantucket.

Mid-July: Edgartown Regatta (tel. 508/627–4361) is three days of yacht racing around Martha's Vineyard. In East Sandwich, the **Cape Cod Antiquarian Book Fair** (tel. 508/888–2331), sponsored by the Burgess Society, features the offerings of more than 60 dealers in old and rare books.

Late July: The Barnstable County Fair (Rte. 151, East Falmouth, tel. 508/563–3200), begun in 1844, is Cape Cod's biggest event. The six-day affair features livestock and food judgings; horse, pony, and oxen pulls and shows; arts and crafts demonstrations; musical and stage entertainment; carnival rides; and lots of food. The traffic is horrendous, but the fair is worth the trip.

Aug.: On Nantucket, an **Annual House Tour** is held by the garden club (tel. 508/228–0340), and a **Sandcastle Contest** at Jetties Beach (tel. 508/228–1700) results in some amazing sculptures. On Martha's Vineyard, **fireworks** (tel. 508/693–0085) explode over the ocean while the town watches from the Oak Bluffs village green and the town band plays on the gazebo.

Early Aug.: The Hyannis Street Festival (tel. 508/775–2201) is a weekend of Main Street shopping, food, and fun. Merchants display sale items on the sidewalk; clowns, jugglers, and other street entertainers stroll the street, and up to 20 bands perform. At the Vineyard's benefit **Possible Dreams Auction** (tel. 508/693–7900), held the first Monday of August, Art Buchwald auctions off such starry prizes as a sailboat ride with Walter Cronkite.

Mid-Aug.: Martha's Vineyard Agricultural Fair (tel. 508/693–4343) is pure Americana, with livestock and food judging, animal shows, a carnival, plus evening musical entertainment, over three days. The **Falmouth Road Race** (Box 732, Falmouth 02541, tel. 508/540–7000) is a world-class race covering 7.1 miles of coast from Woods Hole to Falmouth Heights; apply the previous fall or winter.

Late Aug.: Sails Around Cape Cod (tel. 508/430–1111), a new event in 1991, is a 155-nautical-mile race to Harwich Port and back via Provincetown and the canal. The two-day race, for yachts 30 feet or larger, is accompanied by beach parties and an awards banquet.

Sept.: The Bourne Scallopfest (tel. 508/888–6202), the weekend after Labor Day, attracts thousands of people to Buzzards Bay for three days of fried scallops (and barbecued chicken, hot dogs, and burgers) served under a tent, plus 85 crafts and food booths and entertainment. **The Harwich Cranberry Harvest Festival** (tel. 508/430–2811) is 10 days of festivities, including a country-western jamboree, an arts and crafts show, a parade, fireworks, pancake breakfasts, an antique-car show, and much more.

Mid-Sept.: Tivoli Day (tel. 508/693–0085), an end-of-summer celebration in Oak Bluffs on Martha's Vineyard, features a fishing derby for kids, a world-class 60-mile bike race (**Tour of Martha's Vineyard;** tel. 508/693–1656), and a street fair with live entertainment and crafts.

Mid-Sept.–mid-Oct.: The month-long **Martha's Vineyard Striped Bass and Bluefish Derby** (Box 2101, Edgartown 02539, tel. 508/693–1881) is one of the East Coast's premier fishing contests, offering more than $100,000 in prizes for albacore, bluefish, and bonito catches in shore and boat divisions.

Late Sept.: Bird Carvers' Exhibit and Auction (tel. 508/896–3867) at the Cape Cod Museum of Natural History in Brewster showcases local and regional bird carvers' art over three days.

Oct.: Nantucket Cranberry Harvest (tel. 508/228–1700) is a three-day celebration, including bog and inn tours and a crafts exhibition featuring 60 island artisans.

Thanksgiving Eve: Provincetown Festival of Lights (tel. 508/487–3424), commemorating the Pilgrims' landing, begins with the lighting of 5,000 white and gold bulbs draped over the Pilgrim Monument. The lights are lit nightly until Little Christmas (Jan. 7) and can be seen as far away as the canal. A performance of the "Hallelujah Chorus" accompanies the lighting; the monument museum offers an open house and tours, and local establishments add to the festivities with open houses and refreshments.

Early Dec.: Many Cape and island towns do up the Christmas season in grand style. The best-known celebration is the Nantucket **Christmas** (or **Shopper's**) **Stroll** (tel. 508/228–1700), which takes place the first weekend of the month. Costumed carolers and other musicians entertain hordes of strollers as they walk the festively decorated cobblestone streets and dip into stores to shop and sample seasonal refreshments. Activities include theatrical performances, art exhibitions, crafts sales, and a tour of historic homes. In this most historic town, the old-time celebration is magical. To avoid the throngs, visit on one of the surrounding weekends (decorations go up the weekend before).

On Martha's Vineyard, **Christmas in Edgartown** (tel. 508/627–4711), the second weekend of the month, includes walking tours of historic homes, old-fashioned teas, carriage rides, a parade, caroling, and other entertainment. Vineyard Haven packs events into its **Twelve Days of Christmas** (tel. 508/693–2725).

Falmouth's **Christmas by the Sea** (tel. 508/548–8500), the first full weekend of December, includes lighting ceremonies at the Village Green, caroling at Nobska Light in Woods Hole, an antiques show, a house tour, concerts, cruises, and a parade.

Chatham's **Main Street Open House** (tel. 508/945–0342) takes place the following weekend, with street entertainment, hayrides, caroling, hand-bell ringing, and more, culminating in a dinner dance at the grand Chatham Bars Inn. The open house is part of a monthlong celebration beginning just after Thanksgiving and ending with a lavish First Night celebration (one of many on the Cape), including fireworks, on New Year's Eve.

What to Pack

Only a few restaurants on Cape Cod, Martha's Vineyard, and Nantucket require formal dress; the area prides itself on informality. Do pack a sweater or jacket, even in summer, for the nights can be cool. Also, *see* clothing suggestions in Staying Healthy, *below*, regarding Lyme disease.

Of course, protective sunscreen, sunglasses with UV screen, hats, and insect repellent are important in summer; all are readily available throughout the Cape and islands. And don't forget your raingear.

Carry-on Luggage Passengers aboard major U.S. carriers are usually limited to two carry-on bags. Bags stored under the seat must not exceed 9″ × 14″ × 22″. Bags hung in a closet can be no larger than 4″ × 23″ × 45″. The maximum dimensions for bags stored in an overhead bin are 10″ × 14″ × 36″. Any item that exceeds the specified dimensions will generally be rejected as a carryon and handled as checked baggage. Keep in mind that an airline can adapt these rules to circumstances; on a crowded flight, you may be allowed to take only one carry-on bag aboard.

In addition to the two carryons, passengers may bring aboard: a handbag, an overcoat or wrap, an umbrella, a camera, a reasonable amount of reading material, an infant bag, and crutches, braces, a cane, or other prosthetic device upon which the passenger is dependent. Infant/child safety seats can also be brought aboard if parents have purchased a ticket for the child or if there is space in the cabin.

Checked Luggage Luggage allowances vary slightly among airlines. Many carriers allow three checked pieces; some allow only two. It is best to consult with the airline before you go. In all cases, checked luggage cannot weigh more than 70 pounds per piece or be larger than 62 inches (length + width + height).

Staying Healthy

A problem common on the East Coast is Lyme disease (named after Lyme, Connecticut, where it was first diagnosed). This bacterial infection is transmitted by deer ticks and can be very serious, leading to chronic arthritis and worse if left untreated, which it often is because it is difficult to diagnose. Pregnant women are advised to avoid areas of possible infestation; if contracted during early pregnancy, the disease can harm a fetus.

Deer ticks are most prevalent April through October but can be found year-round. They are about the size of a pinhead; wearing light-colored clothing makes it easier to spot any ticks that might have attached themselves to you. Anyone planning to explore wooded areas or places with tall grasses (including dunes) should wear long pants, socks drawn up over pant cuffs, and a long-sleeve shirt with a close-fitting collar; boots are also recommended. The National Centers for Disease Control recommends that DEET repellent be applied to skin (not face!) and that permethrin be applied to clothing directly before entering infested areas but warns that these repellents should be used very carefully and conservatively with small children.

Avoid walking in pathless brush areas and dune grasses, or brushing against low foliage. On returning from an outing, check your clothes and body for ticks (they also attach themselves to pets). To remove a tick, apply a tweezers to where it is attached to the skin and pull without squeezing the body of the tick — if the tick is squeezed, the body fluids containing the bacteria will be released and spread. Afterward, disinfect the bite with alcohol and save the tick in a closed jar in case symptoms of the disease develop.

The first symptom may be a ringlike rash, or you may experience flulike symptoms, such as malaise, fever, chills, and joint or facial pains. If diagnosed early, Lyme disease can be treated with antibiotics. If you suspect your symptoms may be due to a tick bite, inform your doctor and ask to be tested for the disease. For more information, contact the Centers for Disease Control (tel. 404/332–4555) or the Massachusetts Department of Public Health (305 South St., Jamaica Plains 02130, tel. 617/522–3700, ext. 420). Brochures on the disease are available at many tourist information areas.

Other health risks of a visit to the area are sunburn, poison ivy, and swimming where there are dangerous currents — check on local conditions before diving into unfamiliar waters.

Getting Money from Home

Cash Machines Virtually all U.S. banks belong to a network of ATMs (automated teller machines) that dispense cash 24 hours a day in cities throughout the country. There are some eight major networks in the United States, the largest of which are Cirrus, owned by MasterCard, and Plus, affiliated with Visa. Some banks belong to more than one network. To receive a card for one of these systems, you must apply for it. Cards issued by Visa and MasterCard also may be used in the ATMs, but the fees are usually higher than the fees on bank cards. There is also a daily interest charge on credit card "loans," even if monthly bills are paid on time. Each network has a toll-free number you can call to locate machines in a given city. The Cirrus number is 800/4–CIRRUS; the Plus number is 800/THE PLUS. Check with your bank for information on fees and on the amount of cash you can withdraw on any given day.

Bank Transfers Call your local bank and have money sent to a bank in the area you're visiting; it's easiest if your local bank has a branch in that area (if not, the process may take longer and cost more).

American Express Cardholder Services The company's Express Cash system links your checking account to your American Express card. You may withdraw up to $1,000 in a 7-day period (Gold or Platinum Cardholders have a higher limit); a 2% fee (minimum $2, maximum $6) applies to each transaction. Call 800/227–4669 for more information. Cardholders can also cash personal or counter checks at any American Express office for up to $1,000, of which $500 may be claimed in cash and the balance in traveler's checks, which carry a 1% commission.

Wiring Money You don't have to be a cardholder to have an American Express MoneyGram sent to you, for up to $10,000 in cash. Just have a friend at home head to the nearest American Express MoneyGram agent (tel. 800/543–4080 for information) and fill out a MoneyGram. Up to $1,000 may be paid for with a credit card (AE, D, MC, or V), any additional sum must be paid in cash. Your friend then telephones you with a reference number, and the MoneyGram agent authorizes a transfer of funds to the participating office nearest you. Present proper I.D. and the reference number for payment. Fees are roughly 5% to 10%, depending upon the amount and method of payment.

You can also have money sent through **Western Union** (tel. 800/325–6000). A friend at home can bring cash or a check to the nearest Western Union office or pay over the phone with a credit card. Fees are also about 5% to 10%; delivery usually takes two business days.

Traveling with Film

If your camera is new, shoot and develop a few rolls of film before you leave home. Pack some lens tissue and an extra battery for your built-in light meter. Invest about $10 in a skylight filter: It will protect the lens and reduce haze.

Film doesn't like hot weather, so if you're driving in summer, don't store film in the glove compartment or on the shelf under the rear window. Put it behind the front seat on the floor, on the side opposite the exhaust pipe.

On a plane trip, never pack unprocessed film in checked luggage; if your bags get X-rayed, say goodbye to your pictures. Always carry undeveloped film with you through security and ask to have it inspected by hand. (It helps to keep your film in a plastic bag, ready for quick inspection.) Inspectors at American airports are required by law to honor requests for hand inspection. The newer airport scanning machines used in all U.S. airports are safe for anything from five to 500 scans, depending on the speed of your film.

Traveling with Children

Cape Cod is very much family oriented and provides every imaginable diversion for kids, plus plenty of lodgings and restaurants that cater to them and are affordable for families on a budget. Cottages and condominiums are increasingly popular with families, offering privacy, room, kitchens, and sometimes laundry facilities; often cottage or condo communities have play yards and pools, sometimes even full children's programs.

Publications The Bristol County Development Council (Box BR–976, New Bedford, MA 02741, tel. 508/997–1250) has a calendar of events along south-coastal New England, called "Happenings Especially for Kids." Send $1 for a copy.

Just for Kids: The New England Guide and Activity Book for Young Travelers, by Ed and Roon Frost (Glove Compartment Books, Box 1602, Fort Smith, NH 03801), is available by mail for $7.95 plus $3 shipping and handling.

Family Travel Times is a newsletter published 10 times a year by Travel With Your Children (TWYCH, 45 W. 18th St., 7th floor tower, New York, NY 10011, tel. 212/206–0668). A one-year subscription for $35 includes access to back issues and twice-weekly opportunities to call for specific advice.

Traveling With Children — And Enjoying It (The Globe Pequot Press, Box Q, Chester, CT 06412) offers tips on cutting costs, keeping kids busy, eating out, and packing effectively. Cost: $11.95.

Getting There On domestic flights, children under age 2 not occupying a seat travel free. Various discounts apply to children age 2–12. If possible, reserve a seat behind the bulkhead of the plane; these offer more legroom and usually enough space to fit a bassinet (supplied by the airlines). At the same time, inquire about special children's meals or snacks, which are also offered by most airlines. (See "TWYCH's Airline Guide," in the February 1990 and 1992 issues of *Family Travel Times*, for a rundown on children's services offered by 46 airlines.) Ask the airline if you can bring aboard your child's car seat. For the booklet "Child/Infant Safety Seats Acceptable for Use in Aircraft," write the **Federal Aviation Administration** (APA-200, 800 Independence Ave., SW, Washington, DC 20591, tel. 202/267–3479).

Hotels **Best Western Chateau Motor Inn** in Provincetown, **Hampton Inn Cape Cod** in Hyannis, **Quality Inn** in Falmouth, and **Sheraton Ocean Park Inn** in Eastham allow children under age 18 to share their parents' room for free. **New Seabury Resort** offers summer programs for children through the local YMCA (sports, nature studies, arts and crafts classes, games, overnights), plus tennis and golf clinics. **Chatham Bars Inn, Ocean Edge** in Brewster, and **Tara Hyannis Hotel** offer summer programs for kids, with arts and crafts, outdoor activities, and games; the Tara's program includes pajama parties, supper parties, tennis and golf clinics, and swimming lessons. **Sea Crest** in North Falmouth offers a children's day camp. *See* Lodging in Chapter 3, Cape Cod, for more information.

On Martha's Vineyard (*see* Lodging in Chapter 4, Martha's Vineyard), the **Mattakesett** condominium community has a full children's program and plenty of amenities for kids (pool, tennis clinics, and so forth). At the **Colonial Inn** in Edgartown, children under 16 stay free.

At **Beachside Resort** on Nantucket (*see* Lodging in Chapter 5, Nantucket), children under 17 stay free with parents.

Hints for Disabled Travelers

Lift-van service is available on the Cape and islands (*see* Getting Around in individual chapters). On Cape Cod, the public buses are all accessible (*see* Getting Around by Bus in Chapter 3, Cape Cod). Accessibility regulations passed in 1992 have resulted in increased access across the board, though state laws already in place had covered many of the requirements of the new regulations.

Cape Organization for Rights of the Disabled (CORD; tel. 508/775–8300) will supply information on accessibility of restaurants, hotels, beaches, and other tourist facilities on Cape Cod. **Sight Loss Services** (tel. 508/394–3904 or 800/427–6842 in MA) provides talking-book equipment loans and advice on accessibility.

The **Cape Cod National Seashore** (South Wellfleet 02663, tel. 508/349–3785) has many facilities, services, and programs accessible to disabled visitors. Write for information on what is available, or ask at the Seashore visitor centers (Eastham, tel. 508/255–3421; Provincetown, tel. 508/487–1256).

The Information Center for Individuals with Disabilities (Fort Point Pl., 27-43 Wormwood St., Boston, MA 02210, tel. 617/727–5540) offers useful problem-solving assistance, including lists of travel agents who specialize in tours for the disabled.

Moss Rehabilitation Hospital Travel Information Service (1200 W. Tabor Rd., Philadelphia, PA 19141, tel. 215/456–9603) provides information on tourist sites, transportation, and accommodations on destinations around the world for a small fee.

Travel Industry and Disabled Exchange (TIDE; 5435 Donna Ave., Tarzana, CA 91356, tel. 818/368–5648), for a $15-per-person annual membership fee, provides a quarterly newsletter and a directory of travel agencies that specialize in service to the disabled.

Mobility International USA (Box 3551, Eugene, OR 97403, tel. 503/343–1284) is an internationally affiliated organization with 500 members. For a $20 annual fee, it coordinates exchange programs for disabled people in the United States and around the world and offers information on accommodations and organized study programs.

Amtrak (National Railroad Passenger Corp., 60 Massachusetts Ave. NE, Washington, DC 20002, tel. 800/USA–RAIL) advises that you request redcap service, special seats, or wheelchair assistance when you make reservations. (Not all stations are equipped to provide these services.) All disabled passengers are entitled to a 15% discount on regular coach fares; disabled children also receive discounted fares. Amtrak will provide a free copy of *Access Amtrak,* outlining services for elderly or disabled travelers. Check with Amtrak to be sure discounts are available when you plan to travel. Amtrak's free Travel Planner outlines all its services for the elderly and disabled.

Publications Three useful resources — *Travel for the Disabled* ($19.95), *Directory of Travel Agencies for the Disabled* ($19.95), and *Wheelchair Vagabond* ($9.95) — can be ordered through bookstores or from the publisher, Twin Peaks Press (Box 129, Vancouver, WA 98666, tel. 206/694–2462). When ordering by mail, add $2 postage for one book, $1 for each additional book.

"Fly Rights," a free brochure available on request from the U.S. Department of Transportation (tel. 202/366–2220), gives airline access information for the disabled.

Hints for Older Travelers

More than half of Cape Cod's year-round population is made up of retirees, so the area caters to older people in many ways; for example, senior discounts are widely available, many restaurants offer early-bird specials from around 4 to 7 PM, and wheelchair-access ramps are common. Many inns will accommodate requests for rooms on the ground floor if innkeepers are notified when reservations are made. Older travelers may want to request a room with a shower or ask that they not be put in a room with a Victorian clawfoot tub that requires the bather to climb in and out.

Elder Services of Cape Cod and the Islands (68 Rte. 134, South Dennis 02660, tel. 508/394–4630 or 800/244–4630 in MA; on Martha's Vineyard, Box 2337, Oak Bluffs 02557, tel. 508/693–4393; on Nantucket, 144 Orange St., Nantucket 02554, tel. 508/228–4647) offers information and referrals.

The **American Association of Retired Persons** (AARP; 601 E St., NW, Washington, DC 20049, tel. 202/434–2277) has two programs for independent travelers: (1) the **Purchase Privilege Program,** which offers discounts on hotels, air-fare, car rentals, RV rentals, and sightseeing; and (2) the **AARP Motoring Plan,** provided by Amoco, which furnishes emergency aid (road service) and trip-routing information for an annual fee of $39.95 per couple. (Both programs include the member and member's spouse or the member and another person who shares the household.) The AARP also arranges group tours at reduced rates through **AARP Travel Experience from American Express** (400 Pinnacle Way, Suite 450, Norcross, GA 30071, tel. 800/927–0111). AARP members must be age 50 or older; annual dues are $8 per person or per couple.

Elderhostel (75 Federal St., Boston 02110, tel. 617/426–7788) is an innovative educational program for people age 60 and older. Participants live in dorms on some 1,600 campuses around the world; Martha's Vineyard's Nathan Mayhew Seminars offers one such program. Mornings are devoted to lectures and seminars, afternoons to sightseeing and field trips. Fees for two- to three-week international trips, including room, board, tuition, and round-trip transportation, range from $1,800 to $4,500. The catalog is free for the first 18 months, and $15 after that (or free if you participate in a program).

National Council of Senior Citizens (1331 F St., NW, Washington, DC 20004, tel. 202/347–8800) is a nonprofit advocacy group with some 5,000 local clubs across the country. Annual membership ($12 per person or per couple) brings you a monthly newspaper with travel information and an ID card for reduced-rate hotels and car rentals.

Mature Outlook (6001 N. Clark St., Chicago, IL 60660, tel. 800/336–6330), a subsidiary of Sears Roebuck & Co., is a travel club for people over age 50, with hotel and motel discounts and a bimonthly newsletter. Annual membership is $9.95; there are 800,000 members currently. Instant membership is available at participating Holiday Inns.

Golden Age Passport is a free lifetime pass to all parks, monuments, and recreation areas run by the federal government. People 62 and over can pick one up at any national park that charges admission. The passport also provides a 50% discount on camping, boat launching, and parking (lodging is not included). A driver's license or other proof of age is required.

Saga International Holidays (120 Boylston St., Boston, MA 02116, tel. 800/343–0273), which specializes in group travel for people over age 60, offers a variety of tour packages at various prices.

September Days Club (tel. 800/241–5050) is run by the moderately priced Days Inns of America. The $12 annual membership fee for individuals or couples over age 50 entitles them to reduced car-rental rates and reductions of 15%–50% at most of the chain's 350 motels.

Amtrak (tel. 800/USA–RAIL) offers all passengers over 61 a 15% discount on the lowest available fare. *See also* Hints for Disabled Travelers, *above.*

When using an AARP or other discount identification card, ask for reduced hotel rates when you make your reservation, not when you check out. At restaurants, show your card to the maître d' before you're seated, because discounts may be limited to certain set menus, days, or hours. When renting a car, remember that economy cars, priced at promotional rates, may cost less than cars available with your discount ID card.

Publications *The International Health Guide for Senior Citizen Travelers,* by W. Robert Lange, MD, is available for $4.95 plus $1.50 shipping, and *The Senior Citizens Guide to Budget Travel in the United States and Canada,* by Paige Palmer, is available for $5.95 including shipping, both from Pilot Books (103 Cooper St. Babylon, NY 11702, tel. 516/422–2225).

Further Reading

General The classic works on Cape Cod are Henry David Thoreau's
Cape Cod *Cape Cod,* an account of his walking tours in the mid-1800s, and Henry Beston's 1928 *The Outermost House,* which chronicles the seasons during a solitary year in a cabin at ocean's edge. Both reveal the character of Cape Codders and are rich in tales and local lore, as well as observations on nature and its processes. *Cape Cod: Henry David Thoreau's Complete Text with the Journey Recreated in Pictures,* by William F. Robinson, is a handsome New York Graphics Society edition, illustrated with prints from the period and current photographs. *Cape Cod Pilot,* by Josef Berger (alias Jeremiah Digges), is a WPA guidebook from 1937 that is filled with "whacking good yarns" about everything from religion to fishing, as well as a lot of still useful information.

Martha's Vineyard *On the Vineyard II,* with 38 essays by island authors (including Walter Cronkite, William Styron, and Carly Simon) and more than 200 photographs by islander Peter Simon, captures the Vineyard's many moods.

Nantucket *Nantucket Style,* by Leslie Linsley and Jon Aron (published by Rizzoli), is a look at 25 houses, from 18th-century mansions to rustic seaside cottages, with 300 illustrations. Just reprinted is an architectural classic: *Early Nantucket and Its Whale Houses,* by Henry Chandler Forman.

History *Cape Cod, Its People & Their History,* by Henry C. Kittredge
Cape Cod (first published in 1930), is the standard history of the area, told with anecdotes and style as well as scholarship. *Sand in Their Shoes,* compiled by Edith and Frank Shay, is a compendium of writings on Cape Cod life throughout history. *Of Plimoth Plantation* is Governor William Bradford's descrip-

tion of the Pilgrims' voyage to and early years in the New World. *Art in Narrow Streets,* by Ross Moffett, and *Time and the Town: A Provincetown Chronicle,* by Provincetown Playhouse founder Mary Heaton Vorse, paint the social landscape of Provincetown in the first half of this century.

Martha's Vineyard The many books written by Henry Beetle Hough, the Pulitzer Prize–winning editor of the *Vineyard Gazette* for 60 years, include his 1970 *Martha's Vineyard* and his 1936 *Martha's Vineyard, Summer Resort.*

Nantucket Alexander Starbuck's 1924 *History of Nantucket* (available only in libraries) is the most comprehensive on early Nantucket. *Nantucket: The Life of an Island,* by Edwin P. Hoyt, is a lively and fascinating popular history.

Fiction Herman Melville's *Moby-Dick,* set on a 19th-century Nantucket whaling ship, captures the spirit of the whaling era. *Cape Cod,* by William Martin, is a historical novel and mystery following two families from the *Mayflower* voyage to the present, with lots of Cape history and flavor along the way. *Murder on Martha's Vineyard,* by David Osborn, and Alice Hoffman's lovely *Illumination Night* are set on the island. *Dark Nantucket Noon,* by Jane Langton, is a novel full of island atmosphere. *Nantucket Daybreak* is set in off-season Nantucket and portrays the life of scallopers in a story of love and betrayal.

Photography *A Summer's Day* (winner of the 1985 Ansel Adams Award for Best Photography Book) and *Cape Light* present color landscapes, still lifes, and portraits by Provincetown-associated photographer Joel Meyerowitz. *Martha's Vineyard* and *Eisenstaedt: Martha's Vineyard* are explorations of the island by *Life* magazine photographer Alfred Eisenstaedt, a summer resident for decades.

Periodicals Glossy magazines on the area include *Cape Cod Life* (Box 222, Osterville 02655, tel. 508/428–5706), *Provincetown Arts* (Box 35, Provincetown 02657, tel. 508/487–3167), *Martha's Vineyard Magazine* (Box 66, Edgartown 02539, tel. 508/627–4311), and *Nantucket Journal* (7 Sea St., Nantucket 02554, tel. 508/228–8700).

Arriving and Departing

By Plane

Most flights to Cape Cod land in Hyannis; regular flights are also scheduled year-round between Boston and Provincetown. Service to Martha's Vineyard and Nantucket is available out of Hyannis and New Bedford airports, as well as through nationwide connections; air service also connects the islands. For details, *see* individual chapters.

Smoking The Federal Aviation Administration has banned smoking on all scheduled flights within the 48 contiguous states; to and from the U.S. Virgin Islands and Puerto Rico; and on flights of under six hours to and from Alaska and Hawaii. The rules apply to both domestic and foreign carriers. A request for a seat in a nonsmoking section should be made at the time you make your reservation.

Lost Luggage On domestic flights, airlines are responsible for up to $1,250 per passenger in lost or damaged property. If you're carrying valuables, either take them with you on the plane or purchase additional insurance for lost luggage. Some airlines will issue luggage insurance when you check in, but many do not. Insurance for lost, damaged, or stolen luggage is available through travel agents or directly through insurance companies. Luggage-loss coverage is usually part of a comprehensive travel-insurance package that includes insurance against personal accident, trip cancellation, and sometimes default and bankruptcy. Two companies that issue luggage insurance are **Tele-Trip** (Box 31685, 3201 Farnam St., Omaha, NE 68131–0618, tel. 800/228–9792), a subsidiary of Mutual of Omaha, and **The Traveler** (Ticket and Travel Dept., 1 Tower Sq., Hartford, CT 06183–5040, tel. 203/277–0111 or 800/243–3174). Tele-Trip operates sales booths at airports and issues insurance through travel agents. Tele-Trip will insure checked luggage for up to 180 days. Rates vary according to the length of the trip. The Travelers Insurance Corporation will insure checked or hand luggage with a valuation of $500–$2,000 per person for up to 180 days. Rates for $500 valuation are $10 for one to five days, $85 for 180 days. Other companies with comprehensive policies include **Access America, Inc.,** a subsidiary of Blue Cross–Blue Shield (Box 11188, Richmond, VA 23230, tel. 800/334–7525 or 800/284–8300) and **Near Services** (450 Prairie Ave., Suite 101, Calumet City, IL 60409, tel. 708/868–6700 or 800/654–6700).

By Car

The speed limit in Massachusetts is 55 mph, though, except on Cape Cod's Route 6, you'll find little opportunity to reach it on the Cape and islands. For driving routes to Cape Cod, see Arriving and Departing by Car in Chapter 3, Cape Cod. To get to Martha's Vineyard with your car, you'll have to take a ferry from Woods Hole; to Nantucket, a ferry from Hyannis (*see* Arriving and Departing by Ferry in Chapter 4, Martha's Vineyard, and Chapter 5, Nantucket).

Car Rentals

Avis (tel. 800/331–1212), **Budget** (tel. 800/527–0700), **Dollar** (tel. 800/800–4000), **Hertz** (tel. 800/654–3131), **National Interrent** (tel. 800/227–7368), and **Thrifty** (tel. 800/367–2277) maintain airport and city locations throughout New England. For local rental agencies, see the relevant chapters.

By Train

Amtrak (tel. 800/USA–RAIL) has limited service to Cape Cod in season; in the off-season, trains to Boston connect with bus service to the Cape. For more details, see Arriving and Departing by Train in Chapter 3, Cape Cod.

By Bus

Bus service is available to Cape Cod, with stops at many towns and some connecting service to the islands by ferry; express buses run from Logan Airport in Boston to Hyannis (*see* Arriving and Departing by Bus in Chapter 3, Cape Cod).

By Boat

Provincetown is reached by ferry from Boston and Plymouth in season; Martha's Vineyard, from Woods Hole year-round and from Falmouth, Hyannis, and New Bedford in season; Nantucket, from Hyannis year-round. In season, a passenger ferry connects the islands, and a cruise out of Hyannis makes a one-day round-trip with stops at both islands. *See* Arriving and Departing by Ferry in Chapter 3, Cape Cod; Chapter 4, Martha's Vineyard; and Chapter 5, Nantucket.

Staying on Cape Cod, Martha's Vineyard, and Nantucket

Shopping

Art galleries and crafts shops abound on Cape Cod, Martha's Vineyard, and Nantucket, a reflection of the long attraction the area has held for artists and craftsmen. The region is also a popular antiquing spot. For a directory of area antiques dealers and auctions, contact the Cape Cod Antique Dealers Association (Box 271, Yarmouth Port 02675, tel. 508/362–9508). On the Cape, Provincetown and Wellfleet are the main centers for art. Both the Provincetown Gallery Guild (Box 242, Provincetown 02657) and the Wellfleet Art Galleries Association (Box 916, Wellfleet 02667) issue pamphlets on local galleries. For a listing of crafts shops on the Cape, write to the Society of Cape Cod Craftsmen (Box 791, Sandwich 02563), the Artisans Guild of Cape Cod (Box 258, East Orleans 02643), or Cape Cod Potters (Box 76, Chatham 02633).

Coastal environments and a shared seafaring past account for the proliferation of sea-related crafts on the Cape and the islands (as well as of marine-antiques dealers). A craft form that originated as a time passer on the years-long voyages to faraway whaling grounds is scrimshaw, the art of etching finely detailed designs of sailing ships and sea creatures onto a hard surface. In the beginning, the bones or teeth of whales were used; today's ecologically minded (and legally constrained) scrimshanders use a synthetic substitute like Corian, a DuPont material for countertops.

Another whalers' pastime was the sailor's valentine: a glass-enclosed wood box, often in an octagonal shape (derived from the shape of the compass boxes that were originally used), containing an intricate arrangement of often tiny sea-shells. The shells were collected on stopovers in the West Indies and elsewhere, sorted by color, size, and shape, and then glued into elaborate patterns during the long hours aboard ship. Exquisite examples can be seen at a Nantucket gallery, the Sailor's Valentine (*see* Chapter 5, Nantucket).

The Nantucket lightship basket was developed in the mid-19th century on a lightship placed just off the island's coast to aid in navigation during foggy spells. In good weather there was little to do, and so (the story goes) crew members began weaving intricately patterned baskets of cane, a trade some continued onshore and passed on. Later a woven lid and decoration were added, and the utilitarian baskets were on their way to becoming the handbags that today cost hundreds of dollars.While Nantucket is still the locus of the craft, with a dozen active basket makers, antique and new baskets can be found on the Cape and the Vineyard as well.

Cranberry glass, a light ruby glass made by fusing gold with glass or crystal, is sold in gift shops all over the Cape. It was once made by the Sandwich Glass company (among others) but now retains only the association with Cape Cod, as it is made elsewhere in the United States and in Europe.

On the islands the majority of shops close down in winter; because of the Cape's large year-round population, its shops tend to remain open, though most Provincetown and Wellfleet shops and galleries shut down. Throughout the Cape and islands, shop owners respond to the flow of tourists as well as to their own inclinations; it's best to phone a shop before going out of your way to visit it.

Shop hours are generally 9 or 10 to 5, though in high season many tourist-oriented stores stay open until 10 PM or later. Except in the main tourist areas, shops are often closed on Sunday. The Massachusetts sales tax is 5%.

Sports and the Outdoors

The Cape and the islands are top spots for swimming, surf-ing, windsurfing, sailing, and virtually all water sports. Shipwrecks make for interesting dive sites, but don't expect a tropical underwater landscape. Golfers have many excel-lent courses to choose from, including championship lay-outs, and most remain open nearly year-round. Bicycling is a joy on the mostly level roads, along paved and scenic bike paths, and through the many nature preserves (Massachu-setts law requires a headlight after dark, a red rear reflec-tor, and reflectors visible from either side of the bike). Bird-watchers have an endless variety of habitats to choose from, often in a single nature preserve.

Fishing is extremely popular, especially for bluefish and striped bass, and the area is the site of some major derbies. A license (available at tackle shops) is required for persons age 15 or over to fish in inland waters. The Cape Cod Cham-ber of Commerce (*see* Visitor Information, *above*) puts out a "Sportsman's Guide to Cape Cod," with a map pinpointing boat-launching facilities, surf-fishing access locations, and fishing ponds and streams. The guide also contains information on charter, party, and whale-watch boats; game, bottom, and freshwater fishing (which fish to look for and where); and hunting and fishing regulations.

Spectators can choose from a plethora of bike and running races, golf competitions (including the New England PGA championships at Ocean Edge in Brewster), horse shows, sailboat races around the Cape and islands, and the well-patronized games of the Cape Cod Baseball League, breeding ground of champions.

Beaches

Cape Cod, Martha's Vineyard, and Nantucket are known for long, dune-backed sand beaches, both surf and calm. Swimming season is approximately mid-June–September (sometimes into October). The Cape Cod National Seashore has the Cape's best beaches, with high dunes, wide strands of sand, and no development on the shores. The islands have miles of beautiful, protected coastline as well.

National and State Parks

For further information on the parks mentioned here, as well as on nature and wildlife preserves, see the relevant chapters.

National Parks The **Cape Cod National Seashore** is a 30-mile stretch of the Cape between Eastham and Provincetown that is protected from development. It includes spectacular beaches, dunes, and many other habitats, making for excellent swimming, fishing, bike riding, bird-watching, and nature walks.

State Parks **Manuel F. Correllus State Forest** is 4,000 acres on Martha's Vineyard, laced with hiking, biking, and horse trails.

Nickerson State Park, almost 2,000 acres of forest in Brewster, is a popular camping, biking, boating, fishing, hiking, freshwater swimming, and cross-country skiing area.

Scusset Beach State Reservation in Sandwich is 450 acres with camping, biking, ocean swimming, fishing, and walking trails.

Shawme-Crowell State Forest in Sandwich is 742 acres with camping and walking trails.

Dining

Cape, Vineyard, and Nantucket restaurants offer an endless variety of fresh fish and shellfish. Each restaurant has its version of New England clam chowder, a rich milk- (and sometimes cream-) based dish usually made with the large clams called quahogs (pronounced "KO-hawgs"), chunks of potato, and salt pork. Clams are served in a variety of other ways as well — on the half shell, fried, or baked into a splendid concoction of clams, butter, and bread crumbs called seaclam pie. Clam shacks everywhere serve tasty fried fish and shellfish, accompanied by crisp onion rings — a nice, greasy meal to be savored when you're in a hurry or just on strike against sensible eating.

Other area specialties are the much-prized Wellfleet oysters and the tiny, delicate, buttery-sweet bay scallops (pronounced "SKAWL-lops" here), available fresh from the sea in late fall and winter. The ubiquity of Portuguese dishes — such as kale soup or *linguiça* (a spicy sausage) — on Cape and islands menus is due to a long history of Portuguese immigration; since whaling days, Portuguese have made their living from these seas, particularly around Provincetown. Most Cape restaurants feature traditional New England family fare — pot roast, baked scrod (codfish), chicken pot pie, mashed potatoes and gravy — though a few offer haute cuisine that rivals the best anywhere. Nantucket has spawned a number of first-rate gourmet restaurants, with price tags to match — though most have added lower-priced café or prix-fixe menus in acknowledgment of hard times. Consistency from year to year is a problem, because there is a high turnover among chefs. Because of the short high season and the generally conservative year-round population, in the off-season even adventurous restaurants retreat to more traditional fare, early-bird specials, and buffets in order to survive.

Dress advice in this book's listings refers to dinner only; almost without exception, casual dress is in order at lunch. At establishments where "come as you are" does not always apply, the most that is usually expected is "smart casual," meaning just a neat, minimally dressy look — no shorts, T-shirts, or ripped jeans. The drinking age in Massachusetts is 21; a few towns on Martha's Vineyard are dry. The going rate for tipping in restaurants is 15% of the bill before tax.

Throughout this book, restaurant price ranges are based on the regular dinner menu and include one appetizer, one entrée, and one dessert, without wine, tax, or service. Highly recommended restaurants are indicated by a star ★.

Lodging

Bed-and-breakfasts are especially popular on Cape Cod, Martha's Vineyard, and Nantucket. Many are housed in old sea captains' homes and other 17th- through 19th-century buildings. In most cases, B&Bs are not appropriate for families, because noise travels easily, rooms are often small, and the furnishings are too fragile to withstand normal children's abuse. Usually a B&B will not offer a phone or TV in guest rooms; also, more and more B&Bs no longer allow smoking. The Massachusetts Office of Travel and Tourism (*see* Visitor Information, *above*) offers a free guide to B&Bs and reservation services in Massachusetts.

Besides B&Bs, this highly developed tourist region has all the other lodging options. Luxurious self-contained resorts, beachfront and otherwise, offer all kinds of sporting facilities, restaurants, entertainment, services (including business services and children's programs), and all the assistance one could most likely ever need in making vacation arrangements. Single-night lodgings for those just passing through can be found at countless tacky but cheap and conveniently located little roadside motels, as well as at others that are spotless and cheery yet still inexpensive, or at chain hotels at all price levels; these places often have a pool, TVs, or other amenities to keep children entertained in the evening. Families may want to consider condominiums, cottages, and efficiencies, which offer more space, living areas, kitchens (important if keeping food expenses down is an issue), and sometimes laundry facilities, children's play areas, or children's programs.

There are AYH hostels on Martha's Vineyard and Nantucket, as well as in Hyannis, Eastham, and Truro on Cape Cod (for information and reservations — which are strongly recommended — write to AYH Hostel Dept., Reservations, Box 37613, Washington, DC 20013). Accommodations are simple, dormitories are segregated for men and women, common rooms and kitchens are shared, and everyone helps with the cleanup. Usually it's lights out at 11 PM. The price can't be beat — about $10 a night.

Camping is not allowed on Nantucket, but there are many private and state-park camping areas on Cape Cod and Martha's Vineyard. Write to the Massachusetts Office of Travel & Tourism (*see* Visitor Information, *above*). For state-park campgrounds, see the relevant chapters.

Regarding peak season and the necessity for reservations at various times, *see* When to Go in Before You Go, *above*.

Throughout this book, lodging prices are based on a standard double room (double occupancy) in high season. Unless otherwise noted, a listed establishment's rooms have private baths. Suites are defined here as bedrooms with *separate* sitting rooms. Also, one should be aware that "Continental breakfast" can mean anything from coffee and muffins to elaborate spreads with various fresh-squeezed juices, fruit plate, homemade granola, and many home-baked breads and muffins. Highly recommended lodgings are indicated by a star ★.

Credit Cards

The following credit-card abbreviations are used in this book: AE, American Express; D, Discover; DC, Diners Club; MC, MasterCard; V, Visa.

2 Portraits of Cape Cod, Martha's Vineyard, and Nantucket

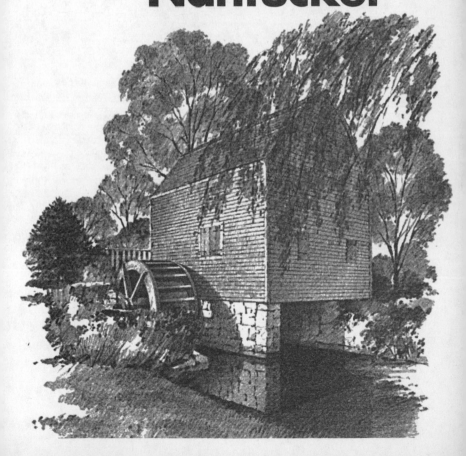

A Brief History

The fortunes of Cape Cod have always been linked to the sea. For centuries, fishermen in search of a livelihood, explorers in search of new worlds, and pilgrims of one sort or another in search of a new life — down to the beach-bound tourists of today — all have turned to the waters around this narrow peninsula arcing into the Atlantic to fulfill their needs and ambitions.

European exploration of Cape Cod dates back at least as far as 1602, when Bartholomew Gosnold sailed from Falmouth, England, to investigate the American coast for trade opportunities. He first anchored off what is now Provincetown and named the cape for the great quantities of cod his crew managed to catch. He then moved on to Cuttyhunk in the Elizabeth Islands (which he named for the queen); on leaving after a few weeks, he noted that the crew were "much fatter and in better health than when we went out of England." Samuel de Champlain, explorer and geographer for the king of France, visited in 1605 and 1606; his encounter with the resident Wampanoag tribe in the Chatham area resulted in deaths on both sides. One theory holds that the Viking Thorwald from Iceland broke his keel on the shoals here in 1004.

None of these visits, however, led to settlement; that began only with the chance landing of the Pilgrims, some of whom were Separatists rebelling from enforced membership in the Church of England, others merchants looking for economic opportunity. On September 16, 1620, the *Mayflower*, with 101 passengers, set out from Plymouth, England, for an area of land granted them by the Virginia Company (Jamestown had been settled in 1607). After more than two months at sea in the crowded boat they saw land; it was far north of their intended destination, but after the stormy passage and considering the approach of winter, they put in at Provincetown Harbor on November 21. Before going ashore they drew up the Mayflower Compact, America's first document establishing self-governance, because they were in an area under no official jurisdiction and dissension had already begun to surface.

Setting off in a small boat, a party led by Captain Myles Standish made a number of expeditions over several weeks, seeking a suitable site for a settlement in the wilderness of woods and scrub. Finally they chose Plymouth, and there they established the colony, governed by William Bradford, that is today re-created at Plimoth Plantation.

Over the next 20 years, settlers spread north and south from Plymouth. The first parts of Cape Cod to be settled were the bay-side sections of Sandwich, Barnstable, and Yarmouth (all incorporated in 1639), along an old Indian trail that is now Route 6A. (Martha's Vineyard was first settled in 1642, and Nantucket in 1659.) Most of the newcomers hunted, farmed, and fished; salt hay from the marshes was used to feed cattle and roof houses.

The first homes built by the English settlers on Cape Cod were wigwams built of twigs, bark, hides, cornstalks, and grasses, which they copied from those of the local Wampanoag Indians who had lived here for thousands of years before the Europeans arrived. Eventually, the settlers stripped the land of its forests to make farmland, graze sheep, and build more European-style homes, though with a New World look all their own. The steep-roofed saltbox and the Cape Cod cottage — still the most popular style of house on the Cape, and copied all over the country — were designed to accommodate growing families.

A newly married couple might begin by building a one- or two-room half-Cape, a rather lopsided 1½-story building with a door on one side of the facade and two windows on the other; a single chimney rose up on the wall behind the door. As the family grew, an addition might be built on the other side of the door large enough for a single window, turning the half-Cape into a three-quarter-Cape; a two-window addition would make it a symmetrical full Cape. Additions built onto the sides and back were called warts. An interesting feature of some Cape houses is the graceful bow roof, slightly curved like the bottom of a boat (not surprising, since ship's carpenters did much of the house-building as well). More noticeable, often, in the older houses is a profusion of small, irregularly shaped and located windows in the gable ends; Thoreau wrote of one such house that it looked as if each of the various occupants "had punched a hole where his necessities required it."

Many historic houses have been turned into historical museums. In some, docents take you on a tour of the times as you pass from the keeping room — the heart of the house, where meals were cooked at a great hearth before which the family gathered for warmth — to the nearby borning room, in whose warmth babies were born and the sick were tended, to the "showy" front parlors where company was entertained. Summer and winter kitchens, backyard pumps, beehive ovens, elaborate raised wall paneling, wide-board pine flooring, wainscoting, a doll made of corn husks, a spinning wheel, a stereopticon, a hand-stitched sampler or glove — each of these historic remnants gives a glimpse into the daily life of another age.

The Wampanoags taught the settlers what they knew of the land and how to live off it. Early on they showed them how to strip and process blubber from whales that became stranded on the beaches. To coax more whales onto the beach, men would sometimes surround them in small boats and make a commotion in the water with their oars until the whales swam to their doom in the only direction left open to them. By the mid-18th century, as the supply of near-shore whales thinned out, the hunt for the far-flung sperm whale began, growing into a major New England industry and making many a sea captain's fortune. Wellfleet, Truro, and Provincetown were the only ports on the Cape that could support deep-water distance whaling (and these were overtaken by Nantucket and New Bedford), but ports along the bay conducted active trade with packet ships carrying goods and passengers to and from Boston. Cape seamen were in great demand for ships sailing from Boston, New York, and other deep-water ports. In the mid-19th century, the Cape saw its most prosperous days, thanks largely to the whaling industry.

The decline in whaling hit the economies of Martha's Vineyard and Nantucket first and hardest, and both islands began cultivating tourism in the 19th century. Martha's Vineyard had played host to annual Methodist Camp Meetings since 1835, and Siasconset, on Nantucket, became a summer haven for New York theater folk when train service reached that remote end of the island in 1884. Whereas previously people traveled from Boston to and along the Cape only by stagecoach or packet boat, in 1848 the first train service from Boston began, reaching to Sandwich; by 1873 it had been extended little by little to Provincetown. At the turn of the century, Cape Cod began to actively court visitors. Creative people, in particular, were lured by the Cape's increasingly Bohemian reputation as artists from New York's Greenwich Village and from Europe discovered the unspoiled beauty, special light, and lively community of Provincetown; by 1916 five art schools flourished here.

In 1914, several successful writers joined the artists in Provincetown for the summer, and the following year, some of these writers, including John Reed (*Ten Days That Shook the World*) and Mary Heaton Vorse (*Footnote to Folly*), began the Cape's first significant theater group, the Provincetown Players, producing plays at a fish house on Lewis Wharf (the theater, where 571 Commercial Street now is, was lost to fire and storm). A young, unknown playwright named Eugene O'Neill joined them in 1916, when his *Bound East for Cardiff* premiered at the fish house theater, and several other O'Neill plays had Provincetown debuts. Though this was to be their last Cape season (they moved on to New York), the Provincetown Players were the germ of Cape com-

munity theater and professional summer-stock companies.

The Barnstable Comedy Club, founded in 1922 and still
going strong, is the most notable of the area's many amateur groups; novelist Kurt Vonnegut acted in its productions in the 1950s and 1960s, and had some of his early
plays produced by the group. Professional summer stock
began with the still-healthy Cape Playhouse in Dennis in
1927, and its early years featured the likes of Bette Davis
(who was first an usher there), Henry Fonda, Ruth Gor-
don, Humphrey Bogart, and Gertrude Lawrence. In
1928, the University Players Guild (today called Falmouth Playhouse) opened in Falmouth, attracting the
likes of James Cagney, Orson Welles, Josh Logan, Tallu-
lah Bankhead, and Jimmy Stewart (who, while on summer vacation from Princeton, had his first bit part during
Falmouth's first season).

T he idea of a Cape Cod canal, linking the bay to the
sound, was studied as early as the 17th century, but
not until 1914 did the privately built canal merge
the waters of the two bays. It was not, however, a thun-
derous success; too narrow and winding, the canal allowed only one-way traffic and created dangerous
currents. The federal government bought it in 1928 and
had the U.S. Army Corps of Engineers rebuild it. In the
1930s three bridges — two traffic and one railroad —
went up, and the rest is the latter-day history of tourism
on Cape Cod.

The building of the Mid-Cape Highway (Route 6) in the
1950s marked the great boom in the Cape's growth, and
the presidency of John F. Kennedy, who summered in
Hyannis Port, certainly added to the area's allure. Today
the Cape's summer population is over 500,000, 2½ times
the year-round population.

Though tourism, construction, and light industry are the
mainstays of the Cape's economy these days, the earliest
inhabitants' occupations have not disappeared. There
are still more than 100 farms on the Cape, and the fishing
industry — including lobstering, scalloping, and oyster
aquaculture, as well as the fruits of fishing fleets such as
those in Provincetown and Chatham — brings in $2 mil-
lion a month.

Visitors are still drawn here by the sea: Scientists come
to delve into the mysteries of the deep, artists come for
the light, and everyone comes for the charm of the beach
towns, the beauty of the white sand, the soft breezes, and
the roaring surf.

The Outermost House

By Henry Beston

The sand bar of Eastham is the sea wall of the inlet. Its crest overhangs the beach, and from the high, wind-trampled rim, a long slope well overgrown with dune grass descends to the meadows on the west. Seen from the tower at Nauset, the land has an air of geographical simplicity; as a matter of fact, it is full of hollows, blind passages, and amphitheatres in which the roaring of the sea changes into the far roar of a cataract. I often wander into these curious pits. On their floors of sand, on their slopes, I find patterns made by the feet of visiting birds. Here, in a little disturbed and claw-marked space of sand, a flock of larks has alighted; here one of the birds has wandered off by himself; here are the deeper tracks of hungry crows; here the webbed impressions of a gull. There is always something poetic and mysterious to me about these tracks in the pits of the dunes; they begin at nowhere, sometimes with the faint impression of an alighting wing, and vanish as suddenly into the trackless nowhere of the sky.

Below the eastern rim the dunes fall in steeps of sand to the beach. Walking the beach close in along these steeps, one walks in the afternoon shade of a kind of sand escarpment, now seven or eight feet high and reasonably level, now 15 or 20 feet high to the top of a dome or mound. In four or five places storms have washed gullies or "cuts" clean through the wall. Dune plants grow in these dry beds, rooting themselves in under old, half-buried wreckage, clumps of dusty miller, *Artemisia stelleriana*, being the most familiar green. The plant flourishes in the most exposed situations, it jumps from the dune rim to the naked slopes, it even tries to find a permanent station on the beach. Silvery gray-green all summer long, in autumn it puts on gold and russet-golden colourings of singular delicacy and beauty.

The grass grows thickest on the slopes and shoulders of the mounds, its tall leaves inclosing intrusive heads and clumps of the thick-fleshed dune goldenrod. Still lower down the slope, where the sands open and the spears rise thin, the beach pea catches the eye with its familiar leaf and faded topmost bloom; lower still, on desert-like floors, are tussock mats of poverty grass and the flat

This essay is excerpted from Henry Beston's 1928 book The Outermost House, *which chronicles a year spent in a solitary cottage at Coast Guard Beach, near Eastham, on Cape Cod.*

green stars of innumerable spurges. The only real bushes of the region are beach plum thickets, and these are few and far between.

All these plants have enormously long taproots which bury themselves deep in the moist core of the sands. The greater part of the year I have two beaches, one above, one below. The lower or tidal beach begins at mean low water and climbs a clean slope to the high-water mark of the average low-course tide; the upper beach, more of a plateau in form, occupies the space between high water and the dunes. The width of these beaches changes with every storm and every tide, but I shall not be far out if I call them both an average 75 feet wide. Unseasonable storm tides and high-course tides make of the beach one vast new floor. Winter tides narrow the winter's upper beach and often sweep across it to the dunes. The whole beach builds up in summer as if each tide pushed more and more sand against it out of the sea. Perhaps currents wash in sand from the outer bars.

It is no easy task to find a name or a phrase for the color of Eastham sand. Its tone, moreover, varies with the hour and the seasons. One friend says yellow on its way to brown, another speaks of the colour of raw silk. Whatever color images these hints may offer to a reader's mind, the color of the sand here on a June day is as warm and rich a tone as one may find. Late in the afternoon, there descends upon the beach and the bordering sea a delicate overtone of faintest violet. There is no harshness here in the landscape line, no hard northern brightness or brusque revelation; there is always reserve and mystery, always something beyond, on earth and sea something which nature, honouring, conceals.

The sand here has a life of its own, even if it is only a life borrowed from the wind. One pleasant summer afternoon, while a high, gusty westerly was blowing, I saw a little "wind devil," a miniature tornado six feet high, rush at full speed out of a cut, whirl itself full of sand upon the beach, and spin off breakerward. As it crossed the beach, the "devil" caught the sun, and there burst out of the sand smoke a brownish prism of burning, spinning, and fantastic color. South of me, the dune I call "big dune" now and then goes through a curious performance. Seen lengthwise, the giant has the shape of a wave, its slope to the beach being a magnificent fan of purest wind-blown sand, its westward slope a descent to a sandy amphitheatre. During a recent winter, a coast guard key post was erected on the peak of the dune; the feet of the night patrols trod down and nicked the crest, and presently this insignificant notch began to "work" and deepen. It is now eight or nine feet wide and as many deep. From across the marshes, it might be a kind of great, roundish bite out of the crest. On windy autumn days, when the sand is still dry and alive, and westerly gusts and currents take on a genuine violence, the loose sand behind the dune is whirled up by the wind and poured eastward through this funnel. At such times the peak "smokes" like a volcano. The smoke is now a streaming blackish plume, now a thin old-ivory wraith, and it billows, eddies, and pours out as from a sea Vesuvius.

Between the dunes and the marshes, an irregular width of salt-hay land extends from the sand slopes to the marshier widths of tidal land along the creeks. Each region has its own grasses, the meadows being almost a patchwork of competing growths. In the late summer and the autumn the marsh lavender, thin-strewn but straying everywhere, lifts its cloud of tiny sun-faded flowers above the tawny, almost deer-coloured grasses. The marsh islands beyond are but great masses of thatch grass rising from floors of sodded mud and sand; there are hidden pools in these unvisited acres which only sunset reveals. The wild ducks know them well and take refuge in them when stalked by gunners.

How singular it is that so little has been written about the birds of Cape Cod! The peninsula, from an ornithologist's point of view, is one of the most interesting in the world. The interest does not centre on the resident birds, for they are no more numerous here than they are in various other pleasant places; it lies in the fact that living here, one may see more kinds and varieties of birds than it would seem possible to discover in any one small region. At Eastham, for instance, among visitors and migrants, residents and casuals, I had land birds and moor birds, marsh birds and beach birds, sea birds and coastal birds, even birds of the outer ocean. West Indian hurricanes, moreover, often catch up and fling ashore here curious tropical and semitropical forms, a glossy ibis in one storm, a frigate bird in another. When living on the beach, I kept a particularly careful lookout during gales.

Eastham bar is only 3 miles long and scarce a quarter of a mile wide across its sands. Yet in this little world nature has already given her humbler creatures a protective coloration. Stop at the coast guard station and catch a locust on the station lawn — we have the maritime locust here, *Trimerotropsis maritima harris* — and, having caught him, study him well; you will find him tinted with green. Go 50 feet into the dunes and catch another, and you shall see an insect made of sand. The spiders, too, are made of sand — the phrase is none too strong — and so are the toads that go beach combing on moonlit summer nights. One may stand at the breakers' edge and study a whole world in one's hand.

* * *

They say here that great waves reach this coast in threes.
Three great waves, then an indeterminate run of lesser
rhythms, then three great waves again. On Celtic coasts
it is the seventh wave that is seen coming like a king out
of the grey, cold sea. The Cape tradition, however, is no
half-real, half-mystical fancy, but the truth itself. Great
waves do indeed approach this beach by threes. Again
and again have I watched three giants roll in one after
the other out of the Atlantic, cross the outer bar, break,
form again, and follow each other in to fulfillment and
destruction on this solitary beach. Coast guard crews are
all well aware of this triple rhythm and take advantage
of the lull that follows the last wave to launch their boats.

It is true that there are single giants as well. I have been
roused by them in the night. Waked by their tremendous
and unexpected crash, I have sometimes heard the last
of the heavy overspill, sometimes only the loud, with-
drawing roar. After the roar came a briefest pause, and
after the pause the return of ocean to the night's long
cadences. Such solitary titans, flinging their green tons
down upon a quiet world, shake beach and dune. Late one
September night, as I sat reading, the very father of all
waves must have flung himself down before the house,
for the quiet of the night was suddenly overturned by a
gigantic, tumbling crash and an earthquake rumbling;
the beach trembled beneath the avalanche, the dune
shook, and my house so shook in its dune that the flame
of a lamp quivered and pictures jarred on the wall.

The three great elemental sounds in nature are the
sound of rain, the sound of wind in a primeval wood,
and the sound of outer ocean on a beach. I have
heard them all, and of the three elemental voices, that of
ocean is the most awesome, beautiful, and varied. For it
is a mistake to talk of the monotone of ocean or of the
monotonous nature of its sound. The sea has many
voices. Listen to the surf, really lend it your ears, and
you will hear in it a world of sounds: hollow boomings and
heavy roarings, great watery tumblings and tramplings,
long hissing seethes, sharp, rifle-shot reports, splashes,
whispers, the grinding undertone of stones, and sometimes vocal sounds that might be the half-heard talk of
people in the sea. And not only is the great sound varied
in the manner of its making, it is also constantly changing
its tempo, its pitch, its accent, and its rhythm, being now
loud and thundering, now almost placid, now furious,
now grave and solemn-slow, now a simple measure, now
a rhythm monstrous with a sense of purpose and elemental will.

Every mood of the wind, every change in the day's
weather, every phase of the tide — all these have subtle
sea musics all their own. Surf of the ebb, for instance, is
one music, surf of the flood another, the change in the

two musics being most clearly marked during the first
hour of a rising tide. With the renewal of the tidal energy,
the sound of the surf grows louder, the fury of battle
returns to it as it turns again on the land, and beat and
sound change with the renewal of the war.

Sound of surf in these autumnal dunes — the continuous-
ness of it, sound of endless charging, endless incoming
and gathering, endless fulfillment and dissolution, endless fecundity, and endless death. I have been trying to
study out the mechanics of that mighty resonance. The
dominant note is the great spilling crash made by each
arriving wave. It may be hollow and booming, it may be
heavy and churning, it may be a tumbling roar. The second fundamental sound is the wild seething cataract roar
of the wave's dissolution and the rush of its foaming waters up the beach — this second sound *diminuendo*. The
third fundamental sound is the endless dissolving hiss of
the inmost slides of foam. The first two sounds reach the
ear as a unisonance — the booming impact of the tons of
water and the wild roar of the up-rush blending — and
this mingled sound dissolves into the foambubble hissing
of the third. Above the tumult, like birds, fly wisps of
watery noise, splashes and counter splashes, whispers,
seething, slaps, and chucklings. An overtone sound of
other breakers, mingled with a general rumbling, fells
earth and sea and air.

Here do I pause to warn my reader that although I
have recounted the history of a breaker — an
ideal breaker — the surf process must be under-
stood as mingled and continuous, waves hurrying after
waves, interrupting waves, washing back on waves, overwhelming waves. Moreover, I have described the sound
of a high surf in fair weather. A storm surf is mechani-
cally the same thing, but it *grinds*, and this same long,
sepulchral grinding — sound of utter terror to all
mariners — is a development of the second fundamental
sound; it is the cry of the breaker water roaring its way
ashore and dragging at the sand. A strange underbody
of sound when heard through the high, wild screaming
of a gale.

Breaking waves that have to run up a steep tilt of the
beach are often followed by a dragging, grinding sound
— the note of the baffled water running downhill again
to the sea. It is loudest when the tide is low and breakers
are rolling beach stones up and down a slope of the lower
beach.

I am, perhaps, most conscious of the sound of surf just
after I have gone to bed. Even here I read myself to
drowsiness, and, reading, I hear the cadenced trampling
roar filling all the dark. So close is the Fo'castle to the
ocean's edge that the rhythm of sound I hear oftenest in
fair weather is not so much a general tumult as an end-

less arrival, overspill, and dissolution of separate great seas. Through the dark, mathematic square of the screened half window, I listen to the rushes and the bursts, the tramplings, and the long, intermingled thunderings, never wearying of the sonorous and universal sound.

Away from the beach, the various sounds of the surf melt into one great thundering symphonic roar. Autumnal nights in Eastham village are full of this ocean sound. The "summer people" have gone, the village rests and prepares for winter, lamps shine from kitchen windows, and from across the moors, the great levels of the marsh, and the bulwark of the dunes resounds the long wintry roaring of the sea. Listen to it a while, and it will seem but one remote and formidable sound; listen still longer and you will discern in it a symphony of breaker thunderings, an endless, distant, elemental cannonade. There is beauty in it, and ancient terror. I heard it last as I walked through the village on a starry October night; there was no wind, the leafless trees were still, all the village was abed, and the whole sombre world was awesome with the sound.

One reason for my love of this great beach is that, living here, I dwell in a world that has a good natural smell, that is full of keen, vivid, and interesting savours and fragrances. I have them at their best, perhaps, when hot days are dulled with a warm rain. So well do I know them, indeed, that were I blindfolded and led about the summer beach, I think I could tell on what part of it I was at any moment standing. At the ocean's very edge the air is almost always cool — cold even — and delicately moist with surf spray and the endless dissolution of the innumerable bubbles of the foam slides; the wet sand slope beneath exhales a cool savour of mingling beach and sea, and the innermost breakers push ahead of them puffs of this fragrant air. It is a singular experience to walk this brim of ocean when the wind is blowing almost directly down the beach, but now veering a point toward the dunes, now a point toward the sea. For 20 feet a humid and tropical exhalation of hot, wet sand encircles one, and from this one steps, as through a door, into as many yards of mid-September. In a point of time, one goes from Central America to Maine.

Atop the broad eight-foot back of the summer bar, inland 40 feet or so from the edge of low tide, other odors wait. Here have the tides strewn a moist tableland with lumpy tangles, wisps, and matted festoons of ocean vegetation — with common sea grass, with rockweed olive-green and rockweed olive-brown, with the crushed and wrinkled green leaves of sea lettuce, with edible, purple-red dulse and bleached sea moss, with slimy and gelatinous cords seven and eight feet long. In the hot noontide they lie, slowly, slowly withering — for their very substance is water — and sending an odor of ocean and vegetation into the burning air. I like this good natural savor. Sometimes a dead, surf-trapped fish, perhaps a dead skate curling up in the heat, adds to this odor of vegetation a faint fishy rankness, but the smell is not earth corruption, and the scavengers of the beach soon enough remove the cause.

Beyond the bar and the tidal runnel farther in, the flat region I call the upper beach runs back to the shadeless bastion of the dunes. In summer this beach is rarely covered by the tides. Here lies a hot and pleasant odor of sand. I find myself an angle of shade slanting off from a mass of wreckage still embedded in a dune, take up a handful of the dry, bright sand, sift it slowly through my fingers, and note how the heat brings out the fine, sharp, stony smell of it. There is weed here, too, well buried in the dry sand — flotsam of last month's high, full-moon tides. In the shadowless glare, the topmost fronds and heart-shaped air sacs have ripened to an odd iodine orange and a blackish iodine brown. Overwhelmed thus by sand and heat, the aroma of this foliage has dissolved; only a shower will summon it again from these crisping, strangely colored leaves.

Cool breath of eastern ocean, the aroma of beach vegetation in the sun, the hot, pungent exhalation of fine sand — these mingled are the midsummer savour of the beach.

3　Cape Cod

In the 1950s, a Patti Page song promised: "If you're fond of sand dunes and salt sea air, quaint little villages here and there, you're sure to fall in love with old Cape Cod." The tourism boom of the next few decades certainly proved her right. So popular did the Cape become, in fact, that today it risks losing much of the charm that brought everyone here in the first place. While the traditional associations — weatheredshingle cottages, long dune-backed beaches, fogenshrouded lighthouses — are still valid, the serenity of the landscape has been eroded. More and more open land so restful to eyes wearied by concrete has been lost to housing developments, condominium complexes, and strip malls, built to service the expanding population. In summer, the large crowds mean having to seek out the tranquillity that once met one at every turn.

Yet, for those who do seek it out, it will be found, for much of the Cape remains compellingly beautiful and unspoiled. Even at the height of the season, there will be no crowds at the less traveled nature preserves and beaches and in wellpreserved old villages off the beaten path. In the off-season, still-beautiful beaches welcome solitary walkers, and life everywhere returns to a small-town hum.

In 1961, the Cape Cod National Seashore was established to preserve virtually the entire eastern shoreline in its natural state for all time, and in 1990 the Cape Cod Commission was created to put a stop to the unplanned development of years past. For the sake of its economy, which is based on the area's continued appeal to tourists, and for the sake of preserving a landscape just as dear to most of the people who live here, Cape Cod has seen the light and has taken its first steps toward it.

Separated from the Massachusetts mainland by the 17.4-mile Cape Cod Canal, the Cape is always likened in shape to an outstretched arm bent at the elbow, with fist turned back toward the mainland at Provincetown. Within the arm's embrace is Cape Cod Bay; to the east is the open Atlantic; to the south, Nantucket Sound. Being surrounded by all this water has its cost: Tides regularly eat away at the land, sometimes at an alarming rate. In his book *Cape Cod,* Henry David Thoreau described the Atlantic-side beach — which he walked from end to end on several trips in the mid-19th century — as "the edge of a continent wasting before the assaults of the ocean." Through the years, many lighthouses — some built hundreds of feet from water's edge — have fallen into the sea, and others are now in danger of being lost. Billingsgate Island off Wellfleet, which once held a number of cottages and a lighthouse, today is a bare sandbar occupied only by resting birds. The U.S. Geological Survey estimates that "at some distant time — not for many generations, however — Cape Cod will be nothing more than a few low sandy islands surrounded by shoals."

The Cape's Atlantic coast is notorious for its shoals, which have accounted for more than 3,000 shipwrecks in 300 years of recorded history. Nicknamed "the graveyard of ships," the area once had 13 lifesaving stations from Monomoy to

Cape Cod Exploring *(Boxes Refer to Detail Maps)*

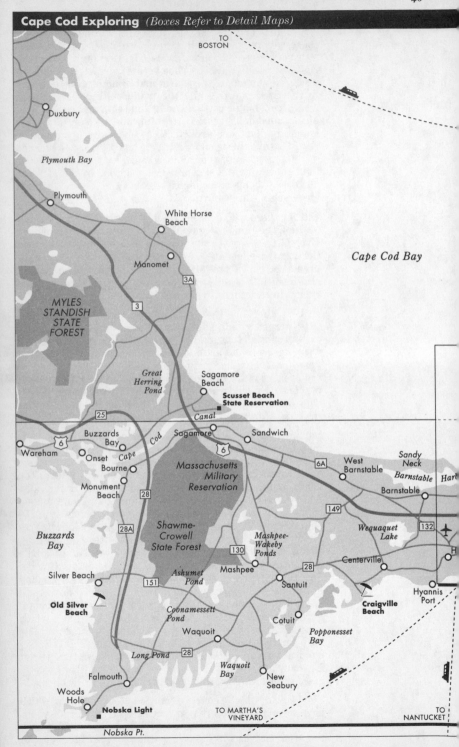

TO
BOSTON

Duxbury

Plymouth Bay

Plymouth

White Horse
Beach

Manomet

3A

3

Cape Cod Bay

MYLES
STANDISH
STATE
FOREST

*Great
Herring
Pond*

Sagamore
Beach

**Scusset Beach
State Reservation**

25

Cod

Canal

Sagamore

Sandwich

Buzzards
Bay

6

Wareham

Onset

Cape

Bourne

Monument
Beach

28

Massachusetts
Military
Reservation

6

6A

West
Barnstable

*Sandy
Neck*

Barnstable

Barnstable

Hart

149

132

*Buzzards
Bay*

28A

*Shawme-
Crowell
State Forest*

130

*Mashpee-
Wakeby
Ponds*

Mashpee

28

*Wequaquet
Lake*

Centerville

H

Silver Beach

151

*Ashumet
Pond*

Santuit

**Old Silver
Beach**

*Coonamessett
Pond*

Waquoit

28

Cotuit

*Popponesset
Bay*

**Craigville
Beach**

Hyannis
Port

Long Pond

*Waquoit
Bay*

New
Seabury

Falmouth

Woods
Hole

Nobska Light

Nobska Pt.

TO MARTHA'S
VINEYARD

TO
NANTUCKET

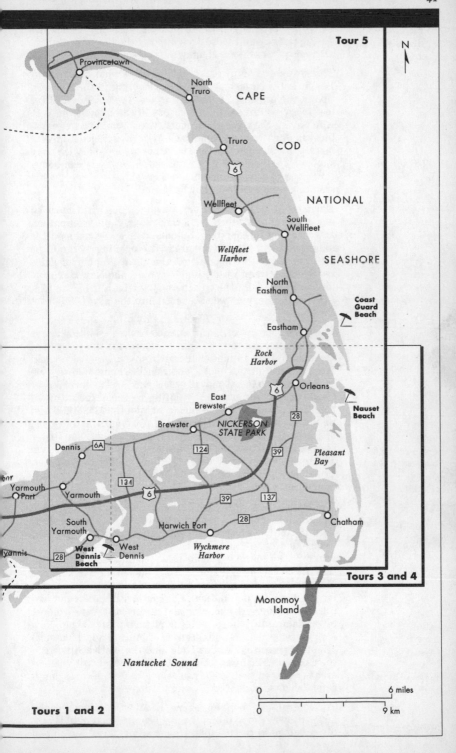

Tour 5

N

Provincetown

North
Truro

CAPE

Truro

6

COD

Wellfleet

NATIONAL

South
Wellfleet

Wellfleet
Harbor

SEASHORE

North
Eastham

Coast
Guard
Beach

Eastham

Rock
Harbor

6 Orleans

East
Brewster

Nauset
Beach

Brewster

28

NICKERSON
STATE PARK

124

Dennis 6A

39

Pleasant
Bay

Yarmouth
Port

134

6

Yarmouth

39

137

South
Yarmouth

Harwich Port

28

Chatham

lyannis 28

West Dennis
Beach

West
Dennis

Wychmere
Harbor

Tours 3 and 4

Monomoy
Island

Nantucket Sound

0   6 miles

0   9 km

Tours 1 and 2

Wood End, at the tip of Provincetown. They were manned by a crew of surfmen who drilled in lifesaving techniques during the day and took turns walking the beach at night in all kinds of weather, watching for ships in distress.

The stories of shipwrecks in Thoreau's book and Henry Beston's *The Outermost House* are riveting in their revelation of the awesome power of the sea, the tragedy of lives lost in icy waters, and the bravery of the men of the U.S. Life Saving Service, whose motto was "You have to go out, but you don't have to come back." (In the service's 43-year history, hundreds of victims were rescued; only twice were surfmen's lives lost.) When the tide is low, you can sometimes see the skeletons of wrecked ships emerge briefly from the sand in which they lie buried.

During the early 20th century, sturdier ships with improved navigational aids (such as Loran, radar, radio, computers, and weather-forecasting equipment) greatly reduced the dangers of shipping in the area. The opening of the Cape Cod Canal in 1914 meant that the great number of ships traveling between Boston and New York and New Haven no longer had to skirt the treacherous coast. In 1915, the U.S. Life Saving Service was absorbed into the new U.S. Coast Guard.

The Cape consists of 15 towns, each broken up into villages (for example, the town of Dennis comprises the villages of Dennis and East Dennis on the north shore, Dennis Port and West Dennis on the south, and South Dennis midway between, much to the dismay of precisionists). The term *Upper Cape* (think "upper arm," relating to the Cape's shape) refers to the towns of Bourne, Falmouth, Mashpee, and Sandwich; *Mid-Cape*, to Barnstable, Yarmouth, and Dennis; and *Lower Cape* ("lower arm"), to Harwich, Chatham, Brewster, Orleans, Eastham, Wellfleet, Truro, and Provincetown. The term *Outer Cape* ("outer reaches") refers to Wellfleet, Truro, and Provincetown, and sometimes is used synonymously with *Lower Cape*.

The Upper Cape, like each of the areas embraced by these designations, contains enough diversity to make generalizations about its character rife with exceptions. The area just before and after the canal and bridges, it encompasses a vast military complex and air base, the Massachusetts Military Reservation; a major training school for seamen, the Massachusetts Maritime Academy; the Cape's second-largest town (in population), Falmouth, still green and historic yet active with shopping and culture; the Cape's oldest town, Sandwich, whose center is picture-postcard old New England; an international center of marine and biological scientific research, Woods Hole; and the Native American township of Mashpee. Along the west coast are wooded areas ending in secluded coves; along the south coast, long-established seaside resort communities.

The central section of the region, the Mid-Cape, includes the largest town, Barnstable; the main commercial hub, Hyannis, a village in Barnstable; Hyannis Port, a well-groomed enclave of wealth and site of the Kennedy Compound; and a number of historic districts and well-preserved back roads.

From the elbow to the fist of the Cape arm is the Lower Cape, the least developed Cape segment, which encompasses Chatham, a traditional and very Capey yet sophisticated town with good shopping and strolling; the Monomoy National Wildlife Refuge, a two-island Audubon bird sanctuary; Nickerson State Park, offering the Cape's prime camping in a forest setting; the beaches, woods, swamps, historic sites, and visitor centers of the Cape Cod National Seashore; the small fishing town of Wellfleet, with a number of art and crafts galleries; the high, sweeping dunes of Truro and the Province Lands; and, last but not least, Provincetown, in winter a quiet fishing village, in summer a wild and crazy place with important galleries, wonderful crafts shops, whale-watch excursion boats, good restaurants and people-watching, and lots of nightlife.

Crossing these boundaries on the north is Route 6A, the Old King's Highway, preserved for miles as a National Historic District, and true to its 17th- to 19th-century origins. On the south, Route 28 is a busy, mostly commercial highway that includes the most overdeveloped areas on the Cape. And everywhere there are bay and sound beaches, calm or wild, dune- or forest-backed, blanket-paved or secluded, which continue to offer just about every option for seekers of sun and sea.

Cape Cod is only about 70 miles from end to end, and you can make a cursory circuit of it in about two days. But it is really a place for relaxing — for swimming and sunning; for fishing, boating, and playing golf or tennis; for attending the theater, hunting for antiques, and making the rounds of the art galleries; for lobsters and fish fresh from the boat; or for leisurely walks, bike rides, or drives along pretty country roads that continue to hold out against modernity.

Essential Information

Important Addresses and Numbers

Tourist Information The **Cape Cod Chamber of Commerce** (junction of Rtes. 6 and 132, Hyannis, tel. 508/362–3225) is open year-round, weekdays 8:30–5; Memorial Day–Columbus Day, also weekends 9–4. It has information booths (open Memorial Day–Columbus Day) at the Sagamore Bridge rotary (tel. 508/888–2438) and just over the Bourne Bridge on Route 28 (tel. 508/759–3814) heading toward Falmouth.

Local chambers of commerce, many open only in season, put out literature on their area:

Brewster Board of Trade (Old Town Hall, Box 1241, 02631, tel. 508/896–8088).
Cape Cod Canal Region, for Sandwich and Bourne (70 Main St., Buzzards Bay 02532, tel. 508/759–3122; information centers at the train depot in Buzzards Bay and on Rte. 130 in Sandwich).

Chatham (533 Main St., Box 793, 02633–0793, tel. 508/945–0342; information center at 553 Main St.).

Dennis (junction of Rtes. 28 and 134, West Dennis; Box 275, South Dennis 02660, tel. 508/398–3568 or 800/243–9920).

Eastham (Rte. 6 at Fort Hill Rd., Box 1329, 02642, tel. 508/255–3444).

Falmouth (Academy La., off Main St., Box 582, 02541, tel. 508/548–8500 or 800/526–8532).

Harwich (Rte. 28, Box 34, Harwich Port 02646, tel. 508/432–1600 or 800/441–3199).

Hyannis Area (319 Barnstable Rd., 02601, tel. 508/775–2201 or 508/790–1079), fax 508/790–0179).

Mashpee (Mashpee rotary, Rte. 28, Box 1245, 02649, tel. 508/477–0792).

Orleans (Rte. 6A and Eldredge Pkwy., Box 153, 02653, tel. 508/255–1386 or 508/240–2474).

Provincetown (MacMillan Wharf, Box 1017, 02657, tel. 508/487–3424); **Provincetown Business Guild** (115 Bradford St., Box 421–89, 02657, tel. 508/487–2313; gay tourism).

Truro (Rte. 6 at Head of the Meadow Rd., Box 26, North Truro 02652, tel. 508/487–1288).

Wellfleet (Rte. 6, Box 571, 02667, tel. 508/349–2510).

Yarmouth Area (911 Rte. 28, Box 479, South Yarmouth 02664, tel. 508/398– 5311; information center on Rte. 6 between Exits 6 and 7).

Emergencies For **police** emergencies, dial 911. For **fire and ambulance** emergencies anywhere on the Cape, call 800/352–7141.

For rescues at sea, call the **Coast Guard** (Woods Hole, tel. 508/457–3277; Sandwich, tel. 508/888–0020; Chatham, tel. 508/945–3830; Provincetown, tel. 508/487–0077).

Hospitals **Cape Cod Hospital** (27 Park St., Hyannis, tel. 508/771–1800). **Falmouth Hospital** (100 Ter Heun Dr., Falmouth, tel. 508/548–5300).

Walk-in Clinics The many Cape clinics include:

Dennis Health Stop (434 Rte. 134, South Dennis, tel. 508/394–7113).

Falmouth Walk-in Medical Center (309 Main St. [Rte. 28], Teaticket, tel. 508/540–6790).

Mashpee Family Medicine (Rte. 28, Deer Crossing, Mashpee, tel. 508/477–4282).

Medi-Center Five (525 Long Pond Dr., Harwich, tel. 508/432–4100).

Mid-Cape Medical Center (Rte. 28 at Bearse's Way, Hyannis, tel. 508/771–4092; Rte. 28, South Yarmouth, tel. 508/394–2151).

Outer Cape Health Services (Rte. 6, Wellfleet, tel. 508/349–3131; Harry Kemp Way, Provincetown, tel. 508/487–9395).

Dentists **Omni Dentix** (Cape Cod Mall, Hyannis, tel. 508/778–1200) is a dental clinic that accepts emergency walk-ins.

Late-night Pharmacies Most of the Cape's 20 **CVS** stores (in the Cape Cod Mall, Hyannis, tel. 508/771–1774) are open Monday–Saturday until 9 PM, Sunday until 6; most have extended hours in summer. They usually accept out-of-town prescription refills with the prescribing doctor's phone verification. Most pharmacies post emergency numbers on their doors.

Other Information **Army Corps of Engineers 24-hour hotline** (tel. 508/759–5991) for events, tide, and fishing information on the canal area.

Tide, marine, and weather forecast (tel. 508/771–5522 or 508/255–8500).

WCOD hotline (tel. 508/790–1061) for time, temperature, weather, beach and marine reports, and concert updates.

Arriving and Departing by Plane

Airports **Barnstable Municipal Airport** (Rte. 28 rotary, Hyannis, tel. 508/775–2020) is the region's main air gateway. **Province-town Municipal Airport** (Race Point Rd., tel. 508/487–0241), through **Cape Air** (tel. 508/487–0240 or 800/999–1616), offers year-round scheduled flights to Boston, regular charters on summer weekends from New York, and other charters. Both airports are just a few minutes from the town center.

Airlines Airline service is extremely unpredictable because of the seasonal nature of Cape travel — carriers come and go, others juggle their routes. The Barnstable airport will always know which carriers fly in, should you encounter difficulty in making reservations. **Business Express/Delta Connection** (tel. 800/345–3400) flies into Hyannis nonstop from Boston (where connections are made with other routes) year-round; on weekends from June through September, it offers flights from New York (LAG). **Cape Air** connects Hyannis with Boston year-round; it also has joint fares with Continental, Delta, and USAir and ticketing-and-baggage agreements with American, Midwest Express, Northwest, and United. **Northwest Airlink** (tel. 800/225–2525) flies to Hyannis nonstop from Boston year-round, from Newark in season, with connections to the Northwest routes.

Arriving and Departing by Car

From Boston (60 miles), take Route 3, the Southeast Expressway, south to the Sagamore Bridge. From New York (220 miles), take I-95 north to Providence; change to I-195 and follow signs for the Cape to the Bourne Bridge. At the Sagamore Bridge, take Route 6 east to reach the Lower Cape and central towns quickly. At the Bourne Bridge, you can also get onto Route 6, or take Route 28 south to Falmouth and Woods Hole (about 15 miles). On summer weekends, when more than 100,000 cars a day cross each bridge, make every effort to avoid arriving there in late afternoon, especially on holidays. Routes 6, 6A, and 28 are heavily congested eastbound on Friday evening and westbound on Sunday afternoon.

Arriving and Departing by Train, Bus, and Boat

By Train **Amtrak** (tel. 800/USA–RAIL) offers limited, weekend service to the Cape, with stops at Buzzards Bay, Sandwich,

West Barnstable, and Hyannis; each year the company re-evaluates the routes, so don't be surprised if you find changes. The *Cape Codder*, on weekends from mid-June through Labor Day, travels between Hyannis and Washington, DC, with stops at Philadelphia, New York, and other points; first-class service is available. Connections with trains on other routes can of course be made at any point along the route. The rest of the year, you can travel to Boston by train and connect with buses there for Hyannis; Amtrak makes the arrangements, and connections are guaranteed. The tour desk (tel. 800/321–8684) offers packages including Hyannis hotels.

By Bus **Bonanza Bus Lines** (tel. 508/548–7588 or 800/556–3815) offers direct service to Bourne, Falmouth, the Woods Hole steamship terminal, and Hyannis from Boston, Providence, Fall River, and New Bedford, and connecting service from New York and Connecticut. **Plymouth & Brockton Street Railway** (tel. 508/775–5524 or 508/746–0378) travels to Hyannis from Boston and Logan Airport, with stops en route.

By Boat **Bay State Cruise Company** makes the three-hour trip between Commonwealth Pier in Boston (tel. 617/723–7800) and MacMillan Wharf in Provincetown (tel. 508/487–9284) from Memorial Day to Columbus Day. *Cost one way/same-day round-trip: $15/$25 adults, $13/$18 children and senior citizens, $5/$10 bicycles.*

Capt. John Boats' passenger ferry makes the 1½- to two-hour trip between Plymouth's Town Wharf and Provincetown from Memorial Day through September. Schedules allow for day excursions. *Tel. 508/747–2400 or 800/242–2469 in MA. Cost, round-trip: $20 adults, $14 children 2–11, $16 senior citizens.*

Getting Around

By Car Traffic on Cape Cod in summer can be maddening, especially on Route 28, which traces the populous south shore. Route 6 is the main artery, a limited-access (mostly divided) highway running the entire length of the Cape. On the north shore, the Old King's Highway, or Route 6A, parallels Route 6 and is a scenic country road lined with crafts and antiques shops. When you're in no hurry, use the back roads — they're less frustrating and much more rewarding.

Rental cars are available at the airport in Hyannis — **Avis** (tel. 508/775–2888), **Hertz** (tel. 508/775–5825), and **National** (tel. 508/771–4353) — or through town branches of the other major chains (*see* Chapter 1, Essential Information).

By Bus The **Cape Cod Regional Transit Authority** (tel. 800/352–7155) provides the SeaLine bus service Monday–Saturday between Hyannis and Woods Hole. Its many stops include Cape Cod Community College, Cape Cod Mall, Mashpee Commons, Falmouth, and the Woods Hole steamship docks (fares 75¢–$4); the driver will stop when signaled along the route, and all buses have lifts for the disabled. **Plymouth & Brockton** (tel. 508/775–5524 or 508/746–0378) has service between Boston and Provincetown, with stops at Sagamore and many towns in between. **Bonanza** (tel. 508/548–7588 or 800/556–3815) plies between Bourne, Falmouth, Woods Hole, and Hyannis. All service is year-round.

By Bicycle Bicycling is a satisfying way of getting around the Cape. There are many flat back roads, as well as a number of well-developed and scenic bike trails (*see* Bicycling in Sports and Outdoor Activities, *below*). The following is a sampling of the many bike-rental shops available.

Upper Cape **Corner Cycle** (115 Palmer Ave., Falmouth, tel. 508/540–4195).
Holiday Cycles (465 Grand Ave., Falmouth Heights, tel. 508/540–3549), with surrey, tandem, and other unusual bikes.
P&M Cycles (29 Main St., Buzzards Bay, tel. 508/759–2830), across from the canal path.

Mid-Cape **All Right Bike & Mower** (627 Main St., West Yarmouth, tel. 508/790–3191).
Cascade Motor Lodge (201 Main St., Hyannis, tel. 508/775–9717).
Outdoor Shop (50 Long Pond Dr., South Yarmouth, tel. 508/394–3819).
Summit Ski and Bike Shop (269 Barnstable Rd., Hyannis, tel. 508/775–3301).

Lower Cape **Arnold's** (329 Commercial St., Provincetown, tel. 508/487–0844).
Bert & Carol's Lawnmower & Bicycle Shop (347 Orleans Rd., Rte. 28, North Chatham, tel. 508/945–0137).
Black Duck Sports Shop (Rte. 6, Wellfleet, tel. 508/349–9801).
Idle Times (Rte. 6A, Brewster, tel. 508/896–9242), at Nickerson State Park just off the Rail Trail.
Summit Ski and Bike Shop (Rte. 6A, Orleans, tel. 508/255–7547).
The Little Capistrano (Rte. 6, across from Salt Pond Visitor Center, Eastham, tel. 508/255–6515).

By Moped **All Right Bike & Mower** and the **Outdoor Shop** (*see* By Bicycle, *above*) also rent mopeds.

By Limousine **Cape Escapes Tours & East Coast Limousine Co.** (tel. 800/540–0808), **Windsor Limousine Service** (tel. 508/420–1306 or 617/958–2489), and **John's Taxi & Limousine** (tel. 508/394–3209) provide 24-hour Cape-wide limo service.

By Taxi There are taxi stands at the Hyannis airport and bus station and at the Cape Cod Mall in Hyannis. A sampling of taxi companies: **All Village Taxi** (Falmouth, tel. 508/540–7200), **Chatham Taxi** (tel. 508/945–0068), **Hyannis Taxi** (tel. 508/775–0400), **Martin's Taxi** (Provincetown, tel. 508/487–0243), **Nauset Taxi** (Orleans, tel. 508/255–6965), and **Town Taxi** (Hyannis, tel. 508/775–5555).

By Horse-drawn Carriage **Rambling Rose Carriage Co.** (tel. 508/487–4246) offers carriage rides in season through Provincetown. The carriage stand is on Commercial Street in front of the town hall.

Guided Tours

Cruises **Hy-Line** offers one-hour narrated tours of Hyannis harbor,
including a view of the Kennedy compound; sunset and evening cocktail cruises are available. *Ocean St. dock, Pier 1, tel.
508/778–2600. Cost: $7 adults, $3 children 5–12.*

Cape Cod Canal Cruises (two or three hours, narrated) leave
from Onset, just before the bridges onto the Cape. A Sunday
jazz cruise, sunset cocktail cruises, and evening dance
cruises are available. *Onset Bay Town Pier, tel. 508/295–3883.
Cost: $6–$8 adults, $3–$4 children 6–12; $1 senior citizen dis-
count Mon. and Fri.*

Patriot Party Boats offers two-hour sunset cruises between
Falmouth and the Elizabeth Islands, past Woods Hole's
Nobska Light and mansions. Charters and schooner day
and evening sails are available. *227 Clinton Ave., Falmouth,
tel. 508/548–2626 or 800/734–0088 in MA. Cost: $10 adults, $6
children 6–12.*

Water Safaris offers 1½-hour tours of Bass River, past
windmills, wilderness areas, and old captains' homes, on a
32-foot aluminum boat with an awning. *Rte. 28, West Dennis,
just east of the Bass River bridge, tel. 508/362–5555. Cost: $8.50
adults, $4.50 children under 13.*

The 68-foot gaff-rigged schooner ***Bay Lady II*** makes two-
hour sails, including a sunset cruise, across Provincetown
Harbor and into Cape Cod Bay. *MacMillan Wharf, Provincetown, tel. 508/487–9308. Cost: $9–$12 adults, $5 children under
12.*

Most of the above operate from May into October. For information on boats and ferries to the islands, *see* Chapter 4,
Martha's Vineyard, and Chapter 5, Nantucket.

Train Tours **Cape Cod Scenic Railroad** runs 1¾-hour excursions (round-
trip) between Hyannis and Sagamore with stops at Sand-
wich and the canal. The train passes ponds, cranberry bogs,
and marshes. A Dinner Train begins and ends in Hyannis (3
hours), and another runs between Buzzards Bay and West
Barnstable; the five-course gourmet meal is elegantly
served as diners watch the passing scenery (floodlighted
after sunset). *Main and Center Sts., Hyannis, tel. 508/771–
3788. Excursions: several departures per day (no service Mon.)
in each direction mid-June–Oct. (weekends starting in May).
Cost: $10.50 adults, $6.50 children 3–12, $9.50 senior citizens.
Dinner train: mid-May–Dec., departs various evenings (reservations required 24 hrs in advance). Cost: $39.95.*

Nature Tours The **Massachusetts Audubon Society** (contact Wellfleet Bay
Wildlife Sanctuary, Box 236, South Wellfleet 02663, tel.
508/349–2615) sponsors naturalist-led wildlife tours year-
round, including a tour of Nauset Marsh and Coast Guard
Beach, with a walk on the tidal flats and a stop at the tern
nesting colony; trips to the bird sanctuary of Monomoy Island; plus canoe trips, bay cruises, bird and insect walks,
hikes, and more.

The Audubon Society's **Ashumet Holly and Wildlife Sanctuary** in East Falmouth (Ashumet Rd., tel. 508/563–6390) offers nature day trips and cruises to Cuttyhunk Island (including seal cruises in winter and spring), with guided birding walks in season. Phone reservations are required.

The **Cape Cod National Seashore** (Salt Pond, tel. 508/255–3421; South Wellfleet, tel. 508/349–3785; Province Lands, tel. 508/487–1256; *see also* Tour 5: Orleans to Provincetown, *below*) has guided walks, canoe trips, and more, daily from Memorial Day to Columbus Day and on weekends in early spring and late fall; plus self-guided walking trails with accompanying leaflets.

Cape Cod Museum of Natural History (*see* Tour 3: Route 6A, Hyannis to Orleans, *below*) offers tours to Monomoy, some including overnights at the lighthouse.

Plane Tours Sightseeing by air is offered by **Cape Cod Airport** (1000 Race Lane, Marstons Mills, near Hyannis, tel. 508/428–8732), **Chatham Municipal Airport** (George Ryder Rd., West Chatham, tel. 508/945–9000), **Hyannis Air Service** (Barnstable airport, tel. 508/775–8171 or 800/321–9912), **Cape Copters** (helicopters; Barnstable airport, tel. 508/790–1998), and **Cape Air** (Provincetown airport, tel. 508/487–0240). Among Cape Air's offerings are helicopter tours and tours in a 1931 Stinson.

Dune Tours **Art's Dune Tours** are hour-long narrated auto tours through the National Seashore and the dunes around Provincetown. *Tel. 508/487–1950 or 508/487–1050. Cost: $8 daytime, $9 sunset. Tours mid-Apr.–mid-Nov.*

Trolley Tours The **P-town Trolley** leaves from Provincetown's Town Hall, with pickups at other locations, on the hour from 10 to 7 and on the half-hour from 10:30 to 5:30. Points of interest on the 40-minute narrated tours include the downtown area and the Province Lands Visitor Center of the Cape Cod National Seashore. Riders can get on and off at four locations. *Tel. 508/487–9483. Cost: $6 adults, $4 children under 13, $5 senior citizens. Tours May–Oct.*

Whale-watching One of the joys of Cape Cod is the opportunity it affords for making trips to the whale feeding grounds at Stellwagen Bank, about 6 miles off the tip of Provincetown. On a sunny day especially, the boat ride out into open ocean is part of the pleasure, but the thrill, of course, is the sightings. You may spot minke, humpback, or finback whales, or the most endangered great-whale species, the right whale; just as welcome are dolphins, which in fact are toothed whales, and the seabirds that tag along for the ride.

Several operators offer whale-watch tours, with morning, afternoon, or sunset sailings lasting three to four hours. Provincetown is the main center. All boats have food service, but remember to bring sunscreen and a sweater or jacket — the breeze makes it chilly. Some boats stock seasickness pills, but if you're susceptible, come prepared!

Dolphin Fleet tours are accompanied by scientists who provide commentary while collecting data on the whale population they've been monitoring for years. They know the whales by name and tell you about their habits and histories. *Ticket office in Chamber of Commerce building at MacMillan Wharf, tel. 508/349–1900 or 800/826–9300. Cost: $15–$16 adults (seasonal variation), $13–$14 children 7–12 and senior citizens. Tours Apr.–Oct.*

The *Portuguese Princess* sails with a naturalist on board to narrate, plus a folk singer or other entertainer on some trips; the snack bar offers Portuguese specialties. Whale sightings are guaranteed. *Tickets available at 70 Shank Painter Rd. ticket office or at Whale Watchers General Store, 309 Commercial St., tel. 508/487–2651 or 800/442–3188 in MA. Cost: $15–$16 adults, $13–$14 children 7–12 and senior citizens. Tours Apr.–Oct.*

The *Ranger V,* the largest whale-watch boat, also has a naturalist on board. *Ticket office on Bradford St. at the corner of Standish St., tel. 508/487–3322, 508/487–1582, or 800/992–9333 in MA. Cost: $14–$17 adults, $10–$12 children 8–12, $12–$14 senior citizens. Tours May–mid-Nov.*

Out of Barnstable Harbor, there's **Hyannis Whale Watcher Cruises.** A naturalist narrates and gives commentary on the sightings and Cape Cod Bay. *Mill Way, Barnstable, tel. 508/362–6088 or 800/287–0374 in MA. Cost: $18–$22 adults, $10 children 4–12, $17–$18 senior citizens. Tours Apr.–Nov.*

Exploring Cape Cod

The bridges over the canal are welcome sights to those approaching the Cape by land — signs every return vacationer eagerly awaits and never takes for granted. They're a bit magical, glistening silver arcs in the air, with boats small and large gliding smoothly below. The **Bourne Bridge** is the longest, at 2,384 feet; the **Sagamore Bridge** is 1,408 feet long. Each is supported by 44 steel cables suspended from the arch. They were completed in 1935, as was the railroad bridge, which has a movable span that lowers on the approach of a train (it takes about 2½ minutes).

Beyond the bridges, Cape Cod is traversed by three main highways. Route 6, the Mid-Cape Highway, passes through the relatively unpopulated center of the Cape, characterized by a landscape of scrub pine and oak. This is the fastest route east–west, and to Provincetown.

Paralleling Route 6 but following the north coast is Route 6A (also known as the Old King's Highway, the Cranberry Highway, and the Grand Army of the Republic Highway), in most sections a winding country road that passes through some of the Cape's best-preserved old New England towns. Here are main streets lined with stately sea captains' mansions and shaded by ancient, leafy trees. The bay side, as the north coast is called, tends to be marshy, and the water in the protected bay is calmer than that of Nantucket Sound and the Atlantic.

The south shore of the Cape, traced by Route 28 and encompassing Falmouth, Hyannis, and Chatham, is heavily populated and is the major center for tourism. Its growth as a resort area has been abetted by its abundance of scenic harbors overlooking Nantucket Sound and its beaches with white sand and gentle surf. Route 28 itself is a busy highway, in summer densely packed with cars. Between about Hyannis and Harwich Port, it is flanked by strip malls, restaurants, motels, and kiddie attractions.

At Orleans, Routes 6A and 28 join with Route 6, which then continues alone through the sparsely populated Outer Cape (also called the back side) to the tip of Cape Cod.

More is included in each of the tours that follow than can be comfortably covered in one day, on the assumption that visitors will select the stops that are of most interest to them. Hyannis and Orleans are used as convenient beginning and end points; Hyannis itself is covered in Tour 1, Orleans in Tour 3.

Highlights for First-time Visitors

Cape Cod Museum of Natural History, Brewster (*see* Tour 3)
Cape Cod National Seashore (*see* Tour 5)
Heritage Plantation, Sandwich (*see* Tour 1)
Julia Wood House, Falmouth (*see* Tour 2)
Kennedy Memorial, Hyannis (*see* Tour 1)
Pilgrim Monument, Provincetown (*see* Tour 6)
Sandy Neck, Sandwich (*see* Tour 1)
Whale watching (*see* Guided Tours, *above*)

Tour 1: Route 6A, Sagamore Bridge to Hyannis

This tour traverses a quiet section of the north shore, on a country road lined with small shops. All of Route 6A from Sandwich east — encompassing the oldest settlements on the Cape — is part of the Old King's Highway historic district and therefore protected from development. In fall, the foliage along the road is bright because of the many ponds and marshes, and along 6A in Sandwich you can stop to watch the berries being harvested in flooded bogs. The whole tour covers about 25 miles.

Numbers in the margin correspond to points of interest on the Tours 1 and 2: The Canal to Hyannis map.

Take the first exit after crossing the Sagamore Bridge, then a right off the exit. Past the Cape Cod Factory Outlet Mall and across the street from the entrance to the Christmas Tree Shop (for both, *see* Shopping, *below*) is **Pairpont Crystal** (formerly Pairpont Glass), where you can watch richly colored lead crystal being hand-blown in the factory, as it has been for 150 years. The shop sells finished wares, including ornamental cup plates (used to hold the cup in the days when tea was poured into the saucer to drink). *Rte. 6A, Sagamore, tel. 508/888–2344 or 800/899–0953. Open daily 9–6; demonstrations weekdays 8:30–4:30.*

1 Continuing along Route 6A, you enter **Sandwich,** the oldest town on the Cape (founded in 1637). Signs direct you to Sandwich center, a perfect old New England village and a good place to walk around a bit. To take the following easy walking tour, turn right at Main St.

Unlike other Cape towns, whose deep-water ports opened the doors to prosperity in the whaling days, Sandwich was an industrial town for much of the 19th century. The main industry was the production of vividly colored glass, called Sandwich glass, which is today a collector's item. The glass was made in the Boston & Sandwich Glass Company's factory here from 1825 until 1888, when competition with glassmakers in the Midwest — and finally a union strike — closed it. The **Sandwich Glass Museum,** across from the town hall, contains relics of the town's early history, a diorama showing how the factory looked in its heyday, and an outstanding collection of blown and pressed glass. *129 Main St., tel. 508/888-0251. Admission: $3 adults, 50¢ children 6-12. Open Apr.-Oct., daily 9:30-4:30; Nov., Dec., Feb., and Mar., Wed.-Sun. 9:30-4; closed Jan.*

Farther down Main Street, across River Street on the left, is the **Yesteryears Doll Museum.** Housed in the unfortunately rundown 1833 First Parish Meetinghouse, the enormous collection includes antique German and French dolls in bisque, china, wax, and many other media; lacquer-and-gold miniatures of a Japanese emperor and empress and their court; Henry VIII and his wives, elegantly clothed in velvets and brocades; samurai warriors; and Balinese shadow puppets. The museum also has some wonderful miniature sets, such as a toy millinery shop with display cases, hatboxes, even ladies trying on hats; period German kitchens, complete with pewter, brass, copper, and tin implements; and an elaborately detailed four-story late Victorian dollhouse with wedding feast going on. A shop sells antique dolls. *143 Main St., tel. 508/888-1711. Admission: $3 adults, $2.50 senior citizens, $2 children under 12. Open mid-May-Oct., Mon.-Sat. 10-4. Closed Nov.-mid-May.*

Just beyond is the **Dan'l Webster Inn,** a reconstruction of a historic inn, and on both sides of the street are antiques and gift shops and art galleries. At School Street, turn right; across Water Street (Route 130) is the **Hoxie House,** a saltbox remarkable in that it has been virtually unaltered since it was built in 1675 — though it was lived in until the 1950s, it was never modernized with electricity or plumbing. Overlooking Shawme Pond, it has been furnished authentically to reflect daily life in the Colonial period; some pieces are on loan from the Museum of Fine Arts in Boston. Highlights are diamond-shaped leaded-glass windows and a collection of small antique textile machines (spinning wheels, yarn winders, a 17th-century harness loom). *Rte. 130, tel. 508/888-1173. Admission: $1.50 adults, 75¢ children 12-16. Open mid-June-mid-Sept., Mon.-Sat. 10-5, Sun. 1-5. Closed mid-Sept.-mid-June.*

Turn left as you leave the Hoxie House and follow Water Street to the **Thornton W. Burgess Museum,** dedicated to

53

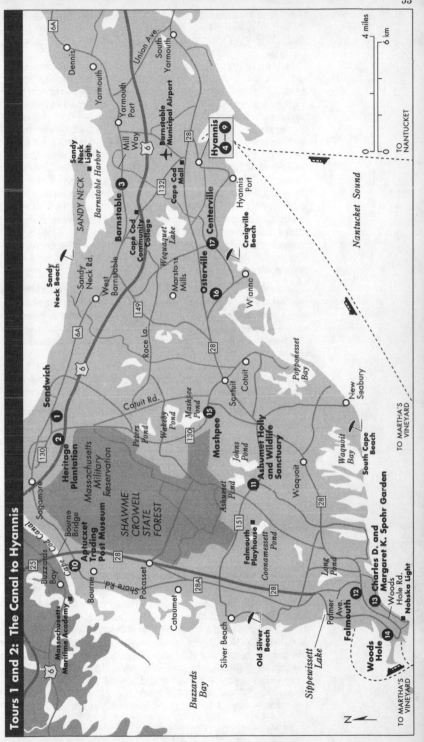

Tours 1 and 2: The Canal to Hyannis

TO NANTUCKET

TO MARTHA'S VINEYARD

Nantucket Sound

Buzzards Bay

Hyannis ④—⑨

Centerville ⑰

Osterville ⑯

Mashpee ⑮

Ashumet Holly and Wildlife Sanctuary ⑪

Charles D. and Margaret K. Spohr Garden ⑫

Falmouth ⑭

Woods Hole

Sandwich ①

Heritage Plantation ②

Barnstable ③

Aptucxet Trading Post Museum ⑩

Massachusetts Maritime Academy

SHAWME CROWELL STATE FOREST

Massachusetts Military Reservation

Cape Cod Mall

Barnstable Municipal Airport

Cape Cod Community College

4 miles
6 km

this Sandwich native whose stories about Peter Rabbit, Reddy Fox, and a host of other creatures of the Old Briar Patch have been part of children's bedtimes for decades. Burgess, an avid conservationist, made his characters behave true to their species in order to educate children as he entertained them. A storytelling session, featuring the live animal that the Burgess story is about, is held regularly in July and August. The museum is best for small children or nostalgic adults; the many displays crowded into the small old house include some of Burgess's 170 books (and information about him), as well as changing exhibits on nature and children's hands-on exhibits. The small gift shop carries inexpensive items, including stuffed animals and Pairpont Glass cup plates decorated with Burgess characters. Out back is a small touch-and-smell herb garden and a labeled herb garden in the shape of a tussie-mussie (a Victorian nosegay). Benches overlook the lovely **Shawme Pond** as ducks and geese bathe along the shore and wander the grounds. *4 Water St. (Rte. 130), tel. 508/888–4668. Donations accepted. Open Mon.–Sat. 10–4, Sun. 1–4; Jan.–Mar., may close Sun. and/or Mon.*

Just beyond is the waterwheel-operated **Dexter Gristmill**, restored in 17th-century style and still grinding corn in season (you can buy the meal). Approach it via a covered wooden bridge over a watercourse in a picturesque park at the pond, where children seem always to be fishing and the ducks love to be fed. Where Main Street joins Water you'll notice the tall, white spire of the **First Church of Christ**, built in 1848 and inspired by a design of London architect Christopher Wren.

② Leaving the village, take Grove Street to **Heritage Plantation,** an extraordinary complex of museum buildings, gardens, and a new café on 76 beautifully landscaped acres overlooking Shawme Pond. The grounds, crisscrossed by paths, include daylily, hostia, heather, herb, fruit-tree, and other gardens, as well as an extensive dell of rhododendrons begun by onetime estate owner Charles O. Dexter, an expert in hybridization. (In 1967, pharmaceuticals magnate Josiah K. Lilly III purchased the estate and turned it into a nonprofit museum.) The Shaker Round Barn showcases classic and historic cars, including a 1931 yellow-and-green Duesenberg built for Gary Cooper, a 1919 Pierce-Arrow, and a 1911 Stanley Steamer. The Military Museum houses antique firearms, a collection of 2,000 hand-painted miniature soldiers, military uniforms, and Native American arts. The Art Museum exhibits Colonial tools, an extensive Currier & Ives collection, Americana (including a mechanical-bank collection), antique toys such as a 1920 Hubley Royal Circus, and a working 1912 "Coney Island–style" carousel. In summer, evening concerts are held in the gardens. Peak bloom time for rhododendrons is mid-May–mid-June; for daylilies, July–early August. *Grove and Pine Sts., tel. 508/888–3300. Admission: $7 adults, $3.50 children 6–18, $6 senior citizens. Open mid-May–Oct., daily 10–5. Closed Nov.–mid-May.*

Return to Sandwich center and from there to Route 6A, then head east. Before you get to Exit 3 you will come to the **Green Briar Nature Center and Jam Kitchen,** owned by the Thornton Burgess Society, which runs the Burgess museum as well. The nature center offers changing exhibits on natural history, such as live frogs or turtles, aquariums, Indian artifacts, and seashells, as well as nature classes, walks, and lectures for adults and children. Great smells waft from the vintage stoves in the Jam Kitchen, and you can watch as jams, cranberry dishes, sun-cooked fruits, and pickles are made according to the recipes used here since 1903. *6 Discovery Hill Rd., off Rte. 6A, East Sandwich, tel. 508/888–6870. Donations accepted. Open Mon.–Sat. 10–4, Sun. 1–4; Jan.–Mar., may close Sun. and/or Mon.*

The center is set on 4 acres of gardens (labeled herb garden, bee garden, wildflower garden) that adjoin 57 acres of town conservation land laced with easy nature trails, dubbed the **Old Briar Patch.** The many varieties of plants and trees here include black locust, white oak, red maple, tupelo, highbush blueberry, American beech and holly, swamp honeysuckle, gray birch, and spice bush; a brochure (with map) of the trails, available at the nature center, helps you identify them.

Sandy Neck Road (3.7 miles farther on 6A, on the left, opposite Michael's at Sandy Neck restaurant) leads to **Sandy Neck Beach.** Even the approach, through duneland, is beautiful. On a peninsula, with the bay to the north and the great salt marshes and Barnstable Harbor to the south, this is a good beach for walking; all you see is dunes and sand and sea in both directions. At the tip of the neck, the **Sandy Neck Light,** nonoperational since 1952 and now privately owned, stands just a few feet from the eroding shoreline. It was built in 1857 (to replace an 1827 light) of steel painted white, and it ran on acetylene gas.

As you continue east on 6A, past fine views of meadows and the bay, you enter the town of **Barnstable,** the Cape's largest, with more than 36,000 year-round residents, and the second oldest, having been founded in 1639, two years after Sandwich. You've just left the cozy Upper Cape for the busy Mid-Cape, but here in the historic district you won't notice the difference.

Past the junction of Route 132 (which leads to the **Cape Cod Community College,** set on 120 wooded acres, and opposite it, the **Cape Cod Conservatory of Music and Arts**), a left at Scudder Lane will bring you to Barnstable Harbor, and a peaceful view of Sandy Neck across the water. At low tide the flats are exposed almost all the way out to the neck. A bit farther on 6A and you're in **Barnstable Village,** a lovely area of large old homes and the county seat. The **Olde Colonial Courthouse,** on the left, built in 1772 as the colony's second courthouse, is the home of the historical society Tales of Cape Cod (tel. 508/362–8927), which is restoring it to serve as a museum; a series of slide-illustrated lectures is held in summer.

Just past the county courthouse, on the left, is the 1644 **Sturgis Library**. Its holdings, which date back to the 17th century, include more than 1,500 maps and land charts, the definitive collection of Cape Cod genealogical material, and an extensive maritime-history collection. *3090 Main St. (Rte. 6A), tel. 508/362–6636. Day use: $5. Open Mon. and Wed. 10–5, Tues. and Thurs. 1–5 and 7–9, Fri. 1–5 (hours changeable).*

Beyond the library is the little village center. Here the Barnstable Village Hall is home to the **Barnstable Comedy Club**, one of the oldest community theater groups in the country. A left onto Mill Way at the traffic light leads to **Barnstable Harbor**, with a fleet of fishing, charter, and whale-watch boats. Beyond the light, on the right, is the **Trayser Museum Complex**, reopened in 1990 after two years of renovation. The downstairs re-creates the way it looked in 1856, when it was a customs house (don't miss the bronze acanthus-leaf capitals on the pillars). Listed on the National Register of Historic Places, the red-painted brick building now houses a small collection of maritime exhibits (telescopes, captains' shaving boxes, items brought back from voyages, ship paintings), plus ivory, Sandwich glass, and Indian arrowheads. On the second floor is the restored customs-keeper's office with the original safe and a harbor view. Also on the grounds are a circa 1690 jail with two cells bearing former inmates' grafitti; and a carriage house with early tools, fishing implements, and a 19th-century horse-drawn hearse. *Rte. 6A, Barnstable, tel. 508/362–2092. Donations accepted. Open July–mid-Oct., Tues.–Sat. 1:30–4:30. Closed mid-Oct.–June.*

If you return to the traffic light, a left there will take you into Hyannis (about 2 miles) along a favorite local traffic-avoiding route. Beyond the intersection with Route 6, a left onto Route 132 leads past the **Cape Cod Mall** to what's called the Airport rotary, with the **Barnstable Municipal Airport** just beyond, on Route 28. Signs at the rotary will lead you to downtown **Hyannis**, the Cape's year-round commercial hub, and a visibly different scene from what you've just left. Now you're well and truly in the Mid-Cape.

❹

Numbers in the margin correspond to points of interest on the Hyannis map.

A right turn onto Main Street will take you through the downtown. Three parallel streets run through the heart of Hyannis. The busy, shop-filled Main Street is one-way, from east to west; South Street runs from west to east; and North Street is open to two-way traffic. At the Old Town Hall on Main Street, a temporary, seasonal exhibition of **photographs from JFK's Cape years**, culled from the archives of the JFK Library in Boston, has been set up pending the realization of the John F. Kennedy Hyannis Museum. At the end of Main Street is the West End rotary; just beyond it, on West Main Street, is the famous **Melody Tent**, opened in 1950 by the actress Gertrude Lawrence and her husband, producer/manager Richard Aldrich, to showcase Broadway musicals and concerts. Today the focus has shifted away from theater to music and stand-up comedy (*see* The Arts, *below*).

❺

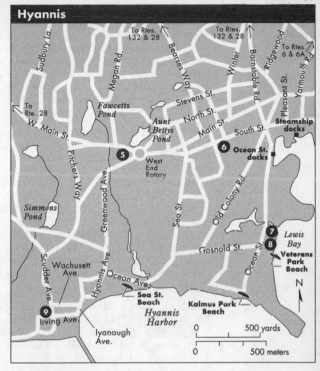

6 Return to the rotary and head toward Main Street; bear
right onto South Street and on your right you'll pass **St.
Francis Xavier Church,** the little church where Rose
Kennedy and her family worshiped during their summers
on the Cape. The pew that John F. Kennedy used regularly
is marked by a plaque. A few doors down is an **octagonal
house,** built in 1850 by a clipper ship master. At Ocean
Street, turn right. Past the bustling docks — with boats for
deep-sea fishing, harbor tours, and ferries to the islands, as
7 well as waterfront seafood restaurants — is the **John F.
Kennedy Memorial,** a quiet esplanade overlooking boat-
filled Lewis Bay, with a plaque and fountain pool erected in
1966 by the people of Barnstable in memory of the president
who loved to sail these waters. Adjacent to the memorial is
8 **Veterans Park,** with a beach, a tree-shaded picnic and barbecue area, and a playground. At the end of Ocean Street is
Kalmus Beach, a long sandy beach with an area for windsurfers.

Hyannis Port was a mecca for Americans during the
9 Kennedy presidency, when the **Kennedy compound** became
the summer White House. The days of hordes of Secret
Service men and swarms of tourists trampling down the
bushes are gone, and the area is once again a community of
quietly posh estates, though the Kennedy mystique is such
that tourists still seek it out. To get a glimpse of the compound, less than 2 miles from the memorial, take a right onto
Gosnold Street across from Veterans Park. At the stop sign,

turn left at Sea Street; bear right onto Ocean Avenue, past
Sea Street Beach; at the next stop sign, turn left onto Hyannis Avenue. If you stop a minute by the stone tower here,
you'll get a good view of the long, narrow dock of the **Hyannis Port Yacht Club,** on Irving Avenue, stretching out into
the harbor. Take the next left onto Iyanough Avenue, right
onto Wachusett Avenue, then left onto Scudder Avenue. The
compound is one block over, bounded by Scudder and Irving
avenues.

Joseph P. and Rose Kennedy bought their house here — the
largest one closest to the water — in 1929, as a healthful
place to summer with their soon-to-be-nine children. Sons
Jack and Bobby bought neighboring homes in the 1950s.
Jack's (now Jacqueline Onassis's) is the one at the corner of
Scudder and Irving, with the six-foot-high stockade fence
on two sides. Bobby's (now Ethel's) is next to it, with the
white fieldstone chimney. Ted bought a home on Squaw Island, a private island connected to the area by a causeway
at the end of Scudder Avenue; it now belongs to his ex-wife,
Joan. And Eunice (Kennedy) and Sargent Shriver have a
house near Squaw Island, on Atlantic Avenue.

The compound is relatively self-sufficient in terms of entertainment: Rose Kennedy's home (with 14 rooms and nine
baths) has a movie theater, and there's a private beach, a
boat dock, a swimming pool, a tennis court, and a sports
field, scene of the famous Kennedy touch-football matches.
The Hy-Line harbor cruise (*see* Guided Tours, *above*) passes
in front of the compound, close enough for a good overview.

Scudder Avenue leads back to the West End rotary and from
there to town.

Tour 2: Route 28, Bourne Bridge to Hyannis

Route 28 from the Bourne Bridge south to Falmouth is commercial in many areas; Route 28A, between Pocasset and
North Falmouth, is more scenic, with side roads leading to
attractive beaches and small harbors. The Falmouth–Hyannis segment traverses some little-developed south-coastal
areas, a situation that quickly changes at Hyannis. The tour
covers about 50 miles.

*Numbers in the margin correspond to points of interest on the
Tours 1 and 2: The Canal to Hyannis map.*

Just over the Bourne Bridge, take a right at the rotary onto
🔟 Trowbridge Road and follow signs to the **Aptucxet Trading
Post Museum,** a monument to the birth of commerce in the
New World. Here, in 1627, Plimoth Plantation leaders established a way station between the Indian encampment at
Great Herring Pond, 3 miles to the northeast; the Dutch
colonists in New Amsterdam (New York) to the south, beyond Buzzards Bay; and the English colonists on Cape Cod
Bay. Before the canal was built, the Manomet River connected the pond with Buzzards Bay (no, scavengers don't
frequent it — it was misnamed for the migrating osprey
that do), and a short portage connected the pond to Scusset

River, which met Cape Cod Bay. The Indians traded furs; the Dutch, linen cloth, metal tools, glass beads, and sugar and other staples; the Pilgrims, wool cloth, clay beads, sassafras, and tobacco (which they imported from Virginia). Wampum was the medium of exchange.

A replica of the post, including the original brick hearth, was erected on the original's foundations; inside are 17th-century cooking utensils, firearms, furniture, and other artifacts, plus Indian arrowhawks, tools, and tomahawks. Also on the grounds are a gift shop in a Dutch-style windmill; a small Victorian railroad station built for the sole use of President Grover Cleveland, who had a summer home in Bourne; a saltworks; herb and wildflower gardens; and a picnic area overlooking the canal. *Aptucxet Rd., tel. 508/759–9487. Admission: $1.50 adults, 50¢ schoolchildren, $1.25 senior citizens. Open May–Columbus Day, Tues.–Sat. 10–5, Sun. 2–5 (July, Aug., and Mon. holidays, also Mon. 10–5). Closed Columbus Day–Apr.*

Return to Route 28 and head south. On your left is the 21,000-acre **Massachusetts Military Reservation,** consisting of the Camp Edwards Army National Guard and Reserve Training Site, the Coast Guard Air Station Cape Cod, and the Otis Air National Guard Base (with the PAVE PAWS radar station, a sophisticated system designed to track military satellites and nuclear missiles). The main entrance is at the so-called Otis rotary on Route 28; others are on Route 130 in Forestdale and on Route 151 in Falmouth. Tours can be arranged (*see* Off the Beaten Track, *below*).

The reservation, more often referred to as Otis Air Base, holds a free two-day open house each summer with exhibitions that may include precision flying by teams of the Air Force's Thunderbirds or the Navy's Blue Angels. Other highlights may be performances by the Air Force Band, the Air Force honor guard and drill team, the National Guard's Equestrian Unit, or the Army's Golden Knights Parachute Team. Military planes are on display, and concession stands serve the crowds. For dates and information, call 508/968–4090 or 508/968–4003.

Leave Route 28 at the Otis rotary for Route 28A, which winds past the little villages of Pocasset and Cataumet, with their old houses, pretty streets, and ocean views. A left toward Cataumet Village takes you on an even more scenic drive along County Road, past cranberry bogs and an old graveyard, then rejoins 28A. A left onto Route 151 leads you to the renowned **Falmouth Playhouse,** one of the Cape's top theater venues.

Beyond the playhouse sign on Route 151, before the fairgrounds, a left leads to the **Ashumet Holly and Wildlife Sanctuary,** a 45-acre tract of woods, shady groves, meadows, and hiking trails (self-guided maps are available). Operated by the Massachusetts Audubon Society, the reservation features more than 1,000 holly trees, including 65 American, Oriental, and European varieties. Like the Heritage Plantation in Sandwich, it was purchased and donated by Josiah

K. Lilly III for preservation purposes. Grassy Pond is home to many turtles and frogs, and in summer, 35 nesting pairs of barn swallows live in open rafters of the barn (they can be viewed Tues.–Sat. 9–4); downstairs is a small gift shop with handcrafted items. In spring, there's an open house when the dogwoods and rhododendrons are in bloom; in September, a festival tied in with the flowering of the Franklinia shrub; in December, a three-day holly sale. Fall through spring, crafts and nature classes are given. *286 AshumetRd., East Falmouth, tel. 508/563–6390. Admission: $3 adults, $2 senior citizens and children under 13. Trails open daily sunrise–sunset; office open Tues.–Sat. 9–4.*

Retrace your route 5 miles on 151 back to 28A and continue south, past a sign leading to **Old Silver Beach,** one of the Cape's prettiest. Shortly after 28A merges into 28, another sign directs you to a scenic drive past **Sippewissett Lake,** or ⑫ continue on Route 28 to the center of **Falmouth.**

The Cape's second-largest town, Falmouth was settled in 1660 by Congregationalists from Barnstable who had been ostracized from their church and deprived of voting privileges and other civil rights for being sympathizers with the Quakers, then the objects of severe repression. The **Village Green** — a spare triangle of grass with a few trees, a flagpole ringed by flowers, and a low white fence — was used as a militia training field in the 18th century and a grazing ground for horses in the early 19th. Today it is flanked by attractive old homes, some built by sea captains, and the 1856 **Congregational Church** (built on the timbers of its 1796 predecessor), with a bell made by Paul Revere. The cheery inscription reads: "The living to the church I call, and to the grave I summon all."

Opposite the green, on Palmer Avenue, are the two museums maintained by the Falmouth Historical Society. The 1790 **Julia Wood House** retains wonderful architectural details (a widow's walk, wide-board floors, leaded-glass windows, a Colonial kitchen with wide hearth), plus antique embroideries, baby shoes and clothes, toys and dolls, portraits, furniture, and an authentically equipped doctor's office (from its onetime owner). Out back is a barn museum with antique farm implements, a 19th-century horse-drawn sleigh, and more. The smaller **Conant House** next door, a 1794 half-Cape, has military memorabilia, whaling items, scrimshaw, sailors' valentines, silver, glass, china, handmade quilts, and a genealogical and historical research library. There's also a collection of books, portraits, and other memorabilia relating to Katharine Lee Bates, the native daughter who wrote "America the Beautiful." Docents lead you through the museums; free walking tours of the town are also available in season (call for meeting times). Adjacent to the museums is a pretty formal **garden,** with a gazebo, statuary, flagstone paths, rosebushes, sculptured boxwood hedges, and labeled plantings. *Palmer Ave., tel. 508/548–4857. Admission: $2 adults, 50¢ children under 13. Open mid-June–mid-Sept., weekdays 2–5.*

On the other side of the green, a right onto Main Street will take you to the white Cape house (at No. 16) that is the **birthplace of Katharine Lee Bates.** Owned by the historical society, the 1812 house is no longer open to the public; a plaque on a rock out front commemorates Bates's birth, in 1859.

Time Out   **Peking Palace** (452 Main St., tel. 508/540–8204) offers good Mandarin, Szechwan, and Cantonese food in a quiet, attractively Oriental setting, and is open until 2 AM nightly in summer, weekends year-round.

Leave town by way of Locust Street (passing the entrance to the **Shining Sea Bikeway** to Woods Hole on your left, across from a small parking lot), which turns into Woods Hole Road; at the stoplights 1.7 miles from town, a left onto Oyster Pond Road and another onto Fells Road takes you to
⓭ the **Charles D. and Margaret K. Spohr Garden,** a private garden of 3 planted acres on Oyster Pond that the generous owner invites the public to enjoy. In spring, there are glorious displays of more than 700,000 daffodils, plus lilies, tulips, azaleas, magnolias, flowering crabs, rhododendrons, climbing hydrangeas, and more. A collection of old millstones, bronze church bells, and ship's anchors are woven into the landscaping. Specimen trees and shrubs are tagged for identification.

At the Cape's southwest tip, about 4 miles from Falmouth
⓮ on 28, is **Woods Hole,** a center for international marine research and home to several major scientific institutions. The National Marine Fisheries Service was here first, established in 1871 to study fish management and conservation. In 1888, the Marine Biological Laboratory (MBL), a center for research and education in marine biology, moved in across the street. In 1930, the Woods Hole Oceanographic Institution (WHOI) joined the group, and in the 1960s the U.S. Geological Survey's Branch of Marine Geology set up shop.

WHOI is the largest of the institutions, with several buildings in the village and a 200-acre campus nearby. During World War II its research focused on underwater explosives, submarine detection, and the development of antifouling paint. Today it is the largest independent oceanography research laboratory in the country, with an $80 million annual operating budget. A graduate program is offered jointly with MIT, in addition to K–12, undergraduate, and postdoctoral studies. WHOI's several research vessels range throughout the world's waters conducting research; its staff led the successful U.S.–French search for the *Titanic* (found about 400 miles off Newfoundland) in 1985.

Most of the year, Woods Hole is a peaceful community of intellectuals, who quietly go about their work. In summer, however, the basically one-street village teems with the 1,000 or more scientists and graduate students from all over the world who come either to participate in summer studies at MBL or WHOI or to work on independent research projects. A handful of waterside cafés and shops along Water Street compete for most bicycles stacked up at the door.

What accounts for this incredible concentration of scientific minds is, first, the variety and abundance of marine life in Woods Hole's unpolluted waters, and the natural deep-water port. Second is the opportunity for easy interchange of ideas and information and the stimulation of daily lectures and discussions (many open to the public) by important scientists. Third, the pooling of resources among the various institutions makes for economies that benefit each while allowing all access to highly sophisticated equipment.

A good example of this pooling of resources is the **MBL-WHOI Library,** possessor of one of the best collections of biological, ecological, and oceanographic literature in the world, including access to over 200 computer data bases and the Internet, and subscriptions to more than 5,000 scientific journals in 40 languages (with complete collections of most from their first issue). During World War II, the librarian arranged with a German subscription agency to have German periodicals sent to neutral Switzerland, to be stored until the end of the war; thus the library's German collections are uninterrupted whereas even many German institutions' are not. All journals are always accessible, because they cannot be checked out and because the library is open 24 hours a day. The Rare Books Room contains photographs, monographs, and prints, as well as journal collections dating back to 1665.

Unless you are a scientific researcher, the only way you'll get to see the library is by taking the **Marine Biological Laboratory tour** (tel. 508/548–3705, ext. 423; call for reservations, at least a week in advance if possible, and meeting instructions). The 1½-hour tours are led by retired scientists (mid-June–Aug., weekdays at 1 PM) and include an introductory slide show, as well as stops at the library, the marine resources center (where live sea creatures collected each day are kept), and one of the many research labs, where scientists will demonstrate the project they are working on.

The Oceanographic Institution is not open to the public, but you can learn about it at the small **WHOI Exhibit Center,** with videos and exhibits on the institute and its various projects. *15 School St., tel. 508/457–2000, ext. 2663. Admission free. Open mid-June–Labor Day, Mon.–Sat. 9:30–5, Sun. noon–5; call for spring and fall hours. Closed mid-Dec.–Mar.*

The **National Marine Fisheries Service Aquarium** displays 16 tanks of regional fish and shellfish, plus microscopes for kids to examine marine life and several hands-on pools with banded lobsters, crabs, snails, starfish, and other creatures. The star attractions are two harbor seals, who can be seen in the outdoor pool near the entrance in summer (they winter in Connecticut). *Corner of Albatross and Water Sts., tel. 508/548–7684. Admission free. Open late June–mid-Sept., daily 10–4; mid-Sept.–late June, weekdays 9–4.*

Leaving town as you entered it, you might stop in at the **Bradley House Museum,** which is devoted to the history of

the town and its scientific institutions. In the archives you'll
find old ships' logs, postcards, newspaper articles, maps,
diaries, photographs; more than 200 tapes of oral history
provided by local residents; and a 100-volume library on
maritime history. In the museum (across from the **Martha's
Vineyard ferry** parking lot entrance) are paintings, tools, a
restored Woods Hole Spritsail boat, boat models, and a
model of the town as it looked in the 1890s. Free guided
walking tours of the village are available on Tuesdays at 4
in July and August. *573 Woods Hole Rd., tel. 508/548-7270.
Donations accepted. Museum open July–Aug., Tues.–Sat. 10–
4. Closed Sept.–June. Archives open year-round, Tues. and
Thurs. 10–2.*

Beyond the museum, a right onto Church Street takes you
past some fine estates. On the left is the 1888 **Episcopal
Church of the Messiah,** a stone church with a conical steeple
and a small medicinal herb garden in the shape of a Celtic
cross. The garden is enclosed by an ilex hedge and provided
with a bench for meditation. Inscriptions on either side of
the carved gate read "Enter in hope" and "Depart in peace."

Turning into a shore road, Church Street leads to **Nobska
Light,** from which the views of the nearby Elizabeth Islands
and of Martha's Vineyard, across Vineyard Sound, are spectacular. The 42-foot cast-iron tower lined with brick was
built in 1876 with a stationary light; depending on a ship's
position, it shows red (indicating dangerous waters) or
white. Since the light was automated in 1985, the adjacent
keeper's quarters have been the headquarters of the Coast
Guard group commander — a fitting passing of the torch
from one safeguarder of ships to another.

Follow the road around, always bearing right, for the coast
road back to Route 28 in Falmouth center; turn right to
continue on 28. At the intersection of Route 130, take a left
⑮ toward **Mashpee,** one of two Massachusetts towns (the other
is Gay Head, on Martha's Vineyard) that have been governed continuously by Native Americans for more than 100
years. More than 600 residents are descended from the
original Wampanoags. On the left is the **Wampanoag Indian
Museum,** a small and somewhat disappointing museum on
the history and culture of the tribe, set in a 1793 half-Cape.
Exhibits include baskets, weapons, hunting and fishing
tools, clothing, arrowheads, and a small diorama depicting
a scene from an early settlement. *Rte. 130, tel. 508/477-1536.
Donations accepted. Open Tues.–Fri. 9–2, Sat. 10–2.*

Across the way, a town landing gives a view of the intercon-
necting **Mashpee and Wakeby ponds,** the Cape's largest
freshwater expanse, popular for swimming, fishing, and
boating.

Return to Route 28; just past the junction is the **Cahoon
Museum of American Art,** in a big Georgian Colonial home.
Its several rooms display selections from the permanent
collection of primitive paintings by Ralph and Martha Cahoon and other 19th- and early 20th-century art, including
a number of pieces from the Hudson River School. Special

exhibitions and demonstrations are held throughout the summer. A gift shop offers books, cards, prints, and so forth. *4676 Falmouth Rd. (Rte. 28), Cotuit, tel. 508/428–7581. Donations accepted. Open Apr.–Dec., Wed.–Sat. 10–4, Sun. 1–4. Closed Jan.–Mar.*

16 Two miles farther you'll see signs for **Osterville,** a wealthy Barnstable enclave, with upscale shopping in its downtown. Off Wianno Avenue is Seaview Avenue, lined with elegant waterfront houses, including a few of the large "cottages" built beginning in the 19th century, when the area became popular with a monied set.

17 The next village along Route 28 is **Centerville.** Once a busy seafaring town, it still boasts 50 or so shipbuilders' and sea captains' homes along its quiet, tree-shaded streets. A right onto Main Street takes you to the **Centerville Historical Society Museum.** Set in a 19th-century house, the museum features furnished period rooms, Sandwich glass, miniature carvings of birds by Anthony Elmer Crowell, models of ships, marine artifacts, perfume bottles dating from 1760 to 1920, and 300 quilts and costumes dating from 1650 to 1950. Guided tours are given (last tour at 3:30). *513 Main St., tel. 508/775–0331. Admission: $2.50 adults, 50¢ children under 12. Open mid-June–mid-Sept., Wed.–Sun. 1:30–4:30. Closed mid-Sept.–mid-June.*

Time Out In summer, sample the homemade offerings at **Four Seas Ice Cream** (360 S. Main St., tel. 508/775–1394), a tradition with generations of summer visitors.

Around the corner is the **1856 Country Store** (555 Main St., tel. 508/775–1856) — what used to be called the penny-candy store, today stocked with nickel and dime candy. It's not the place it once was, but it does have crafts, jewelry, and all kinds of gadgets and toys, and in summer the pickles and slabs of cheddar cheese return.

Follow Main Street to **Craigville Beach,** a busy beach community of weathered-shingle cottages. Main Street continues to rejoin Route 28, which takes you to Hyannis, 3 miles away.

Tour 3: Route 6A, Hyannis to Orleans

For this tour, we return to the Old King's Highway and the north shore (beginning about 2½ miles east of where Tour 1 ended) for attractive old towns, fine beaches, and varied scenery, from marshland and kettle ponds to forest. Also along this stretch are antiques shops and excellent restaurants, several with views of the marsh. The tour covers about 25 miles.

Numbers in the margin correspond to points of interest on the Tours 3 and 4: Hyannis to Orleans map.

Heading east out of Hyannis on Route 28, turn left onto Willow Street. Three miles along you come to Route 6A. Cross 6A onto Mill Lane for a scenic loop (even better on

foot); keep left at the intersection of Water Street to go over
(18) **Keveney Bridge,** a one-lane wooden bridge over marshy Mill
Pond that will make you want to grab a pole and join the
others quietly fishing from it. The loop comes back out onto
Route 6A, west of where you began. Across the street, on
6A, is **Cummaquid Fine Art** (*see* Shopping, *below*), an art
gallery in a lovely old home.

(19) Turn left onto 6A for **Yarmouth Port,** with some impressive
captains' homes, many now B&Bs. On the right, watch for
Hallet's Store, a country drugstore preserved as it was in
1889, when the current owner's grandfather, Thacher Hallet, opened it. Hallet served not only as druggist but as
postmaster and justice of the peace as well. The oak cabi-
netry has ornate carved detailing; at the all-marble soda
fountain with swivel stools, you can order the secret-recipe
ice-cream soda, as well as an inexpensive lunch.

As the first real intersection (Summer St.) approaches, try
to pull over. The 1886 **Village Pump** is on the right, just
before the **Old Yarmouth Inn,** the Cape's oldest inn (1696).
The black wrought-iron pump, long used for drawing household water, is surrounded by ironwork with cutouts of birds
and animals and is topped by a lantern. In front is a stone
trough for watering horses. In an old barn across the street
is **Parnassus Bookshop** (*see* Shopping, *below*), great for
browsing.

Behind the post office, a bit farther on the right, are the
Botanical Trails of the Historical Society of Old Yarmouth,
50 acres of oak and pine woods and a pond, accented by
blueberries, ladyslippers, Indian pipes, rhododendrons,
holly, and more. Stone markers and arrows mark the trails,
and benches are strategically placed for resting and appre-
ciating the view. In the gatehouse's mailbox are trail maps.
Just beyond, a right leads to the little **Kelley Chapel,** built
in 1873 by a father for a daughter grieving over the death
of a child, and moved to this site in 1960. The simple gray-
and-white interior is dominated by an iron wood stove and
a pump organ. *Off Rte. 6A. Admission: 50¢ adults, 25¢ children. Gatehouse open daily 1–4 in summer; trails open any-
time.*

Across 6A, set back, is the 1780 **Winslow Crocker House,** an
elegantly symmetrical two-story Georgian with 12-over-12
small-pane windows and an elaborate doorway. After
Crocker's death, his two sons built a wall dividing the house
in half. It was moved here from West Barnstable in 1935 by
Mary Thacher, who donated it, along with her collection of
17th- to 19th-century furniture, to the Society for the Preservation of New England Antiquities, which operates it as
a museum. *250 Rte. 6A, tel. 508/362–4385. Admission: $4
adults, $2 children 5–12, $3.50 senior citizens. Open June–mid-
Oct., Tues., Thurs., and weekends noon–5. Closed mid-Oct.–
May.*

The next right, before the village green, leads to the **Captain
Bangs Hallet House.** A white Greek Revival building with a
hitching post out front and a weeping beech in back, it was

Tours 3 and 4: Hyannis to Orleans

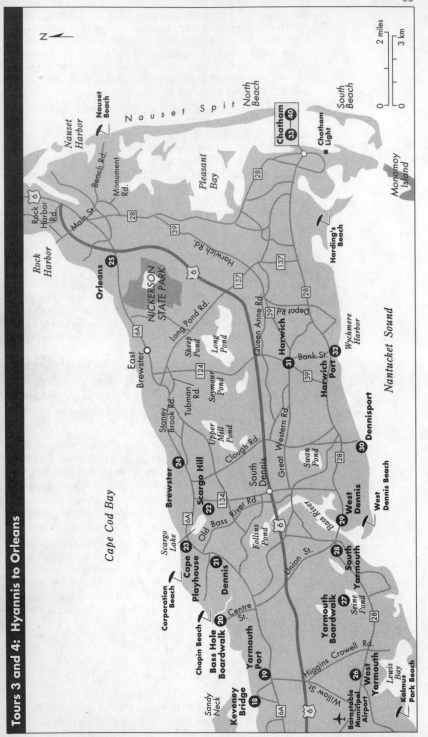

N

2 miles
3 km

Cape Cod Bay

Nauset Spit

North Beach

South Beach

Nauset Harbor

Nauset Beach

Beach Rd.

Monument Rd.

Main St.

28

Pleasant Bay

Chatham 33—40

Chatham Light

Monomoy Island

6 Rock Harbor Rd.

Rock Harbor

Orleans 25

6

NICKERSON STATE PARK

Long Pond Rd.

39

Harwich Rd.

137

28

Sheep Pond

Long Pond

137

28

Queen Anne Rd.

39

Depot Rd

Harwich 31

Bank St. 32

Wychmere Harbor

Harding's Beach

East Brewster

6A

124

Tubman Rd.

Seymour Pond

Stoney Brook Rd.

Upper Mill Pond

Clough Rd.

Great Western Rd.

South Dennis

39

Harwich Port

Dennisport

Swan Pond

28

30

Nantucket Sound

Brewster 24

Scargo Hill 22

134

Old Bass River Rd.

Scargo Lake

Cape Playhouse 23

6A

Dennis 21

Follins Pond

Bass River

West Dennis Beach

West Dennis 29

6

Union St.

South Yarmouth 28

Corporation Beach

Chapin Beach

Bass Hole Boardwalk

Yarmouth Port 20

Centre St.

Yarmouth Boardwalk 27

Seine Pond

28

Sandy Neck

Keveney Bridge 18

6A

Yarmouth 19

Higgins Crowell Rd.

Willow St.

6

West Yarmouth 26

Barnstable Municipal Airport

Lewis Bay

Kalmus Park Beach

built in 1840 (added onto a 1740 rear section) for a sea captain in the China trade, then bought by another, who swapped it with a third (this should give you an idea of the proliferation of sea captains hereabouts). In 1988, six 19th-century paintings and 200 pieces of scrimshaw were among the choice items stolen. Remaining are pewter, china, nautical equipment, antique toys and clothing, and more. The kitchen has the original 1740 brick beehive oven and butter churns. *11 Strawberry La., off Rte. 6A, tel. 508/362-3021. Admission: $1 adults, 25¢ children. Open June, Sun. 2-4; July-Sept., Wed.-Fri. and Sun. 2-4; Oct., by appointment. Closed Nov.-May.*

For a virtually trafficless scenic loop, take a left off Route 6A past the green onto Church Street or Thacher Street, then left again onto Thacher Shore Road. In fall, this route is especially beautiful for its impressive stands of blazing red burning bush. Wooded segments alternate with open views of marsh. Keep bearing right; at the "Water St." sign, the dirt road on the right brings you to a wide-open view of marshland as it meets the bay. (Don't drive in too far, or you may get stuck.) Coming out, a right leads to Keveney Bridge, and back to Route 6A.

Turn left off 6A onto Centre Street (east of Church Street) and follow signs to Gray's Beach. At Homer's Dock Road, keep left; signs on the left point to a parking area for walking trails. Adjacent to Gray's Beach, a little crescent of sand
⓴ with still water good for children, is the **Bass Hole Boardwalk,** which extends over a marshy creek; at the end are benches from which you can observe abundant marsh life and, across the creek, the beautiful, sandy shores of Dennis's Chapin Beach. At low tide you can walk out on the flats for almost a mile.

⓴ Up ahead is **Dennis,** where the back streets, more so than the main route, have a beautifully preserved Colonial charm. The town has a number of conservation areas and nature trails (see the Dennis Chamber of Commerce guide), and many ponds for swimming.

About a mile east of the town line, you'll come to a collection of antiques shops. Just beyond, at an intersection of three roads, across from the Dennis Public Market, a left off Route 6A onto Nobscusset Road leads to the **Josiah Dennis Manse,** a saltbox with add-ons built in 1736 for Reverend Josiah Dennis, after whom the town was named. Inside, the rooms reflect Reverend Dennis's day. One room has marine artifacts (the collection was expanded in 1992); another is set up as a child's room, with antique furniture and toys; the keeping room has an antique fireplace and cooking utensils. Throughout are china, pewter, and portraits of sea captains. On the grounds is a 1770 one-room schoolhouse — furnished with wood-and-wrought-iron desks and chairs — moved in 1974 from a nearby site. *77 Nobscussett Rd., corner of Whig St., tel. 508/385-2232. Donations accepted. Open July and Aug., Tues. and Thurs. 2-4. Closed Sept.-June.*

22 Return to Route 6A; at Old Bass River Road, take a right and follow signs for **Scargo Hill,** the highest spot in the area, at 160 feet. From here the view of wooded Scargo Lake and the village's scattered houses below and of Cape Cod Bay beyond is spectacular — on a clear day, you can see Provincetown. The panoramic view from atop the round tower (up a 38-step spiral staircase) makes sunsets and sunrises equally memorable.

23 Retrace your path to Route 6A and turn right. Just up on the left is the complex built around the **Cape Playhouse,** one of the oldest summer theaters in the country. Californian Raymond Moore — having started a company in Provincetown but finding it too remote — bought an 1820s former Unitarian Meeting House here in 1927 and converted it into a theater. The opening performance was Basil Rathbone in *The Guardsman;* other stars who performed here in the early days, many in their first professional appearances, include Bette Davis, Gregory Peck, and Henry Fonda. Also on the property are the **Cape Cinema,** with a huge ceiling mural designed by Massachusetts artist Rockwell Kent; the **Playhouse Restaurant** (*see* Dining, *below*); and an art museum.

The **Cape Museum of Fine Arts,** founded in 1981 to acquire and house a permanent collection of works by Cape-associated artists, already owns more than 500 artworks. Important works include a 1924 portrait of a Portuguese fisherman's daughter by William Paxton, one of the first artists to summer in Provincetown; a collection of woodblock prints by Varujan Boghosian, a member of Provincetown's Long Point Gallery cooperative; and an oil sketch by Karl Knaths, who painted in Provincetown from 1919 until his death in 1971. In 1990 the museum moved to a new building on the grounds. A classic-film series is held in the basement auditorium. *Tel. 508/385-4477. Donations accepted. Open Tues.–Sat. 10–5 (Wed. and Thurs. until 8).*

A left onto Corporation Road, just after the Playhouse complex, leads to **Corporation Beach.** At one time a packet landing owned by a corporation formed of townsfolk, the beautiful crescent of white sand backed by low dunes now serves a decidedly noncorporate use, as a public beach.

Time Out Before leaving Dennis, you might want to stop for a bite at **Cap'n Frosty's** (219 Main St. [Rte. 6A], near the Yarmouth line, tel. 508/385-8548), a favorite local clam shack, with fried seafood, shellfish, and onion rings, as well as very good lobster rolls with more lobster than celery. For dessert, try homemade ice cream and frozen yogurt at the **Ice Cream Smuggler** (716 Main St., near the Dennis Public Market, tel. 508/385-5307).

24 The next town is **Brewster,** in the early 1800s the terminus of a packet cargo service from Boston and home to many seafaring families. In 1849, Thoreau wrote that "this town has more mates and masters of vessels than any other town in the country." A large number of mansions built for sea captains remain today, and quite a few have been turned into

B&Bs. In the 18th and 19th centuries, the bay side of Brewster was the site of a major salt-making industry. When the tide is low, you can walk out for about a mile on the Brewster Flats among tidal pools rich in sea life.

On a grassy rise on the left is the 1795 **Old Mill.** The octagonal, smock-type mill — shingled in weathered pine, with a roof like an upturned boat — was moved here in 1974 and has been restored. The millstones are original. At night the mill is often spotlit and makes quite a sight. Also on the grounds is a one-room house from 1795, the **Harris-Black House.** Once, amazingly enough, home to a family of 13, the restored 16-foot-square building is today partially furnished and dominated by a brick hearth and original woodwork. *Both no phone, admission free. Open May–June and Sept.–Oct., weekends 1–4; July and Aug., Tues.–Fri. 1–4. Closed Nov.–Apr.*

Farther up on the left is the **Cape Cod Museum of Natural History,** which offers nature and marine exhibits (such as a working beehive and a pond- and sea-life room with live specimens), guided field walks, a natural history library, a museum shop, lectures, classes, and self-guided trails through 80 acres of forest, marshland, and ponds, all rich in birds and other wildlife. The exhibit hall upstairs has a wall display of aerial photographs documenting the process by which a barrier beach off Chatham's shore was split in two (*see* Tour 4, *below*). *Rte. 6A, Brewster, tel. 508/896–3867 or 800/479–3867 in New England. Admission: $3.50 adults, $1.50 children 6–14. Open mid-Apr.–mid-Oct., Mon.–Sat. 9:30–4:30, Sun. 12:30–4:30; mid-Oct.–mid-Apr., Tues.–Sat. 9:30–4:30, Sun. 12:30–4:30, closed Mon.*

Just beyond the bend in the road, turn right onto Paine's Creek Road, then left on Setucket Road, to reach the **Brewster Mill,** a restored 19th-century fulling mill — the area once had four — that is now a museum and gristmill. (Stoney Brook Road leads directly here.) The scene is wonderfully picturesque in true New England fashion: the old weathered-shingle mill, its waterwheel slowly turning, set on a little brook edged with leafy trees. Inside are exhibits, including old mill equipment and looms; during open hours you can watch cornmeal being stone-ground and get a lesson in weaving on a 100-year-old loom. Out back, across little wooden bridges, is a bench with a pleasant view of the pond and of the sluices leading into the mill area. *Stoney Brook Rd., tel. 508/896–6745. Donations accepted. Open July and Aug., Thurs.–Sat. 2–5. Closed Sept.–June.*

Early each spring, Stoney Brook's **Herring Run** is aboil with millions of alewives, which make their way from Cape Cod Bay by way of Paine's Creek to reach Stoney Brook and the ponds beyond to spawn. Walk across the street from the mill and down a path to the rushing stream spilling over rocks. Farther down the path is an ivy-covered stone wishing well and a wooden bridge with a bench.

Head back toward Paine's Creek Road, but instead of turning onto it, keep going straight; you will come out on Route 6A just before the **New England Fire & History Museum.** Set on a re-created 19th-century common with a picnic area, it features vintage fire-fighting apparatus (including the only surviving 1929 Mercedes-Benz fire engine), the late Boston Pops conductor Arthur Fiedler's private collection of fire-fighting memorabilia, an apothecary shop, a diorama of the Chicago Fire of 1871 (complete with smoke and fire), a historic working forge, and medicinal herb gardens. Guided tours are given, and movies about historic fires and the history of apothecaries are shown. *1439 Main St. (Rte. 6A), Brewster, tel. 508/896–5711. Admission: $4.50 adults, $2.50 children 5–12, $4 senior citizens. Open mid-May–Labor Day, weekdays 10–4, weekends noon–4; Labor Day–mid-Oct., weekends 10–4. Closed mid-Oct.–mid-May.*

At the junction of Route 124 is the **Brewster Store** (tel. 508/896–3744), built in 1852. A local landmark, it is a typical New England general store, providing such essentials as the daily papers and penny candy. It's also a good stop for quick grocery-type refreshments, as the bicycles piled up out front in summer attest. Upstairs, the front of the store has been re-created, complete with benches, and memorabilia from antique toys to World War II bond posters are displayed.

Nearby is the handsome **First Parish Church,** with Gothic windows and a capped bell tower. Known as the Church of the Sea Captains, it features pews marked with the names of famous Brewster seamen. Out back is an old graveyard, where militiamen, clergy, farmers, and captains rest side by side. Chowder suppers are held Wednesdays in July and August.

From here Breakwater Road leads to a former packet landing, and a right onto Route 124, then a left onto Tubman Road, takes you to the **Bassett Wild Animal Farm** (*see* What to See and Do with Children, *below*).

Back on 6A, you'll see the **Brewster Historical Society Museum** on the left. Inside the 1830s home are a sea captains' room, with paintings and artifacts; an 1890 barbershop; a child's room with antique toys and clothing; a room of women's period gowns and accessories; and other exhibits on local history and architecture. Out back is a ¼-mile labeled nature trail over dunes leading to the bay. *No phone. Admission free. Open May, June, Sept., and Oct., weekends 1–4; July and Aug., Tues.–Fri. 1–4. Closed Nov.–Apr.*

Farther up Route 6A on the right is **Nickerson State Park** (*see* Nature Areas, *below*). These nearly 2,000 acres were part of a vast estate belonging to Roland C. Nickerson, son of Samuel Nickerson, a Chatham native who became a multimillionaire and founder of the First National Bank of Chicago. At their long private beach or their hunting lodge, Roland and his wife, Addie, lavishly entertained such visitors as President Grover Cleveland in English country house style, with coachmen dressed in tails and top hats and a bugler announcing carriages entering the front gates.

The estate was like a village unto itself. Its gardens provided much of the household's food, supplemented by game from its woods and fish from its ponds. It also had its own electric plant and a nine-hole golf course by the water. The enormous mansion Sam built for his son in 1886 burned to the ground in 1906, and Roland died two weeks later. The even grander stone mansion built in 1908 to replace it is now part of the Ocean Edge resort. In 1934, Addie donated the land for the state park in memory of her son, who died during the 1918 flu epidemic.

㉕ From the park it's about 2 miles to **Orleans.** Named for Louis-Philippe de Bourbon, duc d'Orléans, who reputedly visited the area during his exile from France in the 1790s, it is today the commercial center of the Lower Cape. Historically, it has the distinction of being the only spot in the continental United States to have received enemy fire during either world war. In July 1918, a German submarine fired on commercial barges off the coast; four were sunk, and one shell is reported to have fallen on American soil.

At the junction with Main Street, turn left; Main becomes Rock Harbor Road, a pleasant winding street lined with gray-shingled Cape houses, white picket fences, and neat gardens. At the end is **Rock Harbor,** a former packet landing and the site of a War of 1812 skirmish in which the Orleans militia kept a British warship from landing. In the 19th century Orleans had an active saltworks industry, and a flourishing packet service between Rock Harbor and Boston developed. Today the former packet landing is the base of charter-fishing and party boats in season, as well as of a small commercial fishing fleet whose catch can be sampled at the fish market and small restaurant here. Sunsets over the harbor are memorable.

A right at the junction of Route 6A and Main Street leads east (along what becomes Beach Road) to the town-owned **Nauset Beach,** a long, wide sweep of sand backed by high dunes.

At the intersection of 6A and Route 28, turn right; at Cove Road is the **French Cable Station Museum.** Built in 1890 to house a land extension of the transatlantic cable that originated in Brittany. In World War I, it was an essential link between Army headquarters in Washington and the American Expeditionary Force in France, and was guarded by Marines. In 1959, the station was closed as obsolete; the equipment is still in place. *41 S. Orleans Rd., tel. 508/240–1735. Admission: $2 adults, $1 children 7–17. Open July–Labor Day, Mon.–Sat. 2–4. Closed Labor Day–June.*

Tour 4: Route 28, Hyannis to Chatham

There's no getting around it: The part of the Cape everyone loves to hate is Route 28 where it passes through Yarmouth — one motel, strip mall, nightclub, and miniature golf course after another. In 1989, as *Cape Cod Life* magazine put it, "the town [began] to plant 350 trees in hopes that eventually the trees' leaves, like the fig leaf of Biblical lore, will cover the shame of unkempt overdevelopment."

This tour takes you into the fray; it is a good way to go if you want to intersperse amusements with your sightseeing, because Route 28 is the main locus of such activities. A sensible option if you don't is to take speedy Route 6 to the exit nearest the first place you want to visit, then cut across the interior to 28. This route covers about 30 miles. The proliferation of motels, restaurants, and stores thins out somewhat as you near Chatham.

26 Heading east out of Hyannis, the first village is **West Yarmouth.** A little past the town line, on the left, is the **Baxter Grist Mill,** by the shore of Mill Pond. Built in 1710, it is the only mill on Cape Cod that is powered by an inside water turbine; the others use either wind or paddle wheels. The mill was converted to the indoor metal turbine in 1860 because of the pond's low water level and the damage done to the wooden paddle wheel by winter freezes; the original metal turbine is displayed on the grounds, and a replica powers the restored mill. A videotape tells the mill's history. *Tel. 508/398–2231. Admission free. Days and hours of operation are completely unpredictable; call before you go. Closed Columbus Day–Memorial Day.*

After about 3 miles, a left onto Winslow Gray Road for a mile or so, then a right onto Meadowbrook Lane leads to the
27 **Yarmouth Boardwalk.** A short walk through swamp and marsh takes you to the edge of Swan Pond, a pretty pond ringed with woods.

A bit farther on Route 28 is **Aqua Circus** (*see* What to See and Do with Children, *below*), with dolphin and other shows.

Time Out Next door is **Jerry's Dairy Freeze** (tel. 508/775–9752; open mid-Feb.–mid-Nov.), offering fried clams and onion rings — along with thick frappes, frozen yogurt, and soft ice cream — at good prices. It stays open until 11 at night in season.

A mile up, a right onto Willow Street leads to the 1791 **Judah Baker Windmill,** an octagonal mill with a conical cap. It was moved from South Dennis to West Dennis, then in 1863 to this site on a park with a small public beach on Bass River. There's a nice view of boat and bird life from small benches by the mill.

28 **South Yarmouth** was once called Friends Village, for its large Quaker population. A left off Route 28 onto North Main Street (at a major intersection) takes you to the 1809 **Friends Meeting House,** still open for meetings; the partition down the center was to divide the sexes. The adjacent cemetery has simple Quaker markers with no epitaphs, an expression of the Friends' belief that all are equal in God's eyes.

Bass River forms the dividing line between the southern portions of the towns of Yarmouth and Dennis; the area of

South Yarmouth just before the bridge is commonly referred to as **Bass River.** Here you'll find charter boats and boat rentals, as well as a river cruise, plus seafood restaurants and markets.

29 **West Dennis** (confusingly enough, south of South Dennis) is at the other side of the Bass River Bridge. A right onto School Street at the Texaco station leads to the **West Dennis Beach,** one of the best on the south shore. An aborted breakwater here was begun in 1837 in an effort to protect the mouth of Bass River but abandoned when a sandbar formed on the shore side.

Time Out The 1855 lighthouse that originally watched over the coast here has been converted into part of the aptly named **Lighthouse Inn** (tel. 508/398–2244), a summer resort with a moderately priced restaurant serving three meals a day. Now *you* can watch over the coast, either from behind windows or at tables outside.

Back on Route 28, a left onto Old Main Street leads to the **Jericho House Museum** (at the corner of Trotting Park Road), built in 1801 for a sea captain. (The name was given by a subsequent owner, who said the walls seemed to be tumbling down.) The classic Cape, with a bow roof and large central chimney, has been fully restored. Antique furnishings include 1850s portraits, and Chinese and other items brought home from overseas by sea captains. In the barn museum is antique cranberry-harvesting and woodworking equipment, a model saltworks, marine antiques, and 19th-century sleighs and wagons. Also here is a 150-piece driftwood zoo: a local man collected wood on a beach, then added eyes and beaks to bring out animal shapes. *Tel. 508/398–6736. Donations accepted. Open July and Aug., Wed. and Fri. 2–4. Closed Sept.–June.*

Bear left at the intersection here for the 1835 **South Parish Congregational Church,** which has the oldest working organ in the United States. The cemetery beside the church has markers dating from 1795; many of them are for early sea captains and say simply "Lost at sea," while one says only "The Chinese Woman."

30 Returning to Route 28, the Mid-Cape's last southern village is **Dennisport,** a prime summer resort area, with gray-shingled cottages, summer homes, and condominiums, and lots of white picket fences covered with rambling roses. The Union Wharf Packing Company was located here in the 1850s, and the shore was lined with sailmakers and ship chandlers. The beach where sea clams were once packed is now packed with sunbathers.

Time Out Farther up Route 28, a right onto Sea Street leads to the **Sundae School Ice Cream Parlor** (corner of Lower County Rd., tel. 508/394–9122; open mid-Apr.–mid-Oct.). Set in a rustic mid-19th-century barn decorated with such memorabilia as a working nickelodeon, it serves great homemade ice cream and real whipped cream from an antique marble soda fountain.

A left onto Route 39 takes you into the heart of the quiet
31 New England village of **Harwich.** Just before the junction
of Main Street is the **Brooks Academy,** an 1844 Greek Revival building with fluted pillars that was once a private
school and is now the museum of the Harwich Historical
Society. In addition to a large photo-history collection and
exhibits on artist Charles Cahoon, cranberries, shoemak-
ing, and the Roaring '20s, the museum displays antique
clothing and textiles, china and glass, fans, toys, and much
more. On the grounds is a powder house that was used to
store gunpowder during the Revolutionary War, as well as
a restored 1872 outhouse. *80 Parallel St., tel. 508/432–8089.
Admission free. Open Thurs.–Sun. 1–4. May close for winter.*

Also on Main Street is **Brooks Park,** with a playground,
picnic tables, a ballpark, tennis courts, and a bandstand
where summer concerts are held. Returning to Route 28 via
Bank Street, you pass some of the town's many cranberry
bogs, tours of which are part of the grand Cranberry Harvest Festival in September (*see* Festivals and Seasonal
Events in Chapter 1, Essential Information).

32 Back on Route 28 at the seaside community of **Harwich Port,**
a right onto Harbor Road leads to scenic **Wychmere Harbor,**
busy with pleasure boats.

Time Out The **Augustus Snow House** (528 Main St. [Rte. 28], tel. 508/430–
0528) offers an elegant afternoon tea of finger sandwiches,
scones with cream, and dessert cakes. It is served in the inn's
very Victorian, fireplaced parlors from 1:30 to 4:30 daily year-
round (call to confirm or reserve); creative American dinners
are served by reservation.

33 The next town up is **Chatham.** Situated at the bent elbow of
the Cape, with water on three sides, it has all the charm of
a quiet seaside resort but with relatively little of the com-
mercialism. And it *is* charming: gray-shingled houses with
tidy awnings and cheerful flower gardens, an attractive
Main Street with crafts and antiques stores alongside
homey coffee shops and a five-and-ten. It's a traditional
town, with none of Provincetown's flash yet not overly
quaint; wealthy yet not ostentatious; casual and fun but refined, and never tacky.

*Numbers in the margin correspond to points of interest on the
Chatham map.*

When you cross the town line via Route 28, begin to watch
for **Marion's Pie Shop, Fancy's Farm,** and **Chatham Jam and
Jelly,** all worth stopping for (*see* Farm Stands and Food in
Shopping, *below*), as well as the **Chatham Winery** (tel.
508/945–0300), open for tastings of fruit wines produced
here. Just before you hit downtown, at the intersection with
34 Queen Anne Road, turn left onto Depot Road for the **Railroad Museum,** in a restored 1887 depot. Exhibits include a
1910 New York Central caboose, old photographs, equipment, and thousands of train models. *No phone. Donations
accepted. Open mid-June–mid-Sept., Tues.–Sat. 10–4. Closed
mid-Sept.–mid-June.*

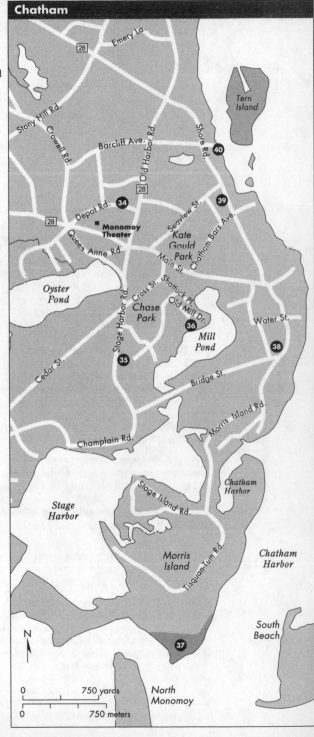

Across from the museum (and behind the school) is the **Play-a-round,** a multilevel wood playground of turrets, twisting tubular slides, jungle gyms, and more. There's a section for the disabled and a fenced-in area for small children. Completed in late 1990, it was designed with the input of local children and built entirely by volunteers.

Return to the Queen Anne Road junction. For a scenic loop, turn down Queen Anne and skirt Oyster Pond, following bike-path signs. Half-Cape houses, open fields, and rolling pastures reveal the area's Colonial and agricultural history.

Winding around Stage Harbor — where Samuel de Champlain anchored in 1606 and was involved in a skirmish that marked the first blood shed in New England between Europeans and Native Americans — keep left at Bridge Street on Stage Harbor Road and you'll come to the **Old Atwood House and Museums** complex. Built by a sea captain in 1752 and occupied by his descendants until it was sold to the Chatham Historical Society in 1926, the Atwood House features a gambrel roof, variable-width floor planking, fireplaces, an old kitchen with a wide hearth and a beehive oven, a collection of antique dolls and toys, and portraits of sea captains. The Joseph C. Lincoln Wing, added in 1949, has the manuscripts and first editions of the Chatham writer. The 1974 Durand Wing houses collections of seashells from around the world (700 in all), threaded Sandwich glass, and Parian ware (unglazed porcelain vases, figurines, and busts). In a remodeled freight shed are a series of murals (1931–1943) by Alice Stallknecht Wight portraying religious scenes in Chatham settings; they have been exhibited at major galleries around the country. On the grounds are an herb garden and the old turret and lens from the Chatham Light. *347 Stage Harbor Rd., tel. 508/945–2493. Admission: $3 adults, $1 children under 12. Open mid-June–Sept., Wed.–Sat. 2–5. Closed Oct.–mid-June.*

A right onto Cross Street takes you past **Chase Park,** with a bowling green and picnic tables, to Shattuck Place; at the end is the **Old Grist Mill,** built in 1797, moved to the hill here from elsewhere in Chatham, and extensively renovated. Closed in 1992 for budgetary reasons, the mill may or may not be open in 1993.

Instead of completing the loop, backtrack and turn left onto Bridge Street, which crosses Mill Pond. There's fishing from the bridge, and "bullrakers" ply the pond's muddy bottom with 20-foot rakes in search of shellfish.

A right onto Morris Island Road and across the dike leads to the **Monomoy National Wildlife Refuge headquarters** (*see* Nature Areas, *below*), on the misleadingly named Morris Island. At the visitor center and new bookstore (tel. 508/945–0594; open daily 8–5, with gaps) you can pick up pamphlets on **Monomoy Island,** a deserted barrier-beach area — once a fishing village — just south of Morris Island that is a paradise for bird-watchers. Actually two islands, North and South Monomoy, since a 1978 storm divided it, Monomoy was itself separated from the mainland in a 1958 storm. A ¾-mile interpretive walking trail (closed at high tide) around Morris Island gives a good view of the refuge and the surrounding waters; there's an observation platform at the visitor center. (For information on visiting the refuge, *see* Guided Tours, *above.*)

㊳ Returning to the junction of Bridge Street, follow the coast road (go straight) to **Chatham Light.** The view from here — of the harbor, the offshore sandbars, and the ocean beyond — justifies the crowds that gather to share it; when fog shrouds the area, pierced with darting beams from the beacon, there's a dreamlike quality about it.

Coin-operated telescopes allow a close look at the famous "Chatham Break," the result of a fierce 1987 storm that blasted a channel through a barrier beach (now known as North and South Beach) just off the coast. The Cape Cod Museum of Natural History in Brewster (*see* Tour 3: Route 6A, Hyannis to Orleans, *above*) has a display of photos documenting the process of erosion leading up to and following the break. If you're looking for a crowd-free sandy beach, boats at Chatham Harbor — such as the **Water Taxi** (tel. 508/945–9378) — will ferry you across to North Beach, a sandspit adjoining Orleans's Nauset Beach. **Outermost Harbor Marine** (Morris Island Rd., tel. 508/945–2030) runs shuttles to South Beach.

㊴ Go straight on Shore Road, where elegant summer cottages share the view with stately houses of purebred Yankee architecture, including some of the finest bow-roof houses in the country. On the left past Main Street, set on a rise overlooking the ocean, is the 1914 **Chatham Bars Inn** (*see* Lodging, *below*). The last of Chatham's grand old resort hotels, it has been thoroughly renovated and is as elegant and charming as it ever was.

Time Out | Even if you're not staying at the inn, you can experience it in several ways, including lunch or dinner in the main dining room (*see* Dining, *below*); breakfast, lunch, or dinner at the more casual **Tavern at the Inner Bar;** or clambakes and lunches of lighter fare at the casual, oceanfront **Beach House Grill** in summer. Call 508/945–0096 for information.

㊵ A bit farther along on the right is the entrance to the **Fish Pier.** The unloading of the boats after Chatham's fishing fleet returns, beginning sometime between noon and 2 PM, is a big local event, drawing crowds who watch it all from an observation deck. From their fishing grounds 10–100 miles offshore, the boats bring in haddock, cod, flounder, and more, which is packed in ice and shipped to New York and Boston.

Main Street, which you passed on Shore Road, takes you to the center of town. On Friday evenings in summer, the place to be is **Kate Gould Park** on Main Street for the Chatham band concert, the town's weekly party (*see* The Arts, *below*).

North of Chatham, Route 28 winds through wooded upland toward **Pleasant Bay,** to which a number of country roads to

the right will take you for a good view of the Nauset spit and
the little islands in between.

Tour 5: Orleans to Provincetown

Starting at Orleans, this tour explores Eastham and the
Outer Cape to the edge of Provincetown (which is covered
in Tour 6: Provincetown, *below*), including the National Seashore. This part of the Cape is markedly different from the
rest; much less populous and largely protected from development, it is an area of high dunes, endless beaches, and
arty communities. The tour covers about 30 miles.

*Numbers in the margin correspond to points of interest on the
Tour 5: Orleans to Provincetown map.*

Traveling down-Cape (toward the tip) from Orleans, head
⑪ east on Route 6. Once in **Eastham,** watch for a sign on the
⑫ right (1½ miles from the town line) directing you to the **Ft.
Hill Area** of the Cape Cod National Seashore (*see below*). On
the approach road is the **Captain Edward Penniman House,**
a large yellow, red, and white house in the French Second
Empire style, built in 1868 by a whaling captain. The impressive exterior is noted for its mansard roof, its cupola
(which once commanded a dramatic view of bay and sea),
and the whale-jawbone entrance gate. To find out when the
interior — which is slowly being renovated — is open for
guided tours (only by reservation) or browsing through
changing exhibits, call the National Seashore at 508/255–
3421.

Ahead, the road curves up over Ft. Hill, dead-ending at a
viewpoint overlooking a lovely pastoral scene: former farmland traced with stone fences, gently rolling down to Nauset
Marsh, a red-maple swamp, and the moors. Winding
through the area are the 1-mile Red Maple Swamp Trail,
which begins outside the Penniman house, and the Ft. Hill
Trail, also 1 mile, beginning at the parking area; a map is
available at trailheads.

Return to Route 6; a half-mile up on the left, at Samoset
Road, is the **Eastham Windmill,** a smock mill built in the
early 1680s, moved to this site in 1808, and now the center-
piece of a park. The only Cape windmill still on a site on
which it was in commercial use, it was recently restored by
local shipwreck historian Bill Quinn and friends. *Rte. 6.
Admission free. Open July–Labor Day, Mon.–Sat. 10–5,
Sun. 1–5. Closed Labor Day–June.*

Opposite the park, next to the post office, is the 1741 **Swift-
Daley House,** once the home of Gustavus Swift, founder of
the Swift meat-packing company. Inside the full Cape with
bow roof you'll find beautiful pumpkin pine woodwork, wide-
board floors, a ship's-cabin staircase (which, like the bow
roof, was built by ship's carpenters), and fireplaces in every
room. The Colonial-era furnishings include an old cannon-
ball rope bed, tools, a melodeon, a stereopticon, and a ceremonial quilt decorated with beads and coins. Antique
clothing includes gloves, lacework, hankies, baby dresses,

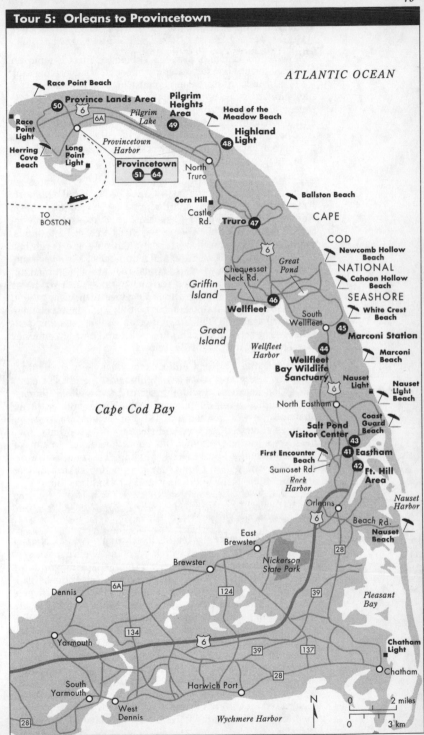

ATLANTIC OCEAN

Race Point Beach

Province Lands Area

50

6

6A

Pilgrim Heights Area

49

Head of the Meadow Beach

Highland Light

48

Pilgrim Lake

Race Point Light

Herring Cove Beach

Long Point Light

Provincetown Harbor

Provincetown

51   64

North Truro

Corn Hill

Castle Rd.

Ballston Beach

CAPE

TO BOSTON

Truro   47

6

COD

Newcomb Hollow Beach

NATIONAL

Chequesset Neck Rd.

Great Pond

Cahoon Hollow Beach

Griffin Island

SEASHORE

White Crest Beach

Wellfleet   46

South Wellfleet

Marconi Station

45

Great Island

Wellfleet Harbor

44

Wellfleet Bay Wildlife Sanctuary

Marconi Beach

6

Nauset Light

Nauset Light Beach

North Eastham

Cape Cod Bay

Salt Pond Visitor Center

Coast Guard Beach

43

First Encounter Beach

41   Eastham

Samoset Rd.

42   Ft. Hill Area

Rock Harbor

Nauset Harbor

Orleans

6

Beach Rd.

Nauset Beach

East Brewster

28

Brewster

Nickerson State Park

Pleasant Bay

Dennis

6A

124

39

134

6

Chatham Light

Yarmouth

39

137

Chatham

South Yarmouth

Harwich Port

28

West Dennis

Wychmere Harbor

N

0   2 miles

0   3 km

28

and a stunning 1850 wedding dress. Out back is a tool museum. *Rte. 6, tel. 508/240–1247. Admission free. Open July and Aug., weekdays 1:30–4:30. Closed Sept.–June.*

Follow Samoset Road, past marshland, to **First Encounter Beach,** a great spot for watching sunsets. Near the parking lot is a bronze marker commemorating the first encounter between the local Indians and the passengers from the *Mayflower,* led by Captain Myles Standish, who explored the entire area for five weeks before moving on to Plymouth. Also here are the remains of a Navy target ship retired after 25 years of battering and now resting on a sandbar about a mile out.

Another half-mile up Route 6, on the right, is the entrance to the first visitor center of the **Cape Cod National Seashore.** Established in 1961 by a bill signed by President John F. Kennedy, the 27,700-acre seashore encompasses and protects 30 miles of superb ocean beaches; great rolling dunes; swamps, marshes, and wetlands; pitch pine and scrub oak forests; all kinds of wildlife; and a number of historic structures. Lacing through these landscapes are self-guided nature trails, as well as biking and horse trails. The two visitor centers, here in Eastham and in Provincetown, offer guided walks, tours, boat trips, demonstrations, and lectures from mid-April through Thanksgiving, as well as evening programs of beach walks, campfire talks, and more in summer (*see* The Arts and Nightlife, *below*).

43 The **Salt Pond Visitor Center** has a museum with displays on the whaling and saltworks industries; exhibits of early Cape Cod artifacts, including scrimshaw; and the journal Mrs. Penniman kept while on a whaling voyage with her husband, as well as some of the Pennimans' possessions (such as their tea service and the captain's top hat). Also here are a bookstore and an air-conditioned auditorium for films on geology, sea rescues, whaling, Thoreau, and Marconi. Something's up every summer evening at the outdoor amphitheater, from slide-show talks to military-band concerts. *Tel. 508/255–3421. Admission free. Open Mar.–June and Sept.–Dec., daily 9–4:30; July and Aug., daily 9–6; Jan. and Feb., weekends 9–4:30.*

From here, hiking trails lead to a red-maple swamp, **Nauset Marsh,** and **Salt Pond,** in which breeding shellfish are suspended from floating "nurseries"; their offspring will later be used to seed the flats. Also here is the Buttonbush Trail, a nature path for the visually disabled. Roads and bicycle trails lead to **Coast Guard Beach** and **Nauset Light Beach,** which begin an unbroken 30-mile stretch of barrier beach extending to Provincetown — the "Cape Cod Beach" of Thoreau's 1865 classic *Cape Cod.* One can still walk its length, as Thoreau did, though the Atlantic continues to claim more of the Cape's eastern shore every year. To the south, near the end of Nauset spit, is the site of the famous beach cottage of Henry Beston's 1928 book *The Outermost House;* designated as a literary landmark in 1964, the cottage was completely destroyed in the Great Blizzard of February 1978.

From the center, signs direct you to Coast Guard Beach, where a turnout gives a good view over marsh and sea. A section of the cliff here was washed away in 1990, revealing remains of a prehistoric dwelling; a video on the archaeological excavation of the area is on view at the visitor center. Other signs lead from here to the much-photographed **Nauset Light,** the red and white lighthouse that tops the bluff where the "Three Sisters" lighthouses once stood. The Sisters themselves can be seen in a little landlocked park surrounded by trees, reached by paved walkways off Nauset Light Beach's parking lot.

How the lighthouses got there is a long story, but briefly it is this: In 1838, three brick lighthouses were built 150 feet apart on the bluffs in Eastham, overlooking a particularly dangerous shoals area; in 1892, after the eroding cliff dropped the towers into the ocean, they were replaced with three wood towers. In 1918, two were moved away, and in 1923 the third was; eventually the National Park Service acquired the Three Sisters and brought them together here, where they would be safe, rather than returning them to the eroding coast. The Fresnel lens from the last working lighthouse is on display at the Salt Pond Visitor Center. Lectures on and guided walks to the lighthouses are conducted throughout the season.

44 A few miles farther on Route 6, on the left just over the Wellfleet line, is the **Wellfleet Bay Wildlife Sanctuary** (*see* Nature Areas, *below*), 750 acres of moors, marsh, and forest supervised by the Massachusetts Audubon Society.

45 A mile and a half farther, on the right, is the **Marconi Station,** the site of the first transatlantic wireless station erected on the U.S. mainland. From here, Italian radio and wireless-telegraphy pioneer Guglielmo Marconi sent the first American wireless message to Europe — "most cordial greetings and good wishes" from President Theodore Roosevelt to Edward VII of England — on January 18, 1903. The station broadcast news for 15 years. An outdoor shelter contains a model of the original station, of which only fragments remain as a result of cliff erosion (parts of the tower bases are sometimes visible on the beach below, where they fell). The Seashore's administrative headquarters is located here, and though it is not an official visitor center, it can provide information at times when the centers are closed; inside is a mock-up of the spark-gap transmitter used at Marconi. Off the parking lot a 1¼-mile (45-minute) trail and boardwalk lead through the Atlantic White Cedar Swamp, one of the most beautiful trails on the Seashore; free maps and guides are available at the trailhead. *South Wellfleet, tel. 508/349-3785. Open Jan. and Feb., daily 9-4:30; Mar.-Dec., weekdays 9-4:30.*

For a scenic loop through a classic Cape landscape, take a left onto LeCount Hollow Road (with scrub and pines on the left, heathland meeting cliffs with ocean below on the right) to **Cahoon Hollow Beach,** a town-managed beach with high dunes and a hot restaurant and night spot, the **Beachcomber** (*see* Nightlife, *below*). Turn left again onto Ocean

View Drive, ending at **Newcomb Hollow**, a less-crowded
town beach with a scalloped shoreline of golden sand; then
backtrack to Cahoon Hollow and take the unmarked right
just across from it to return to Route 6 via Great Pond. Head
east (right) on 6 and turn off at the sign for Wellfleet Center.

46 **Wellfleet** was once the center of a large oyster industry and,
along with Truro to the north, a Colonial whaling and cod-
fishing port. Less than 2 miles wide, it is one of the more
tastefully developed Cape resort towns, with a number of
fine restaurants, historic homes, and more than 20 art galleries.

On the way into town, you pass the **First Congregational
Church of the United Church of Christ** (Main St., tel.
508/349–6877), a handsome 1850 Greek Revival building. It
was originally crowned by a tall spire, but an 1879 north-
easter sent the spire flying across the street, and it was
replaced by a belfry. The clock is said to be the only town
clock in the world to strike on ship's time. The church's
interior is lovely, with pale blue walls, a brass chandelier
hanging from an enormous gilt ceiling rosette, stained glass
windows in unusual subtle colors, and pews curved to form
an amphitheater facing the altar and the 1873, 738-pipe
Hook and Hastings tracker-action organ behind it. (Concerts are given on it in July and August on Sundays at 8 PM.)
To the right is a Tiffany-style window depicting a clipper
ship, with a dedication to the memory of a sea captain and
an inscription beginning "They that go down to the sea in
ships . . . ."

Farther on the right is a public lot where you can park if you
want to wander the town. On Main Street is the **Wellfleet
Historical Society Museum.** Here, and at the **Samuel Rider
House** on Gull Pond Road, north of the Wellfleet turnoff on
Route 6, the society exhibits its collection of shipwreck sal-
vage, needlework, navigation equipment, early photographs, Indian artifacts, clothing, and more. Admission to
one site gets you into the other. *Museum, tel. 508/349–9157;
Rider House, tel. 508/349–3876. Admission: $2 adults and chil-
dren 12 or older. Open late June–mid-Sept., Tues.–Sat. 2–5.
Closed mid-Sept.–late June.*

From Main Street, Bank Street leads to Commercial Street,
which has the flavor of the fishing town Wellfleet is; galleries and shops occupy small weathered-shingle houses that
look like fishing shacks. At the first intersection, turn left
for a short walk across **Uncle Tim's Bridge** — with a much-
photographed view over marshland and a tidal creek —
leading to a small wooded island. Heading back, with the
marsh on your left, follow Commercial Street to the
Wellfleet Pier, busy with fishing boats, sailboats, yachts,
charters, and party boats; at the twice-daily low tides you
can shellfish on the tidal flats for oysters, clams, and quahogs (license required; *see* Shellfishing in Sports and Outdoor Activities, *below*).

Continue on the same road (which becomes Chequesset
Neck Road) for a pretty 2½-mile drive along Cape Cod Bay

past Sunset Hill — a great place to catch one. At the end, on the left, is a parking lot and wooded picnic area, from which nature trails lead off to **Great Island,** perfect for the beachcomber and solitude seeker. Actually a peninsula connected by a sand spit, Great Island offers more than 7 miles of trails (the most difficult on the Seashore, since they're mostly in soft sand) along the inner marshes and the water, and lots of windswept dunes — a beautiful place. The Seashore also offers occasional guided hikes and, from February through April, seal walks. To the right of the Great Island lot, a road leads to **Griffin Island,** with its own walking trail. Both Great and Griffin islands once actually were islands, but a tidal buildup of sand connected them with the mainland.

In the 17th century there were lookout towers for shore whaling, as well as a tavern, on Great Island; animals were pastured here, and oystering and cranberry harvesting were undertaken. By 1800, the hardwood forest that had covered it had been eradicated for use in ship and home building; the pitch pines and other growth you see today were introduced in the 1830s to keep the soil from washing into the sea.

47 Return to Route 6 and follow signs for the center of **Truro,** a town of high dunes, estuaries, and rivers fringed by grasses, rolling moors, and houses sheltered in tiny valleys. Truro is a popular retreat of artists and writers. The most prominent painter to have lived here was Edward Hopper, who found the Cape light ideal for his austere brand of realism.

One of the largest towns in terms of area (almost 43 square miles), it is the smallest in population — only about 1,400 year-round. If you thought Wellfleet's downtown was small, wait until you see — or don't see — Truro's. It's a post office, a town hall, a shop or two; you'll know it by the sign that says "Downtown Truro," at a little plaza entrance. There's also a library, a firehouse, a police station, but that's about it.

From the center, Castle Road leads to Corn Hill Road, where a tablet commemorates the finding of a buried cache of corn by Standish and the *Mayflower* crew on **Corn Hill,** above; they took it to Plymouth and used it as seed, returning later to pay the Indians for the corn they'd taken.

Head east again on Route 6, and follow signs for the Cape Cod Light. As you near the lighthouse, you pass the **Truro Historical Museum,** built at the turn of the century as a summer hotel and now a repository of 17th-century firearms, mementos of shipwrecks, early fishing and whaling gear, ship models, a pirate's chest, scrimshaw, and more. One room exhibits wood carvings, paintings, blown glass, and ship models by Courtney Allen, artist and founder of Truro's historical society. An excellent self-guided historic tour of town is available here. *Lighthouse Rd., North Truro, tel. 508/487-3397. Admission: $2 adults, $1.50 senior citizens, free for children under 12. Open mid-June–mid-Sept., daily 10–5. Closed mid-Sept.–mid-June.*

48 At the end of the road is **Highland Light,** also called Cape
Cod Light, in which Thoreau boarded for a spell in his travels across the Cape's backside (as the Atlantic side of the
Outer Cape is called). One of four active lighthouses on the
Outer Cape, this one's a beauty, and you can drive right up
to it. It is the Cape's oldest lighthouse, and the last to have
become automated (in 1986). The first light on this site,
powered by 24 whale-oil lamps, began warning ships off
Truro's treacherous sandbars in 1798. The dreaded Peaked
Hills Bars alone, to the north, have claimed hundreds of
ships. The current light, a 66-foot tower built in 1857, is
powered by two 1,000-watt bulbs, reflected by a huge Fresnel lens; its beacon can be seen for 20 miles. The lighthouse
could fall into the sea within five to 30 years, depending on
how quickly the 117-foot cliff on which it stands erodes, and
on how successful a local committee is in finding the several
million dollars necessary to move the lighthouse back from
the cliff.

49 Back on Route 6 again, still going east, turn right for the
Pilgrim Heights Area of the Cape Cod National Seashore.
Off the parking lot is a shelter where lectures on the early
history of the region are occasionally given in season (call a
visitor center for a schedule). A short walking trail leads to
the spring where a Pilgrim exploring party stopped to refill
their casks, tasting their first New England water. Another
path leads to a swamp, and a bike trail leads to Head of the
Meadow Beach.

Walking through this still-wild area of oak, pitch pine, bayberry, blueberry, beach plum, and azalea gives you a taste
of what it was like for these voyagers in search of a new
home. "Being thus passed the vast ocean . . ." wrote William
Bradford in *Of Plimoth Plantation,* "they had no friends to
welcome them, no inns to entertain them or refresh their
weatherbeaten bodies; no houses, or much less towns to
repair to, to seek for succour."

50 From here you can take the coastal Route 6A — past countless ticky-tacky beach shacks and tidier rental cottages that
line the bay — straight into **Provincetown,** or follow Route
6 to the Seashore's **Province Lands Area.**

Tour 6: Provincetown

51 This tour explores the 8-square-mile town of **Provincetown**
— the Cape's smallest in area, second-smallest after Truro
in year-round population — and its neighboring segment of
the National Seashore. The town's main thoroughfare, Commercial Street, is 3 miles from end to end; street numbers
are in the 300s around MacMillan Wharf, at the center, and
get lower heading west and higher heading east.

*Numbers in the margin correspond to points of interest on the
Tour 6: Provincetown map.*

Near the Provincetown border the massive dunes begin to
appear on the right; in places they actually meet the road,

turning Route 6 into a sand-swept highway. Scattered
among the dunes are primitive cottages, called dune shacks,
built from flotsam and other found materials, that have
provided atmospheric as well as cheap lodgings to a number
of famous artists and writers over the years — among them
painter Harry Kemp, Eugene O'Neill, e.e. cummings, Jack
Kerouac, and Norman Mailer. The few surviving shacks are
privately leased from the National Seashore, which had
planned to demolish them when their occupancy permits
expire but was halted by their inclusion on the National
Register of Historic Places in 1988.

⑤② Turn right at the traffic light for the **Province Lands Visitor
Center.** Inside you'll find literature and nature-related gifts,
frequent short films (on local geology, the U.S. Life Saving
Service, and more), and changing exhibits. You can also pick
up information on guided walks, birding trips, lectures, bon-
fires, and other current programs throughout the Seashore,
as well as on the Province Lands' own beaches (Race Point
and Herring Cove) and walking, biking, and horse trails.
Don't miss the wonderful 360° view of the dunes and the
surrounding ocean from the observation deck. *Tel. 508/487-
1256. Open Apr.–June and Sept.–Dec., daily 9–4:30; July and
Aug., daily 9–6. Closed Jan.–Mar.*

Beyond the Visitor Center (and the Beech Forest picnic area
and trails, across the way) is the small Provincetown airport, where sightseeing flights are available, and beyond
that, the beautiful **Race Point Beach** (note that in summer
the small parking lot fills up early in the day). Not far from
the present Coast Guard Station is the **Old Harbor Station,**
a U.S. Life Saving Service building towed here by barge
from Chatham in 1977 to rescue it from an eroding beach.
It is reached by a boardwalk across the sand; plaques along
the way tell about the lifesaving service and the whales seen
offshore. Inside are displays of such equipment as Lyle
guns, which shot rescue lines out to ships in distress when
the seas were too violent to launch a surfboat; and breeches
buoys, in which passengers were hauled across those lines
to safety. *No phone. Donations accepted. Open July and Aug.,
daily 10–4. Closed Sept.–June.*

Leaving Race Point Beach, a right onto Province Lands
Road takes you through the heart of the dunes and woods,
past **Herring Cove Beach** (the parking lot on the right is a
great place to catch a sunset), and ultimately into the center
of Provincetown. For this tour, instead return to Route 6 and
turn right; take the next two lefts, then a right onto Winslow
Street. At the top of the hill, a sharp left leads to the parking
⑤③ lot of the **Pilgrim Monument,** commemorating the first
landing of the Pilgrims in the New World and their signing
of the Mayflower Compact, America's first rules of self-governance, before setting off from Provincetown Harbor to
explore the mainland. From atop the 252-foot-high tower
(116 steps and 60 ramps) you get a panoramic view — the
dunes on one side, the harbor on the other, and the entire
bay side of Cape Cod beyond. At the base is a museum of
Lower Cape and Provincetown history, with exhibits on

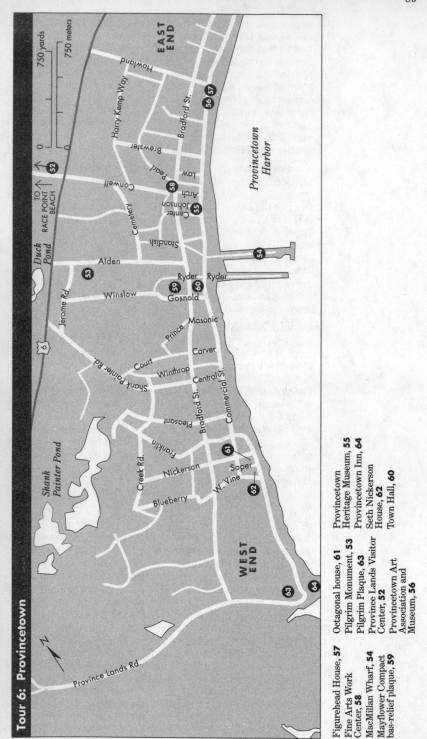

Tour 6: Provincetown

750 yards

750 meters

EAST END

Howland

Harry Kemp Way

Bradford St.

Brewster

Pearl

Law

Cowell

Arch

Cemetery

Center
Johnson

Standish

Provincetown Harbor

57

56

58

55

54

Alden

TO
RACE POINT
BEACH

Duck Pond

52

Ryder

Ryder

Winslow

Gosnold

53

59

60

Jerome Rd.

6

Masonic

Prince

Carver

Court

Shank Painter Rd.

Winthrop

Central St.

Shank Painter Pond

Pleasant

Bradford St.

Commercial St.

Franklin

Creek Rd.

Nickerson

Soper

61

Blueberry

W. Vine

62

WEST END

63

64

Province Lands Rd.

N

Figurehead House, **57**
Fine Arts Work Center, **58**
MacMillan Wharf, **54**
Mayflower Compact bas-relief plaque, **59**

Octagonal house, **61**
Pilgrim Monument, **53**
Pilgrim Plaque, **63**
Province Lands Visitor Center, **52**
Provincetown Art Association and Museum, **56**

Provincetown Heritage Museum, **55**
Provincetown Inn, **64**
Seth Nickerson House, **62**
Town Hall, **60**

whaling, shipwrecks, and scrimshaw; a diorama of the *May-flower* and another of a glass factory; and more. The exhibit on the pirate ship *Whydah*, sunk in a 1717 storm and discovered in 1984 off Wellfleet, includes a working laboratory doing conservation on artifacts from the ship (jewelry, weapons, coins), as well as audiovisual accounts of its discovery. The installation is elaborate, as befits a major find: The *Whydah* is the only pirate shipwreck ever recovered.

The tower was erected of granite shipped in from Maine, to a design modeled on a tower in Siena, Italy; President Theodore Roosevelt laid the cornerstone in 1907, and President Taft attended the 1910 dedication. On Thanksgiving Eve, in a ceremony including a museum tour and open house, 5,000 white and gold lights that drape the tower are lit, creating a display that can be seen as far away as the Cape Cod Canal. They are lit nightly into the New Year. *Tel. 508/487–1310. Admission: $3.50 adults, $1.50 children 4–12; $1.50 surcharge for* Whydah *exhibit. Open July–Sept., daily 9–7; Oct.–June, daily 9–4 or 5. Closed Christmas; may close Dec.–Feb.*

Having looked down upon the town from this great height, it's time to come down and walk around in it. From the bottom of the hill, take a left, then a right, which brings you to MacMillan Wharf. The parking lot here is the most central one, which is why it fills up so fast, but there are other lots. In season especially, driving from one end of the main street to the other could take forever, so walking is definitely the way to go. Narrated trolley sightseeing tours make the downtown circuit throughout the day in season (*see* Guided Tours in Essential Information, *above*); the romantically inclined can hire a horse-drawn carriage (*see* Getting Around, *above*).

Provincetown is a place of creativity, sometimes startling originality, and infinite diversity. In the busy downtown, Portuguese-American fishermen mix with painters, poets, writers, and, in season, whale-watching families, cruise-ship passengers on brief stopovers, and gays and flamboyant cross-dressers who come to enjoy the freedom of a town with a large, visible gay population. In summer, Commercial Street is packed with sightseers and shoppers after the treasures of the many first-rate galleries and crafts shops. At night, raucous music and people spill out of bars, drag shows, and sing-along lounges galore. It's a fun, crazy place, with the extra dimension of the fishing fleet unloading their catch at MacMillan Wharf, in the center of the action.

During the early 1900s, Provincetown became known as Greenwich Village North. Active art schools and inexpensive summer lodgings close to the beaches attracted young rebels and artists, including John Reed, Mabel Dodge, Sinclair Lewis, and Eugene O'Neill. In 1916, O'Neill's play *Bound East for Cardiff* premiered in a tiny wharfside fish house, minimally fitted out as a theater, in the East End. This theater is long since gone, but a model of it and of the old Lewis Wharf on which it stood is on display at the Pilgrim Monument museum.

The Historical Society puts out a series of walking-tour pamphlets, available for less than $1 each at many shops in town, with maps and information on the history of many buildings and the (more or less) famous folk who have occupied them.

The center of town is where the crowds and most of the touristy shops are. The quiet East End is mostly residential, with some top galleries, and the similarly quiet West End has a number of small inns with neat lawns and elaborate gardens. Practically the entire town has been designated part of the Provincetown Historic District — 1,100 buildings spanning many architectural styles, from 18th-century Cape houses to Federals and Victorians.

54 **MacMillan Wharf,** with a large municipal parking facility, is a sensible place to start a tour. One of the remaining five of the 54 wharves that once jutted into the bay, it is the base for whale-watch boats, fishing charters, and party boats. Also here is the **Chamber of Commerce,** which has all kinds of information and schedules of events. Information columns at the wharf have rest room and parking lot locations, bus schedules, and other information for visitors.

55 Head east for two blocks to the **Provincetown Heritage Museum,** on the left. Exhibits include antique fire-fighting equipment, fishing artifacts, art (including donated works by Provincetown-related artists as well as antique prints and watercolors of schooners), wax figures, and a half-scale model (66 feet long, built by a master shipbuilder) of the fishing schooner *Rose Dorothea,* which won the Lipton Cup in 1907. *356 Commercial St., tel. 508/487-7098. Admission: $2 age 12 and over. Open mid-June–Columbus Day, daily 10–6. Closed Columbus Day–mid-June.*

Time Out **Juventino's Portuguese Bakery** (338 Commercial St., tel. 508/487-2303) puts out fresh Portuguese breads and pastries every day year-round, until 9 or 10 at night in summer.

56 Ten more blocks up is the **Provincetown Art Association and Museum (PAAM),** founded in 1914 to collect and show the works of Provincetown-associated artists. Its 1,650-piece permanent collection is displayed in changing exhibits that combine up-and-comers with established artists of the 20th century. Some of the art hung in the four bright galleries is for sale. The museum store has books by or about local artists, authors, and topics, as well as posters, crafts, cards, and gift items. PAAM-sponsored year-round courses (one day and longer) offer the opportunity of studying under such talents as Sal Del Deo and Tony Vevers. *460 Commercial St., tel. 508/487-1750. Admission: $2 adults; $1 children 3–12, senior citizens, and students. Open Nov.–Apr., weekends noon–4 and by appointment; Memorial Day–Labor Day, daily noon–5 and 7–10; May, Sept., and Oct., Mon.–Thurs. noon–5, Fri. and Sat. noon–5 and 7–10 (hours changeable).*

57 In the next block, at No. 476, is the **Figurehead House,** a yellow mansard-roofed house in the Second Empire style. The name comes from the figurehead of a woman — fished out of the sea during a whaling voyage in the early 19th century — that now adorns the front of this house. Turn up Cook Street and left onto Bradford Street, which runs parallel to Commercial Street and is known locally as Back Street. Several blocks up, turn right onto Pearl Street for (58) the **Fine Arts Work Center** (24 Pearl St., tel. 508/487–9960), a nonprofit organization begun in 1968 that sponsors 10 writers and 10 artists from October to May each year with a place to work, a stipend to live on, and access to artists and teachers. The center also has a gallery and sponsors off-season poetry readings and other events. The buildings in the complex around the center, which it owns, were formerly part of Day's Lumber Yard Studios, built above a lumberyard by a patron of the arts to provide poor artists with cheap accommodations.

Farther up are the former studios of two noted artists: Edwin W. Dickinson, at 46 Pearl Street, and Charles W. Hawthorne, at 48 Pearl. Hawthorne's Cape Cod School of Art, established here in 1899, put the town on its path to becoming a major art colony.

Farther along on Bradford Street, on your right, is the Duarte Motors parking lot, on the site of the former railroad depot. The train ran across Bradford and Commercial streets to the wharf, where it picked up passengers from the frequent Boston boats and crates of iced fish from the Commercial Street fish sheds. Train service ended in 1960.

(59) Past Alden Street, in a little park on your right behind the Town Hall, is the **Mayflower Compact bas-relief plaque** by sculptor Cyrus Dalin, depicting the historic signing.

(60) The **Town Hall** was used by the Provincetown Art Association as its first exhibit space, and still exhibits local art — from paintings donated to the town over the years. Two of these are scenes of Provincetown by Charles Hawthorne.

Time Out   **Provincetown Fudge Factory** (210 Commercial St., tel. 508/487–2850), across from the post office, makes silky peanut-butter cups (with milk, dark, or white chocolate, creamy or chunky), fudge, chocolates, butter crunch, saltwater taffy, caramel corn, and yard-long licorice whips — a must stop for those with a dental death wish, and they ship.

All the way at the west end of Commercial Street, at No. 74, between Soper and Nickerson streets, is an interesting (61) piece of Provincetown architecture: an **octagonal house** built in 1850.

Across Soper Street is the oldest building in town, dating to (62) 1746. The small Cape-style **Seth Nickerson House** was built by a ship's carpenter, with massive pegged, hand-hewn oak beams and wide-board floors. Until he passed away in 1992, it was the home of photographer John Gregory.

(63) At the bend in the road, the bronze **Pilgrim Plaque,** set into a boulder at the center of a green space, commemorates the first footfall of the Pilgrims onto Cape soil — Provincetown's humble equivalent of the Plymouth Rock. Across the

street is the **Provincetown Inn**; inside, a series of 19 murals (painted in the 1930s from old postcards) depicts life in the 19th-century town.

What to See and Do with Children

The main component of children's summer vacations on the Cape is the same as their parents': the beach. Swimming, building sand castles, searching for shells and "neat rocks," and checking out the sea creatures and grasses that wash up have been the stuff of happy memories for generations of children.

Still, there are times when kids crave (and nag for) more modern diversions, and this family-oriented resort area offers enough activities to rival Myrtle Beach. Though miniature golf courses, go-cart racetracks, arcades, and the like are ubiquitous, much of the action centers on Route 28 between Yarmouth and Harwich Port. This strip is a monument to overdevelopment and a tangle of traffic in summer, but there's nothing like it when your kids (or you) are in the mood for some tacky fun.

Also, each town has a recreation program open to visitors. The morning activities, including sports, trips, and crafts, provide a good opportunity for your kids to meet others, according to the "Kids' Guide" put out by Brewster-Wellfleet area youngsters and available at the Orleans and Cape Cod chambers.

Amusements   **Batter's Box** has softball and baseball batting cages and pitching machines, including one with fastballs up to 90 mph; a six-game video-arcade room; and video rentals. *322 Main St. (Rte. 28), Harwich Port, tel. 508/430–1155. Cost: $1.50 for 10 pitches, $5 for 50 pitches, or $10 for 40 pitches and a video of yourself. Open Apr.–May and Sept.–mid-Oct., Mon.–Sat. 11–7, Sun. 11–9; June–Aug., Mon.–Sat. 9 AM–11 PM, Sun. 1–11. Closed mid-Oct.–Mar.*

Bayberry Hollow Farm (W. Vine St. Ext., Provincetown, tel. 508/487–6584) offers pony rides year-round.

Bourne Kart Track has go-carts, minibikes, a roller coaster, a Ferris wheel, children's rides, minigolf, an arcade, bumper boats, and batting cages. *Rte. 28, Monument Beach, 2 mi south of Bourne Bridge, tel. 508/759–2636 or 800/535–2787. Cost: $1–$3.25 per ride. Open mid-Mar.–Nov., daily 9 AM–11 PM. Closed Dec.–mid-Mar.*

Bud's Go-Karts offers 20 top-of-the-line go-carts. *364 Sisson Rd., off Rte. 28, Harwich Port, tel. 508/432–4964. Cost: $5 for 6 min. Open June–Labor Day, Mon.–Sat. 9 AM–11 PM, Sun. 1–11 PM. Closed Labor Day–May.*

Cape Cod Storyland Golf is a 2-acre minigolf course set up as a mini–Cape Cod, with each of the 18 holes a Cape town. The course winds around small ponds and waterfalls, a full-size working gristmill, and reproductions of historic Cape buildings. *70 Center St. (by the railroad depot), Hyannis, tel. 508/778–4339. Admission: $5 adults, $4 children under 12.*

Open mid-Apr.–Oct., daily 8 AM–midnight. Closed Nov.–mid-Apr.

Edaville Railroad, about 10 miles west of the canal in South Carver, offers an antique steam engine that traces a 5½-mile narrow-gauge track through 1,800 acres of cranberry bog; rides in a paddle-wheel steamboat, antique trolleys, and mini-Model T's; a carousel; a petting zoo; and more. *Rte. 58, off 495, tel. 508/866–4526. Admission: $12.50 adults, $7.50 children 3–12, $8.50 senior citizens. Open June–Labor Day, daily 10–5:30; Apr., May, and Labor Day–early Jan., hours and days extremely variable. Closed early Jan.–Apr.*

Heritage Plantation (*see* Tour 1: Route 6A, Sagamore Bridge to Hyannis, *above*) has a working 1912 carousel for kids, with chariots and hand-carved horses.

Pirate's Cove is the most elaborate of the Cape's many minigolf emporiums, with a hill, a high waterfall, and a stream. Planned for 1993 is a new 18-hole "Blackbeard's Challenge" course. *728 Main St. (Rte. 28), South Yarmouth, tel. 508/394–6200. Admission: $5 adults, $4 children under 13. Open July and Aug., daily 9 AM–11 PM; Apr.–June, Sept., and Oct., most days 10 AM–7 or 8 PM. Closed Nov.–Mar.*

Play-a-round, a superplayground in Chatham (*see* Tour 4: Route 28, Hyannis to Chatham, *above*).

Rock Night at Orleans's Charles Moore Arena (*see* Sports and Outdoor Activities, *below*) is for kids 9–15 (no parents allowed). From 8 to 10 PM Fridays year-round, kids roller-skate or ice-skate to DJ-spun rock and flashing lights.

Ryan Family Amusement Centers offer video-game rooms, minigolf, bowling, and more. *200 Main St., Buzzards Bay, tel. 508/759–9892; Town Hall Sq., Falmouth, tel. 508/540–4877; Capetown Mall, Rte. 132, Hyannis, tel. 508/775–5566; 441 Main St., Hyannis, tel. 508/775–3411; Cape Bowl, Rte. 28, South Yarmouth, tel. 508/394–5644. Open daily; hours vary for each location.*

Trampoline Center has 12 trampolines at ground level over pits (so kids can't fall very far). *296 Rte. 28, West Harwich, tel. 508/432–8717. Cost: $3 for 10 min. Open mid-June–Labor Day, Mon.–Sat. 9 AM–11 PM, Sun. 1–11; Apr.–mid-June, weekends only (hours very changeable). Closed Labor Day–Mar.*

Water Wizz Water Park has a 50-foot-high water slide with tunnels and dips, a river ride, a kiddies' water park, a six-story tube ride, an arcade, volleyball courts and tournaments, minigolf, and food. *Rtes. 6 and 28, Wareham (west of the Bourne Bridge), tel. 508/295–3255. Admission: $15.75 adults, $9 children under 48" and senior citizens. Open Memorial Day–mid-June, weekends 11–4; mid-June–Labor Day, daily 10–7. Closed Labor Day–Memorial Day.*

Arts   **Academy of Performing Arts** (120 Main St., Orleans, tel. 508/255–5510) offers 8- to 13-year-olds two-week sessions of theater, music, and dance classes, with a show at the end of each session; also, year-round classes for ages 4 to adult in dance, music, and drama.

Harwich Junior Theatre (Division St., Harwich [Box 168, West Harwich 02671], tel. 508/432–2002), a community theater group, presents summer plays for children. Write for information on participation in classes and productions.

Mimsy Puppets (tel. 508/432–1279) give morning performances of fairy tales and folk tales for children late June through August, Wednesdays at Community Hall in West Dennis and Thursdays at First Parish Church in Brewster.

Truro Center for the Arts at Castle Hill (Castle Rd., Box 756, Truro 02666, tel. 508/349–7511), housed in a converted 19th-century horse barn, offers summer arts and crafts workshops for children, as well as courses and single classes in art, crafts, photography, and writing for adults. Teachers have included notable New York– and Provincetown-based artists.

Children's programs are offered by the **Cape Cod Symphony Orchestra**, the **Cape Playhouse**, the **Falmouth Playhouse**, and the **Cape Cod Melody Tent** (*see* The Arts, *below*).

Camps   The Massachusetts Audubon Society offers natural-history day camps for children in grades K–9 in July and August at its **Wellfleet Bay Wildlife Sanctuary** (Box 263, South Wellfleet 02663, tel. 508/349–2615). One-week sessions include classes and excursions. Reserve as early as possible — the camps are very popular. The **Cape Cod Museum of Natural History** (*see* Nature, *below*) and **Cape Cod Community College** (tel. 508/362–2131, ext. 365) also offer summer day camps.

The Cape has a number of other day and residential summer camps; some teach sailing and water sports or horseback riding, such as **Cape Cod Sea Camps** (Box 1880, Brewster 02631, tel. 508/896–3451). **Cape Cod Baseball Camp** (Box 5, Buzzards Bay 02532, tel. 508/295–6046) offers sessions of a week or more, either residential or day-camp, for children 8–19. For more information, write to the **Cape Cod Association of Children's Camps** (Box 38, Brewster 02631).

Museums   **New England Fire & History Museum** (*see* Tour 3: Route 6A, Hyannis to Orleans, *above*) in Brewster has exhibits and picnic grounds.

Plimoth Plantation (*see* Off the Beaten Track, *below*) in Plymouth teaches children despite themselves about 17th-century Cape Cod.

Yesteryears Doll Museum (*see* Tour 1: Route 6A, Sagamore Bridge to Hyannis, *above*) in Sandwich appeals to doll-lovers of all ages.

Nature   **Army Corps of Engineers** (tel. 508/759–4431) has a junior-ranger program of outdoor activities at Bourne Scenic Park for children 6–12.

Aqua Circus of Cape Cod offers dolphin and sea lion shows, a petting zoo, pony rides, wandering roosters and peacocks, shells, aquariums, and more. *Rte. 28, West Yarmouth, tel. 508/775–8883. Admission: $7.50 age 10 and up, $4.50 children 2–9. Open mid-Feb.–June and Sept.–late Nov., daily 9:30–5; July–Aug., daily 9:30–6:30. Closed late Nov.–mid-Feb.*

Bassett Wild Animal Farm has wild and domestic animals, including lions, tigers, and birds, on 20 acres. Hayrides, pony rides, a snack bar, and a picnic area are available. *Tubman Rd., between Rtes. 124 and 137, Brewster, tel. 508/896–3224. Admission: $5.25 age 12 and up, $3.75 children 2–11. Open mid-May–mid-Sept., daily 10–5. Closed mid-Sept.–mid-May.*

Cape Cod Museum of Natural History (*see* Tour 3: Route 6A, Hyannis to Orleans, *above*) has a full program of children's and family activities in summer, including overnights and one- and two-week day camps of art and nature classes for preschoolers through grade 6.

Green Briar Nature Center in East Sandwich (*see* Tour 1: Route 6A, Sagamore Bridge to Hyannis, *above*) offers nature walks and other family activities all summer.

National Marine Fisheries Service Aquarium in Woods Hole (*see* Tour 2: Route 6A, Sagamore Bridge to Hyannis, *above*).

Whale watches (*see* Guided Tours in Essential Information, *above*).

Miscellaneous **Libraries** usually have a children's librarian with whom you can drop kids off for a few hours. Most offer regular children's story hours or other programs — check them out on a rainy day. Hours are listed in the newspapers each week (*see* The Arts and Nightlife, *below*).

Tot Drop (64 Enterprise Rd., Hyannis, tel. 508/778–6777) is a baby-sitting service by the Cape Cod Mall that lets you drop off your children for a few hours. Provincetown's **Council on Aging** (tel. 508/487–9006) also offers babysitting services.

Woodsong Farm Equestrian Center (121 Lund Farm Way, Brewster, tel. 508/896– 5555) has a horsemanship program for children 7–18.

Off the Beaten Track

If you're not from an area like New England, traditional pastimes like church suppers, barbecues, and bazaars are off the beaten track. If you're in the mood for a slice of regional Americana, give them a try — they're advertised in the papers.

Cape Cod Potato Chips (Independence Park, Rte. 132, Hyannis, tel. 508/775–3358) offers a free factory tour weekdays 10–4, including free samples of the all-natural chips handcooked in kettles in small batches.

In front of the **Dennis Police Department** (Rte. 134, South Dennis) is a display of Colonial-era punishment devices: stocks, pillories, and a whipping post.

At the Massachusetts Military Reservation (*see* Tour 2: Route 28, Bourne Bridge to Hyannis, *above*), a tour of **Air National Guard** grounds — including a slide briefing, a film, a look into F-15 fighter planes, and a tour of the museum, with old aircraft engines, missiles, models, and so forth — can be arranged by calling 508/968–4090. An attempt is made to schedule tours around flying activities, so you get to see the Guard in action.

Other of the reservation's tenants give tours as well: **Army National Guard** (tel. 508/968–5975), **Coast Guard** (tel. 508/968–6316), and **PAVE PAWS** (tel. 508/968–3206). It would be possible to see everything in a day, but you would have to reserve a couple days in advance.

Massachusetts Maritime Academy, founded in 1891, is the oldest such academy in the country. At its 55-acre campus in Buzzards Bay, future members of the Merchant Marine receive their training. The library has scale models of ships from the 18th century to the present, as well as changing exhibits, and is open to the public at no charge (hours vary widely; call 508/759–5761, ext. 350). For a 20- to 30-minute tour of the academy weekdays at 10 and 2, call 48 hours in advance (ext. 314).

Plymouth, the settlement site the Pilgrims chose in December 1620 after scouting locations from their base at Provincetown, is just over 20 miles from the Sagamore Bridge via Route 3 or the coastal 3A. In addition to a number of historical museums, visitors can view **Plymouth Rock** (reputed first footfall) and tour a replica of the *Mayflower* as well as **Plimoth Plantation,** a reconstruction of the original settlement. At the last, actors in period costume and speaking Jacobean English carry on the daily life of the 17th century in character as early settlers in the furnished homes and walking the grounds. New in 1992 was a crafts center with demonstrations of early techniques of making pottery, baskets, furniture, and woven goods. Self-guided tours start with a 12-minute film. *Tel. for* Mayflower II *and Plantation: 508/746–1622.* Mayflower II: *State Pier. Admission: $5.75 adults, $3.75 children 5–12. Open Apr.–June and Sept.–Nov., daily 9–5; July and Aug., daily 9:30–5:30. Closed Dec.–Mar. Plantation: Warren Ave. (Rte. 3A). Admission (also includes Mayflower II): $18.50 adults, $11 children 5–12, $17.50 senior citizens. Open Apr.–Nov., daily 9–5. Closed Dec.–Mar.*

At the **Sandwich Fish Hatchery** (Rte. 6A, Sandwich, tel. 508/888–0008; open daily 9–3:30), you'll see some 200,000 brook, brown, and rainbow trout at various stages of development, being raised to stock the state's ponds. The mesh over the raceways is to keep kingfishers and herons from a free lunch. You can buy feed for a dime and watch the fish jump for it.

Libraries The **Nickerson Memorial Room** at the Cape Cod Community College (Rte. 132, West Barnstable, tel. 508/362–2131, ext. 445) has the largest collection of information on Cape Cod, including books, records, ships' logs, oral-history tapes, photographs, films, and more. It also has materials on the islands.

The **Cotuit Library** (Main St., tel. 508/428–8141) has an extensive collection of luxurious leather-bound classics — a donation from a private library — and another of children's books. These may be read on the premises but do not circulate.

Centerville Library (585 Main St., tel. 508/775–1787) has a 42-volume noncirculating set of transcripts of the Nuremberg Trials.

Hyannis Public Library (401 Main St., tel. 508/775–2280) has a large collection of materials on President John F. Kennedy.

Sturgis Library (*see* Tour 1: Route 6A, Sagamore Bridge to Hyannis, *above*) has extensive Cape genealogical and maritime material.

Shopping

Shopping is an important part of a Cape Cod vacation, especially on nonbeach days in summer (and in the rain, when the covered malls and factory outlets are mobbed). Favorite pastimes of many visitors include antiquing and gallery hopping. Throughout the Cape you'll find weavers, candle makers, glassblowers, paper makers, and potters, as well as artists working in metal, enamel, and wood. You'll also find an inordinate number of shops specializing in country crafts, from straw dolls to handmade Christmas-tree ornaments.

Many shops close down for the winter; in season, they tend to stay open late several nights a week, especially in Hyannis and Provincetown. For more on Cape specialties and shop hours, *see* Shopping in Chapter 1, Essential Information.

Shopping Districts

Provincetown has a long history as an art colony and remains an important art center, with many fine galleries and frequent exhibitions of Cape and non-Cape artists. Several artists represented in Provincetown are also shown in prominent New York galleries. Wellfleet has emerged as a vibrant center for art as well. Brochures on galleries in both towns are available by mail (*see* Shopping in Chapter 1, Essential Information).

Provincetown and Wellfleet also attract large numbers of craftsmen, who sell through a number of unique and sophisticated shops. Route 6A, which is the premier area for antiques and antiquarian bookshops, has its share of crafts shops as well, including many focusing on country crafts.

Hyannis's Main Street — the Cape's largest — is lined with bookshops, gift shops, jewelers, clothing stores, summerwear and T-shirt shops, ice-cream and candy stores, plus minigolf places and fun or fancy eating places.

Chatham's pretty Main Street is another main shopping area, with generally more upscale and conservative merchandise than Hyannis. Here you'll find galleries, crafts, and clothing stores, plus a few good antiques shops. Falmouth and Orleans also have a large number of shops of all kinds.

Shopping Malls

Cape Cod Mall (between Rtes. 132 and 28, Hyannis, tel.
508/771–0200), the Cape's largest, has 90 shops, including
Jordan Marsh, Filene's, Marshall's, Sears, F. W. Woolworth,
restaurants, and a food court. It is open Monday–Saturday
9:30–9:30, Sunday noon–6, and is air-conditioned. Wheel-
chairs are available at no charge; strollers, for a small fee.

Falmouth Mall (Rte. 28, Falmouth, tel. 508/540–8329) has
Bradlees, T. J. Maxx, and 30 other shops, generally open
Monday–Saturday 10–9 and Sunday noon–5.

Mashpee Commons (Mashpee Rotary, junction of Rtes. 28
and 151, Mashpee) has more than 50 shops — including The
Gap and an art gallery — and restaurants in an attractive
village square setting. The shops are open Monday–Saturday 10–8, Sunday noon–5. There's also a movie theater.

Department Stores

These include **K mart** (Cape Town Mall, Rte. 132, Hyannis,
tel. 508/771–0012); in the Cape Cod Mall, **F. W. Woolworth**
(tel. 508/775–5212), **Jordan Marsh** (tel. 508/771–7111),
Filene's (tel. 508/775–3800), and **Sears** (tel. 508/771–1700);
and in the Falmouth Mall, another **Sears** (tel. 508/548–9580).

Factory Outlets

Cape Cod Factory Outlet Mall (Factory Outlet Rd., Exit 1
off Rte. 6, Sagamore, tel. 508/888–8417) has a food court and
more than 20 outlets, including Corning/Revere, Carter's,
Gitano, Bass Shoe, Bugle Boy, Van Heusen, and Toy Liqui-
dators.

Factory Shoe Mart (Rte. 28, Dennisport, tel. 508/398–6000;
Rte. 28 at Deer Crossing plaza, Mashpee, tel. 508/477–0017)
has such brand names as Penaljo, Nickels, 9 West, Evan
Picone, Etienne Aigner, Nike, Reebok, and Rockport for
men, women, and children.

Victorian Village (851 Rte. 28, South Yarmouth, no phone)
has several outlets, including Cape Cod Crafters Outlet (tel.
508/760–1677), Gitano (tel. 508/760–2170), and Crazy Horse
(tel. 508/394–1236) and is open daily year-round.

Flea Markets

The **Wellfleet Drive-In Theater** (Rte. 6, Eastham–Wellfleet
line, tel. 508/349–2520) is the site of a giant flea market
(mid-Apr.–June, Sept., and Oct., weekends and Mon. holidays 8–4; July and Aug., Mon. holidays, Wed., Thurs., and
weekends 8–4). There's a snack bar and playground.

Dennisport Indoor Flea Market (677 Main St. [Rte. 28], tel.
508/394– 6752), with both flea and antiques markets, is open
year-round.

Farm Stands

Fancy's Farm Stands (199 Main St., East Orleans, tel. 508/255–1949; The Cornfield, Rte. 28, West Chatham, tel. 508/945–1949) sell local and exotic produce, fresh-baked breads and pastries, dried flowers, baskets, hand-dipped candles, frozen prepared gourmet foods, spices and pot-pourri by the ounce, and more.

Tony Andrews Farm and Produce Stand (398 Old Meeting House Rd., East Falmouth, tel. 508/548–5257) lets you pick your own strawberries (mornings from mid-June), as well as peas, beans, and tomatoes (late June–late Aug.).

Auctions

You'll find an auction going on somewhere on the Cape all year long, from country-barn types to the internationally known Eldred's and Bourne auctions. Though the high-end auctions deal in very fine antiques, they always include some lower-priced merchandise. (Write for schedules.) Church auctions often yield interesting Cape pieces, such as old sea chests, at good prices.

Eldred's (1483 Rte. 6A, Box 796, East Dennis 02641, tel. 508/385–3116) deals in mostly top-quality antiques, such as marine, Oriental, American, and European art; Americana; and estate jewelry. Its "general antiques and accessories" auctions feature less-expensive wares.

Merlyn Auctions (204 Main St., North Harwich, tel. 508/432–5863) are homey affairs with moderate to inexpensive prices for old and new merchandise.

Richard A. Bourne (Corporation St., Hyannis [Box 141, Hyannis Port 02647], tel. 508/775–0797) has theme auctions, such as art glass, marine art, watches and clocks, fishing and sporting goods, and duck decoys.

Sandwich Auction House (15 Tupper Rd., Sandwich, tel. 508/888–1926) has events weekly, usually estate sales.

Specialty Stores

"Cape Cod Antiques & Arts" (Box 39, Orleans 02653, tel. 800/660–8999), a monthly supplement of *The Register* and *The Cape Codder,* is chock-full of information on galleries, upcoming shows, Cape artists, antiques shops, auctions, and so forth. *The Review: Cape Cod's Arts & Antiques Magazine* (60 Benjamin Franklin Way, Suite C, Hyannis 02601, tel. 508/362–2002) is a glossy magazine with gallery ads and articles. Both are available at local newsstands.

Antiques **B. D. Hutchinson** (1274 Long Pond Rd., Brewster, tel. 508/896–6395), a watch- and clockmaker, sells antique and collectible watches, clocks, and music boxes.

Brown Jug (Main St. at Jarves St., Sandwich, tel. 508/833–1088) specializes in antique glass, such as Sandwich glass and Tiffany iridescent glassware, as well as Staffordshire china.

Ellipse Antiques (427 Main St. [Rte. 6A], Dennis, tel. 508/385–8626) specializes in mostly museum-quality early glass, such as rare Sandwich glass pieces, as well as Staffordshire, Spatterware, and Americana.

Horsefeathers (454 Rte. 6A, East Sandwich, tel. 508/888–5298) sells antique linens, lace, bird cages, baby things, and Victoriana such as valentines.

H. Richard Strand (Town Hall Sq., Sandwich, tel. 508/888–3230), in an 1800 home, displays very fine pre-1840 and Victorian antique furniture, paintings, American glass, and more.

Kingsland Manor (440 Main St. [Rte. 6A], West Brewster, tel. 508/385–9741) is like a fairyland, with ivy covering the facade, fountains in the courtyard, and everything "from tin to Tiffany" — including English hunting horns, full-size antique street lamps, garden and house furniture, weathervanes, jewelry, and chandeliers.

Paul Madden Antiques (146 Main St., Sandwich, tel. 508/888–6434 or 888–6886; only by appointment or chance) specializes in Americana, with a selection of choice scrimshaw pieces, Nantucket lightship baskets, paintings, furniture, and accessories.

Remembrances of Things Past (376 Commercial St., Provincetown, tel. 508/487–9443) deals with articles from the 1920s to the 1960s, including Bakelite and other jewelry, telephones, photographs of old movie stars, and neon items.

Salt & Chestnut (651 Rte. 6A, West Barnstable, tel. 508/362–6085) has antique and custom-designed weathervanes displayed indoors and in the yard — a fun place to browse.

Shirley Walker Antiques at the Carriage House (3425 Rte. 6A, Brewster, tel. 508/896–6570) has American folk art, painted furniture, quilts, toys, and a roomful of garden accessories.

The Spyglass (618 Main St., Chatham, tel. 508/945–9686) carries telescopes, barometers, writing boxes, sea charts, and other nautical antiques.

Whitman House Gift Shop (Rte. 6, North Truro, tel. 508/487–3204) has Amish quilts and other country items.

Art **Berta Walker Gallery** (208 Bradford St., Provincetown, tel. 508/487–6411) deals in Provincetown-affiliated artists, including Selina Trieff and Nancy Whorf, working in various media.

Blue Heron Gallery (Bank St., Wellfleet, tel. 508/349–6724) is one of the Cape's best galleries, with representational contemporary art by regional and nationally recognized artists, including Donald Voorhees.

Cummaquid Fine Arts (4275 Rte. 6A, Cummaquid, tel. 508/362–2593) has works by Cape Cod and New England artists, plus decorative antiques, beautifully displayed in an old home.

Ellen Harris Gallery (355 Commercial St., Provincetown, tel. 508/487–1414 or 508/487–0065), in its 24th year, deals in art and crafts, including jewelry, art glass, sculpture, and all media.

Hell's Kitchen Gallery (439 Commercial St., Provincetown, tel. 508/487–3570) features Provincetown-associated artists, including photographer Joel Meyerowitz and painter John Dowd.

Kendall Art Gallery (East Main St., Wellfleet, tel. 508/349–2482) carries contemporary art, including paintings by March Avery and gallery owner Walter Dorrell, bronzes by Harry Marinsky, and wonderful ceramics by John Ffrench — brightly colored, high-gloss renderings of real and whimsical building facades.

Long Point Gallery (492 Commercial St., Provincetown, tel. 508/487–1795) is a cooperative of 13 well-established artists — including Varujan Boghosian, Robert Motherwell, Paul Resika, Judith Rothschild, and Tony Vevers — founded in 1977.

Woods Hole Gallery (14 School St., Woods Hole, tel. 508/548–7594) deals in 19th- and 20th-century New England art.

Books   The Cape has a dozen bookshops that sell rare and out-of-print books (at any, ask for the brochure listing them), along with plenty of all-purpose bookstores.

Chart House Books (Liberty Sq., Rte. 132, Hyannis, tel. 508/771–4880) is a good new-book store with helpful staff.

Kings Way Books and Antiques (774 Rte. 6A, Brewster, tel. 508/896–3639) has out-of-print and rare books, including a large medieval section, plus small antiques, china, glass, silver, coins, linens, and clothing.

Parnassus Book Service (Rte. 6A, Yarmouth Port, tel. 508/362–6420), in an 1840 former general store, has a huge selection of old and new books — Cape Cod, maritime, antiquarian, and others — and is a great place to browse. They also carry Robert Bateman's nature prints.

Provincetown Art Association and Museum (460 Commercial St., Provincetown, tel. 508/487–1750) has a gift shop with many books on Provincetown and its artists.

Punkhorn Bookshop (672 Rte. 6A, Brewster, tel. 508/896–2114), an antiquarian- and rare-book seller, specializes in books on the sea and some antique prints and portfolios.

Titcomb's Bookshop (432 Rte. 6A, East Sandwich, tel. 508/888–2331) has used, rare, and new books, including a large collection of Cape and nautical titles and Americana and a new section with quality children's books.

Yellow Umbrella Books (501 Main St., Chatham, tel. 508/945–0144) has an excellent selection of new books, many on Cape Cod, plus used books.

Clothing   **Cape Sailboards** (661 Main St., Falmouth, tel. 508/540–8800) has surf-type beachwear, Body Glove wet suits, and other beach gear, plus sail, boogie, and skim boards.

Hannah (47 Main St., Orleans, tel. 508/255–8234; Main St., Wellfleet, tel. 508/349–9884) has high-end women's fashions in unusual styles by such labels as Hannah, No Saint, and Leon Max, and shoes by Chinese Laundry.

Howlingbird (91 Palmer Ave., Falmouth, tel. 508/540–3787) carries detailed, hand-silkscreened, marine-theme T-shirts and sweatshirts, plus silver and shell jewelry, hand-painted cards, and batik-print summer clothing.

Kidstuff (381 Commercial St., Provincetown, tel. 508/487–0714) carries unusual, colorful children's wear.

Maxwell & Co. (200 Main St., Falmouth, tel. 508/540–8752) has traditional men's and women's clothing with flair, from European and American designers; handmade Italian shoes and boots; and leather goods and accessories.

Northern Lights Leather (361 Commercial St., Provincetown, tel. 508/487–9376) has high-fashion clothing, boots, shoes, and accessories of very fine, soft leather, plus silk clothing. Its shop nearby sells all kinds of rope hammocks.

Silk and Feathers (377 Commercial St., Provincetown, tel. 508/487–2057) has some of the most interesting young women's shoes and boots on the Cape, plus clothing, wild and tame lingerie, and jewelry.

Crafts **The Blacks Handweaving Shop** (597 Rte. 6A, West Barnstable, tel. 508/362–3955), in a barnlike shop with looms upstairs and down, makes beautiful hand-woven goods in traditional and jacquard weaves.

Cape Cod Cooperage (1150 Queen Anne Rd., Chatham, no phone) features woodenware made in a century-old tradition by a barrelmaker on site.

Chatham Glass Co. (17 Balfour La., Chatham, tel. 508/945–5547) is a glassworks where you can watch glass being blown, and buy it, too — objects including marbles, Christmas ornaments, jewelry, art glass, and antique reproductions.

Impulse (188 Commercial St., Provincetown, tel. 508/487–1154) has contemporary American crafts, including jewelry and an extraordinary kaleidoscope collection. The Autograph Gallery features framed photographs, letters, and documents signed by celebrities.

Kemp Pottery (Rte. 6A, Orleans, tel. 508/255–5853; 258 Rte. 6A, West Brewster, tel. 508/385–5782) has functional and decorative stoneware and porcelain, fountains, and garden sculpture.

Linda's Originals & the Yankee Craftsman (220 Rte. 6A, West Brewster, tel. 508/385–2285) brings together the work of 500 craftsmen in handcrafted country furnishings and gifts.

Oak & Ivory (1112 Main St., Osterville, tel. 508/428–9425) specializes in Nantucket lightship baskets made on the premises, as well as gold miniature baskets and scrimshaw.

Pewter Crafters of Cape Cod (927 Main St. [Rte. 6A], Yarmouth Port, tel. 508/362–3407) handcrafts traditional and contemporary pewter objects from baby's cups to tea services.

Scargo Pottery (off Rte. 6A, Dennis, tel. 508/385–3894) is set in a pine forest, where potter Harry Holl's unusual wares — such as his signature castle birdhouses — sit on tree stumps and hang from branches. Inside are the workshop and kiln, plus work by Holl's four daughters and others, including glassware and special exhibits.

The Spectrum (Rte. 6A, Brewster, tel. 508/385–3322; 342 Main St., Hyannis, tel. 508/771–4554) showcases imaginative American arts and crafts, including pottery, stained glass, art glass, and more.

Sydenstricker Galleries (Rte. 6A, Brewster, tel. 508/385–3272) features glassware handcrafted by a unique process, which you can watch in progress at the studio on the premises.

Tree's Place (Rte. 6A at Rte. 28, Orleans, tel. 508/255–1330), one of the Cape's best and most original shops, has a huge collection of handcrafted kaleidoscopes, plus art glass, hand-painted porcelain and pottery, hand-blown stemware, Russian lacquer boxes, jewelry, imported ceramic tiles, and much more.

Wellfleet Collection (Baker Ave., Wellfleet, tel. 508/349–9687) carries folk art, quilts, baskets, pottery, and country antiques.

Whippletree (Rte. 6A, West Barnstable, tel. 508/362–3320) is a large barn, decorated for each season and filled with country gift items and a year-round Christmas section. Offerings include German nutcrackers, from Prussian soldiers to Casanova, plus characters from *The Nutcracker* ballet.

Food   **Chatham Jam and Jelly Shop** (10 Vineyard Ave. at Rte. 28, West Chatham, tel. 508/945–3052) sells preserves (cranberry with strawberries and honey, Maine wild blueberry), nutty conserves, and ice-cream toppings, all made on site in small batches.

Chocolate House Fudge and Gift Shop (11 Cranberry Hwy., Sagamore, tel. 508/888–7065), just over the Sagamore Bridge on the Cape side, sells creamy fudge in 12 flavors, hand-dipped chocolates and truffles, and saltwater taffy and penny candy. The gift shop has cranberry glass and other Cape items.

Clambake Celebration (5 Giddiah Hill Rd., Orleans, tel. 508/255–3289 or 800/423–4038) prepares full clambakes, including lobster, clams, mussels, corn, potatoes, onions, and sausage, for you to take away — or they'll deliver or air-ship year-round. The food is layered in seaweed in a pot and ready to steam.

Marion's Pie Shop (2022 Main St. [Rte. 28], West Chatham, tel. 508/432–9439) sells homemade and home-style fruit breads, pastries, prepared foods (lasagna, Boston baked beans, chowder base), and, of course, pies, both meat and fruit.

Gifts   **Crystal Pineapple** (1540 Rte. 6A, West Barnstable, tel. 508/362–3128 or 800/462–4009) has cranberry glass, Dept. 56, Snowbabies, Swarovski crystal, beer steins, and more.

Home for the Holidays (154 Main St., Sandwich, tel. 508/888–4388) carries decorations, gifts, and handcrafted cards for nearly every holiday or special occasion — baby gifts, Christmas ornaments and papers, goblin lights for Halloween — as well as elegant glassware and china. Set in an old home, it's a lovely place to browse, with something magical at every turn.

Odds and Ends   **Baseball Shop** (26 Main St., Orleans, tel. 508/240–1063) sells everything relating to baseball (and other sports) — cards (new and collectible), hats, clothing, videos, and more.

Bird Watcher's General Store (36 Rte. 6A, Orleans, tel. 508/255–6974 or 800/562–1512) has everything avian: feeders, paintings, houses, books, fountains, calls, ad infinitum. **Christmas Tree Shops** (main shop at Exit 1 off Rte. 6, Sagamore, tel. 508/888–7010; others at Falmouth, Hyannis, Orleans, West Dennis, West Yarmouth, and Yarmouth Port) sell everything, period: discounted paper goods, candles, furniture, toys, kitchen goods. This is not high-concept shopping, it's pure fun. The multicolor, Victorian-style Hyannis shop (Rte. 132, tel. 508/778–5521) is the largest.

Sports and the Outdoors

Bicycling

The Dennis Chamber of Commerce's guidebook includes bike tours and maps, and the Wellfleet chamber's pamphlet "Bicycling in Wellfleet" includes an annotated map (*see* Tourist Information in Essential Information, *above*). Also, a booklet on the marked and unmarked bike trails of Cape Cod, *The Cape Cod Bike Book,* is available in Cape bookstores and bike shops, or send $3.25 to Box 627, South Dennis 02660. For bike-rental shops, see Getting Around by Bicycle, above. **Cape Cod Cycle Tours** (Box 1356, North Eastham 02651, tel. 508/255–8281) offers guided tours with van support and deluxe accommodations.

For a brochure on the **Claire Saltonstall Bikeway** between Boston and Provincetown (135 miles) or Woods Hole (85 miles), using mostly bike paths and little-traveled roadways, send $2 and a business-size SASE to American Youth Hostels (1020 Commonwealth Ave., Boston 02215). It is also available in area bike shops and bookstores.

Bike Paths **Cape Cod Rail Trail,** the paved right-of-way of the old Penn Central Railroad, is the Cape's premier bike path. It is 20 miles long, from Dennis to Eastham, and passes salt marshes, cranberry bogs, ponds, and Nickerson State Park, which has its own path (*see below*). Along the way you can veer off to spend an hour or two on the beach, or stop for lunch. The terrain is easy to moderate. The trail begins in South Dennis (the start is at the parking lot off Rte. 134, south of Rte. 6, near Theophilus Smith Rd.) and ends at the entrance to the Salt Pond Visitor Center. There are parking lots along the route if you want to do only a segment: across from Pleasant Lake Store (on Pleasant Lake Ave.) in Harwich and at Nickerson State Park in Brewster. The Butterworth Company (Box 296, Harwich Port 02646, tel. 508/432–8200) sells a guide to the trail for $2.95.

On either side of the **Cape Cod Canal** is an easy straight trail (6½ miles on the south side, almost 8 miles on the north), offering a view of the bridges and canal traffic. They are accessed from many points along the trails.

The **Shining Sea Bikepath** is an easy 3½-mile route between Locust Street, Falmouth, and the Woods Hole ferry parking lot. It follows the coast, giving views of Vineyard Sound and dipping into oak and pine woods; a detour onto Church Street takes you to Nobska Light. A brochure is available at the trailheads.

The Cape Cod National Seashore maintains three bicycle trails (maps available at visitor centers). **Nauset Trail** is 1⅗ miles, from Salt Pond Visitor Center in Eastham through groves of apple and locust trees to Coast Guard Beach. **Head of the Meadow Trail** is 2 miles of easy cycling between dunes and salt marshes from High Head Road, off Route 6A in North Truro, to the Head of the Meadow Beach parking lot. **Province Lands Trail** is a 5¼-mile loop off the Beech Forest parking lot on Race Point Road in Provincetown, with spurs to Herring Cove and Race Point beaches and to Bennett Pond. The paths wind up and down hills amid dunes, marshes, woods, and ponds, and offer spectacular views (on a really clear day, you can see the Boston skyline); there's a picnic grove at Pilgrim Spring.

Nickerson State Park (*see* Nature Areas, *below*) has 3 miles of trails through forest (trail map available).

Fishing

Fishing is one of the Cape's main pastimes (the Cape Cod Chamber's "Sportsman's Guide" gives fishing regulations, surf-fishing access locations, a map of boat-launching facilities, and more). The "Fishing Around" column in the Friday *Cape Cod Times* tells the latest in fishing on the Cape — what's being caught and where. A good source for Cape fishing books is Cape Cod Rod & Reel (*see below*).

The Cape Cod Canal is a good place to fish, from the service road on either side, for blues, cod, flounder, mackerel, and black and striped bass (Apr.–Nov.). The Army Corps of Engineers offers a **hotline on Canal fishing** (tel. 508/759–5991).

Hundreds of freshwater ponds offer good fishing; a license for freshwater fishing (along with rental gear) is available at tackle shops, such as **Cape Cod Rod & Reel** (210 Barnstable Rd., Hyannis, tel. 508/775–7543 or 800/734–6658 in MA), **Eastman's Sport & Tackle** (150 Main St., Falmouth, tel. 508/548–6900), **Goose Hummock Shop** (Rte. 6A, Orleans, tel. 508/255–0455), and **Truman's** (Rte. 28, West Yarmouth, tel. 508/771–3470). For rental boats, see Water Sports, below.

Fishing Trips Charter boats and party boats (per-head fees, rather than the charters' group rates) take you offshore for tuna, mako and blue sharks, swordfish, and marlin; bottom fishing for flounder, tautog, scup, fluke, cod, and pollock.

Fishing trips are operated on a walk-on basis from spring through fall by **Cap'n Bill & Cee Jay** (MacMillan Wharf, Provincetown, tel. 508/487–4330 or 800/675–6723), **Double Eagle Cruises** (Town Marina, Falmouth, tel. 508/548–2929), **Hy-Line** (Ocean St. docks, Hyannis, tel. 508/778–2600; bottom fishing), the *Naviator* (Town Pier, Wellfleet, tel. 508/349–6003), and **Patriot Party Boats** (Falmouth Harbor, tel. 508/548–2626 or 800/734–0088 in MA). Many of these offer charters as well, as do **Barnstable Harbor Charter Fleet** (186 Millway, tel. 508/362–3908) and **Rock Harbor Charter Boat Fleet** (Rock Harbor, Orleans, tel. 508/255–9757 or 800/287–1771 in MA).

Golf

The Cape Cod Chamber of Commerce has a "Golf Map of Cape Cod," locating 48 courses on the Cape and Islands. The Cape's mild climate makes golf possible almost year-round, and most of its 20 public courses stay open, though January and February do get nippy (temperatures average in the 30s).

Blue Rock Golf Course (off Highbank Rd., South Yarmouth, tel. 508/398–9295) is a highly regarded, easy-walking 18-hole, par-54 course.

Captain's Golf Course (1000 Freeman's Way, Brewster, tel. 508/896–5100), with 18 holes, was voted among the top 25 public courses in the country by *Golf Digest* in 1990.

New Seabury Country Club (Shore Dr., New Seabury, tel. 508/477–9110) is one of the state's best golf resorts, with one superior 18-hole par-72 championship layout on water, and another good 18-hole par-70 course. Both are open to the public September–May (space-available basis, proper attire required).

Ocean Edge Golf Course (1 Villagers Rd., Rte. 6A, Brewster, tel. 508/896–5911), an 18-hole, par-72 course, is the home of the New England PGA Championship. It features Scottish-style pot bunkers, challenging terrain, and one hole over a cranberry bog. Weeklong residential or commuter golf schools are offered in spring and fall.

Tara Hyannis Hotel & Resort (West End Circle, Hyannis, tel. 508/775–7775) has a beautifully landscaped, challenging 18-hole, par-3 course.

Other courses: **Chatham Seaside Links** (the old Chatham Bars Inn course, now town owned; tel. 508/945–4774), nine holes, a good beginner's course; and **Cranberry Valley Golf Course** (Oak St., Harwich, tel. 508/430–7560), 18 holes.

Health and Fitness Clubs

Falmouth Sports Center (Highfield Dr., Falmouth, tel. 508/548–7433) is a huge facility with three all-weather tennis, six indoor tennis, one squash, and three racquetball/handball courts; a sauna and a steam room; Nautilus, Biocycle, Airdyne, StairMaster, Cybex, and Gravitron machines; treadmills; a physical therapist; step and low-impact aerobics; and a large free-weights room.

Fitness Club of Cape Cod (55 Attucks Way, Independence Park, off Rte. 132, Hyannis, tel. 508/771–7734) has five racquetball/wallyball courts; basketball; Nautilus, Universal, Lifecycle, StairMaster, rowing, and other cardiovascular machines; treadmills; free weights; aerobics; personal trainers, myotherapy, massage, sauna, whirlpool; day care; and a bar/restaurant with pool table and dart boards.

Mid-Cape Racquet Club (193 White's Path, South Yarmouth, tel. 508/394–3511) has one all-weather tennis, nine indoor tennis, two racquetball, and two squash courts; indoor and outdoor basketball; free weights; treadmills and Nautilus, Lifecycle, StairMaster, and rowing machines; aerobics; personal trainers and racket sports pros; plus whirlpool, steam room, and sauna.

Norseman Athletic Club (Rte. 6, North Eastham, tel. 508/255–6370 or 508/255–6371) has four racquetball, two squash, six indoor tennis, and indoor basketball courts; Nautilus, StairMaster, Lifecycle, Biocycle, Versa/Climber, and rowing machines; treadmills and free weights; an indoor Olympic-size heated pool; Red Cross swimming lessons; aerobics and children's self-defense classes; saunas, steam room, and whirlpools; plus a pro shop and a restaurant.

The Tara Club (Tara Hyannis Hotel & Resort, West End Circle, tel. 508/775– 7775) has two lighted outdoor tennis courts; indoor and outdoor pools; aerobics; Nautilus, Cybex, Lifecycle, Liferower, StairMaster, and treadmill machines; sauna, steam rooms, whirlpool, massage, free weights, and more.

Hiking/Walking

The **Cape Cod Museum of Natural History** (*see* Tour 3: Route 6A, Hyannis to Orleans, *above*), **Cape Cod National Seashore** (*see* Tour 5: Route 6, Orleans to Provincetown, *above*), and **Nickerson State Park** (*see* Nature Areas, *below*) offer guided walks and hikes in season. The **Army Corps of Engineers** (tel. 508/759–4431) sponsors guided walks, bike trips, and hikes from its visitor center in Bournedale on Route 6; outside the center, on a bank of the canal with an excellent view, are a herring run, picnic tables, access to the canal bike path, and a short self-guided walking trail through woodland.

The **Cape Cod National Seashore** has nine trails through varied terrain (brochures at visitor centers and trailheads). Among them are the moderately difficult 1½-mile Ft. Hill Trail in Eastham, exploring a red-maple swamp, and Wellfleet's 1¼-mile Atlantic White Cedar Swamp Trail. Easy trails in Truro include the ¾-mile Pilgrim Spring Trail through woodland in the Pilgrim Heights Area and the ½-mile Cranberry Bog Trail.

Horseback Riding

The **Province Lands Horse Trails** are three two-hour trails to the beaches through or past dunes, cranberry bogs, forests, and ponds — great at sunset. At press time, no area stables were renting horses, but inquire at the Province Lands Visitor Center. Stables offering trail rides elsewhere: **Deer Meadow Riding Stables** (Rte. 137, East Harwich, tel. 508/432–6580), **Haland Stables** (Rte. 28A, West Falmouth, tel. 508/540–2552), and **Holly Hill Farm** (Flint St., Marstons Mills, tel. 508/428–2621). **Woodsong Farm** (121 Lund Farm

Way, Brewster, tel. 508/896–5555) offers instruction and day camps.

Ice-skating/Roller-skating

Fall through spring, ice-skating is available at several town rinks, including the **Charles Moore Arena** (O'Connor Way, Orleans, tel. 508/255–2971), **Falmouth Ice Arena** (Palmer Ave., Falmouth, tel. 508/548–9083), **John Gallo Ice Arena** (231 Sandwich Rd., Bourne, tel. 508/759–8904), **Kennedy Memorial Skating Rink** (Bearses Way, Hyannis, tel. 508/775–0397), and **Tony Kent Arena** (8 Gages Way, South Dennis, tel. 508/760–2400). Some offer roller-skating and rollerblading in summer. In winter, ponds and shallow flooded cranberry bogs sometimes freeze hard enough for skating; check conditions with the local fire department before venturing onto unfamiliar territory.

Jogging/Running

Aside from the state parks and forests, which have paved trails (*see* Nature Areas, *below*), the beaches are great places to run, as are the paths alongside the canal.

Lifecourse (Access and Old Bass River Rds., South Dennis) is a 1½-mile jogging trail through woods, with 20 exercise stations along the way. It is part of a recreation area that includes basketball and handball courts, a ball field, a playground, and a picnic area.

Many road races are held in season, including the world-class **Falmouth Road Race** (*see* Festivals and Seasonal Events in Chapter 1, Essential Information) in August and the **Cape Codder Triathlon** (Box 307, West Barnstable 02668) at Craigville Beach in July.

Shellfishing

For shellfishing licenses and information on sites, contact the local town hall.

Tennis and Racquetball

Public tennis courts abound: Falmouth, for example, has more than 20. To locate one near you, call the town chamber of commerce (*see also* Health and Fitness Clubs, *above*).

Bissell's Tennis Courts (Bradford St. at Herring Cove Beach Rd., Provincetown, tel. 508/487–9512; open Memorial Day–Sept.) has five clay courts and offers lessons.
Chatham Bars Inn (Shore Rd., Chatham, tel. 508/945–0096, ext. 1155) offers four waterfront all-weather tennis courts, lessons, and a pro shop.
Chequessett Yacht & Country Club (Chequessett Neck Rd., Wellfleet, tel. 508/349–3704) is a semiprivate club with a nine-hole golf course and five hard-surface tennis courts across from the bay. From mid-March to mid-December, the public may use the facility on a space-available basis. Lessons are available.

Melrose Tennis and Sport Shop (606 Rte. 28, Harwich Port, tel. 508/430–2444) offers three new Omni courts (synthetic grass and a sand layer, so it plays soft) and six Har-Tru courts, a pro shop, and lessons. You can also rent Rollerblades or bikes and buy sporting goods here.

Ocean Edge (Rte. 6A, Brewster, tel. 508/896–9000) has six all-weather courts; offers lessons and round-robins; and hosts Tim Gullikson's World-Class Tennis School, including weekend packages and video analysis.

Spectator Sports

The **Cape Cod Baseball League** (tel. 508/432–0340), begun in 1885, is an invitational league of college players that boasts Carlton Fisk, Ron Darling, and the late Thurman Munson as alumni. Considered the country's best summer league, it is scouted by all the major-league teams. Ten teams play a 44-game season from mid-June to mid-August; games are free.

Many annual bike races, road races, marathons, triathlons, and golf and tennis tournaments are held on the Cape. Watch the local papers for upcoming events, and *also see* Festivals and Seasonal Events in Chapter 1, Essential Information.

Water Sports

Boating, Canoeing, and Kayaking

See also Sailing and Windsurfing, below.

Cape Cod Boats (Rte. 28 at Bass River Bridge, West Dennis, tel. 508/394–9268) rents powerboats, sailboats, and canoes.

Cape Cod Waterways (16 Rte. 28, Dennisport, tel. 508/398–0080) rents canoes, solo and tandem kayaks, and manual and electric paddleboats for leisurely travel on the Swan River, as well as Windsurfers and sailboats delivered on the Mid-Cape.

Eastern Mountain Sports (Village Marketplace, 233 Stevens St., Hyannis, tel. 508/775–1072) rents kayaks.

Wellfleet Bay Wildlife Sanctuary (*see* Nature Areas, *below*) and the **Cape Cod National Seashore** (*see* Tour 5: Orleans to Provincetown, *above*) run canoe trips.

Sailing and Windsurfing

Aqua Venture Para-sailing (MacMillan Wharf, Provincetown, tel. 508/487–6386 or 800/300–3787) offers parasailing.

Arey's Pond Boat Yard (off Rte. 28, South Orleans, tel. 508/255–0994) has a sailing school with individual and group lessons.

Cape Water Sports (Rte. 28, Harwich Port, tel. 508/432–7079; other locations) rents Sunfish, Hobie Cats, Lasers, powerboats, sailboards, day sailers, paddleboats, and canoes, and gives instructions; sailboat charters are available.

Flyer's Boat Rental (131A Commercial St., Provincetown, tel. 508/487–0898) rents Sunfish, sailboats, outboards, canoes, rowboats, and fishing poles and teaches sailing.
Jack's Boat Rentals (Rte. 6, Wellfleet, tel. 508/349–9808; locations on Flax Pond, Nickerson State Park, Brewster; Gull Pond, Wellfleet; Beach Point, Rte. 6A, North Truro) rents paddleboats, Sunfish, Hobie Cats, canoes, kayaks, boogie boards, surfboards, and sailboards, and offers sailing and windsurfing lessons and guided "Canoe Eco-Tours" — sunset tours of connecting kettle ponds to observe wildlife.
Monomoy Sail & Cycle (275 Orleans Rd. [Rte. 28], North Chatham, tel. 508/945–0811) rents sailboards and Sunfish and gives lessons.
Windsurfing Unlimited (277A Commercial St., Provincetown, tel. 508/487–9272) rents sailboards, Sunfish, day sailers, and kayaks and provides instruction.

Scuba

Water temperatures vary from 50° to 70° in Nantucket Sound, and from 40° to 65° on the ocean side and in Cape Cod Bay. Check with a dive shop about local conditions and sites, as well as on dive boats. Wrecks in area waters include a steamship and schooners. Rentals, instruction, group dives, and information are available through **Aquarius Diving Center** (3239 Cranberry Hwy., Buzzards Bay, tel. 508/759–3483), Cape Cod Aquarium (281 Main St. [Rte. 6A], Brewster, tel. 508/385–9252), and Cape Cod Divers (tel. 800/348–4641 in MA; 269 Barnstable Rd., Hyannis, tel. 508/775–3301; 815 Main St. [Rte. 28], Harwich Port, tel. 508/432–9035; Rte. 6A, Orleans, tel. 508/255–7547).

Surfing

The Outer Cape beaches, including North Beach in Chatham, Nauset Beach in Orleans, Marconi Beach and White Crest Beach in Wellfleet, and Long Nook in Truro, are the best spots for surfing, which is best when there's a storm offshore. **Cinnamon Rainbows Surf Co.** (9 Cranberry Hwy., Orleans, tel. 508/255–5832) rents body boards, surfboards, and wet suits.

Swimming

Cape Cod Divers in Harwich Port (*see* Scuba, *above*) offers an indoor, heated pool and swimming lessons year-round.

Beaches

Cape Cod has more than 150 ocean and freshwater beaches, with something for just about every taste. Bayside beaches generally have colder water, carried down from Maine and Canada, and gentle waves. Southside beaches, on Nantucket Sound, have rolling surf and are warmed by the Gulf Stream. Open-ocean beaches on the Cape Cod National Seashore are cold and have serious surf. Shell collecting is best on Nantucket Sound beaches, just after high tide or a storm; also check tidal pools and around jetties and wharf pilings.

To avoid the crowds, arrive either early in the morning or later in the afternoon (when the water is warmest, anyway). Parking lots fill up by 10 AM or so. Those beaches not restricted to residents charge (sometimes hefty) parking lot fees; for weekly or seasonal passes, contact the local town hall.

Cape Cod National Seashore

All of the Atlantic Ocean beaches on the National Seashore, though cold, are otherwise superior — wide, long, sandy, dune-backed, with great views. They're also contiguous: from Eastham to Provincetown, you can walk virtually without ever leaving sand. Seashore beaches also offer the luxury of length: You can always keep walking if you want privacy, whereas most everywhere else there's no escape from the crowds. Wellfleet beaches from late July through August are sometimes troubled with red algae in the water, which, while harmless, can be annoying; check with the Seashore on conditions.

All the Seashore beaches have lifeguards, showers (except Head of the Meadow Beach), and rest rooms; only Herring Cove has food. Beginning June 25, parking costs $5 per day, or $15 for a yearly pass good at all Cape beaches; walk-ins pay $2; senior citizens with Golden Eagle passports and disabled persons with Golden Age Passports (*see* Hints for Older Travelers and Hints for Disabled Travelers in Chapter 1, Essential Information) are admitted free.

Coast Guard Beach in Eastham is a long beach backed by low grass and heathland. (It doesn't have a parking lot; park at the Salt Pond Visitor Center and take the free shuttle to the beach.) The adjacent **Nauset Light Beach** is similar, with the lighthouse for a little extra Cape atmosphere. **Marconi Beach** in South Wellfleet is a narrow but long strand of golden sand backed by high dune cliffs. **Head of the Meadow Beach** in Truro is often less crowded; it has only temporary rest room facilities and no showers since the bathhouse burned down.

In Provincetown, **Race Point Beach** has a remote feeling, with a wide swath of sand stretching far off into the distance and around the point and Coast Guard Station. Behind the beach is pure duneland; bike trails lead off the parking lot. Because of its position, on a point facing north, the beach gets sun all day long, whereas the east-coast beaches tend to be sunniest early in the day. **Herring Cove Beach,** also in Provincetown, is calmer, a little warmer, and not as pretty, since the parking lot is not hidden behind dunes. There's a hot dog stand here, and sunsets from the parking lot to the right of the bathhouse are great.

Town and State Beaches

Chapin Beach in Dennis is an attractive, dune-backed bay beach with long tidal flats at low tide that allow walking far out, but no lifeguards or services.

Corporation Beach in Dennis is an attractive crescent of white sand with lifeguards, showers, rest rooms, and a food stand.

Craigville Beach, near Hyannis, is a long, wide strand that is extremely popular, especially with the roving and volley-ball-playing young (hence its nickname, "Muscle Beach"). It has lifeguards, showers, rest rooms, and food nearby.

Kalmus Beach, in Hyannis Port, is a fine, wide sandy beach with an area set aside for Windsurfers and a sheltered area good for children. It has a snack bar, rest rooms, showers, and lifeguards.

Nauset Beach in Orleans is 10 miles of wide, sandy beach with large waves good for bodysurfing or board surfing. There are lifeguards, rest rooms, showers, and a food concession.

Old Silver Beach in North Falmouth is a long, beautiful crescent of soft white sand, with the Sea Crest resort hotel at one end. It is especially good for small children because a sandbar keeps it shallow at one end and makes tidal pools with crabs and minnows. There are lifeguards, rest rooms, showers, a snack bar, and lots of parking.

Sandy Neck Beach in West Barnstable, a 6-mile barrier beach between the bay and marshland, is one of the Cape's most beautiful, a wide swath of pebbly sand backed by dunes extending to what looks like forever in both directions. Camping and four-wheel-drive vehicles are allowed on parts of the beach.

South Cape Beach in Mashpee is a mile-long state beach on warm Nantucket and Vineyard sounds, reachable via Great Neck Road South from the Mashpee Rotary. Wide, sandy (pebbly in parts), with low dunes, it's a beach where you can walk a bit for privacy. Its only services are portable toilets and parking.

Veterans Park in Hyannis has a small beach that is especially good for children since it is sheltered from waves and fairly shallow. It offers picnic tables, barbecue facilities, showers, rest rooms, and a playground.

West Dennis Beach is a popular, long and wide sandy beach on the warmer south shore. There's a very open feeling, since the beach goes on for 1½ miles, with marshland and Bass River across from it. Windsurfer rentals are available, as are bathhouses, lifeguards, a playground, food, and parking for 1,000 cars.

Freshwater Beaches

Flax Pond in Nickerson State Park (*see* Nature Areas, *below*) offers picnic areas, a bathhouse, a snack bar, lifeguards, a playground, and water sports rentals.

Scargo Lake in Dennis has two beaches (access off Route 6A or Scargo Hill Road) that offer rest rooms and a picnic area. The sandy-bottomed lake is shallow along the shore (good for kids), surrounded by attractive woods, and stocked for fishing.

Nature Areas

Ashumet Holly and Wildlife Sanctuary (*see* Tour 2: Route 28, Bourne Bridge to Hyannis, *above*).

Cape Cod National Seashore (*see* Tour 5: Orleans to Provincetown, and Tour 6: Provincetown, *above*).

Monomoy National Wildlife Refuge is a 2,750-acre preserve on Monomoy Island, a fragile, 9-mile-long barrier-beach area (actually composed of two islands) south of Chatham (*also see* Tour 4: Route 28, Hyannis to Chatham, *above*). An important stop along the North Atlantic Flyway for migratory waterfowl and shore birds (peak migration times are May and late July), it provides nesting and resting grounds for 285 species, including large nesting colonies of great black-backed, herring, and laughing gulls and several tern species. White-tailed deer also live on the islands, and harbor and gray seals frequent the shores in winter.

Monomoy is a very quiet, peaceful place of sand and beach grass; of tidal flats, dunes, marshes, freshwater ponds, thickets of bayberry and beach plum and a few pines. Because the refuge harbors several endangered species, visitors' activities are limited; certain areas are fenced off to protect nesting areas of terns and the endangered piping plover. The Audubon Society and others conduct tours of the island (*see* Guided Tours in Essential Information, *above*); the *Rip Ryder* (tel. 508/587–4540 or 508/945–5450) will taxi you over in season for some lone bird-watching. The only structure on Monomoy is the South Island Lighthouse. Built in 1849, the shiny red-orange structure, along with the keeper's house, was refurbished in 1988.

Roland C. Nickerson State Park (Rte. 6A, Brewster 02631, tel. 508/896–3491; map available on-site) is almost 2,000 acres of white pine, hemlock, and spruce forest dotted with eight freshwater kettle ponds (formed by glacial deposits). Ponds are stocked with trout; other recreational opportunities are biking along 8 miles of paved trail (with access to the Rail Trail), canoeing, sailing, motorboating, picnicking, bird-watching (thrushes, wrens, warblers, woodpeckers, finches, larks, Canada geese, cormorants, great blue herons, loons, hawks, owls, osprey), and ice-skating and cross-country skiing in winter. Wildlife includes red foxes and white-tailed deer. Tent and RV camping (420 sites; no hookups) is extremely popular here, and visitor programs are offered.

Scusset Beach Reservation (Scusset Beach Rd., off Rte. 3, Sandwich [Box 1292, Buzzards Bay 02532], tel. 508/888–0859) is 450 acres near the canal, with a cold-water beach on the bay. Its pier is a popular fishing spot; other activities include biking, hiking, picnicking, and tent and RV camping on its 104 sites.

Shawme-Crowell State Forest (Rte. 130, Sandwich 02563, tel. 508/888–0351) is 742 acres less than a mile from the canal. Activities include wooded tent and RV camping (280 sites; no hookups), biking, and hiking; campers get free day use of Scusset Beach.

Waquoit Bay National Estuarine Research Reserve (Great Neck Rd., off Rte. 28, Mashpee; Box 3092, Waquoit 02536, tel. 508/457–0495) is 2,500 acres of estuary and barrier beach around the bay. It encompasses South Cape Beach (*see* Beaches, *above*), where interpretive walks are held; Washburn Island (reachable by private boat or reserve tour), offering 330 acres of pine barrens and trails, 11 primitive campsites (permit required), and swimming; and reserve headquarters, a 23-acre estate where evening talks are held (*see* Nightlife, *below*) and trail hikes and guided field trips begin.

Wellfleet Bay Wildlife Sanctuary is a 750-acre haven for more than 250 species of birds, attracted by the varied habitats found here. Hiking trails lead through woods, past moors and salt marshes that rim Cape Cod Bay. The Massachusetts Audubon Society refuge sponsors many activities, including walks, hikes, birding, nature classes, day camps for children (*see* What to See and Do with Children, *above*), and week-long field schools for adults, camping, seabird and marsh cruises, snorkeling, canoe and kayak trips, evening slide shows, an evening lecture series under the stars (bring insect repellent), and evening bat watches; a schedule is available on-site, or write for one. *Off Rte. 6 (Box 236), South Wellfleet 02663, tel. 508/ 349–2615. Admission: $3 adults, $2 children 5–15 (free to MA Audubon Society members). Open daily 8 AM–dusk.*

Dining

Reviews by Malcolm Wilson

Malcolm Wilson is the longtime restaurant reviewer for the Cape Cod Times.

New England cooking — hearty meat-and-potatoes fare — is the cuisine of choice on the Cape, plus, of course, the ubiquitous New England clam chowder and fresh fish and seafood. A number of extraordinary gourmet restaurants coexist with the bastions of tradition, however, along with the occasional purveyor of ethnic cuisines. Portuguese specialties such as kale soup or *linguiça* are found on many menus, thanks to the long history of seafaring Portuguese who have settled on the Cape. In Provincetown you'll find over 80 restaurants — some excellent — in season, and a few hearties year-round. At these little waterfront or back-street places, Italian and Portuguese cuisines and seafood predominate, but there's a wide variety.

In the off-season especially, many Cape restaurants offer "early-bird specials" — low-price dinners in early evening — and Sunday brunches and buffets, often with musical accompaniment. These are advertised in the newspapers.

Category	Cost*
Very Expensive	over $40
Expensive	$25–$40
Moderate	$15–$25
Inexpensive	under $15

per person, excluding drinks, service, and sales tax (5%)

Upper Cape

Buzzards Bay
Inexpensive
Stir Crazy. Southeast Asian dishes are served at this little box of a restaurant, given a bit of exotic flavor with baskets and posters from the owner's native Cambodia. There are no tame flavors here. The Thai *me-siam* is sautéed minced pork, tofu, soybean, coconut milk, and chili on a bed of bean sprouts and rice noodles topped with peanut sauce; the deep-fried finger egg roll appetizer is filled with chopped pork and vegetables and served with a very hot sauce. *100 Main St., tel. 508/759–1781. No reservations. Dress: casual. MC, V. BYOB. No lunch Sun. Closed Mon.*

East Sandwich
Moderate
Michael's at Sandy Neck. The twin-lobster special — in peak season, Michael's sells at least 3,000 lobsters a week — is the trademark of this relaxed restaurant, with a pubby dining room of exposed beams and white plaster walls, and a glassed-in porch with paper-covered tables you can color on. Fresh swordfish is a specialty, broiled, grilled, or blackened; the liver and onions is impeccable, with crunchy onions and a rich, nutty sauce. Homemade loaves of bread accompany meals. *674 Rte. 6A, tel. 508/362–4303 or 800/362–4303. Reservations advised. Dress: casual. MC, V. No smoking.*

Falmouth
Expensive
★
Regatta of Falmouth-by-the-Sea. A spectacular view of the Inner Harbor and the Vineyard Sound is matched by the spectacularly creative French and American cuisine, typified by the signature dish, rack of lamb *en chemise:* the lamb is carved from the bone and, surrounded by *chèvre*, spinach, and pine nuts, wrapped in puff pastry, then served with a cabernet sauvignon sauce. Seafood choices may include soft-shell crab with a three-basil butter sauce. Newly renovated after extensive damage during 1991's Hurricane Bob, the restaurant has a soft, elegant look, with contemporary decor in pinks, mauve, and white, and tables set with Limoges porcelain and hand-blown oil lamps. *217 Clinton Ave., Falmouth harbor, tel. 508/548–5400. Reservations advised. Dress: smart casual. AE, MC, V. Closed Oct.–Memorial Day.*

Moderate–
Expensive
★
Coonamessett Inn. A classic New England hostelry, this elegant place built in 1796 retains all its old-fashioned charm. The main dining room features paintings by Ralph

Cahoon; his signature hot-air balloons are re-created in copper and enamel to form hanging sculptures-cum-planters that add a touch of whimsy to an otherwise subdued and romantic room. The mostly white garden room has a window wall overlooking a leafy pond. The regional American menu focuses on fresh fish and seafood, such as lobster pie: crunchy chunks baked in a ramekin with a light breading and a filling of cream, butter, and sherry. A heart-healthy dish is offered each night. *Jones Rd., tel. 508/548–2300. Reservations advised. Dress: smart casual. AE, DC, MC, V.*

Moderate   **Amigo's.** This busy strip-mall restaurant, its rough barnboard and plaster walls brightened with Mexican art and Tiffany lamps, serves good traditional Mexican fare — try the *sopa de elote*, a creamy soup of ground corn with nubbles of niblets, tomato, and crunchy onion — as well as "gringo food" and nightly specials such as blackened fish. A children's menu has several offerings for $3. *Tataket Sq., Rte. 28, tel. 508/548–8510. Reservations for 6 or more. Dress: casual. MC, V.*

Mashpee   **The Flume.** This clean, plain fish house, decorated only with
Inexpensive–   a few Indian artifacts and crafts (the owner is a Wampanoag
Expensive   chief), offers a small menu of straightforward food guaran-
★   teed to satisfy. The chowder is perhaps the Cape's best, rich with salt pork, onions, quahogs, butter, and cream. Other specialties are fried smelts and clams, Indian pudding, and fresh broiled fish. *Lake Ave. (off Rte. 130), tel. 508/477–1456. Reservations limited. Dress: casual. MC, V. Closed some weekdays in the off-season.*

New Seabury   **Popponesset Inn.** Combine a magnificent ocean view with
Moderate–   comfortable dining in the ultimate Cape summer restaurant
Expensive   and you have this charming spot, which attracts a loyal cli-
★   entele year after year. Gray-shingled buildings house a series of bright and airy white-and-blue dining rooms, some open to the sky, others enclosed by glass, but all witness to the varying moods of Nantucket Sound beyond the waving beach grass. Weather permitting, there's beachfront dining under a tent. The cuisine is traditional New England with a strong emphasis on seafood, such as clam chowder; baked stuffed lobster with shrimp, scallops, and lobster; or herb-roast rack of lamb. In the oceanview lounge, Poppy's serves a new lighter, less expensive menu. *Mall Way, tel. 508/477–1100 or 508/477–8258. Reservations advised. Jacket preferred. MC, V. Closed Nov.–Mar.; closed Mon. and Tues. before May 1 and after Labor Day; no lunch before mid-June and after Labor Day.*

Sagamore   **The Bridge.** Known for good food and a warm welcome, The
Inexpensive–   Bridge has several small dining rooms with recessed light-
Moderate   ing. Helen Trout has been cooking Yankee pot roast for 30
★   years, and the menu doesn't lie when it says "nobody can cook a bottom round like Helen." The eclectic menu also offers *bijoux de la mer* — lobster, scallops, and shrimp with lemon and tarragon on spinach pasta with a smoky mushroom cream sauce — and homemade tortellini *casagrande*, stuffed with chicken and topped with meat sauce. *Rte. 6A,*

tel. 508/888–8144. Reservations advised on weekends. Dress: casual. D, DC, MC, V.

★ **Sagamore Inn.** Seek out this diamond in the rough for home-style Italian and Yankee dishes and seafood served in a family atmosphere. Inside, the look is old Cape, with captain's chairs, Formica-topped tables, wood booths, stamped-tin ceilings, and bare varnished floors. The food is top-notch: the fried shrimp are very large and sweet, the chicken cacciatore rich and simple, the eggplant Parmesan flawless, the onion rings tasty enough to merit a special trip. Also on the menu are lobsters, pot roast, and homemade bread pudding and grapenut custard. *Rte. 6A, tel. 508/888–9707. No reservations. Dress: casual. AE, MC, V. Closed Tues. and Dec.–Mar.*

Sandwich **Dan'l Webster Inn.** The Colonial New England patina of this
Moderate– congenial inn, conveyed in the decor and the costumed serv-
Expensive ers, belies its construction in 1971, on the ruins of the
★ landmark original inn. The glassed-in conservatory has Colonial-style chandeliers and lush greenery. The regional American and Continental menu emphasizes seafood, such as lobster sautéed with *crimini* and chanterelle mushrooms in Fontina sauce on pasta; early-bird specials and Sunday brunch are offered year-round. The wine cellar has many times won the *Wine Spectator* Award of Excellence. *149 Main St., tel. 508/888–3622. Reservations advised. Dress: smart casual. AE, D, DC, MC, V.*

West Falmouth **Domingo's Olde Restaurant.** Owner-chef Domingo Pena
Moderate– turned his grandfather's 1841 Greek Revival home into a
Expensive charming restaurant with two small dining rooms. The ambience is friendly and intimate, with stucco and antique green walls, wide-board pine floors, hanging plants, fresh flowers on glass-top tables, and chandeliers. Domingo, who shops the markets daily for fresh ingredients, describes the cuisine as international, with an emphasis on seafood. Star dishes are bouillabaisse or lobster Americal (wok-sautéed lobster meat, mussels and oysters in the shell, scallops, cognac, garlic, leeks, onions, and mushrooms). *850 Rte. 28A, tel. 508/540–0575. Reservations advised. Dress: casual. AE, DC, MC, V. Dinner only.*

Mid-Cape

Barnstable **Mattakeese Wharf.** Extending over the water on pilings,
Moderate with a view of the warehouses and general helter-skelter of the harbor, this relaxed restaurant has a popular waterside bar and a nautical-looking dining area lit by tiny twinkling lights. Seafoods, pastas, and steaks are served simply. Try the lightly breaded broiled scrod or roast prime rib. *271 Mill Way, Barnstable Harbor, tel. 508/362–4511. Reservations requested. Dress: casual. AE, D, DC, MC, V. Closed Nov.–Apr.*

Cotuit **Regatta of Cotuit.** This sister restaurant to the Regatta in
Expensive Falmouth is set in an 18th-century landmark stagecoach inn
★ (the restored original taproom offers an inexpensive light bar menu and piano music). Its nine intimate and romantically lit dining rooms are perfectly furnished in period, with Venetian mirrors, Chippendale furniture, and Oriental car-

peting. The cuisine is American, with grilled foods a specialty (like the mixed grill of two fish, each with its own sauce) as well as sautés and pâtés of rabbit, veal, or venison. Boneless sliced rack of lamb with Cabernet sauce is outstanding. *Rte. 28, tel. 508/428–5715. Reservations advised. Dress: smart casual. AE, MC, V. Dinner only. Closed Jan.–Mar.*

Dennis
Moderate–Expensive

Gina's by the Sea. An intimate little bistro by the bay (perfectly situated for an after-dinner beach walk), Gina's serves some of the tastiest food on the Cape, as the owners of the BMWs and Mercedeses that fill the parking lot seem to agree. The interior has exposed beams, knotty pine walls, a fireplace, and nicely set tables with white cloths, flowers, and candles. The Northern Italian menu is supplemented with seafood specials. Chicken Gismonda is a moist breast of chicken lightly breaded, sautéed in butter, and served on a bed of spinach, garnished with mushrooms sautéed in Madeira sauce — a polished dish. *134 Taunton Ave., tel. 508/385–3213. No reservations. Dress: casual. AE, MC, V. Closed Jan.–Mar.; June–Aug., lunch and dinner daily; Apr., May, and Sept.–Dec., dinner only, and closed Mon.–Wed.*

Red Pheasant Inn. The main dining room is pleasantly intimate and rustic, with stripped pine floors, exposed beams, candlelighted tables, Victorian lighting, and two fireplaces. The cuisine is American regional, with a French twist in the sauces. The large menu always features a lamb special — such as medallions in a hearty garlic-and-rosemary sauce of wine and veal stock — as well as sweetbreads, game, and seafood. The long wine list is a *Wine Spectator* award winner. *905 Main St. (Rte. 6A), tel. 508/385–2133. Reservations strongly advised. Dress: smart casual. MC, V. Dinner only.*

Moderate

Rose's. Rose and Angelo Stocchetti opened the place in 1946; today the family still takes care of business, some in the kitchen, some waiting tables, Rose presiding over all. There are several New England–style dining rooms, as well as a glassed-in white room with a flagstone floor and a wishing well with (fake) birds on branches. Veal is the specialty, as in saltimbocca or veal scallops sautéed in lemon butter on fettuccine. The *calamaretti alla Ronaldo,* squid in a lobster-tomato sauce, and the mussels in cream and wine, both served on linguini, are delicious. *Black Flats Rd., tel. 508/385–3003. Reservations advised on weekends. Dress: casual. MC, V. Dinner only. Closed Feb.–Mar.; also Mon. Apr.–May and mid-Oct.–Jan.*

Scargo Cafe. Across 6A from the Cape Playhouse is this romantic old sea captain's house. One cozy room has a fireplace and exquisite, highly polished golden oak paneling, another has large windows that let in the sun at lunch, a third has nautical prints of whaling ships. The menu mixes simple Italian dishes and pastas, fish, and several specials, including chicken Wildcat (sautéed with apricot brandy, mushrooms, raisins, and sausage) and grapenut pudding that made *Bon Appétit.* Food is served until midnight in summer. *799 Rte. 6A, tel. 508/385–8200. Reservations advised for 5 or more. Dress: casual. AE, D, MC, V.*

Inexpensive–Moderate **Playhouse Restaurant.** This institution of pre- and post-theater dining (where the chance of rubbing elbows with the performers adds an element of excitement) offers such simply prepared dishes as broiled and baked fish, chicken pie in puff pastry, and lots of sautés, such as shrimp with raisins, pine nuts, garlic, and basil. The front room is bright and airy, surrounded on three sides by small-pane windows and decorated in soft peach and powder blue under a white cathedral ceiling. The back dining room, by the bar, is a crowded, cozy spot prettily decorated with flowered chintz. Charcoal etchings of stage stars add to the theatrical ambience. *36 Hope La., off Rte. 6A, tel. 508/385–8000. Reservations advised. Dress: casual. D, MC, V. Usually dinner only (lunch on some matinee days). Closed mid-Jan.–Mar.*

Dennisport *Inexpensive* **Bob Briggs' Wee Packet.** This little restaurant has maintained an enviable reputation for good food and good value since its opening in 1949. The decor is Cape kitsch, with canary-yellow wood tables, watercolors in driftwood frames, and shells, glass buoys, starfish, lobster claws, and nets everywhere. From the kitchen — open to view and immaculate — comes New England fare with an emphasis on fresh local seafood (such as fish-and-chips, charbroiled swordfish, Cape bay scallops fried or broiled), a light menu, and a long list of sandwiches. Desserts include blueberry shortcake and bread pudding with lemon sauce. *Depot St., tel. 508/398–2181. No reservations. Dress: casual. MC, V. Closed Oct.–Apr.*

Hyannis *Moderate–Expensive* ★ **The Paddock.** Long the benchmark of consistent quality dining, this formal restaurant is decorated in Victorian style, from the dark, pubby bar to the airy summer-porch area filled with green wicker and large potted plants. The main dining room is a blend of dark beams, frosted-glass dividers, sporting art, upholstered banquettes, and Victorian armchairs. The wine list has won *Wine Spectator* awards for years. The traditional Continental-American menu emphasizes seafood (including 2-pound lobsters) and beef, such as steak *au poivre* — pounded with crushed peppercorns, sautéed in shallot butter, and flamed with cognac. *W. Main St. rotary (next to Melody Tent), tel. 508/775–7677. Reservations advised. Dress: smart casual. AE, DC, MC, V. Closed mid-Nov.–Mar.*

Roadhouse Cafe. This consistently fine downtown restaurant serves a mix of New England seafood, Italian pastas, milk-fed veal, and other dishes. The cioppino is popular, as is the chicken Homard (stuffed with lobster and Swiss cheese with lemon herb butter). The interior is cozy and attractive, with Oriental carpets on polished hardwood floors, exposed beams, lots of hanging plants, and a fireplace; in season, there's outdoor dining, and early-bird specials are offered year-round. *488 South St., tel. 508/775–2386. Reservations advised. Dress: casual. AE, D, DC, MC, V.*

Three Thirty One Main. Also called "Penguins Go Pasta" — its logo is a tuxedoed penguin — this sophisticated Northern Italian restaurant focuses on seafood and homemade pastas and breads. The dining room is a two-level affair, the upper section set off by brass railings. On the walls, mirrors alternate with wood paneling and brick; soft lighting and romantic music add to the ambience of this warm and attractive room. A signature dish is veal chops Pasetto, stuffed with prosciutto and Fontina cheese, lightly breaded and panfried, and served with a sauce of shallots, capers, prosciutto, and fresh tomatoes. The wine list is extensive. *331 Main St., tel. 508/775–2023. Reservations advised. Dress: smart casual. AE, DC, MC, V. No lunch weekends.*

Moderate **Fazio's Trattoria.** Chef/owners Tom and Eileen Fazio, re-
★ cently of San Francisco's North Beach area, have brought their considerable talents to Hyannis's West End. The trattoria is small and warm, dressed mostly in restaurant moderne, with candles on red-and-white-checkered tablecloths, black-and-white photographs of Sicily, and robust Italian ballads adding the right atmospheric note. The minestrone is a deeply flavorful dish with a rich, dark broth; also recommended is the *penne salsiccia,* pasta with a sauce of sausages, roasted peppers, olives, onions, and fresh tomatoes. The sausages, along with desserts like cannoli and zabaglione, are strictly homemade. *586 Main St., tel. 508/771–7445. Reservations advised weekends. Dress: casual. MC, V. No lunch Sun.*

Harry's. A great place for consistently good food featuring Continental dishes with Cajun specials and local seafood, Harry's offers seating at benches with wrought-iron arms or at tables. New Orleans and Toulouse-Lautrec posters decorate the walls, with plants and art-deco glass as accents. The hopping John (white rice and black-eyed peas), jambalaya, and blackened fish are all excellent, as are the substantial sandwiches. Sundays feature live jazz, blues, or rock. *700 Main St., tel. 508/778–4188. No reservations. Dress: casual. AE, MC, V.*

Inexpensive– **Barbyann's.** The success of this place is due to its casual,
Moderate comfortable interior — exposed-beam ceilings, subdued
★ lighting, and green, pink, and red color scheme — as well as its low-priced, tasty food. The menu mixes fish, steak, teriyaki, Mexican dishes, pizza, burgers, fun appetizers, and sandwiches. The Buffalo chicken wings, fried clams, and serious homemade chili are excellent. *120 Airport Rd., tel. 508/775–9795. No reservations. Dress: casual. AE, D, DC, MC, V.*

Baxter's Fish N' Chips. Right on busy Lewis Bay, the ever-popular Baxter's gets a lot of swimsuit-clad back-in boaters at its picnic tables for possibly the best fried clams on the Cape, as well as other fried, baked, and broiled fresh fish and seafood, lobsters, steamers, and mussels (plus burgers, chicken, and Cajun steak for landlubbers) and offerings from a raw bar on wheels in season. It's a fun place to watch boats at play while you dine. The indoor Baxter's Boat House Club — an airy, open room with sliding glass doors leading to deck tables, paintings of ships, copper lanterns, and a busy bar — has the same menu, plus specials. *Pleasant St., tel. 508/775–4490. No reservations. Dress: casual. MC, V. Closed Oct.–Apr.*

Sam Diego's. Traditional Mexican dishes are served until midnight amid a charming Mexican ambience — ornamental toucans, draped serapes, plants, and polished wood tables — and a crowded good-time bar. An interesting dessert is the crusty deep-fried ice cream, served in a giant goblet. *950 Iyanough Rd. (Rte. 132), tel. 508/771–8816. No reservations. Dress: casual. AE, D, MC, V.*

Starbuck's. The decor is sort of Hard Rock Café but without a theme — from the rafters and on the walls of this "Good Time Eating and Drinking Place" hang flags, a sled, a mannequin, a miniature Fokker D-7, carved pigs, a tuba, and weather vanes. Everything is orchestrated in a glitzy, with-it way, from the marquee lights that trim the striped awnings to the bar, raised like a motionless carousel. The menu is huge and eclectic, including fun Chinese, Japanese, Italian, Cajun, and Mexican dishes, seafood, barbecue, and lots of exotic and frozen drinks; appetizers are half-price at the bar from 4 to 7 PM. *Rte. 132, tel. 508/778–6767. Reservations 1 hr in advance advised weekends. Dress: casual. AE, D, DC, MC, V.*

★ **Up the Creek.** This comfortable, casual spot with a busy hum about it serves fine food at very good prices with an almost effortless competence. House specialties include the broiled seafood platter (half-lobster, scallops, scrod, baked stuffed shrimp) and seafood strudel — two hollandaise-sauced pastries filled with lobster, shrimp, crab, cheese, and more. The baked stuffed lobster is excellent. *36 Old Colony Rd., tel. 508/771–7866. Reservations advised. Dress: casual. AE, D, DC, MC, V. 10% senior discount at lunch.*

Osterville
Moderate–
Expensive
★
East Bay Lodge. Bought back from bankruptcy, the inn reopened in May 1992 following a major overhaul, and with the new top-notch staff, including a full-time pastry chef, the dining experience is first-class. The casually elegant main dining room, part glassed-in veranda, suggests the 1880 summer house the inn once was. The "country Continental" menu — featuring pheasant, sweetbreads, salmon, lobster, and 21-day-aged beef — may include wild-mushroom tart, lobster-and-oyster strudel, saltimbocca, or the signature dish, lobster Royale: sautéed lobster, shrimp, and scallops with tarragon-mustard sauce on green fettuccine. Sundays there's a lavish brunch buffet, followed by an evening shellfish buffet. The 450-item wine list boasts some extraordinary bottles. Renowned jazz pianist Dave McKenna plays in the lounge most nights (*see* Nightlife, *below*). *199 East Bay Rd., tel. 508/428–5200. Reservations advised. Jacket requested. AE, D, DC, MC, V. Dinner and Sun. brunch only.*

South Yarmouth
Moderate–
Expensive
Riverway Lobster House. Owned and run by the same family since 1945, this favorite of bus crowds delivers traditional New England food and hospitality. Lobster is featured in several forms, including baked with a crab stuffing. Also on the menu are many other fish and seafood dishes, served panfried, deep-fried, baked, broiled, and Newburg style, along with plenty of choices for landlubbers. Early-bird and children's menus are available. The many dining rooms all have a New England feel, some with barn-board walls. *1328*

*Rte. 28, tel. 508/398–2172. Reservations advised. Dress: casual.
AE, D, DC, MC, V.*

West Dennis **Christine's.** Lebanese dishes — such as the sampler of lamb
Moderate shish kebab, stuffed grape leaves, and more — make up part
of the menu. The rest consists of Italian dishes such as
homemade meatballs and sausages, excellent steaks, and
baked and fried seafood. The dining room has etched glass,
Tiffany lamps over low, vinyl-back booths and Formica tables, lots of greenery, and watercolors and lithographs. A
small nightclub has entertainment and dancing year-round
(*see* Nightlife, *below*). *Rte. 28, tel. 508/394–7333. No reservations. Dress: casual. AE, D, DC, MC, V.*

Yarmouth Port **Abbicci.** The Cranberry Moose is dead, long live Abbicci.
Expensive Marietta Hickey has scrapped her successful restaurant
★ and started anew — in the same 18th-century cottage but
now with contemporary Italian cuisine. The new decor,
designed by Marietta's architect son, is also very contemporary, in white, black, and bright yellow and blue, including
a black slate bar with steel-back chairs. Her cooking still
emphasizes a clean taste, though, with light use of oils and
fats in such dishes as calves' liver with polenta and balsamic
vinegar, grilled veal chop with wild mushrooms, or roast
duck with vinegar-apricot sauce. Also on the menu are a
dozen elegant pasta dishes and a few Moose favorites, like
rack of lamb. *43 Main St. (Rte. 6A), tel. 508/362–3501. Reservations advised. Dress: casual. AE, D, DC, MC, V.*

Moderate– **Anthony's Cummaquid Inn.** The main dining room is a spa-
Expensive cious, genteel place with window walls that reveal a water
view of great beauty. Complemented by an impressive wine
list is a traditional New England menu featuring bouillabaisse, baked stuffed fillet of sole (moist, flaky pieces of sole
rolled and stuffed with bread crumbs and lobster and
topped with Newburg sauce), and an exceptionally good,
oversize roast beef *au jus. Rte. 6A, tel. 508/362–4501. Reservations advised. Jacket requested. AE, D, MC, V. Dinner and
Sun. lunch only. Jan.–Mar., closed Mon. and Tues.*

Moderate **Inaho.** Relocated from its Main Street, Hyannis, storefront
to the more spacious quarters vacated by La Cipollina,
Inaho continues to offer tempura, teriyaki, and other traditional Japanese fare in a setting with such authentic details
as *noren* screens and a sushi bar. *157 Main St., tel. 508/362–
5522. Reservations advised. Dress: casual. AE, MC, V. Dinner
only.*

Inexpensive– **Jack's Outback.** Though renovation has seen the rummage-
Moderate sale decor replaced by simple wood booths and tables that
★ actually match, Jack's remains a quirky place where cus-
tomers get their own coffee while exchanging barbs with the
staff. The food is basic American home cooking: pot roast
with mashed potatoes and gravy, prime rib, fresh fish and
seafood, superb soups, and simple but exceptional desserts.
(Jack's is hidden "out back," down the driveway by Inaho.)
*161 Main St., tel. 508/362–6690. No reservations. Dress: casual.
No credit cards. No dinner Sun. and Mon. No liquor.*

Lower Cape

Brewster
Very Expensive
★

Chillingsworth. The Cape's best restaurant, this elegant little jewel, lit by candles and decorated in Louis XV antique and reproduction furnishings, offers award-winning French and nouvelle cuisine and an outstanding wine cellar. The frequently changing dinner menu is a five-course prix fixe ($40–$50), served at seatings (lunch is à la carte, no seatings), and features such entrées as venison with celery-root puree and fried pumpkin; sweetbreads and foie gras with wild mushrooms and ham julienne, asparagus, and smoky sauce; and peppered striped marlin with lemon basil sauce. Desserts, made in-house, are glorious and are available to take out. *2449 Main St. (Rte. 6A), tel. 508/896–3640. Reservations usually necessary (sometimes difficult to get). Jacket preferred at dinner. AE, DC, MC, V. Mid-June–mid-Oct., closed Mon., no lunch Tues.; Memorial Day–mid-June and mid-Oct.–Thanksgiving, closed weekdays. Closed Thanksgiving–Memorial Day.*

Expensive

High Brewster. A classic country inn overlooking a pond, the restored farmhouse offers a glimpse of a more romantic past: low ceilings, dark exposed beams, richly patinated wide paneling, small oil paintings in gilt frames, Oriental carpeting on polished floors. Five-course prix-fixe menus ($33–$38) featuring American regional cuisine change seasonally; a fall menu might include pumpkin-and-sage bisque, tenderloin medallions with chives and cheese glaze, and apple crisp with maple syrup, walnuts, and apple rum ice cream. A six-course tasting dinner is offered once a week. Accommodations are available. *964 Satucket Rd., tel. 508/896–3636. Reservations required. Jacket suggested. MC, V. Dinner only. Closed 1st 2 wks in Jan.; many weekdays in the off-season (call for days).*

Chatham
Expensive–
Very Expensive
★

Café at the Queen Anne Inn. Now operated by Brewster's Chillingsworth, the kitchen offers a menu that combines the best of Continental and new American, with a move toward lighter cuisine. Entrées may include oak-grilled tuna with coriander and wasabi-lemon butter or marinated, pan-seared veal rib eye with onion marmalade and balsamic veal juice. Homemade pastas are available in appetizer or entrée portions. Appetizers (like roast quail over creamy polenta with shiitake and fresh parmesan) and desserts are creative, wonderful, and beautifully presented. The main dining room has a country French look, from the French countryside landscapes to the elegant curtains of white lace and light blue and white stripes. The wine list is extensive. *70 Queen Anne Rd., tel. 508/945–0394. Reservations required. Dress: smart casual. AE, DC, MC, V. Dinner only. Closed Nov.–mid-May.*

Expensive

Chatham Bars Inn. There's no mistaking style, and this grande dame of Cape Cod hostelries has plenty of that — from the delightful airy lightness of the white-wicker-and-chintz reception area to the elegant-summerhouse look of the high-ceilinged formal dining room. The latter is a study in white, from the painted brick walls and woodwork to the ceiling fans, lantern wall sconces, and crisp linens — set off admirably by the rich deep green rug and the blue of the ocean seen through the picture windows that wrap the room. (Try for a seat facing the sea.) The $30 prix-fixe menu of creative American cuisine — using local products whenever possible, from cheese to poultry — features peerless crab cakes spiced with a generous hand and set in a pool of tomato coulis (puree); an excellent smoked seafood chowder; braised sweetbreads with sea scallops and lobster cream sauce; and noisettes of lamb niçoise, a magnificent dish in a dark, dense olive-tomato sauce. *Shore Rd., tel. 508/945–0096 or 800/527–4884. Reservations required. Jacket and tie requested at night. AE, DC, MC, V.*

Christian's. Billed as "an elegant Yankee restaurant," Christian's does have a certain panache. The look of the 1818 house's downstairs dining room is a mix of French country and old Cape Cod: exposed beams painted Colonial blue, wall sconces with parchment shades, Vanity Fair prints, Oriental runners on dark wood floors, lace-covered tables. The cuisine is creative Continental and American, represented by such dishes as boneless roast duck with raspberry sauce, chicken with macadamia-nut breading and a grain-mustard cream sauce, or superior sautéed sole with lobster and a lemon-butter sauce. The mahogany-paneled piano bar/bistro upstairs serves a light, fish-based menu, and there's dining on an outdoor deck. *443 Main St., tel. 508/945–3362. Reservations advised. Dress: casual. AE, D, DC, MC, V.*

Moderate–Expensive **The Impudent Oyster.** A longtime favorite in this part of the Cape, this restaurant just off Main Street is a big, comfortable room with a high ceiling, exposed beams, large hanging plants, and soft lighting from frosted-glass fixtures. The most popular menu items are grilled veal piccata — medallions with French mustard, rosemary, and lemon-butter sauce — and in summer, bouillabaisse and seafoods *fra diavolo. 15 Chatham Bars Ave., tel. 508/945–3545. Reservations requested in summer. Dress: casual. AE, MC, V.*

Harwich Port **Cafe Elizabeth.** A Cape captain's house has been converted *Expensive–* into a French country inn with a number of intimate dining *Very Expensive* areas decorated with white lace curtains, hanging pans and baskets, gilt mirrors, art glass, and velvet upholstery. The hallmark dish on the classical French menu is the sampler called La Pa-lette Duchesse: shrimp with a tomato-oregano sauce, veal with wild mushrooms, rack of lamb with tarragon, and filet mignon with béarnaise sauce. Appetizers include homemade gravlax (salmon marinade) with dill and sweet mushroom sauce, and caviar *blini* (small, thin pancakes) with homemade frozen cranberry vodka. Four vegetables accompany entrées. *31 Sea St., tel. 508/432–1147. Reservations advised. Jacket suggested. DC, MC, V. Dinner only. Closed late Oct.–Apr.; also Mon. and Tues. before Memorial Day and after Labor Day.*

Moderate– **Thompson's Clam Bar.** A perennial favorite for fresh fish, *Expensive* Thompson's has been renovated extensively over the past few years. The new look is swanky/clubby nautical, with a window wall overlooking the scenic harbor, varnished wood tables, brass marine instruments, hanging green-glass ship's lanterns, a huge mahogany circular bar and mahogany paneling, and a cranberry-glass clerestory. The harborfront patio is a popular spot for lunch or watching sunsets over cocktails and selections from the raw bar. Menu highlights are lobster served several ways, a fisherman's platter (an oversize assortment of fried fish and shellfish, onion rings, and shoestring potatoes), and a true shore dinner (chowder, steamers, boiled lobster, corn on the cob, and watermelon, plus sausage); nonfish choices are available, as is a children's menu. The HarborWatch Room offers a more expensive Continental menu in more formal surroundings, with a harbor view (reservations advised; dress: smart casual; closed mid-Sept.–May). *Snow Inn Rd., off Rte. 28, tel. 508/432–3595. No reservations. Dress: casual. AE, D, DC, MC, V. Closed Labor Day–late June.*

North Truro **Whitman House.** An inn since 1894, this elegant tavern has
Moderate a cozy Early American feel, with brick and dark barnboard walls, handhewn posts, exposed ceiling beams, and hurricane lanterns on cloth-draped tables. Crackers and cheese, lavish salads, and loaves of homebaked bread accompany such finely prepared traditional entrées as lobsters and prime rib, several surf-and-turf combinations, teriyakis, or lightly blackened swordfish or chicken. *Rte. 6, tel. 508/487–1740. Reservations advised on weekends, nightly in summer. Dress: casual. AE, MC, V. Dinner only. Closed Jan.–Mar.*

Orleans **Captain Linnell House.** Framed by huge trees, this neoclas-
Moderate– sic structure with dramatic Ionic columns looks like an an-
Expensive tebellum mansion transported to Cape Cod. Inside is a
★ series of small dining rooms: one with a Normandy fireplace, exposed beams, and white plaster; another with a pecan-paneled fireplace, oil lamps, Aubusson rug, and ceiling rosette; another with English rose chintz drapes framing windows overlooking a Victorian folly garden. Among offerings on the classic American menu are oysters Linnell, Wellfleet oysters with Champagne sauce and julienned vegetables; rack of lamb; and scrod in parchment with a lime-vermouth sauce. *137 Skaket Beach Rd., tel. 508/255–3400. Reservations required in season. Dress: casual. AE, MC, V. No lunch June–Oct. (except Sun. buffet brunch year-round).*

Off the Bay Cafe. This is an easygoing storefront restaurant with pressed-tin ceiling, antique brass fixtures, lots of polished woodwork (including golden pine wainscoting), a hunter-green-and-white color scheme softened with floral-print linens, and Cape maps and pictures of seals and birds. The regional American cooking centers on fresh grilled seafood, aged beef, wild game, and pastas. Highlights may include paillard of veal with garlic, shallot, and lemon cream sauce; simple broiled scrod with lemon butter and capers; smoked fish and meats; and rotisseried game birds and duck. An inexpensive light menu is always available. There's a jazz brunch on Sunday. *28 Main St., tel. 508/255–5505. Reservations advised on Sat., nightly in season. Dress: casual. AE, D, DC, MC, V.*

Moderate **Nauset Beach Club.** On the road to the beach is this casual
★ restaurant, set in an old duck-hunting cottage, that serves
superb, moderately priced Northern Italian dinners and is
packed in summer. Entrées include meat dishes such as osso
bucco, fish dishes such as swordfish cacciatore, and homemade pastas, including *penne* with *pancetta* in carbonara
sauce. The wine cellar is extensive. *222 E. Main St., tel.
508/255–8547. No reservations. Dress: casual. AE, DC, MC, V.
Dinner only. Thanksgiving–Mar., closed Sun. and Mon.*

Old Jailhouse Tavern. Tucked away on a rural side road is
this 100-year-old house, renovated with a prize-winning architectural design and an all-glass conservatory addition.
The chic, hard-edged contemporary interior — a stunning
display of brass, etched glass, and the original grouted stone
(the stone room was once used as a jail by the sheriff who
lived in the house, hence the restaurant's name) — is softened with natural oak and greenery. The cuisine is eclectic,
including everything from barbecued chicken and ribs to
filet mignon and broiled seafood sampler. Toast Nelson is a
taste bud–popping entrée, crusty French bread smothered
with bacon, crunchy onion, crabmeat, shrimp, and scallops,
topped with hollandaise sauce and Parmesan cheese. Sunday brunch is served year-round, and there's a late-night
menu til midnight. *West Rd., tel. 508/255–5245. No reservations. Dress: casual. MC, V.*

Inexpensive– **Land Ho!** Walk in, grab a newspaper from the lending rack,
Moderate take a seat, and relax — for 20 years Land Ho! has been
making folks feel right at home. Decorated in a jumble of
quarter boards and business signs, this casual spot serves
kale soup that has made *Gourmet* magazine, plus burgers,
hearty sandwiches, fresh native seafood, and very good
chicken wings, chowder, and fish-and-chips. *Rte. 6A, tel.
508/255–5165. No reservations. Dress: casual. MC, V.*

Wellfleet **Aesop's Tables.** Set in an 1800s house built from ships' tim-
Moderate– bers, Aesop's Tables has since 1965 served consistently fine
Expensive meals. The many dining areas include a summer porch, a
new brick patio, a romantic room with a fireplace, the bar
(with marble-topped antique tables), and a large, partly art-
deco room. The cuisine is new American, as in pan-roasted
lamb chops with a port-rosemary demiglaze. Death by
Chocolate, a heavy mousse cake made from imported chocolate, was voted Best Dessert on Cape Cod by *Boston* magazine. *Main St., tel. 508/349–6450. Reservations advised. Dress:
smart casual. AE, DC, MC, V. Dinner and Sun. brunch only.
Closed Columbus Day–Mother's Day.*

Provincetown

Moderate– **Ciro's.** After 30 years, Ciro's stage-set Italian restaurant —
Expensive raffia-covered Chianti bottles hanging from the rafters,
★ plaster and brick walls, slate flooring, strains of Italian
opera — plays out its role with all the confidence of years
on the boards. Hand-cut veal and pasta dishes are specialties; the extensive seafood selections include scampi *alla
griglia*, grilled shrimp with lemon, parsley, garlic, butter,
leeks, and shallots. *4 Kiley Ct., tel. 508/487–0049. Reservations*

strongly advised in summer and Sat. night year-round. Dress:
casual. MC, V. Nov.–Memorial Day, closed Mon.–Thurs.

Euro Island Grill & Café. An umbrella table on Euro's
second-floor deck is a great vantage point for observing the
Commercial Street parade while dining on Caribbean, Sicilian, or New England dishes, choosing from the raw bar, or
sipping drinks from the outdoor Tiki bar. Other offerings,
served outdoors or in the dramatic nightclub (*see* Nightlife,
below), include Sicilian pizzas cooked on a stone hearth,
clambakes, or grilled ribs, chicken, and lobsters. *258 Com-*
mercial St., tel. 508/487–2505. No reservations. Dress: casual.
AE, DC, MC, V. Closed Halloween–Memorial Day.

Lobster Pot. A wide selection of seafood (including sashimi,
lobsters, full clambakes), award-winning chowder, and
homebaked breads and desserts (there's a takeout chowder
and lobster market and bakery on the premises) are the
specialties at this bustling family-run restaurant. The unfussy glass-walled dining room and the outdoor deck upstairs overlook MacMillan Wharf and the harbor. *321*
Commercial St., tel. 508/487–0842. No reservations. Dress: cas-
ual. AE, D, DC, MC, V. Closed Jan.

The Mews. The location is super, right on the harbor; the
bar extends out over the water. Follow cobblestone paths
down to the glassed-in dining room or the intimate Mermaid
Bar with mahogany paneling, antiques, gas lamps, and mer-
maids in etched glass. In season, the emphasis is on fresh
seafood and shellfish, such as the popular mixed grill (three
kinds of fish, each with its own sauce). Nonfish entrées may
include ratatouille — a sauté of baby eggplants, zucchini,
tomatoes, Italian peppers, onions, and fresh herbs —
served with saffron couscous. *359 Commercial St., tel.*
508/487–1500. Reservations advised. Dress: casual. D, DC, MC,
V. Closed mid-Nov.–mid-Feb.; also Mon.–Thurs. before late
June and after Labor Day.

The Moors. This unique restaurant, constructed of flotsam
and jetsam found on Cape beaches, specializes in seafood
and Portuguese cuisine, such as kale, *chourico,* and *linguiça*
soups; marinated swordfish steaks; and chicken with Madeira. The atmosphere is nautical and informal, and there's
entertainment in the lounge (*see* Nightlife, *below*). *5 Brad-*
ford St. Ext., tel. 508/487–0840. Reservations advised. Dress:
casual. AE, D, DC, MC, V. Closed late Nov.–Mar.

★ **Napi's.** A Provincetown institution, Napi's serves original
and well-prepared food in a warm, casual art- and antiques-
filled house of natural wood, exposed beams and brickwork,
stained-glass windows, Tiffany lamps, and hanging plants.
The menu is large and eclectic: Middle Eastern, Moroccan,
European, Oriental, vegetarian. Shrimp feta is shrimp
flamed with Ouzo and Metaxa, baked in tomato sauce, and
topped with feta cheese. Chicken *chambeaux* is boneless
chicken in white wine, tarragon, and a mushroom cream
reduction. *7 Freeman St., tel. 508/487–1145. Reservations re-*
quired in summer; advised off-season. Dress: casual. D, DC,
MC, V. May–Oct., dinner only.

Sal's Place. Everything at this waterfront trattoria is homemade, from breads and pastas to *tiramisù* and other des-

serts. Shrimp Adriatica is shrimp and calamari with pesto sauce; other specialties on the southern Italian menu are saltimbocca and spinach lasagna. The decor leans to wine basket-bottles and old photos and posters out front; the dining room overlooking the water, or outdoor dining in summer, is a treat. *99 Commercial St., tel. 508/487–1279. Reservations advised. Dress: casual. MC, V. Dinner only. Closed Nov.–Apr.; also Mon.–Thurs. before mid-June and after Oct. 1.*

Lodging

With a tourism-based economy, the Cape naturally abounds in lodging places, including self-contained luxury resorts, grand old oceanfront hotels, chain hotels, mom-and-pop motels, antiques-filled bed-and-breakfasts, cottages, condominiums, and apartments. The Cape Cod Chamber of Commerce's "Resort Directory" lists hundreds of establishments, as well as many real-estate agencies dealing in rentals (*see also* Lodging in Chapter 1, Essential Information). Local chambers' guidebooks all carry information on realtors in their area, and the monthly full-color "Real Estate Book" (Box 10, West Hyannisport 02672, tel. 800/841–3401) includes rentals.

Choosing where to stay depends on the kind of vacation you have in mind. Beach lovers may choose on the basis of water temperature (bay and National Seashore waters are coldest, south-shore sound waters are warmest) or beach scenery and atmosphere (Seashore beaches are the dune-backed, windswept ones with no development allowed along the shore and miles of contiguous beaches for long walking and private sunning; Mid-Cape and Falmouth beaches are generally more circumscribed and crowded with families, though some are quite pretty, wide, and sandy).

Quiet, traditional villages with old-Cape flavor and several charming B&Bs with gardens and sometimes woodland settings are found in Sandwich and other towns along the north-shore Route 6A historic district. Access to the bay beaches and a number of shops and historical museums combine with the real country-road feeling of 6A to make for a leisurely getaway. Falmouth has village charm while providing all the amenities of the Cape's second-largest town, as well as proximity to the warmer south-shore beaches and to the ferry to Martha's Vineyard. Quiet, traditional Chatham, with upscale shops and superior accommodations, is well-positioned for day trips to Provincetown, Seashore beaches, and Hyannis.

Those who like more action should head for the Mid-Cape. The center of it all is Hyannis, with a busy Main Street and plenty of nightlife, along with some fine warm-water beaches; if you want to be near but not in it, consider one of the pretty surrounding villages, such as Centerville. Yarmouth encompasses the most developed stretch of Route 28 and is wall-to-wall tourist amenities, from motels with pools to seafood restaurants to minigolf and other activities —

possibly a good choice for families with action-oriented children — as well as fishing and boating on Bass River.

For the austere Cape of dunes and sea, try the beach cottages of the sparsely developed Lower Cape between Wellfleet and Provincetown. Except in these two towns of artists and fishermen, there's not a lot of activity here, but especially in Truro there's escape and open vistas not possible elsewhere on the Cape, as well as spectacular long beaches. Provincetown is something completely different, a fun and (in summer) frantic wall-to-wall jumble of shops and houses bursting with colorful people, and a very active nighttime scene. Staying in town makes getting to everything by foot or bike possible; the edges of Commercial Street, away from the center, are relatively quiet. For a more secluded setting, you can stay in nearby Truro or Wellfleet and make day (or night) trips to town; the bayfront motels and cottages on Route 6A in North Truro, just outside Provincetown, are perhaps the best option for families, offering long sandy beaches, picnic areas, and often pools.

Finally, remember that the Cape is only 70 miles from end to end, so wherever you stay, you can always get there from here.

In summer, lodgings should be booked as far in advance as possible — several months for the most popular cottages and B&Bs. Assistance with last-minute reservations is available at the Cape Cod Chamber of Commerce information booths (*see* Essential Information, *above*). Off-season rates are much reduced, and service may be more personalized.

Reservations Services B&B services include **House Guests Cape Cod and the Islands** (Box 1881, Orleans 02653, tel. 800/666–HOST), with more than 100 B&Bs, cottages, and efficiencies; **Bed and Breakfast Cape Cod** (Box 341, West Hyannisport 02672–0341, tel. 508/775–2772, fax 508/775–2884), with about 90 on the Cape and islands; and **Orleans Bed & Breakfast Associates** (Box 1312, Orleans 02653, tel. 508/255–3824 or 800/541–6226), with 75 host homes and small inns on the Lower Cape from Harwich to Truro. **Provincetown Reservations System** (tel. 508/487–2400 or 800/648–0364) makes reservations year-round for accommodations, shows, restaurants, transportation, and more. **DestINNations** (tel. 800/333–INNS) handles a limited number of hotels and B&Bs on the Cape and islands but will arrange any and all details of a visit.

Hostels The homey **HyLand AYH-Hostel** (465 Falmouth Rd., Hyannis 02601, tel. 508/775–2970), on 3 acres of pine woods, offers 42 dormbeds and rental bikes March–November. **Mid-Cape AYH-Hostel** (75 Goody Hallet Dr., Eastham 02642, tel. 508/255–2785; open mid-May–mid-Sept.), on 3 wooded acres a 15-minute walk to the bay, has eight cabins sleeping six to eight each, plus volleyball and ping-pong. **Little America AYH-Hostel** (N. Pamet Rd., Box 402, Truro 02666, tel. 508/349–3889; open mid-June–Labor Day), in a former Coast Guard station, has 42 beds.

Camping The Cape has many private campgrounds (ask the Cape Cod Chamber of Commerce for its listing), as well as camping at state parks and forests; tent and sleeping-bag rentals are available from **Eastern Mountain Sports** (Village Marketplace, 233 Stevens St., Hyannis, tel. 508/775–1072). Most popular with nature lovers is **Nickerson State Park** (*see* Nature Areas, *above,* for more on this and other state facilities). A surprise in this very traditional area is a family nudist campground, **Sandy Terraces** (Box 98, Marstons Mills 02648, tel. 508/428–9209). Although private campgrounds serve the area, the only camping permitted on the Cape Cod National Seashore itself is in nonrental, self-contained ORVs at Race Point Beach.

Category	Cost*
Very Expensive	over $150
Expensive	$100–$150
Moderate	$70–$100
Inexpensive	under $70

*all prices are for a standard double room in high season, excluding 5.7% state tax and 4% local tax

Upper Cape

East Sandwich **Earl of Sandwich Motor Manor.** Single-story Tudor-style
Moderate buildings are ranged in a *U* around a wooded lawn in the back, set with lawn chairs. The newer buildings (1981–83) have air-conditioning, unlike the main building (1963), which has room fans; all rooms have phones. The decor is rather somber, with dark exposed beams on white ceilings, dark paneled walls, quarry-tile floors with Oriental throw rugs, olive leatherette wing chairs, and chenille bedspreads, but the rooms are a good size and have large Tudor-style windows and small tiled baths. *378 Rte. 6A, 02537, tel. 508/888–1415 or 800/442–3275. 24 rooms. Facilities: minifridges available. AE, D, MC, V.*

Falmouth **Coonamessett Inn.** Since 1953, this inn has been providing
Expensive gracious accommodations and fine dining. One- or two-bed-
★ room suites are located in five buildings ranged around a broad, landscaped lawn that spills down to a scenic wooded pond — a tranquil country setting. Three suites directly overlook the pond. Rooms are casually decorated, with bleached wood or pine paneling, New England antiques or reproductions, upholstered chairs and couches, color TV, and phones. A large collection of art by Ralph Cahoon is displayed throughout the inn. *Jones Rd. and Gifford St., Box 707, 02541, tel. 508/548–2300. 25 suites, 1 cottage. Facilities: 2 restaurants, clothing shop. AE, DC, MC, V.*

Quality Inn. Across from a pond, a mile outside Falmouth center, the inn's three buildings were remodeled in 1989–90. Rooms are large, with plush carpeting, contemporary pastel decor, wood-tone furniture, cable TV/HBO, and phones; suites have minifridges. The large pool area is bright and nicely arranged with patio furniture and greenery. Discount packages are available. *291 Jones Rd., 02540, tel. 508/540–2000 or 800/228–5151, fax 508/548–2712. 88 rooms, 5 suites. Facilities: heated indoor pool, room service, sauna, video game room, restaurant (in season), lounge with top-40s entertainment, children under 18 stay free. AE, D, MC, V.*

Moderate–Expensive **Admiralty Resort.** This large all-suite hotel on the highway outside Falmouth offers rooms with a Murphy bed and a queen bed or two queen-size beds. Every unit has cable TV, a wet bar, a minifridge, and a coffee-maker and is furnished in pastel Formica and wood, with rose wall-to-wall carpeting. Townhouse suites have cathedral ceilings with skylights; a loft; a living room with queen-size Murphy or king-size bed, sofabed, and table and chairs; and a whirlpool bathtub. Golf and other packages are available. *51 Teaticket Hwy. (Rte. 28), 02540, tel. 508/548–4240 or 800/341–5700. 98 suites. Facilities: outdoor pool, new heated indoor pool with spa, restaurant, lounge with live entertainment and dancing. AE, D, DC, MC, V.*

Moderate **Capt. Tom Lawrence House.** Set back from the street, just steps from downtown, is this pretty white house with a cupola and green shutters, surrounded by flowers and bushes and a lawn shaded by old maple trees. Built in 1861 for a whaling captain, it is now an intimate B&B. All rooms look fresh and romantic, with antique and painted furniture, French country wallpapers, soft colors, and thick carpeting; the beds, all queen-size canopy or king-size, have firm mattresses, Laura Ashley or Ralph Lauren sheets, and down comforters in winter. *75 Locust St., 02540, tel. 508/540–1445. 6 rooms. Facilities: full breakfast, pay phone. MC, V. No smoking.*

★ **Mostly Hall.** Set in a landscaped park far back from the street and separated from it by tall bushes, trees, and a wrought-iron fence, this inn looks very much like a private estate. The 1849 house itself is imposing, with a wraparound porch and a dramatic cupola (fitted out as a guest den with TV and travel library). Accommodations are in large corner rooms, with leafy views through shuttered casement windows, reading areas, antique pieces and reproduction queen-size canopy beds, floral wallpapers, wall-to-wall carpeting, and Oriental accent rugs. First-floor rooms have 13-foot ceilings; most baths are small. *27 Main St., 02540, tel. 508/548–3786 or 800/682–0565. 6 rooms. Facilities: full breakfast, central air-conditioning, bicycles, common phone and TV, lending library, lawn games. MC, V. No smoking. Closed Jan.–mid-Feb.*

Village Green Inn. In 1986, two former schoolteachers turned this turreted Victorian building into a B&B inn. Guest rooms are spacious and decorated tastefully: antique beds, lovely wallpapers, comforters, dust ruffles, beautiful hardwood floors, elaborate woodwork, and some working fireplaces. The more modern suite has 12 windows, Danish walnut furniture, and a full-size cable TV. The breezy front porch — which faces the Falmouth green — is set with white wicker furniture and hung with colorful potted geraniums. *40 W. Main St., 02540, tel. 508/548–5621. 4 rooms, 1 suite.*

Facilities: full breakfast, afternoon beverages or snacks, common piano and TV. AE, MC, V. No smoking. Closed Jan.–Mar.

New Seabury **New Seabury Resort and Conference Center.** On a 2,000-acre
Very Expensive point surrounded by the waters of Nantucket Sound, this
★ self-contained resort community of private homes and "villas" (condominium units) consists of 13 "villages," three of
which offer rentals. The oceanfront Maushop Village is a
Nantucket-style complex of gray-shingled, cottagelike
buildings set among narrow lanes of crushed seashells, with
rugosa roses trailing white picket fences and trellises. The
interiors offer an attractive mix of reproduction Cape-style
antiques and casual modern furnishings. The Mews, overlooking the beautifully landscaped championship golf
courses, offers contemporary California-style condos with
cathedral ceilings, lots of white and natural wood, and some
private pools and hot tubs. Villas have full kitchens,
washer/dryers, cable TV, and phones; The Mews has air-conditioning. Among the resort's many amenities are fine
oceanfront dining, a lounge and restaurant overlooking the
fairways and the sound, a vast tennis facility, warm sea
bathing and an oceanfront pool, miles of jogging trails
through the woods, a marketplace of more than 20 shops and
cafés, and weekend concerts. A health club was added in
1992. Golf and other packages are available. *Box 549, 02649,
tel. 508/477–9111 or 800/999–9033. 167 1- and 2-bedroom units.
Facilities: 4 restaurants, health club (Nautilus, Stairclimbers,
Airdyne, rowers, recumbent bikes, aerobics), 2 18-hole golf
courses, 16 all-weather tennis courts, pro shops and lessons,
3½-mi private beach, water-sports and bike rentals, beach
clubs, 2 outdoor pools (1 waterfront), children's activities (including tennis and golf clinics; fee), soccer and baseball fields,
jogging and bike trails, minigolf. AE, DC, MC, V.*

North Falmouth **Sea Crest.** Extensive flood damage caused by 1991's Hurri-
Moderate– cane Bob was a good excuse to spruce up some of the older
Expensive rooms and the now-tropical-look restaurant at this oceanfront resort on beautiful Old Silver Beach. Many rooms in
the six buildings connected by a glass-enclosed walkway
have ocean views; some rooms in unattached building 8 have
fireplaces, but most overlook the parking lot. Newer rooms
are modern, done in pastels with a flashy painting of flowers
above each bed; others date from the 1940s and are traditional Cape Cod. All rooms have TVs, phones, and minifridges. Packages may include buffet breakfasts or dinner
(the restaurant is good in a pinch) or any configuration of
meals. *350 Quaker Rd., 02556–2903, tel. 508/540–9400 or
800/225–3110, fax 508/548–0556. 260 rooms (5 disabled accessible), 6 suites. Facilities: restaurant, lounge, bar, deli, health
club (StairMaster, Nautilus, rowing machines, indoor pool,
whirlpool, dry and steam saunas), 4 tennis courts, unheated
outdoor pool and cabana bar, shuffleboard, putting green, video
arcade, children's day camp, room service, movie room, 8 conference and meeting rooms, 2 ballrooms, bike and water-sports
equipment for rent. AE, DC, MC, V.*

Sandwich **Dan'l Webster Inn.** A re-creation of an 18th-century inn that
Moderate– stood on the site, this is a classy, quiet, traditional New
Expensive England inn with an excellent restaurant. Guest rooms
★ (which are mostly in the main inn and wings; two nearby
historic homes have four suites each) have been recently
redecorated, with some canopy beds and fine reproduction
furnishings. All rooms have phones, cable TV, and air-conditioning; some suites have fireplaces or whirlpools, and one
has a baby grand piano. *149 Main St., Sandwich 02563, tel.
508/888–3622 or 800/444–3566, fax 508/888–5156. 38 rooms, 9
suites. Facilities: outdoor pool, membership in local health
club, access to private golf club, room service, turndown service,
no-smoking rooms, gift shop, restaurant, lounge with piano
bar and weekend dance bands. AE, D, DC, MC, V. 2-night minimum year-round.*

Mid-Cape

Barnstable **Ashley Manor.** Set back from the Old King's Highway by
Expensive high boxwood hedges and a wide lawn is this fine B&B, just
a walk from the village and the bay beach. Begun in 1699,
with later additions, the inn preserves the antique wide-
board floors (some spatter-painted), the two living rooms'
big open-hearth fireplaces with beehive ovens, and the recently hand-glazed carved woodwork. Antique and country
furnishings, Oriental rugs, brass and crystal accents create
an elegant atmosphere. All but one room has a working
fireplace or open-hearth wood stove, and all provide such
amenities as crystal glasses and coffee-makers; a country-
Colonial one-room cottage has a kitchenette for light cooking. Breakfast is served on the backyard terrace, looking
onto fruit trees, a gazebo, and the tennis court, or in the
formal dining room with candlelight, china, and crystal. *3660
Rte. 6A, Box 856, 02630, tel. 508/362–8044. 4 rooms, 2 suites.
Facilities: full breakfast, afternoon snacks, complimentary
wine (or sherry or port), all-weather tennis court, bikes, croquet, access to yacht club, beach chairs, common grand piano
and phone. AE, MC, V.*

★ **Beechwood.** A yellow and pale green 1853 Queen Anne Victorian, Beechwood is trimmed with a touch of gingerbread,
wrapped by a wide porch with wicker and tinkling wind
chimes, and shaded by big old beech trees. Guest rooms are
beautifully decorated with antiques in the unheavy early
Victorian style; all have minifridges, and some have fireplaces. While classical music plays softly, breakfast is
served by candlelight in the dining room, with pressed-tin
ceiling, fireplace, and tables set with lace, flowers, and crystal. *2839 Main St. (Rte. 6A), 02630, tel. 508/362–6618. 6 rooms.
Facilities: full breakfast, afternoon tea, common phone. AE,
MC, V. No smoking in common areas.*

Centerville **Inn at Fernbrook.** The most striking feature of this inn is
Expensive the grounds, originally landscaped by Frederick Law Olm-
sted, designer of New York's Central Park. Paths wind past
duck ponds stocked with Japanese *koi* and blooming with
water lilies; a sunken, heart-shaped sweetheart garden of
red and pink roses; exotic trees; a windmill; and, of course,

a fern-rimmed brook. The house itself, an 1881 Queen Anne Victorian mansion on the National Register of Historic Places, is a beauty, from the turreted exterior to the fine woodwork and furnishings within. Most rooms have garden views; some have bay-windowed sitting areas, canopy beds, pastel Oriental carpets, and working fireplaces. Breakfast is elaborate, formally served, friendly, and delicious. *481 Main St., 02632, tel. 508/775-4334, fax 508/778-4455. 4 rooms, 1 suite, 1 cottage (no kitchen). Facilities: full breakfast, afternoon tea, common phone. AE, MC, V.*

Hyannis **Tara Hyannis Hotel & Resort.** For its beautifully landscaped
Expensive– setting, extensive services and pampering, and superior re-
Very Expensive sort facilities (including a well-equipped health club, an 18-
★ hole golf course, a large indoor pool with a window wall overlooking the golf course, and a popular night spot), it's hard to beat the Tara. The lobby area is elegant, but rooms are decorated a bit boringly in pale colors and standard contemporary hotel style; a revamp is in the works. All rooms have color TV, phone, desk, table and chairs, and a private balcony or patio. Rooms overlooking the golf greens or the courtyard garden have the best views. *West End Circle, 02601, tel. 508/775-7775 or 800/843-8272, fax 508/790-4221. 224 rooms, 2 suites. Facilities: golf course (fee), 2 putting greens, 2 lighted tennis courts, indoor pool with Roman bath, outdoor pool with grill, health club (fee; see Sports and Outdoor Activities, above), restaurant, lounge, hair salon, gift shop, full children's program (school vacations and summer), business services, room service, minifridges (fee). AE, D, DC, MC, V.*

Moderate– **Capt. Gosnold Village.** An easy walk to the beach and town,
Expensive this colony of newly upgraded motel rooms and one- to three-bedroom cottages is ideal for families. Children can ride their bikes around the quiet street and compound; the pool is fenced in and is manned by a lifeguard. In some rooms, walls are attractively paneled in knotty pine; floors are carpeted; furnishings are colonial or modern, simple, and pleasant. All units have cable TV and heat; most have decks. Motel rooms have fridges and coffee-makers. *230 Gosnold St., 02601, tel. 508/775-9111. 18 cottages (divisible into rooms, efficiencies, and 1- to 3-bedroom cottages). Facilities: outdoor pool, basketball area, game nets, picnic areas, gas grills, daily maid service. MC, V. Closed Nov.–mid-Apr.*

Moderate **Hampton Inn Cape Cod.** In 1990, Hampton Inns (Holiday Inn's lower-priced division) bought the Iyanough Hills Motor Lodge and put $2 million into renovations, including all-new decor and white-oak-veneer furnishings. All the rooms at this business- and family-oriented cinderblock motel just off the highway now have two double beds or one king-size bed, and either a table and chairs or a desk and chair, a wardrobe, air-conditioning, cable TV with remote, and a phone; some have microwaves and minifridges; some king rooms have sofabeds. The quietest rooms are those on the top floor that face the pond and woods. *1470 Rte. 132, 02601, tel. 508/771-4804 or 800/999-4804, fax 508/790-2336. 104 rooms (no-smoking rooms available). Facilities: Continental breakfast, indoor pool, whirlpool, saunas, sun deck, children* *under 18 stay free, senior discounts available. AE, D, DC, MC, V.*

★ **Inn on Sea Street.** There's news at this charming, relaxed B&B a walk away from the beach and downtown Hyannis: the addition of a home across the street, with a common living room and large guest rooms with queen-size canopy beds and TVs in armoires. It and the restored 1849 Victorian main house have been furnished with country antiques and lacy fabrics by the personable innkeepers (car buffs will enjoy the antique cars J. B. keeps around). Delicious breakfasts are served with china, silver, and crystal in a dining room with antiques and lace or in the glassed-in sun porch. *358 Sea St., 02601, tel. 508/775–8030. 9 rooms, 2 with shared bath. Facilities: full breakfast, central phone and TV, games. AE, MC, V. Smoking discouraged. Closed mid-Nov.–Mar.*

Hyannis Port **Harbor Village.** Set in pine woods by a salt marsh is this
Expensive community of one- to four-bedroom Cape-style cottages, most with a water view (the ones *on* the marsh are booked far in advance). Each cottage is individually owned (rented out for the summer only), homey, nicely furnished, and clean; each has a fully equipped kitchen with microwave, a TV, a fireplace, a barbecue grill, and a deck with patio furniture, and most have phones and dishwashers. *Marstons Ave., Box 635, 02647, tel. 508/775–7581. 20 units. Facilities: daily maid service, children's play area. No credit cards. Closed Nov.–Apr.*

Simmons Homestead Inn. A rambling 1820 captain's house in a quiet area less than a mile from downtown Hyannis was converted in 1987 into an unusual-looking inn. Each guest room is decorated with an animal theme, such as the Rabbit Room or the wild Jungle Room. The large common rooms feature a mantel-top duck collection and huge Mexican papier-mâché birds. The style of the rooms varies from country to colonial to modern; some have decks, fireplaces, or canopy beds, either antique or fine reproduction. *288 Scudder Ave., 02647, tel. 508/778–4999 or 800/637–1649. 10 rooms. Facilities: full breakfast, evening wine and cheese, common TV and phone. AE, MC, V as guarantee only. No smoking in guest rooms.*

Yarmouth Port **Wedgewood Inn.** This handsome Greek Revival building is
Expensive on the National Register of Historic Places and dates from
★ 1812. White with black shutters, the facade has a front door with sidelights and fanlight and a large fan ornament over a third-floor window. Inside, the decor is sophisticated country, a mix of fine antiques, upholstered wing chairs, Oriental rugs, large Stobart and English sporting prints and maritime paintings, brass accents, handcrafted cherry pencil-post beds, antique quilts, period wallpapers, and wide-board floors. All rooms are large and air-conditioned and two have fireplaces; most baths are large. Two suites have canopy beds, fireplaces, and porches; one has a separate den. *83 Main St., 02675, tel. 508/362–5157. 4 rooms with bath, 2 suites. Facilities: air-conditioning, common TV, bicycles, full breakfast, afternoon tea. No smoking in common areas; no pets. AE, DC, MC, V.*

Moderate
★ **Liberty Hill.** The 1825 Greek Revival mansion stands on a rise set back from Route 6A, in an attractive setting of trees and flower-edged lawns. The large rooms, with tall windows and high ceilings, are romantically but unfussily decorated with fine antiques, upholstered chairs, and thick carpets. The third-floor Waterford Room has a king-size bed, an oversize bath, and bay and garden views. *77 Main St. (Rte. 6A), 02675, tel. 508/362–3976 or 800/821–3977. 5 rooms. Facilities: full breakfast, afternoon tea, dinner on request (fee), common TV and phone, guest fridge with mixers. AE, MC, V.*

Lower Cape

Brewster
Expensive–
Very Expensive
Ocean Edge. This huge, self-contained resort is more like a town, with 17 "villages" of residential and rental condominiums, as well as a major conference center. The sports facilities are superior, including a world-class golf course; activities such as concerts, tournaments, and clambakes are scheduled throughout the summer. Accommodations range from oversize hotel rooms with sitting areas in the conference center, with direct access to the health club and tennis courts, to luxurious one- to three-bedroom condos in the woods. All are tastefully decorated in modern style, are air-conditioned, and have TVs and phones; condos have washer/dryers and some fireplaces; some units have ocean views. The resort is very spread out; you may need your car to get from your condo to the pool. Weekend packages are available. *Rte. 6A, 02631, tel. 508/896–9000 or 800/343–6074, fax 508/896–9123. 125 condominium units, 90 hotel rooms. Facilities: 1,000-foot private beach, championship golf course, golf and tennis schools, driving range and putting greens, 2 heated indoor pools (1 lap pool, 1 with whirlpool), heated Olympic-size outdoor pool, ponds, 6 all-weather tennis courts, well-equipped fitness room, saunas, jogging and bike trails, 3 restaurants, pub entertainment, room service (hotel), concierge, basketball court, bicycle rentals, children's program, playground. AE, D, DC, MC, V.*

Inexpensive–
Moderate
Isaiah Clark House. The 18th-century main house retains much of the flavor of its origins, in variable-width floorboards, old fireplace mantels and moldings, narrow staircases, and the authentically furnished breakfast room, with original keeping-room hearth. The decor is colonial in furnishings and colors, accented with homey antique pieces. Some rooms have canopy beds, fireplaces, cable TV, or phones; rooms in the main house are air-conditioned. The wooded backyard is perfect for picnicking, lying in the hammock, walking through 5 acres of gardens, fruit trees, and berry patches, or relaxing by the pond. *1187 Rte. 6A, Box 169, 02631, tel. 508/896–2223 or 800/822–4001. 7 rooms (all private baths, 4 detached) in main house, 5 rooms (1 private bath, 4 share 2 baths) in cottage. Facilities: full breakfast, afternoon tea, turndown service, bikes, games, beach chairs and towels, airport or train station pickup; common phone, piano, TV, VCR, stereo. AE, MC, V. No smoking in bedrooms.*

★ **Old Sea Pines Inn.** The inn, fronted by a white-columned portico and wraparound veranda overlooking a broad lawn, strongly evokes the feel of a summer estate of an earlier day. The living room is spacious, with an appealing seating area before the fireplace. A sweeping staircase leads to guest rooms decorated with antique-look wallpaper, framed old photographs, and nicely matching antique furnishings. Many rooms are very large; fireplaces are available, including one in the inn's best room, which has a sitting area in an enclosed sun porch. Rooms in a newer building are well but sparely decorated, with bright white modern baths, and have TVs. The shared-bath singles are very small but sweetly done, and a steal at $40 in summer. *2553 Main St. (Rte. 6A), Box 1026, 02631, tel. 508/896–6114. 19 rooms (5 share 2¹/₂ baths), 2 suites. Facilities: full breakfast, afternoon tea Nov.–Mar., pay phone, board games. AE, DC, MC, V. No smoking in bedrooms.*

Chatham
Very Expensive
★

Chatham Bars Inn. The ultimate oceanfront resort in the old style, this Chatham landmark comprises the main building, with its grand-hotel lobby and formal restaurant, and 26 one- to eight-bedroom cottages on 20 beautifully landscaped acres. The entire inn has been renovated to create a casual Cape Cod elegance, though you'll feel free to dress in your best. Some rooms have TVs or ocean-view porches; all have phones and traditional Cape-style furnishings. Service is attentive and extensive. Theme weekends are scheduled in the off-season. MAP rates are available; a service charge is added to all bills (no tipping allowed). *Shore Rd., 02633, tel. 508/945–0096 or 800/527–4884, fax 508/945–5491. 152 rooms. Facilities: private beach, 4 tennis courts, fitness room, putting green, heated outdoor pool, shuffleboard, launch service to North Beach, baby-sitting, children's program (July and Aug.), 3 restaurants, clambakes, lounge with entertainment, bar, 9-hole golf course adjacent. AE, DC, MC, V.*

Wequassett Inn. This tranquil, traditional resort offers first-rate accommodations in 19 Cape-style cottages along a little bay and on 22 acres of woods, plus luxurious dining, attentive service, evening entertainment, and plenty of sunning and sporting opportunities. The recently renovated guest rooms have received design awards; the decor is Early American, with country pine furniture and homey touches such as handmade quilts and duck decoys. Each room has air-conditioning, a minifridge, cable TV/HBO, and a phone; some have fireplaces or wet bars. *Pleasant Bay, 02633, tel. 508/432–5400 or 800/225–7125, fax 508/432–5032. 98 rooms, 6 suites. Facilities: 5 all-weather tennis courts, heated outdoor pool, fitness equipment, boat tours, beach dropoff, transport to town, restaurant, poolside grill, piano lounge, room service, walking path; for extra fee, sailboats, Windsurfers, sailing school (5- to 7-day courses), seaplane rides (sightseeing, islands visits). AE, DC, MC, V. Closed mid-Oct.–Apr.*

Expensive

Bradford Inn and Motel. Just off Main Street are this family-owned inn's cheery yellow awnings and colorful gardens. Accommodations are in several buildings, ranging from the 1860 main house to the 1978 motel section to the 1987 Jonathan Gray luxury building. Rooms run the gamut from small and basic to luxurious and spacious with fireplaces and canopy beds; all have phones, TVs, minifridges, and air-conditioning. *26 Cross St., Box 750, 02633, tel. 508/945–1030 or 800/562–4667, fax 508/945–9652. 25 rooms. Facilities: full breakfast, dinner available (fee), 18 x 40 heated outdoor pool, lounge with fireplace, library. AE, D, MC, V.*

★ **Captain's House Inn.** Finely preserved architectural details, superb taste in decorating, opulent home-baked goods, and an overall feeling of warmth and quiet comfort are just part of what makes this one of the Cape's finest small inns. Each room in the three inn buildings has its own personality. Some are quite large, some have fireplaces; some are lacy and feminine, some refined and elegant. The general style of the inn is Colonial Williamsburg. The spacious Hiram Harding Room in the Captain's Cottage is spectacular, with 200-year-old handhewn ceiling beams, a wall of raised walnut paneling centered by a large working fireplace, and a rich red Oriental carpet. Teatime provides a good chance to meet fellow guests. *371 Old Harbor Rd., 02633, tel. 508/945–0127, fax 508/945–9406. 14 rooms, 2 suites. Facilities: Continental breakfast, afternoon tea, guest phone. AE, MC, V. No smoking. Closed mid-Nov.–mid-Feb.*

★ **Moses Nickerson House.** Warm, thoughtful service and a love of fine antiques and decorating characterize this B&B. Queen-bedded guest rooms in the 1839 house feature wideboard pine floors; some have wood or gas-log fireplaces. Each room has an individual look: one with dark woods and leathers and Ralph Lauren fabrics and accessories; another with green and white beach stripes, white walls, and white iron bed; another with a high canopy bed, puffy feather mattress, exquisite 100-year-old white bedspread, and Nantucket hand-hooked rug. Breakfast is served on family china and crystal. Through an arbor is a lovely flower garden with fish pond and fountain. *364 Old Harbor Rd., 02633, tel. 508/945–5859 or 800/628–6972. 7 rooms. Facilities: full breakfast, afternoon wine or tea, complimentary fruit and sherry, turndown service. AE, MC, V. No smoking. Closed Jan.*

Queen Anne Inn. A short walk from Chatham center, and perfectly situated for walks and bike rides around scenic Oyster Pond, this member of the Romantik Hotels group has the feel of a European country inn. Built in 1840 (with later additions) as a parsonage, the stately gray-shingled building became an inn in 1874 and today offers an intimate restaurant (*see* Dining, *above*), tree-fringed tennis courts, and comfortable accommodations. The decor is simple, with country wallpapers, locally made (and some antique) furniture, chenille bedspreads, and some fishnet canopies; ongoing redecoration aims at a Nantucket/country feel. All rooms have phones; some have air-conditioning, fireplaces, or private balconies looking onto the back lawn and gardens. *70 Queen Anne Rd., 02633, tel. 508/945–0394 or 800/545–4667, fax 508/945–4884. 30 rooms, 1 suite. Facilities: Continental breakfast, 3 Har-Tru tennis courts, tennis pro (2-day refresher courses available), bikes, game room, whirlpool room, common TV and VCR, restaurant. DC, MC, V.*

Eastham **Sheraton Ocean Park Inn.** Located at the entrance to the *Expensive* National Seashore, with a nicely landscaped atrium pool area at its center, this Sheraton offers standard modern-decor rooms with TV, phone, two double beds or one king-size bed, and tiled baths. Rooms have views of the pool or the woods; the outside rooms are a little bigger and brighter and have minifridges. *Rte. 6, 02642, tel. 508/255–5000 or 800/533–3986, fax 508/240–1870. 105 rooms, 2 suites. Facilities: fitness room with Universal and other equipment, whirlpool, 2 outdoor tennis courts (lighted in summer), saunas, outdoor pool with poolside bar, heated indoor atrium pool, restaurant, lounge with dancing, game arcade, no-smoking rooms, room service, children under 18 stay free. AE, D, DC, MC, V.*

East Orleans **Nauset Knoll Motor Lodge.** On a low rise overlooking
Expensive Nauset Beach, two minutes' walk away — the closest accommodation to an ocean-side beach you'll find in this area — a row of adjoining Cape houses offers basic, ground-level motel rooms. Each is sparsely furnished (Formica and pine, acoustical tile ceilings) but light and bright, with six-foot ocean-view picture windows, tiled baths, new carpeting, and color cable TV. Book well in advance. *Nauset Beach, 02643, tel. 508/255–2364. 12 rooms. Facilities: public phone. MC, V. Closed late Oct.–mid-Apr.*

Harwich Port **Augustus Snow House.** Luxury is the operative word at this
Expensive inn, a Princess Anne Victorian with gabled dormers and wraparound veranda, from the whirlpools in some baths to the Gucci amenity baskets. The rooms are done up in Victorian style, down to reproduction furnishings and wallpapers and authentic period brass bathroom fixtures. All rooms have phones and color TV. An afternoon English tea and dinner most evenings are open to the public and served in the lovely Victorian drawing rooms. *528 Main St., 02646, tel. 508/430–0528 or 800/339–0528 in MA. 5 rooms. Facilities: full breakfast, turndown service. AE, MC, V.*

Moderate **Coachman Motor Lodge.** This clean, well-maintained single-story motel just off the highway offers cheerful guest rooms with basic motel-colonial furnishings, including two double beds, a desk, and a sitting area. Each room has a tiled bath, air-conditioning, a phone, and cable TV. *Rte. 28, 02646, tel. 508/432–0707 or 800/524–4265. 27 rooms, 1 efficiency. Facilities: outdoor pool, restaurant. AE, MC, V. Closed Nov.–Apr.*

North Eastham **Captain's Quarters.** Set back from the highway and sur-
Moderate rounded by woods is this single-story motel and small conference center, built between 1982 and 1987. Guest rooms are roomy, with white walls, blond-wood-grain-Formica motel furniture, and pastel fabrics. All have cable TV/HBO, minifridges, phones, individual heat and air- conditioning, one queen-size or two double beds, and table and chairs; luxury rooms have somewhat nicer fabrics and are newer. *Rte. 6, Box Y, 02651, tel. 508/255–5686 or 800/327–7769, fax 508/240–0280. 75 rooms, 4 suites. Facilities: Continental breakfast, small heated outdoor pool, shuttle to beach (July and Aug.), bikes, 2 tennis courts, picnic/barbecue area, sand volleyball court, basketball hoop, horseshoes. AE, D, DC, MC, V. Closed Dec.–Mar.*

North Truro **East Harbour.** This meticulously maintained complex out-
Moderate side Provincetown offers simple accommodations ranged

around a manicured lawn separated from the bay beach by low grasses. The two-bedroom cottages have paneled walls, colonial-style furnishings, and full kitchens. Motel rooms have large picture windows, minifridges and coffee-makers, light paneling, and '60s motel-style furnishings. A new apartment is all white and bright, with skylights, Shaker-reproduction furnishings, a modern kitchen, and second-floor views of the harbor from a private deck. All units have individual heat and color cable TV. *Rte. 6A, Box 183, 02652, tel. 508/487–0505, fax 508/487–6693. 7 cottages, 8 rooms, 1 apartment. Facilities: beach, laundry, gas grills, picnic tables, umbrellas. AE, D, MC, V. In season, 1-wk min. for cottages, 2-night min. for rooms. Closed Nov.–Mar.*

Kalmar Village. Another good choice on this bayfront strip is this cheerful, family-owned (for 30 years) complex of cottages grouped around landscaped lawns and a large pool. Nicest and closest to the water are the six new two-bedroom cottages, all white and bright with lots of windows and blond wood and new kitchens. Other two-bedrooms have fireplaces but less living area than the somewhat nicer one-bedrooms (knotty-pine walls, large living room with two sofabeds). All cottages have cable TV, individual heat, picnic tables, and hibachis. *Rte. 6A, Box 745, 02652, tel. 508/487–0585; in winter, 246 Newbury St., Boston 02116, tel. 617/247–0211. 50 cottages, 6 efficiencies, 4 motel rooms. Facilities: heated outdoor pool, laundry, daily maid service. D, MC, V. Closed Columbus Day–Memorial Day.*

South Harwich
Inexpensive

Handkerchief Shoals Motel. Located about 2 miles from Harwich Port and 3 miles from downtown Chatham, the single-story property is set back from the highway and surrounded by well-maintained lawn and trees. Rooms are sparse but large and sparkling clean, with sitting and desk areas, tiled baths, and color cable TV with remote, fridge, and microwave — a very good value for the money. *Rte. 28, Box 306, South Harwich 02661, tel. 508/432–2200. 26 units. Facilities: morning coffee, outdoor pool, lawn games, ping-pong. AE, D, MC, V. Closed mid-Oct.–mid-Apr.*

South Wellfleet
Moderate–Expensive

Wellfleet Motel & Lodge. A mile from Marconi Beach and opposite an Audubon sanctuary is this well-maintained and tasteful complex. Rooms in the single-story motel, built in 1964, have attractive knotty-pine paneling. Those in the two-story lodge, built in 1986, are bright and spacious, with white walls, oak furniture, king- or queen-size beds, and patios. Each room has a minifridge, a color TV and radio, a phone, air-conditioning, and a coffee-maker. *Rte. 6, Box 606, 02663, tel. 508/349–3535 or 800/852–2900. 65 rooms. Facilities: heated indoor pool and whirlpool in cedar-lined room, small heated outdoor pool, coffee shop (breakfast only), bar, basketball hoop, disabled-accessible rooms. AE, DC, MC, V. Lodge and facilities closed Thanksgiving–Mar.*

Wellfleet
Inexpensive–Moderate

Inn at Duck Creek. A walk from town is this old-time inn with a sweet country feel. Set on 5 wooded acres by a pond, creek, and salt marsh, it consists of the 1800s main inn and two other old houses. Rooms in the main inn (except rustic third-floor rooms) and in Saltworks have a simple charm, with a few rough edges; typical furnishings include clawfoot tubs, country antiques, light floral wallpapers, lace curtains, chenille spreads, and rag rugs on hardwood floors. The two-room Carriage House is cabiny, with rough barnboard and plaster walls. The inn's parlors, screened porches, and marsh-view deck invite relaxation — a concept reinforced by the absence of phones and TVs. There's elegant dining at Sweet Seasons or pub dining with entertainment at The Tavern Room (*see* Nightlife, *below*). *Main St., Box 364, 02667, tel. 508/349–9333. 26 rooms, 17 with private bath. Facilities: Continental breakfast, 2 restaurants, guest fridge. AE, MC, V. Closed mid-Oct.–mid-May; 2-night min. weekends in season.*

Provincetown

Expensive **Best Western Chateau Motor Inn.** The personal attention of the owners, whose family has run the place since it was built in 1958 (additions completed in 1972; total remodeling in 1986), shows in the beautifully landscaped lawn and garden that surround the pool, as well as in the well-maintained modern hotel rooms, with wall-to-wall carpeting and tiled baths. All rooms have color cable TV with HBO, satellite, and remote; two phones; shower-massage heads; card-key locks; and individual heat and air-conditioning. Atop a hill with expansive views from picture windows of marsh, dunes, and sea, the motel is just a longish walk to the center of town, yet at a remove from it all. *Bradford St. W, Box 558, 02657, tel. 508/487–1286 or 800/528–1234, fax 508/487–3557. 55 rooms. Facilities: morning coffee, heated outdoor pool, fax service; minifridges and room safes available. Children under 18 stay free ($5 extra in high season). AE, D, DC, MC, V. Closed Nov.–Apr.*

★ **Hargood House.** This apartment complex on the water, a half-mile from the town center, is a great option for longer stays and families. Many of the individually decorated units have decks and large water-view windows; all have full kitchens and modern baths. No. 8 is like a light, bright beach house: on the water, with three glass walls, cathedral ceilings, private deck, dining table and chairs. A newly redone cottage, No. 20, has a fireplace and a home-style kitchen. Rental is mostly by the week in season; two-night minimum off-season. *493 Commercial St., 02657, tel. or fax 508/487–9133. 19 apartments. Facilities: private beach, daily maid service in season, barbecue grills, parking. AE, MC, V.*

Moderate– **Anchor Inn.** A short walk from town center, this 1912 shin-
Expensive gled guest house with turret and porch offers small rooms with sliding doors that open out to a deck overlooking or on the water (corner rooms also have a window, making them brighter). The decor is very simple but pleasant, with light-painted wood furnishings; all rooms have TVs and ceiling fans. *175 Commercial St., 02657, tel. 508/487–0432 or 800/858–2657 outside MA. 24 rooms. Facilities: beach. AE, MC, V.*

Dinghy Dock. In the quiet West End, this waterfront apartment house is a vestige of old Provincetown, as is the funny and wise proprietress. The decor is minimal and baths are small, but the apartments are cheerful and comfortable and have full kitchens (some TVs). The nicest have picture windows and decks overlooking the water and the lighthouse on the sand spit just across the harbor; one has sliding doors that open out to a small deck and garden. For summer, book by April 1 (one-week minimum). *71 Commercial St., 02657, tel. 508/487–0075. 8 apartments. Facilities: laundry, grills, beach (no parking, but can be arranged). No credit cards.*

Inexpensive–Expensive **The Masthead.** Families in particular are welcome at these unpretentious but homey seaside cottages and apartments — some with room for seven — within walking distance of town, but far enough away to escape the frenetic summer pace. This is classic Provincetown — friendly, down-to-earth, with cooking facilities, plants, phones, color cable TV, air-conditioning, and private decks. The best and most expensive units overlook the water. Cottage #35 is like a ship's cabin, with wainscoting on the walls and ceiling. *31–41 Commercial St., Box 577, 02657, tel. 508/487–0523 or 800/395–5095. 6 apartments, 4 cottages, 3 efficiencies, 8 rooms. Facilities: beach, free moorings and launch service, daily* New York Times. *Children under 14 stay free. AE, D, DC, MC, V.*

Moderate **Fairbanks Inn.** On the next street over from Commercial Street is this comfortable and nicely decorated inn that includes the 1776 main house and auxiliary buildings. Guest rooms have four-poster or canopy beds, Oriental rugs on wide-board floors, and antique furnishings; some have color cable TV, fireplaces (10 rooms), or kitchens. The wicker-filled sun porch with guest bar or the garden are good places for afternoon cocktails. *90 Bradford St., 02657, tel. 508/487–0386. 14 rooms, 10 with private bath. Facilities: Continental breakfast; common TV, VCR, stereo, phone, and rooftop sun deck; BYOB bar and fridge. AE, D, MC, V.*

Holiday Inn. This two-story motor court built in 1969 offers clean, spacious rooms at the edge of town. The rooms were refurbished in 1989 and are bright and modern, with pastels and florals; each has two double beds, cable TV/HBO, a phone, and air-conditioning. Second-floor rooms facing the parking lot have a water view, but this side gets noisy. *Rte. 6A, Box 392, 02657, tel. 508/487–1711 or 800/465–4329, fax 508/487–3929. 78 rooms. Facilities: nonsmoking rooms, large outdoor pool, poolside bar, restaurant (Apr.–Oct.), lounge with dancing or movies, fax service. AE, D, DC, MC, V.*

The Arts and Nightlife

Arts and entertainment events are listed in the *Cape Cod Times*'s "CapeWeek" section on Friday or in its daily editions. Also check out the Tuesday "What's On Cape" section or Friday "Weekend" page of *The Register* and *The Cape Codder.* In Provincetown, look for *The Advocate,* a weekly.

The Arts

Since before the turn of the century, creative people have been drawn to Cape Cod summers, and their legacy and ongoing contribution is a thriving arts scene. Vital art galleries exist in Provincetown and elsewhere (*see* Shopping, *above*). In addition to the professional theaters, which offer top-name talent in season, almost every town has a community theater that provides quality entertainment — often mixing local players with visiting pros — throughout the year. The Cape also gets its share of music stars, from pop to classical, along with local groups ranging from barbershop quartets to Bach chorales to early music or chamber ensembles, often playing at school auditoriums or town halls.

Theater The top summer-stock venues, often featuring name performers, are the Equity **Cape Playhouse** (off Rte. 6A, Dennis, tel. 508/385–3911 or 508/385–3838) and the **Falmouth Playhouse** (off Rte. 151, North Falmouth, tel. 508/563–5922). Both offer Broadway-style shows and morning children's plays.

The **Barnstable Comedy Club** (Village Hall, Rte. 6A, Barnstable, tel. 508/362–6333), the Cape's oldest amateur theater group, gives much-praised performances of musicals and dramas throughout the year.

Monomoy Theater (776 Main St., Chatham, tel. 508/945–1589) presents eight summer productions — thrillers, musicals, classics, modern drama — by the Ohio University Players.

The **College Light Opera Company** (Highfield Theatre, Depot Ave., Falmouth, tel. 508/548–0668), founded in 1969, presents Oberlin and other college music majors in summer operettas and musical comedies. The company includes more than 30 singers and an 18-piece orchestra.

The **Wellfleet Harbor Actors Theater** (**W.H.A.T.;** by town pier, tel. 508/349–6835) presents less summer-oriented fare — including satires, farces, black comedies, and dramas — than most Cape theaters in its May–October season.

The **Academy Playhouse** (120 Main St., Orleans, tel. 508/255–1963), one of the oldest community theaters on the Cape, presents 10–12 productions year-round, including original works.

The **Provincetown Theatre Company** (Provincetown Inn, tel. 508/487–3466) presents new works by local authors year-round, as well as staged readings.

The **Cape Cod Melody Tent** (*see* Music, *below*) hosts a Wednesday-morning children's theater series in July and August.

Music **Heritage Plantation** (*see* Tour 1: Route 6A, Sagamore Bridge to Hyannis, *above*) sponsors summer jazz and other concerts in its gardens from June to mid-September; bring chairs or blankets. Most concerts are free with admission to the complex.

The **Provincetown Playhouse Mews Series** (Town Hall, 260 Commercial St., tel. 508/487–0955) presents classical chamber, folk, ethnic, and jazz concerts in summer.

Popular   The Cape's top venue for popular music concerts and comedy is the **Cape Cod Melody Tent** (21 W. Main St., Hyannis 02601, tel. 508/775–9100), an institution since 1950. Performances are held late June–early September in a 2,300-seat theater-in-the-round under a tent. Performers have recently included Ray Charles, the Preservation Hall Jazz Band, Willie Nelson, Alabama, the Pointer Sisters, and Bill Cosby.

The **Beach Plum Music Festival,** held in August at the Provincetown Town Hall (260 Commercial St., tel. 508/349–6874), is a series of popular folk and jazz concerts by such performers as Wynton Marsalis, Arlo Guthrie, Queen Ida, and Holly Near.

Club Euro (258 Commercial St., Provincetown, tel. 508/487–2505 or 487–2511; *see* Nightlife, *below;* Euro Island Grill in Dining, *above*) embarked on an ambitious program for the 1992 season, lining up international name acts in world music for weekend concerts, including African music, Jamaican reggae, Chicago blues, and Cajun zydeco.

Classical   The 100-member **Cape Cod Symphony Orchestra** (Mattacheese Middle School, Higgins Crowell Rd., West Yarmouth, tel. 508/362–1111), under former D'Oyly Carte Opera conductor Royston Nash, gives regular and children's concerts, with guest artists, October–May; in summer, two outdoor pops concerts are given, in Mashpee and Orleans.

The **Cape & Islands Chamber Music Festival** (Box 2721, Orleans 02653, tel. 508/349–7709) is three weeks of top-caliber performances and master classes at various locations in August.

Band Concerts   Traditional New England town band concerts are held weekly each summer in many Cape towns; bring along chairs, blankets, and a picnic supper if you like, and go early to get a good spot. **Chatham's** (Kate Gould Park, Main St., tel. 508/945–0342), beginning at 8 PM on Friday, draws up to 6,000 people; as many as 500 fox-trot on the roped-off dance floor, and there are special dances for children and sing-alongs for all.

Other locations: **Buzzards Bay** (Buzzards Bay Park, off Main St., tel. 508/888–6202), Thursdays at 7. **Falmouth** (Marina Park, Scranton Ave., tel. 508/548–2416), Thursdays at 8. **Harwich** (Brooks Park, tel. 508/432–1600), Tuesdays at 7:30. **Hyannis** (Bismore Park, Ocean St. docks, tel. 508/775–2201), Wednesdays at 7:30. **Sandwich** (bandstand, Henry T. Wing Elementary School, Rte. 130, tel. 508/888–5281), Thursdays at 7:30. **West Yarmouth** (Mattacheese Middle School, off Higgins Crowell Rd., tel. 508/398–5311), Mondays at 7:30.

Opera   Two performances a year, in spring and fall, are given at Sandwich High School (Quaker Meetinghouse Rd., East Sandwich) by the touring group from New York City's Opera Northeast under Donald Westwood. For dates, contact **Opera New England of Cape Cod** (tel. 508/775–3974).

(*See also* College Light Opera Company under Theater, *above.*)

Film Besides the first-run theaters, the **Cape Museum of Fine Arts Cinema Club** (Cape Playhouse complex, Rte. 6A, Dennis, tel. 508/385–4477) presents classic and avant-garde movies in an intimate setting year-round.

That fast-disappearing American tradition, the drive-in movie, is living still on Cape Cod: At the **Wellfleet Drive-In Theater** (Rte. 6, tel. 508/349–7176 or 508/255–9619), films start at dusk nightly in season, and there's a minigolf course.

Dance The **Cape Ballet** (Canterbury Plaza, Cotuit Rd., Sandwich, tel. 508/833–0699 or 508/477–8052), a semiprofessional company, performs classical and contemporary ballet year-round.

Nightlife

Nighttime on Cape Cod can be very special, in many ways. In the less developed areas, the stars are amazingly bright and make beach walks in blackness and silence even more wondrous — more of an experience in the elemental. Also, the power of the lighthouse beacons as they cut through the night sky has a fascination impossible to resist. If you're up *really* late, you might head for Chatham Light to catch a terrific sunrise.

Many daytime activities, such as fishing, take on a completely different aspect at night. Scuba enthusiasts might consider night diving; colors are more vivid by flashlight, a lot of sea life is phosphorescent or bioluminescent, and nocturnal species come out to play. It's important to know the tides and safe locations — ask at a dive shop before setting out.

A number of organizations sponsor outdoor activities at night, including the **Cape Cod Museum of Natural History**'s stargazing sessions (*see* Tour 3, *above*) and **Wellfleet Bay Sanctuary**'s bat walks, night hikes, and lecture series (*see* Nature Areas, *above*). The **Army Corps of Engineers** (tel. 508/759–4431), which maintains the Cape Cod Canal, offers free evening programs in summer, including slide shows about the canal, sing-alongs, night walks, and storytelling around campfires at the Bourne Scenic Park and Scusset Beach State Park. The **Cape Cod National Seashore** offers summer evening programs, such as slide shows, sunset beach walks, concerts (local groups, military bands), and sing-alongs, at its Salt Pond Amphitheater (Eastham, tel. 508/255–3421) and Province Lands Visitor Center (Provincetown, tel. 508/487–1256) and sunset campfire talks at the beaches at Eastham and Provincetown. **Waquoit Bay reserve** (*see* Nature Areas, *above)* holds July "Evenings on the Bluff," talks for families (who are invited to bring picnics) on environmental, historical, and artistic subjects; activities for children are often provided.

In summer, just walking Main Street in Hyannis or Commercial Street in Provincetown is nightlife in itself. The streets are filled with a fascinating array of people who are from everywhere and into everything, all on vacation and having a great time. All you require to be a part of "the stroll" is an appreciation of life's infinite variety — and maybe an ice-cream cone.

Of course, the Cape certainly has plenty of what is more traditionally defined as nightlife, though live music has become increasingly scarce, edged out by economic hard times and replaced by DJs and dance music.

Hyannis and Yarmouth have a lot of rowdy dance clubs, bars, and restaurant lounges packed with college students on summer vacation. Most of the Upper and Lower Cape is quiet, except for Provincetown (with the added spice of drag shows) and a few places in Chatham. And scattered throughout the Cape are places to dine and dance in elegant style. In season, many restaurant and hotel lounges have entertainment nightly; in the off-season, those that remain open cut back to weekends.

Mixed Menu **Chatham Wayside Inn** (Main St., tel. 508/945–1800) has dinner cabaret six nights a week (reservations required) in season; off-season weekends, there's dining and dancing to piano music, and sometimes rock bands later in the evening. The tavern features piano duos and acoustic folk and blues nightly in season, weekends year-round.

Christine's (Rte. 28, West Dennis, tel. 508/394–7333; *see* Dining, *above*) has entertainment nightly in season, whether jazz, comedy, concerts by name bands from the 1950s–1970s, or Top-40 bands. Off-season, there's live entertainment and dancing to a DJ on weekends, plus special events. The piano bar offers jazz and show tunes weekends year-round, nightly in season.

Crown & Anchor Complex (247 Commercial St., Provincetown, tel. 508/487–1430) consists of a number of bars under one roof, including a leather bar, a disco (with new light shows), a cabaret of gay and straight comics and drag shows, a pool bar, and a game room with pool tables and video games.

Bars and Lounges **Bobby Byrne's Pubs** (Rte. 28, Harwich Port, tel. 508/430–1100; Rte. 28, Hyannis, tel. 508/775–1425; Mashpee Commons, Rtes. 28 and 151, tel. 508/477–0600; Rte. 6A, Sandwich, tel. 508/888–6088) offer a comfortable pub atmosphere, a jukebox, and good light and full menus. **Chatham Squire** (487 Main St., Chatham, tel. 508/945–0945), with four separate bars (including a raw bar), is a rollicking year-round local hangout, drawing a young crowd to the bar side and a mixed crowd of locals to the quieter restaurant side. A jukebox and the crowd itself are the only entertainment. **Oliver's** restaurant (Rte. 6A, Yarmouth Port, tel. 508/362–6062) has duos performing on weekends in its tavern. **The Tavern Room** (Main St., Wellfleet, tel. 508/349–7369), set in an 1800s building, with beamed ceiling, fireplace, and a bar covered in nautical charts, features live entertainment from jazz to pop to Latin ensembles. Munchies are served along-side the menu of traditional and Latin/Caribbean-inspired dishes. **The Woodshed** (Rte. 6A, Brewster, tel. 508/896–7771), the rustic bar at the Brewster Inn, is a good place to soak up local color and dance to pop duos or bands that perform most nights. **The Yacht Club,** the sophisticated lounge of the Tara Hyannis Hotel (West End Rotary, tel. 508/775–7775), has live pop entertainment nightly in season, mostly DJs in the off-season. The bar has a wide-screen TV for sports events and a window wall overlooking the pool and golf course.

The Moors restaurant (Bradford St. Ext., Provincetown, tel. 508/487–0840; *see* Dining, *above*) has presented Lenny Grandchamp in its lounge for the past 15 years, and the town never tires of him; he plays the piano, sings, does jokes, and leads sing-alongs from about 7, three to six nights a week in season. **Napi's** (7 Freeman St., Provincetown, tel. 508/487–1145; *see* Dining, *above*) offers easy-listening piano in its upstairs lounge on weekends, nightly in season. The **Surf Club** (315A Commercial St., Provincetown, tel. 508/487–1367), a waterfront bar/restaurant, has for 20+ years featured the Provincetown Jug Band — playing everything from bluegrass to rock on everything from trombones to jugs — nightly in summer.

Dance Clubs **Beachcomber** (Cahoon Hollow Beach, off Rte. 6, Wellfleet, tel. 508/349–6055) — an oceanfront restaurant with live Boston rock bands most nights, a Saturday happy hour with live reggae, and dancing nightly in summer — is hot with the college crowd at night and on breaks from the sun. The menu features fun appetizers, salads, burgers, seafood, barbecue, frozen drinks, and weekend raw bar. Eat indoors or at tables by the outdoor bar.

Champions (Rte. 132, near Airport rotary, Hyannis, tel. 508/790–0100) is a sports bar/restaurant that is extremely popular with a 20s crowd. Part of a chain, it features 18 TVs, lots of sports paraphernalia (such as the 2,000 baseball cards laminated onto the bar), and DJ dancing nightly.

Club Euro (*see* The Arts, *above*) in Provincetown has world-music concerts weekends in season, plus vintage videos for dancing five nights (and at concert intermissions) in a great room — 1843 Congregational church, later movie theater — done in an eerie ocean dreamscape: oceanic-green-sea walls with half-submerged 3D mermaid and sprouting fish, black ceiling high above. A late-night menu (*see* Euro Island Grill in Dining, *above*) is available.

Guido Murphy's (615 Main St., Hyannis, tel. 508/775–7242) is a hopping bar bursting with college kids and young professionals. Entertainment includes dancing to live and DJ music, as well as Sunday-night comedy.

Mill Hill Club (164 Rte. 28, West Yarmouth, tel. 508/775–2580) has dancing to a DJ nightly and Top-40 dance bands Thursday–Saturday year-round, plus videos and satellite sports on large-screen TVs, a regular hypnotist act, and a singer/guitarist at happy hour in season.

Pufferbellies (Rte. 28, Hyannis, tel. 508/775–2922) is a huge, 1,500-seat summer club across from the airport, with three dance floors and two stages, as well as a volleyball court and a pool. Entertainment includes a guitarist and sing-along at happy hour and dancing to Top-40 and dance bands nightly, plus weekly male and female body contests and Pro-Beach Volleyball Tour games.

Rascals Saloon (261 Rte. 28, West Yarmouth, tel. 508/790–1799) has dancing to a DJ nightly in season.

Safari Club (formerly the Kasbar; Rte. 28, South Yarmouth, tel. 508/760–1616) has dancing to a DJ, male-dancer night, and occasional reggae and other bands year-round. The large disco has a high-tech sound and laser system and a 15-foot video screen.

Starbuck's in Hyannis (*see* Dining, *above*) has live acoustic entertainment many nights.

Sundancer's (116 Rte. 28, West Dennis, tel. 508/394–1600) has dancing to a DJ and live bands year-round and Sunday-afternoon reggae bands in season.

Ballroom Dancing **Betsy's Ballroom** (Yarmouth Senior Center, 528 Forest Rd., South Yarmouth, tel. 508/362–9538) has Saturday-night dancing to bands on the Cape's largest dance floor year-round. A free half-hour lesson and exhibitions are given at each dance.

Chatham Bars Inn (Shore Rd., tel. 508/945–0096; *see* Dining, *above*) has dancing in its South Lounge (jacket and tie required) in July and August and to a pianist or other soft music year-round in its dark and clubby Tavern at the Inner Bar restaurant (jacket required in season).

Coonamessett Inn (Jones Rd. and Gifford St., Falmouth, tel. 508/548–2300; *see* Dining, *above*) has dancing to soft piano, jazz trios, or other music in its lounge on weekends year-round, as well as ballroom dancing a few Sunday nights in winter.

East Bay Lodge (East Bay Rd., Osterville, tel. 508/428–6961; *see* Dining, *above*) has dancing weekends in season to jazz ensembles centered by renowned jazz pianist Dave McKenna, who plays most nights year-round.

Popponesset Inn (Mall Way, New Seabury, tel. 508/477–1100 or 8258; *see* Dining, *above*) has dancing to bands in its waterview lounge, on a large dance floor, in season.

Rof-Mar Diplomat Club (Popple Bottom Rd., Sandwich, tel. 508/428–8111; reservations required), a function room, has ballroom dinner dances and dancing to country bands year-round. There's a large dance floor and seating on outdoor porches.

Country and Western **Bud's Country Lounge** (Bearses Way and Rte. 132, Hyannis, tel. 508/771–2505) has pool tables and features live country music year-round. (*See also* Rof-Mar, *above*.)

Folk The Cape's three coffeehouses present a mixture of professional and local folk and blues in a no-smoking, no-alcohol environment, with refreshments available during intermission.

Benefit Coffeehouse of the Liberty Folk Society (Liberty Hall, Main St., Marstons Mills, tel. 508/428–1053) opened in 1989 and holds concerts the first Saturday of each month, featuring mostly local and some professional musicians, to benefit local organizations.

First Encounter Coffee House (Chapel in the Pines, Samoset Rd., Eastham, tel. 508/255–5438 or 508/255–1710) has since 1974 offered professional folk concerts, held the first and third Saturday of each month (every Saturday in summer; closed May and September).

Woods Hole Folk Music Society (Community Hall, Water St., Woods Hole, tel. 508/540–0320), in existence since 1973, offers concerts on the first and third Sundays of the month from October through May.

Irish Music **Cape Cod Irish Village** (512 Main St., West Yarmouth, tel. 508/771–0100) has dancing to two- or three-piece bands performing traditional and popular Irish music year-round. The crowd is mostly couples and over-35s.

Clancy's (8 Upper County Rd., Dennisport, tel. 508/394–6661; 175 Rte. 28, West Yarmouth, tel. 508/775–3332) has singer/guitarists year-round.

Irish Pub (126 Main St. [Rte. 28], West Harwich, tel. 508/432–8808) has dancing to bands doing "ballads and blarney" — a mix of Irish, American, and dance music and sing-alongs — plus pool, darts, and sports TV in the bar.

Shamrock Lounge (Mitchells Steak and Rib House, 451 Iyanough Rd. [Rte. 28], Hyannis, tel. 508/775–6700) has duos performing Irish and American songs, sing-alongs, and comedy year-round.

Jazz The Cape Cod Jazz Society operates a 24-hour hotline (tel. 508/394–5277) on jazz events throughout the Cape.

Bishop's Terrace restaurant (Rte. 28, West Harwich, tel. 508/432–0253) has dancing to jazz most of the year in its small lounge. Set in a converted barn, it has tools hanging on walls of rustic barn boards.

Dome Restaurant (State Rd., Woods Hole, tel. 508/548–0800) has dancing to a Dixieland jazz band in its lounge, under a geodesic dome, Sundays in July and August; there is easy-listening piano on Friday and Saturday in season.

Wequassett Inn (Pleasant Bay, Chatham, tel. 508/432–5400; *see* Lodging, *above*) has a jazz duo nightly in its lounge (jacket requested).

Yarmouth Inn (Rte. 6A, Yarmouth Port, tel. 508/362–3191) has jazz trios in its country French restaurant's lounge Wednesday–Saturday nights year-round.

Dinner Theater **Mystery Cafe Cape Cod** (reservations required, tel. 508/771–1955 or 800/532–9572), based at different restaurants each year, presents a murder mystery over a 2½-hour four-course dinner and lets diners join in. It's a fully orchestrated theatrical evening laced with plenty of humor; on breaks, actors mingle with the audience in character.

Cruises **Hy-Line** in Hyannis and **Cape Cod Canal Cruises** in Onset (*see* Guided Tours in Essential Information, *above*), as well as the *Island Queen* in Falmouth (tel. 508/548–4800), run sunset or moonlight cruises in season. Falmouth's includes dancing under the stars to live music.

Miscellaneous **Boatslip** (161 Commercial St., Provincetown, tel. 508/487–1669) has a tea dance on its huge beachfront deck and indoor dance floor to DJ dance music from 3:30 to 6:30 on summer afternoons (weekends May–Sept.; also weekdays in high season). The crowd is mostly gay, and the place is always packed.

Town House (291 Commercial St., Provincetown, tel. 508/487–0292) has drag shows or other entertainment for a mixed crowd in its "Backroom Cabaret" most nights in season.

Johnny Yee's Polynesian/Chinese restaurant (228 Rte. 28, West Yarmouth, tel. 508/775–1090) has dinner-show entertainment, including a Hawaiian revue and a late-night adult comedy show.

Cape Cod Ocean Waves (Yarmouth Senior Center, 528 Forest Rd., South Yarmouth, tel. 508/945–3196) and the **Nausets** (Willy's Gym, Orleans, tel. 508/430–1718 or 255–5079) hold square dances weekly most of the year.

Coconuts Comedy Club (Cape Cod Plaza Hotel, Rte. 132 and Bearses Way, Hyannis, tel. 508/771–3000 or 800/365–3207), new in 1992, promises "the hottest comics in the country" Thursday–Saturday nights in season.

4 Martha's Vineyard

Much less developed — by stringently enforced design — than Cape Cod, yet more diverse and cosmopolitan than neighboring Nantucket Island, Martha's Vineyard is an island with a split personality. From Memorial Day through Labor Day it is a vibrant, star-studded place. Edgartown is flooded with seekers of chic who've come to wander the tidy streets lined with boutiques and stately whaling captains' homes. The busy main port, Vineyard Haven, welcomes day-trippers from the ferries and private yachts to browse in its own array of shops. Oak Bluffs has a boardwalk-town air, with less pricey shops, pizza and ice-cream emporiums, and several night spots that cater to the high-spirited, tanned young. Those too long in city pent find escape on the many bike paths, in nature preserves, and on miles of spectacular white-sand beaches paved with multicolor beach towels. Summer regulars return, including a host of celebrities such as William Styron, Art Buchwald, Walter Cronkite, Katherine Graham, Jacqueline Onassis, Beverly Sills, and Carly Simon. Concerts, theater and dance performances, and lecture series draw top talent to the island, while a county agricultural fair, weekly farmer's markets, and fireworks displays viewed from the village green offer earthier pleasures.

This summer persona is the one most people know, but in many ways the Vineyard's other self is even more appealing, for in the off-season the island becomes a place of peace and simple beauty. On drives along country lanes through the agricultural center of the island, there's time to linger over pastoral and ocean vistas without deference to a throng of other cars, bicycles, and mopeds. In the many conservation areas, the voices of the summer crowds are gone, leaving only the sounds of birdsong and the crackle of leaves underfoot. The beaches, always lovely, now can be appreciated in solitude, and the water seems to sparkle more under the crisp blue skies.

The locals, too, are at their best now. After struggling to make the most of the short money-making season, they reestablish contact with friends and take up pastimes previously crowded out by work. The result for visitors — besides the extra dose of friendliness they are likely to encounter — is that cultural, educational, and recreational events continue to be offered year-round.

Bartholomew Gosnold charted Martha's Vineyard for the British Crown in 1602 and is credited with naming it, supposedly after his infant daughter and the wild grapes he found growing in profusion. Later, a Massachusetts Bay Colony businessman, Thomas Mayhew, was given a grant to the island, along with Nantucket and the Elizabeth Islands, from King Charles of England. Mayhew's son, Thomas Mayhew, Jr., founded the first European settlement here in 1642, at Edgartown, finding the resident Wampanoag Indians good neighbors. Among other survival skills, they taught the settlers to kill whales on shore; when moved out to sea, this skill would bring the island great prosperity, at least for a while. (Historians estimate a Wampanoag population of

Martha's Vineyard

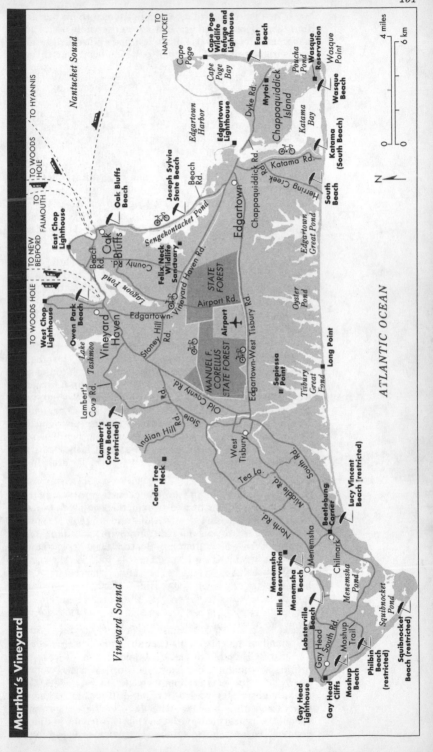

Vineyard Sound

Nantucket Sound

TO WOODS HOLE

TO NEW BEDFORD FALMOUTH

TO WOODS HOLE

TO FALMOUTH

TO HYANNIS

TO NANTUCKET

West Chop Lighthouse

East Chop Lighthouse

Oak Bluffs Beach

Joseph Sylvia State Beach

Owen Park Beach

Vineyard Haven

Lake Tashmoo

Lambert's Cove Rd.

Lambert's Cove Beach (restricted)

Cedar Tree Neck

Indian Hill Rd.

State Rd.

Old County Rd.

Stoney Hill Rd.

Beach Rd.

County Rd.

Oak Bluffs

Sengekontacket Pond

Lagoon Pond

Felix Neck Wildlife Sanctuary

Vineyard Haven Rd.

Edgartown

Airport Rd.

STATE FOREST

Airport

MANUEL F. CORELLUS STATE FOREST

Edgartown-West Tisbury Rd.

West Tisbury

Tea La.

Middle Rd.

North Rd.

South Rd.

South Rd.

Sepiessa Point

Tisbury Great Pond

Long Point

Oyster Pond

Edgartown Great Pond

Beach Rd.

Edgartown Harbor

Edgartown Lighthouse

Chappaquiddick Rd.

Dyke Rd.

Cape Page

Cape Page Bay

Cape Page Wildlife Refuge and Lighthouse

East Beach

Mytoi

Chappaquiddick Island

Katama Bay

Poucha Pond

Wasque Reservation

Wasque Point

Wasque Beach

Katama (South Beach)

Herring Creek Rd.

Katama Rd.

South Beach

ATLANTIC OCEAN

Beetlebung Corner

Lucy Vincent Beach (restricted)

Menemsha

Chilmark

Menemsha Pond

Menemsha Hills Reservation

Menemsha Beach

Lobsterville Beach

Gay Head Lighthouse

Gay Head Cliffs

Gay Head

South Rd.

Moshup Trail

Moshup Beach

Philbin Beach (restricted)

Squibnocket Pond

Squibnocket Beach (restricted)

N

0   4 miles

0   6 km

3,000 upon the arrival of Mayhew; today there are fewer than 300. The tribe is now working hard to reclaim and perpetuate its cultural identity, as it has reclaimed ancestral lands in the town of Gay Head.)

Settled as a community of farmers and fishermen (both of which occupations continue to flourish here today), the island made a decided shift in the early 1800s to whaling as the basis of its economy. Never as influential as Nantucket or New Bedford, Martha's Vineyard still held its own, and many Vineyard whaling masters returned home wealthy men. Especially during the golden age of whaling — around 1830 to 1845 — the captains built impressive homes with the profits, and these, along with many graceful houses from earlier centuries, still line the streets of the onetime whaling towns of Vineyard Haven and Edgartown. After the Civil War the industry went into decline, but by that time, a new industry was on the rise, and it has continued to hold sway to this day: tourism.

The story of this development begins in 1835, when the first Methodist Camp Meeting — a two-week gathering of far-flung parishes for group worship and a healthy dose of fun — was held in the then-undeveloped Oak Bluffs area. From the original meeting's nine tents, the number grew to 250 by 1857.

Little by little, permanent platforms ranged around the large central tent of the preachers were built by returning campers; then the odd cottage popped up, fit into the same space a tent would occupy. By 1880, Wesleyan Grove, as it was called (after Methodism founder John Wesley), was a community of about 500 tiny cottages. Lacy filigree insets began to appear along the facades, becoming more and more ornate as neighbors tried to outdo one another. The style, emerging from Gothic Revival styles imported from Europe, was known as Carpenter Gothic, for the filigree work produced with jigsaws.

Meanwhile, burgeoning numbers of cottagers coming to the island each summer helped convince speculators of its desirability as a resort destination, and in 1867 a separate secular community was laid out alongside the Camp Ground. Steamers from New Bedford, Boston, New York, and elsewhere began bringing in fashionable folk for the bathing and the sea air, for picking berries or playing croquet. Grand hotels sprung up around Oak Bluffs Harbor; a railroad followed, connecting the town with the beach at Katama. The Victorian seaside resort became known as Cottage City; later, the name was changed to Oak Bluffs.

Today, more than 300 of the Camp Ground cottages remain, and just as Edgartown and Vineyard Haven attest to their origins as whaling ports, so Oak Bluffs — with its grassy, open parks, its porch-wrapped beach houses, and its village green and gazebo, where families still gather to hear the town band play — evokes the days of Victorian summer ease. If you close your eyes, the Day-Glo orange bikinis and cones of frozen yogurt seem to fade away, replaced for just a moment by flowing white dresses and parasols held languidly against the sun.

Essential Information

Important Addresses and Numbers

Tourist Information **Martha's Vineyard Chamber of Commerce** is two blocks from the Vineyard Haven ferry. *Beach Rd., tel. 508/693–0085. Open weekdays 9–5; also Memorial Day–Labor Day, Sat. 10–2.*

Emergencies Dialing 911 will connect you with a **communications center,** where messages are quickly relayed to the hospital, physicians, ambulance services, police, fire departments, or Coast Guard. There's a 24-hour emergency room at **Martha's Vineyard Hospital** (Linton La., Oak Bluffs, tel. 508/693–0410). **Island Medical Services** (261 Main St., Edgartown, tel. 508/627–5181) and **Vineyard Medical Services** (State Rd., Vineyard Haven, tel. 508/693–6399) provide walk-in care; call for days and hours.

Late-night Pharmacies The **Oak Bluffs Pharmacy** (Circuit Ave., tel. 508/693–4501; night number 508/627–5067) and **Triangle Pharmacy** (245 Vineyard Haven Rd., Edgartown, tel. 508/627–5107; night number 508/627–3175) are open daily until 9 or 10 PM in July and August. These, as well as **Leslie's Drug Store** (Main St., Vineyard Haven, tel. 508/693–1010), are open daily year-round and have pharmacists on 24-hour call for emergencies.

Cash Machines ATMs are operated by the **Edgartown National Bank** (2 S. Water St. and 251 Upper Main St. [next to the A&P] in Edgartown; 129–131 Circuit Ave., near post office, in Oak Bluffs; tel. 508/627–3343) and by the **Martha's Vineyard National Bank** (opposite steamship offices in Vineyard Haven and Oak Bluffs; 19 Lower Main St., Edgartown; Up-Island Cronigs Market, State Rd., West Tisbury; tel. 508/693–9400).

Arriving and Departing by Plane

Airport **Martha's Vineyard Airport** (tel. 508/693–7022) is in West Tisbury, about 5 miles west of Edgartown.

Airlines **Cape Air** (tel. 508/771–6944 or 800/999–1616), which absorbed Edgartown Air in late 1991, connects the Vineyard year-round with Boston, Hyannis, Nantucket, and New Bedford; it also offers joint fares with Continental, Delta, and USAir and ticketing-and-baggage agreements with American, Midwest Express, Northwest, and United. **Continental Express** (tel. 800/525–0280) has nonstop flights from Newark Memorial Day to Labor Day. **Coastal Air** (tel. 508/693–5942; 508/228–3350 on Nantucket; 203/448–1001 in Groton, CT; 516/537–5200 on Long Island, NY; 401/348–2323 on Block Island, RI) and **Direct Flight** (tel. 508/693–6688) are charter services with island bases.

Arriving and Departing by Ferry

Car-and-passenger ferries travel to Vineyard Haven from Woods Hole on Cape Cod year-round. In season, passenger ferries from Falmouth and Hyannis on Cape Cod, and from New Bedford, serve Vineyard Haven and Oak Bluffs. All provide parking lots for leaving cars overnight (cost: $6–$10 a night).

From Woods Hole The **Steamship Authority** operates the only car ferries, which make the 45-minute trip to Vineyard Haven year-round, and to Oak Bluffs from late May through September. *Tel. 508/540–2022 for auto reservations; on the Vineyard, 508/693–0367 or 508/693–0125 for information, 508/693–9130 for auto reservations; TDD 508/540–1394. Cost, one-way, mid-Oct.–mid-May/mid-May–mid-Oct.: $4/$4.50 adults, $2/$2.25 children 5–12; cars, $23/$36. Bicycles, $2.75 each way year-round.*

If you plan to take a car to the island (or to Nantucket) in summer or fine weekends in fall, you *must* reserve as far ahead as possible; weekend spaces are often sold out months in advance. In season, call weekdays from 7 to 9 PM for faster service. Those with reservations must be at the terminal 30 minutes (45 in season) before sailing time. If you're without a reservation, get there very early and be prepared to wait, possibly for hours, for a space to open up. A standby policy guarantees same-day passage from Woods Hole or Vineyard Haven daily in summer to vehicles in the standby line by 2 PM.

A number of parking lots in Falmouth hold the overflow of cars when the Woods Hole lot is filled; free shuttle buses take passengers to the ferry, about 15 minutes away. Signs along Route 28 heading south from the Bourne Bridge direct you to open parking lots, as does AM radio station 1610, which can be picked up within 5 miles of Falmouth.

Available at the ticket office in Woods Hole is a free reservations phone connecting you with many lodgings and car- and moped-rental firms on the island.

From Hyannis **Hy-Line** makes the 1¾-hour run to Oak Bluffs May–October. It's a good idea to reserve a parking space in the lot in high season if you're leaving your car. From June to mid-September, the "Around the Sound" cruise makes a one-day round-trip from Hyannis with stops at Nantucket and Martha's Vineyard ($31 adults, $15.50 children 5–12, bicycles $13.50). *Ocean St. dock, tel. 508/778–2600, 508/778–2602 for reservations; in Oak Bluffs, tel. 508/693–0112. Cost, one-way: $10.50 adults, $5.25 children 5–12, $4.50 bicycles.*

From Falmouth The ***Island Queen*** makes the 40-minute trip to Oak Bluffs from late May through Columbus Day. *Falmouth Harbor, tel. 508/548–4800. Cost: round-trip, $9 adults, $4.50 children under 13, $6 bicycles; one way, $5 adults, $2.50 children under 13, $3 bicycles. Children under 5 sail free Fri.–Mon.*

If you miss your ferry and you're willing to pay $90 or more, **Patriot Party Boats** (tel. 508/548–2626) operates a 24-hour water-taxi service.

From New Bedford The *Schamonchi* travels between Billy Woods Wharf and Vineyard Haven from mid-May to mid-October. The 450-passenger ferry makes the 1½-hour trip at least once a day, several times in high season, avoiding Cape traffic. *Tel. 508/997–1688; Beach Rd., Vineyard Haven, tel. 508/693–2088. Cost, one-way/round-trip same day: $8.50/$15 adults, $4.50/$7.50 children under 12, $2.50/$5 bicycles. Senior citizens get a 10% discount.*

From Nantucket **Hy-Line** makes 2¼-hour runs to and from Oak Bluffs from mid-June to mid-September — the only interisland passenger service. (To get a car from the Vineyard to Nantucket, you must return to the mainland.) *Tel. 508/778–2600 in Hyannis, 508/693–0112 in Oak Bluffs, 508/228–3949 on Nantucket. Cost, one-way: $10.50 adults, $5.25 children 5–12, $4.50 bicycles.*

Arriving and Departing by Private Boat

Town harbor facilities are available at **Vineyard Haven** (tel. 508/693–4200), **Oak Bluffs** (tel. 508/693–4355), **Edgartown** (tel. 508/627–4746), and **Menemsha** (tel. 508/645–2846). Private companies include **Vineyard Haven Marina** (tel. 508/693–0720 or 693–0728), **Dockside Marina** (tel. 508/693–3392) in Oak Bluffs, and **Edgartown Marine** (tel. 508/627–4388).

Arriving and Departing by Bus and Train

Buses and trains connect with the ferry at Woods Hole — **Amtrak** (tel. 800/USA–RAIL) in summer, **Bonanza Bus Lines** (tel. 800/556–3815, from New York, Providence, and Boston) year-round.

Getting Around

By Car In season, the Vineyard gets overrun with cars and many innkeepers will advise you to leave your car home, saying you won't need it. This is true if you are coming over for just a few days and plan to spend most of your time in the three main towns, Oak Bluffs, Vineyard Haven, and Edgartown, which are connected in summer by a shuttle bus. Otherwise, you'll probably want a car. Driving on the island is fairly simple; there are few main roads, and these are all well marked. Sample distances from Vineyard Haven: to Oak Bluffs, 3 miles; to Edgartown, 8 miles; to Gay Head, 18 miles.

Rentals can be booked through the Woods Hole ferry terminal free phone; at the airport desks of **Budget** (tel. 508/693–7322), **Hertz** (tel. 508/693–2402), **All Island** (tel. 508/693–6868), and others; or from companies in the towns, including **Atlantic** (tel. 508/693–0480 or 508/693–9780). **Adventure Rentals** (Beach Rd., Vineyard Haven, tel. 508/693–1959) rents cars as well as mopeds, Jeeps, and buggies, and offers half-day rates. Cost: $25–$65 per day for a basic model car. See also By Bicycle, below.

By Four-wheel-drive Four-wheel-drive vehicles are allowed on parts of South Beach with $30 annual permits sold on the beach in summer, or anytime at the Dukes County Courthouse (Treasurer's Office, Main St., Edgartown, tel. 508/627–4250). In addition to the payment of fees, Wasque Reservation (*see* Nature Areas, *below*) requires that vehicles carry certain equipment, such as a shovel; call the rangers before setting out for the dunes. Jeeps are a good idea for exploring areas approachable only by dirt roads, but for over-sand travel, even in a Jeep the going can be difficult. Also, most rental companies (*see* By Car, *above*; By Bicycle and Moped, *below*) don't allow their Jeeps to be driven over sand, for insurance reasons. Cost: $40–$140 per day (prices fluctuate widely with the season).

By Bus For information on bus service, call Martha's Vineyard Transportation (tel. 508/693–1589). Schedules are included in Steamship Authority schedule pamphlets. Mid-May to mid-October, shuttles operate between Vineyard Haven (pickup on Union Street in front of the steamship wharf), Oak Bluffs (by the Civil War statue), and Edgartown (on Church Street). The buses operate daily from 8 AM to midnight or so in high season (on the hour and the half hour out of both Vineyard Haven and Edgartown), from 8 to 7 other times (on the hour out of Vineyard Haven, the half hour out of Edgartown); in shoulder seasons, sometimes weekends only. Cost: $1.50–$3 one-way; three-town combination ticket, $4.

Buses from Edgartown to Gay Head — with stops at the airport, West Tisbury, and Chilmark — run between 9 AM and 5 PM in July and August; at other times, call to confirm. Cost: $1–$5 one-way.

By Trolley The Martha's Vineyard Transit Authority (tel. 508/627–7448) offers two trolley routes in Edgartown.

Downtown From mid-May to mid-September, trolleys make a continuous circuit of downtown, beginning at two free parking lots on the outskirts — at the Triangle off Upper Main Street and at the Edgartown School on Robinson Road (a right off the West Tisbury Road before Upper Main). It's really worth doing to avoid parking headaches in town, and it's cheap (25¢) and convenient. Trolleys run every 10 minutes from 7:30 AM to 11:30 PM daily (mid-May–June, 7:30–7) and can be flagged along the route.

South Beach Trolley service to South Beach from town is available mid-June–Labor Day for $1.50 one-way. Pickup is at the corner of Main and Church streets every 15 minutes 9–5:30 daily, hourly in inclement weather, or you can flag a trolley whenever you see one. Weekend service begins on Memorial Day. For information on weekly, monthly, or seasonal passes, call 508/627–9663.

By Taxi Taxis meet all scheduled ferries and flights; there are taxi stands by the Flying Horses Carousel in Oak Bluffs, at the foot of Main Street in Edgartown, and by the Steamship office in Vineyard Haven. Companies serving the island include **All Island** (tel. 508/693–3705), **Marlene's** (tel. 508/693–0037), **Martha's Vineyard Taxi** (tel. 508/693– 8660), and **Up Island** (tel. 508/693–5454). Fares range from $3 within a town to $35 one way from Vineyard Haven to Gay Head; rates double between 2 and 7 AM.

By Limousine **Muzik's Limousine Service** (tel. 508/693–2212) and **Holmes Hole Car Rental & Limo Service** (tel. 508/693–8838) provide limo service on-island and sometimes travel off-island.

By Bicycle Martha's Vineyard is a great place for bicycling, though
and Moped Up-Island roads are hilly, and in season all are often crowded. There are several paved, scenic bike paths (*see* Sports and Outdoor Activities, *below*). To rent a moped, a driver's license is required; remember that many Vineyard roads are narrow, and watch out for loose gravel and sand. There are many accidents each year.

Rent bikes in Vineyard Haven just up from the ferry at **Martha's Vineyard Scooter and Bike** (tel. 508/693–0782), in Oak Bluffs at **Anderson's** (tel. 508/693–9346), and in Edgartown at **R.W. Cutler Bike** (1 Main St., tel. 508/627–4052; bikes only). Rent bikes and mopeds in Oak Bluffs at **De Bettencourt's** (tel. 508/693–0011; also Jeeps), **King's Bike & Moped** (tel. 508/693–1887), and **Ride-On Mopeds** (tel. 508/693–2076), all on Circuit Avenue Extension near the ferry docks, or at **Sun 'n' Fun** (Lake Ave., tel. 508/693–5457; also cars and Jeeps). Cost: $7–$15 per day for bikes, $25–$50 for mopeds.

By Ferry The three-car **On Time** ferry — so named because it has no printed schedules and therefore can never be late — makes the five-minute run to Chappaquiddick Island (*see* Off the Beaten Track, *below*) June–mid-October, daily 7:30 AM–midnight; less frequently off-season. *Dock St., Edgartown, tel. 508/627–9427. Cost, round-trip: $1 individual, $4 car and driver, $2.50 bicycle and rider, $3.50 moped or motorcycle and rider.*

By Horse-drawn **Lysander Drives** (tel. 508/693–3789) offers rides in an an-
Carriage tique surrey with Victorian-costumed driver.

Guided Tours

Orientation The bus companies (tel. 508/693–1555, 508/693–4681, or 508/693–0058) offer two-hour narrated tours of the island spring through fall, with a stop at the Gay Head Cliffs. Buses meet the ferries. See the island another way if possible.

Special-Interest See the Vineyard by silent sailplane with **Soaring Adven-**
Sailplane **tures of America** (Katama Airfield, Herring Creek Rd., Edgartown, tel. 508/627–3833). Tours are given daily in summer. It's just you and the pilot; you can even take a turn at the controls.

Cruises Day sails, sunset cruises, and overnights to Nantucket or Cuttyhunk on the 54-foot Alden ketch *Laissez Faire* (tel.

508/693–1646) are offered in season out of Vineyard Haven. Cost (including meals): $85 full day, $50 half-day, $300 overnight.

Day sails with lunch on the *Shenandoah* (tel. 508/693–1699), a square topsail schooner, are available one week each summer (call for schedule) and depart from Coastwise Wharf (south of Steamboat Wharf) in Vineyard Haven. Cost: $75. From mid-June through mid-September the schooner offers six-day cruises ($700, including three hearty meals). Passengers are ferried to ports, which may include Nantucket, Cuttyhunk, New Bedford, Newport, Block Island, or others.

Ayuthia Charters (tel. 508/693–7245) offers half-day ($50 per person), full-day ($550–$650 for up to 10 persons), and overnight sails to Nantucket or the Elizabeth Islands (wide price variation) on a teakwood sailing yacht, also leaving from Coastwise Wharf in Vineyard Haven from late May through October.

Exploring Martha's Vineyard

The island is roughly triangular, with maximum distances of about 20 miles east to west and 10 miles north to south. The west end of the Vineyard, known as Up-Island (from the nautical expression of going "up" in degrees of longitude as you sail west), is more rural and wild than the east end, known as Down-Island (Vineyard Haven, Oak Bluffs, and Edgartown). Almost a fifth of the island (over 11,400 acres) is conservation land, and more is being acquired all the time by organizations — including the Land Bank, funded by a 2% tax on real estate transactions — that exist in order to preserve as much of the island in its natural state as is possible and practical.

Highlights for First-time Visitors

Dukes County Historical Society (*see* Tour 3: Edgartown)
Felix Neck or **Cedar Tree Neck** (*see* Nature Areas)
Gay Head Cliffs (*see* Tour 4: Up-Island)
Menemsha (*see* Tour 4: Up-Island)
Oak Bluffs Camp Ground (*see* Tour 2: Oak Bluffs)
West Tisbury town center (*see* Tour 4: Up-Island)

Tour 1: Vineyard Haven

Numbers in the margin correspond to points of interest on the Vineyard Haven map.

Because most visitors to the island come by the Vineyard Haven ferry (the town is officially named Tisbury, but commonly referred to as Vineyard Haven, the name of the port), we begin here. A short walk from the steamship terminal

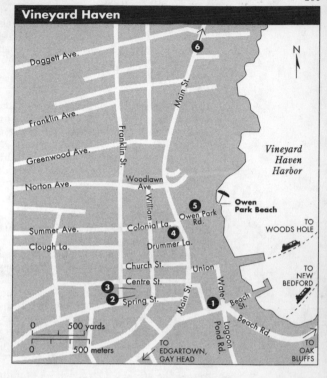

Vineyard Haven

① along Water Street and a right onto Beach Road will take you to the **Martha's Vineyard Chamber of Commerce** for maps and information.

Time Out On Water Street, across from the A&P, is the **Black Dog Bakery** (tel. 508/693–4786), with fresh breads and pastries, quick-lunch items, and Black Dog gift items (*see* Shopping, *below*).

② The next right after the chamber building is Main Street, with shops and places to eat. From here, a left onto Spring Street brings you to the **Association Hall.** The 1844 neoclassical structure houses the town hall as well as the Katharine Cornell Memorial Theatre, created in part with funds the actress — a longtime summer resident — donated in her will. The walls of the theater, on the second floor, are painted with murals depicting such island scenes as whaling and an Indian gathering; overhead is a blue sky with seagulls. Island artist Stan Murphy painted the murals on the occasion of the town's tercentenary, in 1971. In addition to theatrical performances, concerts and dances are held here.

③ A path to the left of the hall leads to the **Centre Street Cemetery,** where tall pine trees shade grave markers dating as far back as 1817. Some stones are simple gray slate slabs; others are engraved with such motifs as the death's-head, or skull, common on early tombstones. A more recent grave is that of Katharine Cornell, who died in 1974.

Leave the cemetery via Center Street, turning right; past the town tennis courts is **William Street,** a quiet, pretty stretch of white picket fences and Greek Revival houses, many of them built for prosperous sea captains. Now a part of a National Historic District, the street was spared when the Great Fire of 1883 claimed much of the old whaling and fishing town.

At **108 William Street,** set back on a wide lawn behind a wrought-iron fence just before Colonial Lane, is an imposing monument to a later source of the town's prosperity: tourism. Though the three-story, 1873 white house with front gable, elegantly detailed porch, black shutters, and cupola was also built by a sea captain, this one — Benjamin C. Cromwell — piloted not a whaling ship but a steamer that brought New Bedford folk to the island.

Turn down the unmarked Colonial Lane. At the intersection of Main Street is the **Old Schoolhouse Museum,** built in 1829 as the first town school. Exhibits include items brought back from voyages during whaling days, including Polynesian and Inuit tools, as well as antique musical instruments, clothing, and records of 19th-century schoolchildren. Out front is the **Liberty Pole,** erected by the Daughters of the American Revolution in commemoration of three patriotic girls who blew up the town's liberty pole in 1776 to prevent it from being taken for use on a British warship. *110 Main St., tel. 508/693–3860. Donations accepted. Open mid-June–mid-Sept., weekdays 10–2. Closed mid-Sept.–mid-June.*

Across the street and a block up Main is **Owen Park,** with swings, a bandstand where summer band concerts are held (*see* The Arts, *below*), and tree-shaded benches with a fine view of the harbor. At the end of the lawn is a public beach with a swing set and a close-up view of the boats coming in and out.

In the 19th century, this harbor was one of the busiest ports in the world, welcoming thousands of coastwise vessels each year. The headlands on either side — West Chop in Vineyard Haven and East Chop in Oak Bluffs — each came to have a lighthouse at its tip to help bring ships safely into port. Both areas were largely settled in the late 19th to early 20th centuries, when the very rich from Boston and Newport built expansive bluff-top "summer cottages." These houses — built in what is called the Shingle Style, characterized by broad gable ends, dormers, and, of course, natural shingle siding that weathers to gray — were meant to eschew show, though they were sometimes gussied up a bit with a turret or two.

Today beautiful, green **West Chop** retains its exclusive air and boasts some of the island's most distinguished residents. A 2-mile drive or bike ride along Main Street, which becomes increasingly residential, will take you there. The 52-foot white-and-black **West Chop Lighthouse,** on the right, was built in 1881 of brick, to replace an 1817 wood light. It has been moved back twice from the edge of the eroding bluff. Just beyond the lighthouse, on the point, is a scenic overlook with a landscaped area and benches.

If you return to town via Franklin Street you pass the **West Chop Woods,** an 85-acre conservation area with marked walking trails through pitch pine and oak; there's parking off Franklin Street and a bike rack on Main Street.

Tour 2: Oak Bluffs

Numbers in the margin correspond to points of interest on the Oak Bluffs map.

Beach Road leads east out of Vineyard Haven across a narrow strip of land between the harbor on the left and Lagoon Pond: a haven for boats passing in storms, a good scalloping and water-sports area, and the site of the **State Lobster Hatchery** (*see* Off the Beaten Track, *below*). A left onto Highland Drive, after the drawbridge, takes you past **Crystal Lake** and the wildlife preserve that surrounds it. Beyond

❼ the lake is **East Chop** and the **East Chop Lighthouse.** Built of cast iron in 1876 to replace an 1828 tower — used as part of a semaphore system between the island and Boston — that burned down, the 40-foot tower stands high atop a bluff from which the views of Nantucket Sound are spectacular. The lighthouse is open Friday and Sunday in summer for sunsets, and private tours can be arranged (tel. 508/693–4922 or 508/645–9954). Keeping to the coast road, you'll come eventually to **Oak Bluffs Harbor.** Once the setting for

❽ a number of grand hotels — the 1879 **Wesley Hotel** on Lake Avenue is the last of them — the still colorful harbor now specializes in gingerbread-trimmed guest houses and mini-malls hawking fast food and souvenirs.

This walking tour of town begins where Lake Avenue runs into Oak Bluffs Avenue (which ends at the steamship dock). A good first stop in season is the new gingerbread-trimmed

❾ **information booth** here. Across the way is the building that

❿ houses the **Flying Horses,** arguably the nation's oldest carousel, and a National Historic Landmark. Handcrafted in 1876 and extensively renovated in 1990–91, it offers small children entertainment from a Nintendo-less time. While waiting in line, sample another old-time treat: sinfully sugary cotton candy. In the waiting area are a number of 20th-century diversions: i.e., ping-ing arcade games. *Oak Bluffs Ave., tel. 508/693–9481. Rides cost $1; $8 for a book of 10. Open mid-June–Labor Day, daily 10–10; spring and fall, weekends only; closed in winter.*

Time Out **Standby Diner** (Oak Bluffs Ave., tel. 508/693–5525), across the street, is light and bright, with lots of small-paned windows and a marble countertop salvaged from an old diner by the owner/cook, Jack. Eggs and omelets are served all day, along with lunches and dinners of homemade soups (like pork-and-green-chili stew), burgers and clubs, fresh seafood, and $6–$8 blue-plate specials (shepherd's pie, grilled pork chops, steak, fried chicken). Senior citizens get a 10% discount.

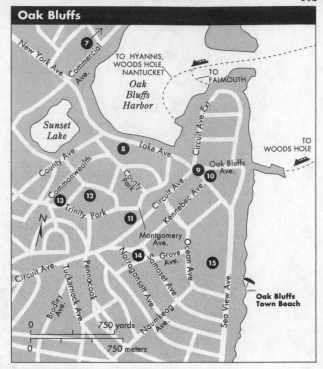

Just beyond the Flying Horses is Circuit Avenue, the center of the Oak Bluffs action, with most of the town's shops, bars, and restaurants. Here, on the right, is the entrance to the

⑪ Oak Bluffs Camp Ground, a 34-acre warren of streets tightly packed with more than 300 Carpenter Gothic Victorian cottages, gaily painted in pastels with wedding-cake trim. As you wander through this fairy-tale setting, imagine it at night, lit by the warm glow from hundreds of Japanese paper lanterns hung from every cottage porch. This is what happens each summer on Illumination Night, when the end of the Camp Meeting season — attended these days by some fourth- and fifth-generation cottagers — is marked as it has been for more than a century, with lights, singing, and open houses for families and friends. (Because of overwhelming crowds of onlookers in seasons past, the date is not announced until the week before.)

⑫ As you enter the grounds, before you is the **Tabernacle,** an impressive open-air structure of iron at the center of Trinity Park. On Wednesdays at 8 PM in season, visitors are invited to join in on an old-time community sing. If you know tunes like "The Erie Canal" or just want to listen in (music books are available for a donation), drop by the Tabernacle and take a seat. Also in the park is the 1878 **Trinity Methodist Church.**

⑬ The Cottage Museum, in an 1867 cream-and-orange cottage near the Tabernacle, exhibits cottage furnishings from the early days, including photographs, hooked rugs, quilts, and old Bibles. The gift shop offers Victorian and nautical items. *1 Trinity Park, tel. 508/693–0525. Admission: $1. Open mid-June–Sept., Mon.–Sat. 10:30–4. Closed Oct.–mid-June.*

Exit the Camp Ground as you entered, but don't leave until you've spotted what's called the **Wooden Valentine** (25 Washington Ave.); just think purple. At Circuit Avenue, cross the street and turn right. At the junction of the next street, again cross the street and head left. The octagonal **(14)** building you see is the nonsectarian **Union Chapel,** built in 1870 for the Cottage City resort folk who lived outside the Camp Ground's seven-foot-high fence. In summer, concerts are held here. Follow Grove Avenue to Ocean Avenue, a crescent of large Shingle-style cottages, with lots of turrets, **(15)** breezy porches, and pastel facades, circling **Ocean Park.** Band concerts take place at the gazebo here on summer nights, and in August the park hosts hordes of island families and visitors for a grand fireworks display over the ocean, across Sea View Avenue.

Tour 3: Edgartown

Numbers in the margin correspond to points of interest on the Edgartown map.

The third main town is approached from Oak Bluffs via a scenic 6-mile section of Beach Road. On your left is Nantucket Sound and one of the island's best beach areas; soon the road narrows to an ever-eroding strip separating the Sound from Sengekontacket Pond, on your right. A protected bike path also runs the distance.

Edgartown, a world away from the honky-tonk of Oak Bluffs, is a tidy, polished town of upscale boutiques, elegant 17th- and 18th-century sea captains' houses, well-manicured lawns, and picturesque flower gardens. To orient yourself historically a bit before touring the town, you might want to stop off at a complex of buildings and lawn exhibits **(16)** belonging to the **Dukes County Historical Society.** The following service information applies to all the exhibits, which are detailed below. *Cooke St., corner of School St., tel. 508/627–4441. Admission: mid-June–mid-Sept., $4 adults, $2 senior citizens and children under 16; mid- Sept.–mid-June, $2 adults, $1 senior citizens and children. Open mid-June–mid-Sept., Tues.–Sat. 10–4:30; rest of year, Wed.–Fri. 1–4, Sat. 10–4.*

The one property open in summer only is the **Thomas Cooke House,** set in the 1765 home of a customs collector. The house itself is part of the display, including the low doorways, the wide-board floors, the original raised-panel woodwork with fluted pilasters, and the hearths in the summer and winter kitchens. Docents conduct tours of the 12 rooms, whose exhibits document the island's history through furniture, tools, costumes, portraits, toys, crafts, and various household objects. One room is set up as a 19th-century parlor, illustrating the opulence of the golden age of whaling through such period pieces as a two-foot-long inlaid Swiss-movement music box and a pianoforte. Upstairs are ship

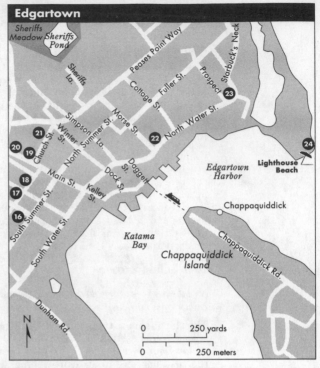

models, whaling paraphernalia, and old customs documents, as well as a room tracing the evolution of the Camp Meeting through photographs and objects.

The **Francis Foster Museum** houses a small collection of whaling implements, scrimshaw, navigational instruments, and lots of old photographs. One interesting exhibit is a collection of 19th-century miniature photographs of 110 Edgartown whaling masters, grouped by family. In the same building is the **Gale Huntington Reference Library,** with genealogical records, rare island books, and ships' logs from the whaling days, plus some publications for sale. The **Capt. Francis Pease House,** an 1850s Greek Revival adjacent to the library, houses a permanent exhibit of Native American, prehistoric, pre-Columbian, and later artifacts, including arrowheads and pottery, plus changing exhibits from the collection.

The **Carriage Shed** displays a number of vessels and vehicles, including a whaleboat, a snazzy 1855 fire engine with stars inlaid in wood, and an 1830 hearse, considerably less ornate than the fire engine, and rightly so. The shed also houses some peculiar gravestones that once marked the eternal resting places of some strangely beloved chickens. In the yard outside it are a replica of a 19th-century **brick tryworks,** used to process whale oil from blubber aboard ship; and the 1,008-prism **Fresnel lens** installed in the Gay Head Lighthouse in 1854 and removed when the light was automated in 1952. In summer, the lens lamp is lighted briefly on Sunday nights at 8, and the official lighthouse keeper is on hand to talk with aficionados about its operation.

The Historical Society sells an excellent Edgartown walking-tour booklet ($4.95) that is full of anecdotes, as well as history, about the people who have lived in the houses along the route over the past three centuries. The following tour takes you along the most interesting streets.

Leaving the complex, proceed down School Street toward ⑰ Main Street. On the left, at **60 Davis Lane,** is a handsome white clapboard Greek Revival with black shutters and fan ornament, surrounded by gardens. It was built in 1825 as a ⑱ private school. At **20 School Street,** also on the left, is a white monumental Greek Revival fronted with four big Doric columns; built as a Baptist church in 1839, it is now a private residence.

At the end of School Street, turn left onto Main Street. On ⑲ the right is the **Old Whaling Church,** begun in 1842 as a Methodist church and now a performing-arts center. The massive Greek Revival building has a six-column monumental portico, unusual three-sash windows, and a 92-foot clock tower that can be seen for miles. The simple yet graceful interior is bright with 27-foot-tall windows and retains the original box pews. *89 Main St., tel. 508/627–8017. Admission free. Open mid-June–mid-Sept., daily 10–2. Open only for performances mid-Sept.–mid-June.*

⑳ Next door is the graceful **Dr. Daniel Fisher House,** with wraparound roofwalk, small front portico with fluted columns topped by acanthus capitals, and a simple but elegant side portico with thin fluted columns. It was built in 1840 for one of the island's richest men, who was not only a doctor but also the owner of a whale-oil refinery, a spermaceti candle factory, and a gristmill, among other things. The house is now used for functions, and the local Historical Preservation Society has offices upstairs.

In back of the Fisher House is one of the oldest dwellings ㉑ on the island: the 1672 **Vincent House,** a weathered-shingle farmhouse moved to this site in 1977, restored, and now maintained as an architectural museum. Most of the original wide-board floors, glass, brick, and hardware remain; parts of walls have been exposed to reveal the early construction methods. *Main St., tel. 508/627–8017. Donations welcome. Open June–Sept., weekdays 10–2. Closed Oct.–May.*

Heading back down Main Street toward the harbor, you enter the commercial district of Edgartown. A left onto North Water Street brings you past Daggett Street, at the end of which is the ferry to Chappaquiddick (*see* Getting Around by Ferry, *above*).

The upper part of North Water Street is the most photographed strip of architecture in town, for its many fine captains' houses. There's always some interesting detail you never noticed before — like a widow's walk with a mannequin poised, spyglass in hand, watching for her seafaring husband to return. The 1832 house where this piece of whimsy can be seen is at **86 North Water Street,** which the Society for the Preservation of New England Antiquities maintains as a rental property.

At the bend in the road is the gray-shingled Victorian **Harbor View Hotel,** on the left. Built in the 1890s and a major player in the Vineyard's early resort days, the very upscale property was totally renovated in 1990, including the addition of such period details as a gazebo off the wraparound veranda and new turrets. A path off to the right just before the hotel leads down to the **Edgartown Lighthouse,** surrounded by a public beach with a good view but seaweedy bathing. The original light guarding the harbor was built in 1828 on an island made from granite blocks. The island was later connected to the mainland by a bridge. By the time the 1938 hurricane made a new light necessary, sand had filled in the gap between the island and the mainland. The current white-painted cast-iron tower was floated over from Ipswich, Massachusetts, on a barge in 1939.

This area, called Starbuck's Neck, is a good place to wander about in, with views of ocean, harbor, a little bay, and moorland. Return to town by continuing past the hotel and turning left onto Fuller Street.

Tour 4: Up-Island

Much of what makes the Vineyard special is found here, in the agricultural heart of the island and the largely undeveloped lands along the perimeter, from West Chop in the north to Edgartown in the southeast. Country roads meander through woods and tranquil farmland; dirt side roads lead past crystalline ponds, abandoned cranberry bogs, and conservation lands. In Chilmark, West Tisbury, and Gay Head, nature lovers, writers, artists, and others have established close ongoing summer communities. In winter, the isolation and bitter winds send even many year-round Vineyarders from their Up-Island homes to places in the Down-Island towns.

Numbers in the margin correspond to points of interest on the Up-Island map.

This tour starts from State Road in Vineyard Haven. Just outside the center of town, on the right just past Sears, is a turnout. Called the **Tashmoo Overlook,** it is a scenic viewpoint overlooking a meadow leading down to Lake Tashmoo and Vineyard Sound beyond.

Time Out   Before the overlook, turn in at John's Fish Market for **Sandy's Fish & Chips** (tel. 508/693–1220), a seasonal clam shack, with takeout fried fish and seafood, burgers, and soft ice cream.

After a mile or so, a sign on the left directs you to **The Winery at Chicama Vineyards** (Stoney Hill Rd., tel. 508/693–0309). (From Edgartown, take the Edgartown–

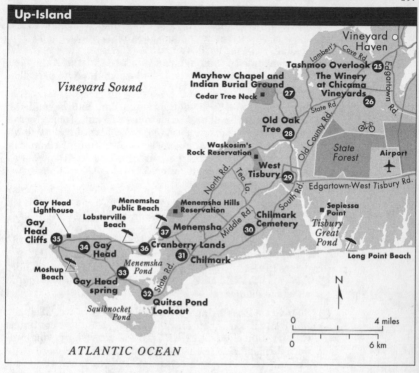

Vineyard Haven Road and turn off at the sign for Thimble
Farm.) From 35 acres of trees and rocks, the Mathiesen
family — George, a broadcaster from San Francisco; his
wife, Cathy; and their six children — have created a
vineyard, starting in 1971 with 75 vinifera vines. Today the
winery produces 100,000 bottles a year, from chardonnay,
cabernet, Riesling, Pinot noir, and other European grapes.
Free tours and tastings are given daily Memorial Day–
Columbus Day; tastings only for the rest of the year on a
limited schedule (call for details). A shop selling wines and
herbed vinegars, mustards, jellies, and other foods prepared on the premises is open year-round (closed July 4 and
Labor Day). A Christmas shop with glassware, gift baskets,
wreaths, and more is open mid-November through New
Year's Eve.

Farther down this woodsy lane is **Thimble Farm** (tel.
508/693–6396), with pick-your-own — or already boxed, if
you're not feeling so rural — strawberries and raspberries
in season (mid-June–early Oct.; closed Mon.). Also available
are cut flowers, melons, pumpkins, and other produce
grown here.

Return to State Road and bear right (toward Gay Head) at
the next fork, remaining on State Road. Just beyond is Indian Hill Road; turning into a dirt road, this leads to the
② **Mayhew Chapel and Indian Burial Ground.** The small
chapel, built in 1829 to replace an earlier one, and a memo-

rial plaque are dedicated to the pastor Thomas Mayhew, Jr., leader of the original colonists who landed at Edgartown in 1642. Mayhew was an enlightened man, noted for his fair dealings with the local Wampanoags. Within a few years, he had converted a number of them to Christianity; called Praying Indians, they established a community here called Christiantown.

Near the chapel is a wildflower garden, and beyond the boulder with the plaque are stones marking Indian grave mounds (the dead are not named, for fear of calling down evil spirits). Behind the chapel is the beginning of a loop trail through the woods (there's a map at the first trail fork), which leads to a lookout tower.

A sign just before you rejoin State Road leads to the **Cedar Tree Neck** nature preserve (*see* Nature Areas, *below*). Back on State Road, turn right. Soon thereafter you'll pass **Takemmy Farm** (*see* What to See and Do with Children, *below*) — keep an eye out for llamas by the fence on the right. Just before the intersection of North Road (the sign points to Menemsha), in a field on the right, is what's fondly

28 known as the **Old Oak Tree**, a massive, ancient oak that is an island landmark.

29 Soon State Road brings you into the center of **West Tisbury.** For centuries a sheep-farming region, the town continues its agricultural tradition with several active horse and produce farms; it also encompasses half of the 4,000-acre **State Forest.** West Tisbury's center looks very much the small New England village, complete with white, steepled church. **Alley's General Store** (State Rd., tel. 508/693–0088), here since 1858, sells everything from hammers to dill pickles.

Time Out | Behind Alley's is **Back Alley's** (tel. 508/693–7366), serving sandwiches, grocery items, and pastries to go.

Past the mansard-roofed town hall is the 1859 **Agricultural Hall,** where a county fair, including livestock and produce judging, is held in August (*see* Festivals and Seasonal Events in Chapter 1, Essential Information) and weekly farmer's markets are held in summer (*see* Shopping, *below*). The Agricultural Society purchased a nearby parcel of land in 1992; when construction on a new, larger Ag Hall is finished, the fair and market will be moved there. Across from the present site is the **Field Gallery** (tel. 508/693–5595), where Tom Maley's large white sculptures, like a colonial horse and rider or a whimsical piper, are displayed on a wide lawn. Inside are changing summer exhibitions of island artists. Just after the First Congregational Church, on the right, is **Music Street,** a street of old sea captains' homes once noted for a preponderance of pianos bought with whaling profits.

About 3 miles out of West Tisbury center, on the right, is

30 **Chilmark Cemetery,** where John Belushi is buried. His tree-shaded grave, near the entrance, is marked by a boulder in which his name is deeply engraved. Visitors often leave tokens of remembrance. Lillian Hellman, a longtime summer resident of the island, is also buried here. Two miles past the cemetery, a dirt road on the left (look for a big telephone pole at the center of a paved street entrance leads to **Lucy Vincent Beach,** perhaps the island's most beautiful.

The crossroads you soon come to is called **Beetlebung Corner,** named for the stand of beetlebung, or black gum, trees
③¹ on your right. This is the center of **Chilmark,** whose scenic ocean-view roads, rustic woodlands, and lack of crowds have drawn chic summer visitors and, hard on their heels, stratospheric real estate prices. At Beetlebung are the town's public buildings, including the firehouse and the post office, as well as the **Chilmark Community Center,** where everything from town meetings to auctions to chamber music concerts are held. In summer, a general store, a clothing boutique, a restaurant and breakfast café, a gallery, and a bank turn the little crossroads into a metropolis almost.

Continue on State Road. After about 1½ miles, a paved road on the left leads to **Squibnocket Beach,** a rocky beauty with a tranquil, covelike look. Beyond the next bend on State Road
③² is the **Quitsa Pond Lookout,** with a good view of the adjoining Menemsha and Nashaquitsa ponds, the woods, and the ocean beyond. Just past the Gay Head town line, on the left,
③³ is the **Gay Head spring;** from an iron pipe gushes water cold enough to slake a cyclist's thirst on the hottest day. Feel free to fill a canteen; locals come from all over the island to fill jugs.

③⁴ **Gay Head** is an official Native American township: In 1987, after more than a decade of struggle in the courts, the Wampanoag tribe won guardianship of 420 acres of land, which are being held in trust by the federal government in perpetuity and constitute the Gay Head Native American Reservation.

At the fork beyond the spring, take a left onto Moshup Trail, the coastal route, with views of dunes and sea. In this area is the 380-acre estate bought by Jacqueline Onassis in the mid-1970s. A stretch of beachfront property belonging to tribe members but surrounded by her land was for years the cause of much legal dispute. The Wampanoags considered the ground hallowed, as the final resting place of tribal founder Chief Moshup and his wife, Squant, but were unable to reach it except by trespassing on Onassis land. In 1990 a compromise was reached, involving the exchange of another piece of sacred ground for the disputed beachfront, along with a cash settlement.

③⁵ Continue to the western tip of the island and the **Gay Head Cliffs,** a National Historic Landmark and part of the reservation land. These dramatically striated walls of red clay are the island's major tourist attraction, as evidenced by the tour bus–filled parking lot. Native American crafts and food shops line the approach to the overlook, from which you can see the Elizabeth Islands, north across Vineyard Sound, and Noman's Land Island (part wildlife preserve, part military bombing-practice site — with fake bombs), 3 miles off the Vineyard's southern coast.

Time Out The **Aquinnah** (tel. 508/645–9654), at the end of the row of shops, is a Wampanoag-owned restaurant with a great view from the deck: of the 135-foot cliffs over which it is perched, of the long white stretch of beach 135 feet below, of the sea and islands, and of spectacular sunsets over the water. Highlights of the simple menu are fresh fish, homemade chowder and pies, and delicious breakfasts, like pancakes with fresh raspberries or pecans.

Adjacent to the overlook is the **Gay Head Lighthouse** (the largest of the Vineyard's five), precariously stationed atop the rapidly eroding cliffs. In 1798, a wood lighthouse was built here — the island's first — to warn ships away from Devil's Bridge, an area of shoals ¼ mile offshore. The current incarnation, built in 1856 of red brick, carries on with its alternating pattern of red and white flashes. Despite the light, the Vineyard's worst wreck occurred here in January 1884, when the *City of Columbus* sank, taking with it into the icy waters more than 100 passengers and crew. The original Fresnel lens was removed when the lighthouse was automated in 1952, but it is preserved at the Dukes County Historical Society in Edgartown (*see* Tour 3: Edgartown, *above*). The lighthouse is open to the public summer weekends for sunsets, weather permitting; private tours can also be arranged (tel. 508/693–4922 or 508/645–9954).

Head out from the cliffs area via State Road, which will take you past the "center" of Gay Head. This consists of a combination fire and police station, the town hall, a Tribal Council office, and a public library, formerly the little red schoolhouse (because the town's year-round population is only about 650, Gay Head children attend schools in other towns). A left onto Lobsterville Road and a right onto West Basin Road (off which another right leads to a parking lot for Menemsha Pond) take you along the shore of Menemsha ❸❻ Bight and through the **Cranberry Lands,** an area of cranberry bog gone wild that is a popular nesting site for birds. No humans can nest here, but you can drive by and look. At the end of the road, with marshland on the right and low dunes and grasses and the long blue arc of the bight on the left, you get a terrific view of the quiet fishing village of Menemsha, across the water.

Return to State Road via Lobsterville Road, and at Beetle- ❸❼ bung Corner, follow signs to **Menemsha.** If you think you've seen it before, you probably have: It was used for location shots in the film *Jaws.* The jumble of small fishing and pleasure boats and the drying nets and lobster pots create a picturesque scene not lost on myriad photographers and artists. But this is very much a working village. The catch of the day can be bought from markets along Dutcher's Dock, or from the restaurant Home Port (*see* Dining, *below*). Along with fishing shacks, you'll find a Texaco station where locals gather for morning coffee, a few boutiques, good fishing from the jetty, and a public beach to which romantics repair for picnic suppers before watching the perfect sunsets over the water.

Back at Beetlebung, turn left onto **Middle Road** to enjoy pastoral Chilmark at its best, with gently rolling farmland and woodland marked off by low stone fences, as well as ocean views here and there from elevated points. A right at the end of Middle Road brings you back to West Tisbury center, from which roads lead anywhere you want to go on the island. Alternatively, go straight toward Edgartown at Beetlebung on the busier South Road to catch the view at Chilmark's **Allen Farm** — an impressive vista across pastureland and moors, now protected by the Land Bank. A shop here (tel. 508/645–9064) sells handwoven blankets and knitted items made from the farm's wool.

What to See and Do with Children

The **Chilmark Community Center** (Beetlebung Corner, tel. 508/645–9484) has activities for children of all ages in summer, including dances, concerts, and movies. It's a great place for kids to meet other kids. The other towns have recreation programs as well: Edgartown (tel. 508/627–6145), Gay Head (tel. 508/645–9265), Oak Bluffs (tel. 508/693–2303), Vineyard Haven (tel. 508/693–0272), and West Tisbury (tel. 508/693–2723).

The **Children's Theatre** in Oak Bluffs (at the high school, Edgartown–Vineyard Haven Rd., tel. 508/693–4060) has weekday classes for children in summer. **Vineyard Playhouse** (*see* The Arts, *below*) has theater-related activities for children and teens in summer.

Island Cove Mini Golf (State Rd., Vineyard Haven, tel. 508/693–2611), new in 1992, is a small, nine-hole course featuring bridges, a cave, fake rocks, sand traps, and lots of running water, including a stream that powers a watermill. It uses ropes, pilings, and old boats to create a nautical feel and is accessible to the disabled.

Storytelling hours for children are offered by all the island's libraries. Call about days and times: **Chilmark** (Beetlebung Corner, tel. 508/645–3360), **Edgartown** (N. Water St., tel. 508/627–4221), **Oak Bluffs** (Circuit Ave., tel. 508/693–9433), **Vineyard Haven** (Upper Main St., tel. 508/696–4210), and **West Tisbury** (Music St., tel. 508/693–3366).

In summer, **Oak Bluffs** has all kinds of attractions to keep kids entertained. In a big white building across the street from the **Flying Horses Carousel** (*see* Tour 2: Oak Bluffs, *above*) is **The Game Room** (Oak Bluffs Ave., tel. 508/693–5163), with 75 arcade games, as well as pool tables, air hockey, and skeeball. At **Dockside Minigolf** (upstairs at Dockside Marketplace, Oak Bluffs Harbor, tel. 508/696–7646) each of the 18 holes — half indoors, half in the open — has an island motif, such as a ferryboat, a lighthouse, or a gingerbread house. **South Pole Slush Co.** (124½ Circuit Ave., tel. 508/693–7545) has at least 20 flavors of slush, like canteloupe, tangerine, and piña colada, plus comic books, cool sunglasses, and lots of goofy candy, like wax lips.

At **Katama Farm** (Katama Rd., Edgartown, tel. 508/627–9272), a working dairy farm, children can go for a free ride on a wagon pulled by Belgian horses, buy fresh ice cream, watch cows be milked, or pet the puppies, goats, or other farm animals that are always around. The farm is open daily year-round; wagon rides are given by appointment on weekends from mid-May to mid-June, daily 2–5 PM from mid-June through September.

Nip 'n' Tuck Farm (State Rd., West Tisbury, tel. 508/693–1449) offers pony-cart rides in July and August from 3 to 5 PM (and by arrangement), as well as hayrides for groups.

Arrowhead Farm (*see* Horseback Riding, *below*).

Takemmy Farm (State Rd., North Tisbury, tel. 508/693–2486) invites children to visit with the llamas (raised as pets and breeding stock) and miniature donkeys on Wednesday and Saturday afternoons year-round. Every day year-round, the farm stand sells eggs, as well as natural wool yarn (no colors); in season, there are vegetables, flowers, and honey as well.

Gymnastics and movement day camps for children from age 3½ through high school are available in one-week summer programs through the U.S. Academy of Gymnastics (Sept.–mid-June, 11 Allen Rd., Norwalk, CT 06851, tel. 203/847–4994; mid-June–Aug., Box 2271, Vineyard Haven 02568, tel. 508/693–5225).

Felix Neck Wildlife Sanctuary (*see* Nature Areas, *below*) runs the **Fern & Feather Day Camp,** with one- or two-week sessions (including campouts) in which children learn about wildlife, plants, and the stars. Early registration is advised and begins in February.

Spinnaker Lanes (State Rd., Vineyard Haven, tel. 508/693–9691) offers 12 lanes of candlepin bowling and six tournament pool tables. Lanes are disabled-accessible.

Off the Beaten Track

The **Nathan Mayhew Seminars** (167 N. William St., Box 1125, Vineyard Haven 02568, tel. 508/693–6603) offer college-level two-day to seven-week courses in humanities, social science, business, and visual and performing arts year-round, as well as lectures, music and arts events, and workshops. New in 1992 were week-long, live-in Elderhostel academic programs and an accredited associate of arts degree program. The **Henry Beetle Hough Memorial Library,** in the same building (open by appointment only), is a research library on island studies. The basis of the collection is the personal library of the Pulitzer Prize–winning journalist who was editor of the *Vineyard Gazette* from 1920 to 1985.

A memorial to Thomas Mayhew, Jr. — called **Place on the Wayside** — was erected on the Edgartown–West Tisbury Road, just east of the airport entrance, on the opposite side. A plaque identifies the spot where Mayhew had his "last worship and interview with them before embarking for England" in 1657, never to return. (The ship was lost at sea.) Wampanoags passing this spot would leave a stone in Mayhew's memory; the stones were later cemented together to form the memorial.

June through August, the **State Lobster Hatchery** (end of Shirley Ave. on Lagoon Pond, Oak Bluffs, tel. 508/693–0060) allows weekday tours of its visitor room, with hatching and rearing tanks and wall displays. The hatchery stocks all of coastal Massachusetts and conducts research on marine life.

Martha's Vineyard Shellfish Group (tel. 508/693–0391) grows seed clams, scallops, and oysters to stock lagoons and beds throughout the county. From spring through fall, tours of the solar shellfish hatchery on Lagoon Pond in Vineyard Haven can be arranged with advance notice.

Chappaquiddick Island, reached by ferry from Edgartown (*see* Getting Around by Ferry, *above*) or by oversand vehicle from South Beach, is a sparsely populated area with a number of nature preserves, among them Cape Poge Wildlife Refuge, Wasque Reservation, and Mytoi Japanese gardens (*see* Nature Areas, *below*).

Shopping

A specialty of the island is wampum — black, white, or purple beads made from shells that are fashioned into jewelry — sold at the cliffs and elsewhere. Antique and new scrimshaw jewelry and the ultra-expensive, sometimes scrimshaw-topped pocketbooks called Nantucket lightship baskets can be found at many island shops. Many Vineyard shops close for the winter, though quite a few in Vineyard Haven and a few elsewhere remain open; call to make sure a shop is open before making a special trip.

Shopping Districts The three main towns have the largest concentrations of shops. Most of Vineyard Haven's line Main Street. Edgartown's, the toniest, are clustered together within a few blocks of the dock, on Main, Summer, and Water streets. Primarily fun, casual clothing and gift shops line Circuit Avenue in Oak Bluffs. At Gay Head Cliffs, you'll find touristy Native American crafts and souvenirs in season.

Shopping **Tisbury Marketplace,** on Beach Road between Oak Bluffs
Complexes and Vineyard Haven across from the Mobil station, has crafts and gift shops, a toy store, a music store, a sporting-goods shop, and a pizza parlor. In Edgartown, the **Colonial Inn Shops** (38 N. Water St.) sell art, crafts, and sports gear; the adjacent **Nevin Square** (Winter St.) has leather, clothing, art, antiques, and crafts. **Crispin's Landing** in Vineyard Haven (Main St.) has shops selling leather, pottery, jewelry, and crafts.

Department Store **The Fligors** (27 N. Water St., Edgartown, tel. 508/627–8811) is the closest thing to a department store on the island, with varied offerings, including preppy clothing and a bargain basement.

Food and Flea   A **flea market** is held on the grounds of the Chilmark Com-
Markets   munity Church (Menemsha Cross Rd., tel. 508/645–3177)
Wednesday and Saturday in season from about 7 AM until
2:30 or 3 PM.

Farmers markets — offering fresh flowers, plants, fruits
and vegetables, homemade baked goods and jams, honey,
and fun — are held at the Agricultural Hall (tel. 508/693–
9549) on South Road in West Tisbury mid-June–mid-October on Saturday from 9 to noon, and at Up-Island Cronig's
on State Road in West Tisbury July–mid-September on
Thursdays 3:30–6.

Specialty Stores   **All Things Oriental** (Beach Rd., Vineyard Haven, tel.
Antiques   508/693–0190) has jewelry, porcelains, paintings, furniture,
and more.
Bramhall & Dunn (Main St., Vineyard Haven, tel. 508/693–
6437; Red Barn Emporium, Old County Rd., West Tisbury,
tel. 508/693–5221, antiques only) carries stripped 19th-
century English country pine furniture, as well as fine
crafts, linens, and housewares.
C. W. Morgan Marine Antiques (Beach Rd., Vineyard
Haven, next to MV Shipyard, tel. 508/693–3622) offers a
wide range of museum-quality nautical items (instruments,
sea chests, ship models, paintings, prints, and so forth).
Soulagnet Collection (Colonial Inn Shops, Edgartown, tel.
508/627–7759; Basin Rd., Menemsha, tel. 508/645–3735) has
Americana, including furniture, folk art, and crafts, as well
as local photographs and prints, educational gifts for children, and a garden center.

Art   **Edgartown Art Gallery** (27 S. Summer St., Edgartown, tel.
508/627–5991), in the Charlotte Inn, has 19th- and 20th-cen-
tury oils and watercolors, including English sporting prints,
marine art, and works by major local artists, plus small
English antiques.
Goff's Gallery & Book Store (State Rd., North Tisbury, tel.
508/693–4484) sells books by Vineyard writers, Clark Goff's
New England–theme prints and notepapers, Heather
Goff's painted pottery (including her signature plates with
farmscapes, cows, and other Vineyard scenes), Ingrid
Goff's jewelry, and yarn from Vineyard sheep — a complete
island and family enterprise.
Granary Gallery (Red Barn Emporium, Old County Rd.,
West Tisbury, tel. 508/693–0455 or 800/GRANARY) showcases mostly representational paintings, as well as sculptures, by island and international artists, including the
photographs of Alfred Eisenstaedt. Weekly shows spot-
lighting a local artist are preceded by Sunday-evening receptions.
Hermine Merel Smith Gallery (Edgartown Rd., West Tisbury, tel. 508/693–7719) specializes in paintings and draw-
ings by contemporary American impressionists.

Books   The **Bunch of Grapes Bookstore** (Main St., Vineyard Haven,
tel. 508/693–2291) and **Bickerton & Ripley Books** (Main St.,
Edgartown, tel. 508/627–8463) carry a wide selection of new

books, including many island-related titles, and sponsor book signings — watch the papers for announcements.

Book Den East (New York Ave., Oak Bluffs, tel. 508/693–3946) has 20,000 out-of-print, antiquarian, and paperback books housed in an old barn.

Clothing **Bramhall & Dunn** (*see* Antiques, *above*) in Vineyard Haven carries fine hand-knit sweaters and original women's accessories and shoes.

Island Children (Main St., Vineyard Haven, tel. 508/693–6130) has children's and women's clothing in 100% cotton, hand-block-printed with unique African- and Caribbean-inspired designs.

Lakota (66 Main St., Vineyard Haven, tel. 508/693–9044) has sophisticated, upscale women's dresses (some with a summery island feel), suits, and blouses in natural fibers, all designed by Lorraine Parrish (who, incidentally, designed Carly Simon's wedding dress); some clothing uses fabrics designed by island designers.

Laughing Bear (138 Circuit Ave., Oak Bluffs, tel. 508/693–9342) has fun children's and women's wear made of Balinese or Indian batiks and other unusual materials.

Murray's of the Vineyard (Main St., Vineyard Haven, tel. 508/693–2640), sister shop of Nantucket's Murray's Toggery, has classic men's and women's fashions, shoes, and accessories, from names such as Ralph Lauren and Liz Claiborne.

Nature Knits (Tisbury Marketplace, Beach Rd., Vineyard Haven, tel. 508/693–7776) sells natural-fiber clothing for children, as well as adult and maternity items.

Crafts **Chilmark Pottery** (off State Rd., West Tisbury, tel. 508/693–7874; Crispin's Landing, Main St., Vineyard Haven) is a workshop and gallery of hand-formed stoneware, porcelain, and Raku by Geoffrey Borr and other island potters.

Edgartown Scrimshaw (Main St., tel. 508/627–9439) carries a large collection of scrimshaw, including some antique pieces, as well as Nantucket lightship baskets and jewelry.

Michaela Ltd. Gallery of American Crafts (Towanticut Ave., Oak Bluffs, tel. 508/693–8408) has pottery, blown glass, jewelry, soaps, candles, baskets, woven goods, and more.

Indian & Mexican Crafts (128 Circuit Ave., Oak Bluffs, tel. 508/693–4040) has shells; Native American beadwork and wampum jewelry; imports from Africa (masks, Kenyan cloth, Zulu beadwork, malachite); and colorful Colombian *retalbo,* wood-and-ceramic shadowboxes with doors that open to reveal little people.

Gifts **Black Dog Bakery** (*see* Tour 1: Vineyard Haven, *above*) sells T-shirts, sweatshirts, beach towels, and many other gift items, all emblazoned with the signature Black Dog logo.

Chilmark Chocolates (State Rd., near Beetlebung Corner, tel. 508/645–3013) sells superior chocolates and buttercrunch that you can sometimes watch being made in the back room.

The Secret Garden (148 Circuit Ave., Oak Bluffs, tel. 508/693–4759), set in a yellow gingerbread cottage, has linens, lace, baby gifts, wicker furniture, prints, and more.

Tashtego (29 Main St., Edgartown, tel. 508/627–4300) is one of the island's most interesting shops, with small antiques, island crafts, and home furnishings.

At **Vineyard Photo Emporium** (Circuit Ave., Oak Bluffs, tel. 508/693–6435), you can have your picture taken in costume before exotic backdrops; inexpensive sepia prints make fun gifts.

Jewelry **Optional Art** (35 Winter St., Edgartown, tel. 508/627–5373) sells fine jewelry in 18-karat gold handcrafted by 30 award-winning American artisans.

Sioux Eagle Designs (Crispin's Landing, Main St., Vineyard Haven, tel. 508/693–6537) offers unusual handmade pieces.

Vivian Wolfe & Co. (Main St., Edgartown, tel. 508/627–5822) has antique and estate jewelry, as well as antique silver tea services, and so forth.

Sporting Goods **Brickman's** (Main St., Vineyard Haven, tel. 508/693–0047; Main St., Edgartown, tel. 508/627–4700) sells beach and sports gear, such as camping, fishing, snorkeling equipment and boogie boards; also sportswear and surfer-type clothing.

Wind's Up! (Tisbury Market Place, Beach Rd., Vineyard Haven, tel. 508/693–4340) sells swimwear, windsurfing and sailing equipment, and other outdoor gear.

Sports and the Outdoors

Edgartown Recreation Area (Robinson Rd., tel. 508/627–9726) has four tennis courts, a basketball court, a softball field, a roller hockey court, a picnic area, and playground equipment. All areas are lighted some nights in summer. Activities (published in the papers) include tennis round-robins; softball, soccer, and basketball games; arts and crafts; and rainy-day events. Also see the "Island Recreation" section of *The Vineyard Gazette*'s calendar for open Frisbee, rugby, and other games.

Bicycling There are paved paths along the coast road from Oak Bluffs to Edgartown, inland from Vineyard Haven to Edgartown, and from Edgartown to South Beach. These connect with scenic paths that weave through the State Forest. For information on unofficial group rides, call Cycleworks (tel. 508/693–6966). For bike rentals, *see* Getting Around by Bicycle and Moped, *above*.

The biggest race of the year is the **Tour of Martha's Vineyard** (tel. 508/693–1656), held on Tivoli Day in September, and beginning and ending in Oak Bluffs. The 60-mile race attracts contestants from all over the world.

Fishing Huge trawlers unload their catch daily at the docks in Vineyard Haven and Menemsha, attesting to the richness of the waters surrounding the island. One of the most popular spots for sport fishermen is **Wasque Point** (*see* Nature Areas, *below*) on Chappaquiddick. Another is **South Beach** (*see* Beaches, *below*) and the jetty at the mouth of the **Menemsha Basin.** Striped bass and bluefish are island stars.

The annual **Martha's Vineyard Striped Bass & Bluefish Derby** (Box 2101, Edgartown 02539, tel. 508/627–8342), from mid-September to mid-October, offers daily, weekly, and derby prizes in four categories, for bluefish, bonito, and false albacore catches, from boat or shore.

Pick up the current listing of fishing regulations at **Larry's Tackle Shop** (25 Dock St., Edgartown, tel. 508/627–5088), **Coop's Bait and Tackle** (147 West Tisbury Rd., Edgartown, tel. 508/627–3909), and **Dick's Bait and Tackle** (New York Ave., Oak Bluffs, tel. 508/693–7669). All rent gear and sell accessories and bait.

The party boat *Skipper* (tel. 508/693–1238) leaves out of Oak Bluffs Harbor in season. Several outfits offer fishing charters, including **North Shore Charters** (Menemsha, tel. 508/645–2993), **Big Eye Charters** (Edgartown, tel. 508/627–3649), and the *Slapshot II* (Edgartown, tel. 508/627–8087).

Golf **Farm Neck Golf Club** (Farm Neck Rd., Oak Bluffs, tel. 508/693–3057), a semiprivate club on Sengekontacket Pond, has 18 holes in a championship layout, plus a driving range. The public **Mink Meadows Golf Course** (Golf Club Rd., off Franklin St., Vineyard Haven, tel. 508/693–0600), on West Chop, has nine holes and ocean views.

Health and Fitness Clubs **Health Club at the Tisbury Inn** (Main St., Vineyard Haven, tel. 508/693–7400) has Lifecycle, Nautilus, Universal, NordicTrak, turbo-rower, and stair machines, plus bikes, a free-weight room, an indoor lap pool, a sauna, a hot tub, tanning, aerobics classes, and baby-sitting.

Vineyard Racquet & Fitness Center (12 Mariner's Way, off Vineyard Haven Rd., Edgartown, tel. 508/627–7760) has Nautilus, Universal, Lifecycle, and StairMaster machines; treadmills and Concept II rowers; free weights; sauna and steam room; two racquetball courts; aerobics and body-conditioning classes; tanning; personal trainers; massage; and day care.

Hiking The nature preserves and conservation areas (*see* Nature Areas, *below*) are laced with well-marked, scenic trails through varied terrains and ecological habitats. The miles of uninterrupted beaches are perfect for long walks.

Horseback Riding **Arrowhead Farm** (Indian Hill Rd., West Tisbury, tel. 508/693–8831) offers lessons for adults and children year-round, as well as children's summer horsemanship programs. The farm has an indoor ring and leases horses out but does not offer trail rides. **Martha's Vineyard Riding Center** (across from the airport, off the Edgartown Rd., West Tisbury, tel. 508/693–3770) offers English and Western riding lessons; it also has indoor and outdoor rings, a hunt course, and beach and other scenic trails. Dawn, sunset, and moonlight rides are available. **Misty Meadows Horse Farm** (Old County Rd., West Tisbury, tel. 508/693–1870) has a large indoor riding area and offers trail rides and lessons. At any stable, be sure to call ahead to reserve. The **State Forest** (*see* Nature Areas, *below*) has horse trails through it.

Ice-skating **Martha's Vineyard Ice Arena** (Edgartown–Vineyard Haven Rd., Oak Bluffs, tel. 508/693–4438) is open in the off-season.

Jogging The **State Forest** (*see* Nature Areas, *below*) has a 2-mile par-course adjacent to the high school.

Sailing and The **Harborside Inn** in Edgartown (S. Water St., tel.
Boating 508/627–4321 or 800/627–4009) rents O'Day 17s, Hobie Cats, and Boston Whalers. **Wind's Up!** (Beach Rd., Vineyard Haven, by Lagoon Pond, tel. 508/693–4252) rents day sailers, catamarans, and Sunfish, as well as Windsurfers and boogie boards. Both provide instruction. **Vineyard Boat Rentals** (Dockside Marketplace, Oak Bluffs Harbor, tel. 508/693–8476) rents Boston Whalers, Bayliners, and Jet Skis. For chartered cruises, *see* Guided Tours, *above*.

Scuba-diving Vineyard waters hold a number of sunken ships, including several schooners and freighters off East Chop. **Vineyard Scuba** (5 Circuit Ave., Oak Bluffs, tel. 508/693–0288) has diving information and equipment rental.

Shellfishing Each town issues shellfish licenses for the waters under its jurisdiction. Contact the town hall of the town in which you wish to fish for a permit, as well as information on good spots and a listing of areas closed because of seeding projects or contamination: **Chilmark** (tel. 508/645–2651), **Edgartown** (tel. 508/627–6180), **Gay Head** (tel. 508/645–9915), **Oak Bluffs** (tel. 508/693–5511), **Vineyard Haven** (tel. 508/696–4200), and **West Tisbury** (tel. 508/693–9659).

Tennis Tennis is very popular on the island, and at all times reservations are strongly recommended. Public courts (reserve court with the attendant the previous day) are on Church Street in Vineyard Haven (clay courts; in season only; fee), in Niantic Park in Oak Bluffs, on Robinson Road in Edgartown, and at the grammar school on Old County Road in West Tisbury (all hard surface; open year-round; fee in season).

Farm Neck Tennis Club (County Rd., Oak Bluffs, tel. 508/693–9728; open mid-Apr.–mid-Nov.) is a semiprivate club with four clay courts and a pro shop. **Island Country Club** (Beach Rd., Oak Bluffs, tel. 508/693–6574; open May–Columbus Day) has three Har-Tru courts and a pro shop.

Water Sports Martha's Vineyard is an ideal place for windsurfing. With the many bays and inlets there is always a patch of protected water for the neophyte; the oceanside surf provides plenty of action for the expert. Surfing is good at South Beach and Long Point. Coast Guard–licensed captain **Mark Clarke** (tel. 508/693–2838) offers waterskiing lessons and rides at all skill levels, including pair, slalom, and trick riding. He'll also take you for a spin in an inner tube towed by a pull-rope.

Wind's Up! (*see* Sailing, *above*) provides windsurfing lessons and rentals, plus an invaluable brochure including best locations and safety tips.

In Oak Bluffs, **Vineyard Boat Rentals** (Dockside Marina, tel. 508/693–8476) rents Jet Skis and Boston Whalers, and

Sun 'n' Fun (Lake Ave., tel. 508/693–5457) rents Jetboats, sailboats, and Jet Skis.

Beaches

The beaches on the south shore, on the Atlantic Ocean, offer strong surf. Those on the Nantucket or Vineyard soundside tend to be protected and calmer. Inns sometimes make available to guests a parking sticker for town beaches that are otherwise limited to residents; these restricted beaches are often much less crowded than the popular public beaches, and some, such as Lucy Vincent and Lambert's Cove, are the most beautiful. There are, however, miles of superb public beaches on which a couple minutes' walk will get you a private patch of sand. Surprisingly, beach rest rooms are in short supply.

Public **Bend-in-the-Road Beach,** Edgartown's town beach, is a protected area (marked by floats) adjacent to the state beach, beginning at, appropriately enough, the bend in the road. The beach, backed by low, grassy dunes and wild roses, offers calm, shallow waters, some parking, and lifeguards. It can be reached by bike path or shuttle bus.

East Beach, on Chappaquiddick Island, one of the area's best beaches, is part of the Cape Poge Wildlife Refuge and Wasque Reservation (*see* Nature Areas, *below*). It offers heavy surf, good bird-watching, and relative isolation in a lovely setting, but it is accessible only by boat or Jeep from Wasque.

Joseph A. Sylvia State Beach, between Oak Bluffs and Edgartown, is a mile-long sandy beach with a view of Cape Cod across Nantucket Sound. The calm, warm water and food vendors make it popular with families. There's parking along the roadside, and the beach is accessible by bike path or shuttle bus.

Lake Tashmoo Town Beach, at the end of Herring Creek Road in Vineyard Haven, offers swimming in the warm, relatively shallow brackish lake or in the cooler Vineyard Sound, with gentle waves. There is a lifeguarded area and some parking.

Lobsterville Road Beach is 2 miles of beautiful sandy barrier beach and dune land on the Vineyard Sound in Gay Head. It is a seagull nesting area and a favorite fishing spot. Though the water tends to be cold, the beach is protected and suitable for children. There is no public parking.

Long Point (*see* Nature Areas, *below*) has a beautiful beach on the Atlantic, as well as freshwater and saltwater ponds for swimming, including the brackish Tisbury Great Pond.

Menemsha Public Beach, adjacent to Dutcher's Dock, is a pebbly beach with gentle surf on Vineyard Sound. Located on the western side of the island, it is a great place to catch the sunset. The fishing boats and people angling from the jetty add atmosphere. There are rest rooms and lifeguards, and snack shops and restaurants are just a walk away from the parking lot.

Moshup Beach, in Gay Head, off Moshup Trail, is a Land Bank property offering surf and sand backed by low grasses. At the cliffs are food shops and rest rooms. From the parking lot, signs lead along a boardwalk path to the beach, a five-minute walk away; there's a drop-off point at the edge of the beach. Heading to the right along the shore, you can walk eventually to the beach below the cliffs, but PLEASE, *do not climb them!* The cliffs are eroding much too quickly even without the added stress of human erosion tactics; it's also against the law.

Oak Bluffs Town Beach, between the steamship dock and the state beach, is a crowded, narrow stretch of calm water on Nantucket Sound, with snack joints, lifeguards, parking, and rest rooms at the steamship office.

Owen Park Beach, a small, sandy harbor beach off Main Street in Vineyard Haven, is a convenient spot, with a children's play area, lifeguards, and a harbor view.

South Beach (aka Katama Beach), the island's largest and most popular, is a 3-mile ribbon of sand on the Atlantic, with strong surf and sometimes riptides (check with the lifeguards before swimming). From Edgartown, take the bike path to Katama or catch the trolley. There is limited parking. The beach is a good spot for expert windsurfers and for body surfers. Activities such as sand-castle-building contests and nature walks are held on the beach throughout the summer.

Uncle Seth's Pond is a freshwater pond on Lambert's Cove Road in West Tisbury, with a small beach area right off the road.

Wasque Beach, at the Wasque Reservation on Chappaquiddick (*see* Nature Areas, *below*), is an uncrowded ½-mile sandy beach with sometimes strong surf and current, a parking lot, and rest rooms.

Restricted **Lambert's Cove Beach** (West Tisbury), one of the island's prettiest, has fine sand and very clear water. On the Vineyard Sound side, it has calm waters good for children and views of the Elizabeth Islands.

Lobsterville Beach, off Lobsterville Road in Gay Head, is a shallow, calm, sandy beach on Menemsha Pond with resident-only parking and an attractive setting.

Lucy Vincent Beach (Chilmark), on the south shore, is a very beautiful, wide strand of fine sand and surf backed by high clay bluffs. Keep walking to the left for the unofficial nude beach.

Squibnocket Beach (Chilmark), on the south shore, offers an appealing boulder-strewn coastline; a narrow beach that is part smooth rocks and pebbles, part fine sand; and gentle waves.

Nature Areas

Several of the island's nature areas offer bird walks, special kids' programs, and a schedule of events (listed in the newspapers year-round; also in the *Best Read Guide,* available free in shops and hotels, in season). All have nature trails. A free map to the islands' conservation lands, including detailed directions, parking information, and usages permitted, is available from the Martha's Vineyard Land Bank (167 Main St., Edgartown 02539, tel. 508/627-7141).

Cape Poge Wildlife Refuge and Wasque Reservation on Chappaquiddick Island is 509 acres of refuge and 200 adjacent acres of reservation. This wilderness of dunes, woods, moors, salt marshes, ponds, tidal flats, and barrier beach is an important migration stopover or nesting area for many sea and shore birds. There's excellent surfcasting at Wasque (pronounced "WAYCE-qwee") Point and a special parking lot with easy access (ask the attendant at the gate for directions to the fishermen's lot). Much of the area is accessible only by four-wheel-drive vehicles with a $50–$75 annual Trustees of Reservations beach permit, available on site or through Coop's Bait & Tackle (147 West Tisbury Rd., Edgartown, tel. 508/627-3909). Natural-history Jeep tours of Cape Poge are available (tel. 508/627-3599). Access was once via the Dyke Bridge — infamous as the scene of the 1969 accident in which a young woman was killed in a car driven by Edward M. Kennedy — but the rickety bridge was dismantled in 1991. Until it is replaced, the only way to Cape Poge and its lighthouse is by boat or via the Wasque Reservation (it's 4½ miles from Wasque Point to the cape). You can also walk or drive over from South Beach across Katama Bay to Chappy (it's a 2¾-mile killer walk). The beautiful East Beach is here, as is Wasque Beach (*see* Beaches, *above*), just west of the dangerous currents around Wasque Point. There's parking by Wasque Beach and Wasque Point; scenic walkways lead to the beach. *Take the Chappy ferry (see Getting Around, above), then follow the main road to the end; from there a ¾-mi dirt road leads to gatehouse. Tel. 508/627-7260. Admission: $3 cars, $3 adults over 15 mid-June–Labor Day; free rest of year. Property open 24 hrs; gatehouse open mid-June–Columbus Day, daily 9–5.*

Cedar Tree Neck, 300 hilly acres of unspoiled West Tisbury woods managed by the Sheriffs Meadow Foundation, offers varied environments, rich wildlife, freshwater ponds, brooks, low stone walls, and wooded trails ending at a stony but secluded North Shore beach (swimming, picnicking, and fishing prohibited). *Indian Hill Rd. (off State Rd.) for 2 mi, then right 1 mi down steep, rocky dirt road to parking lot. Tel. 508/693-5207. Admission free. Open daily 8:30–5:30.*

Felix Neck Wildlife Sanctuary, 3 miles out of Edgartown, has 350 acres, including 6 miles of hiking trails traversing marshland, fields, oak woods, seashore, a pond with a large variety of wildfowl, and a reptile pond. Affiliated with the Massachusetts Audubon Society (members admitted free), it offers a full schedule of events throughout the year, including sunset hikes along the beach, exploration of salt marsh, stargazing, snake or bird walks, snorkeling, and more, all led by trained naturalists. An exhibit center has aquariums, snake cages, and a gift shop. *Off Edgartown–Vineyard Haven Rd., tel. 508/627–4850. Admission: $2 adults, $1 children under 13 and senior citizens. Open June–Oct., daily 8–4; Nov.– May, Tues.–Sun. 8–4.*

Long Point, a 633-acre Trustees of Reservations preserve, is an open grassland area bounded on the east by the freshwater Homer's Pond; on the west by the saltwater West Tisbury Great Pond, and on the south by the Atlantic Ocean. Dense heathland of bayberry, rugosa rose, and goldenrod give way to the beach grass of vast dune, ending at a mile of South Beach, with swimming, surf fishing, and picnicking. Tisbury Great Pond and Long Cove Pond (a sandy freshwater swimming pond) are ideal spots for duck- and birdwatchers. *Mid-June–mid-Sept., turn left onto the unmarked dirt road (Waldron's Bottom Rd., look for mailboxes) ³/₁₀ mi west of airport on Edgartown–West Tisbury Rd.; at end, follow signs to Long Point parking lot. Mid-Sept.–mid-June, follow unpaved Deep Bottom Rd. (1 mi west of airport) for 2 mi to lot. Tel. 508/693–7392. Admission: $6 per vehicle, $3 adults over 15 mid-June–mid-Sept.; free rest of year. Open daily 10–6.*

Manuel F. Correllus State Forest. At the center of the island is a 4,000-acre forest of pine and scrub oak laced with hiking trails and circled with a paved bike trail (mopeds are prohibited). Also here is a 2-mile nature trail, a 2-mile parcourse, and horse trails. *Headquarters on Barnes Rd., between Edgartown–Vineyard Haven Rd. and Edgartown–West Tisbury Rd., tel. 508/693–2540. Admission free. Open daily sunrise–sunset.*

Menemsha Hills Reservation. Opened to the public in 1991, this 210-acre property includes a mile of rocky shoreline and high sand bluffs along Vineyard Sound; excellent views of the Elizabeth Islands and beyond; hilly walking trails through scrub oak and heathland, with interpretive signs at viewpoints; and Prospect Hill, the island's highest at 309 feet. *Off North Rd., Chilmark, 1 mi east of Menemsha Cross Rd., tel. 508/693–7662. Call ahead about naturalist-led tours. Admission free. Open daily sunrise–sunset.*

Mytoi. Though 1991's Hurricane Bob wiped out 60% of the trees and 50% of the flowers and shrubs in this 14-acre Japanese park on Chappaquiddick, a five- year replanting plan is already under way. First on the replacement list were Japanese maples, rhododendrons, and Japanese azaleas. Mytoi is still a tranquil sanctuary, with grassy hillsides sweeping down to a pool with goldfish, spanned by a bridge. Adjacent walking trails lead to a salt marsh with views to the barrier beach. *From ferry landing, follow paved road to sharp bend, then take dirt Dyke Rd. for ¹/₄ mi and look for sign. Tel. 508/693–7662. Admission free. Open daily sunrise–sunset.*

Sepiessa Point. This new Land Bank property, 164 acres on Tisbury Great Pond, offers expansive pond and ocean views, walking trails and bird-watching around fresh- and saltwater marshes, horse trails, and swimming and boating. *1.2 mi on right down Tiah's Cove Rd., off West Tisbury Rd., West Tisbury, tel. 508/627–7141. Admission free. Open daily sunrise–sunset.*

Waskosim's Rock Reservation. Purchased by the Land Bank in 1990, this 145-acre preserve (and hundreds of adjoining acres to which access has been granted by neighbors) is a unique property comprising very diverse habitats, from wetlands to open fields to oak and beetlebung woods. Also on the property are the ruins of an 18th-century homestead. The rock itself — deposited by the retreating glacier and said to resemble the head of a breaching whale — is on a high ridge above the Mill Brook Valley, from which there is a spectacular panorama of 1,000 acres of protected land; in the distance, the Atlantic can sometimes be seen. A map to a 3-mile walking trail is available at the trailhead. *Parking areas are in Chilmark: on North Rd. or off Tea La., a rough dirt road. Tel. 508/627–7141. Admission free. Open daily sunrise–sunset.*

Dining

The focus of island cuisine is seafood fresh from the surrounding waters, though you will find Mexican, Chinese, and other more exotic cuisines. Dining out here is not the highly developed, gourmet experience it is on Nantucket, but a few establishments do offer sophisticated cooking in equally sophisticated settings.

Note: Only Edgartown and Oak Bluffs allow the sale of liquor. In the "dry" towns, restaurants are glad to provide setups for patrons' bottles.

Box or picnic lunches are provided by **Vineyard Gourmet** (Main St., Vineyard Haven, tel. 508/693–5181) and **Savoir Faire** (14 Church St., Edgartown, tel. 508/627–9864). **Bill Smith** (tel. 508/627–8809 or 800/828–6936) and **New England Clambake Co.** (tel. 508/627–7462) prepare clambakes to go.

Category	Cost*
Very Expensive	over $40
Expensive	$25–$40
Moderate	$15–$25
Inexpensive	under $15

*per person, excluding drinks, service, and 5% tax

Edgartown

Very Expensive ★ **L'étoile.** The Charlotte Inn's restaurant is set in a glass-wrapped summerhouse, with a flagstone floor and a skylight-punctuated peaked roof. An open, airy room with lots of white and lots of greenery — hanging ferns, citrus trees in big clay pots — it has the civilizing influence of liberally caviar cream, or filet mignon with béarnaise sauce and sun-dried tomatoes. Soft music from a white piano, along with two window walls to catch memorable sunsets, make this a romantic setting for a special evening out. A $25 early-evening menu is available. *North Rd., tel. 508/645-9454. Reservations required. Dress: casual. AE, D, MC, V. BYOB. Breakfast and dinner only. Closed Nov.-Apr.*

Moderate   **Home Port.** Here you'll find very fresh fish and seafood (the
★   specialties are lobsters and swordfish) simply baked, broiled, or fried, served in four-course prix fixe menus ($15–$26) that include hot little loaves of bread. The decor, too, is no-nonsense, with plain wood tables and a family atmos-phere; window walls overlooking the harbor provide more than enough visual pleasure at sunset. The wait for a table is often very long; take a seat outside and order from the raw bar or the takeout menu, or use the time to wander around the fishing village. *North Rd., tel. 508/645-2679. Reservations required. Dress: casual. AE, MC, V. BYOB. Dinner only. Closed Nov.-Apr.*

Oak Bluffs

Expensive–   **Oyster Bar.** Subtitled "An American Bistro," the Oyster Bar
Very Expensive   (named for its 35-foot mahogany raw bar) has a sophisti-
★   cated art-deco look in white and pink, with a high embossed-tin ceiling, faux-marble and fluted columns, tropical greenery on Ionic-column pedestals, and a line of pink neon along the walls. Though the extensive menu includes pastas, pizzas, hearty soups, and specials, the stars are the many varieties of fish available each night — local catch as well as exotics like mahimahi — cooked any way you like: broiled, sautéed, grilled, steamed, *wasabi*-glazed, blackened, au poivre. Specials may include gumbo filé with duck and shrimp; quail and polenta; or grilled muscovy duck breast with spaetzle and a dried cranberry sauce. *162 Circuit Ave., tel. 508/693-3300. Reservations strongly advised. Dress: casual. MC, V. Dinner only. Closed mid-Oct.–mid-May; Tues. and Wed. in May and Oct.*

Moderate–   **David's Island House.** Northern Italian risottos, lots of pas-
Expensive   tas, and Polynesian or other exotic dishes supplement a full traditional menu. Pianist David Crohan owns the place and entertains most evenings with dinner music from classical to contemporary. The decor is island casual and New Eng-landy, with a fun mix of antique tables. The lounge is a civi-lized spot for drinks, a light menu, and conversation. *118–120 Circuit Ave., tel. 508/693-4516. Reservations required for 6 or more. Dress: casual. MC, V. Closed Labor Day–Memorial Day.*

Moderate   **Zapotec.** Warm tortilla chips and coriander-scented salsa accompany authentic and creative regional Mexican dishes at this little place with heart and style; top choices include the lobster quesadilla or the grilled catch of the day, served perhaps with a fiery fruit salsa and pumpkin-seed tamales. Tag sales supplied the decor, all vaguely Mexican (like the used piñata) or just fun (like the EARTH 1 and EARTH 2 license plates). The outdoor porch, lighted by red and green caviar cream, or filet mignon with béarnaise sauce and sun-dried tomatoes. Soft music from a white piano, along with two window walls to catch memorable sunsets, make this a romantic setting for a special evening out. A $25 early-evening menu is available. *North Rd., tel. 508/645-9454. Reservations required. Dress: casual. AE, D, MC, V. BYOB. Breakfast and dinner only. Closed Nov.-Apr.*

Moderate ★ **Home Port.** Here you'll find very fresh fish and seafood (the specialties are lobsters and swordfish) simply baked, broiled, or fried, served in four-course prix fixe menus ($15–$26) that include hot little loaves of bread. The decor, too, is no-nonsense, with plain wood tables and a family atmosphere; window walls overlooking the harbor provide more than enough visual pleasure at sunset. The wait for a table is often very long; take a seat outside and order from the raw bar or the takeout menu, or use the time to wander around the fishing village. *North Rd., tel. 508/645-2679. Reservations required. Dress: casual. AE, MC, V. BYOB. Dinner only. Closed Nov.-Apr.*

Oak Bluffs

Expensive–Very Expensive ★ **Oyster Bar.** Subtitled "An American Bistro," the Oyster Bar (named for its 35-foot mahogany raw bar) has a sophisticated art-deco look in white and pink, with a high embossed-tin ceiling, faux-marble and fluted columns, tropical greenery on Ionic-column pedestals, and a line of pink neon along the walls. Though the extensive menu includes pastas, pizzas, hearty soups, and specials, the stars are the many varieties of fish available each night — local catch as well as exotics like mahimahi — cooked any way you like: broiled, sautéed, grilled, steamed, *wasabi*-glazed, blackened, au poivre. Specials may include gumbo filé with duck and shrimp; quail and polenta; or grilled muscovy duck breast with spaetzle and a dried cranberry sauce. *162 Circuit Ave., tel. 508/693-3300. Reservations strongly advised. Dress: casual. MC, V. Dinner only. Closed mid-Oct.-mid-May; Tues. and Wed. in May and Oct.*

Moderate–Expensive **David's Island House.** Northern Italian risottos, lots of pastas, and Polynesian or other exotic dishes supplement a full traditional menu. Pianist David Crohan owns the place and entertains most evenings with dinner music from classical to contemporary. The decor is island casual and New Englandy, with a fun mix of antique tables. The lounge is a civilized spot for drinks, a light menu, and conversation. *118-120 Circuit Ave., tel. 508/693-4516. Reservations required for 6 or more. Dress: casual. MC, V. Closed Labor Day-Memorial Day.*

Moderate **Zapotec.** Warm tortilla chips and coriander-scented salsa accompany authentic and creative regional Mexican dishes at this little place with heart and style; top choices include the lobster quesadilla or the grilled catch of the day, served perhaps with a fiery fruit salsa and pumpkin-seed tamales. Tag sales supplied the decor, all vaguely Mexican (like the used piñata) or just fun (like the EARTH 1 and EARTH 2 license plates). The outdoor porch, lighted by red and green

Christmas lights in the shape of chile peppers, is more intimate, even romantic. *10 Kennebec Ave., tel. 508/693–6800. No
reservations. Dress: casual. With $5 surcharge, AE, MC, V.
Dinner only. Closed Thanksgiving–Easter; Mon.–Tues. in
shoulder seasons.*

Inexpensive–
Moderate
★
Giordano's. Bountiful portions of simply prepared Italian
food (pizzas, pastas, cacciatores, cutlets) and fried fish and
seafood at excellent prices keep Giordano's — run by the
Giordano family since 1930 — a family favorite. Several different children's meals are available for about $5 (including
milk and Jell-O). The ambience suits the clientele: hearty,
noisy, and cheerful, with sturdy booths, bright green-topped
wood tables, and hanging greenery. Lines often wrap
around the corner. *107 Circuit Ave., tel. 508/693–0184. No reservations. Dress: casual. No credit cards. Closed late Sept.–
early June.*

Linda Jean's. For quick and easy American classics such as
meat loaf, fish-and-chips, and baked chicken, try this homey,
diner-style eatery in the middle of the action. It opens at 6
AM for hearty breakfasts. *34 Circuit Ave., tel. 508/693–4093.
No reservations. Dress: casual. No credit cards.*

Vineyard Haven

Expensive–
Very Expensive
Le Grenier. At this classic French restaurant, owner/chef
Jean Dupon from Lyons offers a menu of more than 20 entrées, such as quail flamed with cognac and grapes, maigret
of duck in crème cassis, and poached salmon with cream of
leeks. The *feuilleté d'escargot* appetizer is a puff pastry filled
with a sauté of escargots, shallots, lemon juice, tarragon,
and more, flamed with cognac and combined with garlic butter and heavy cream. Delectable desserts include dark-
chocolate mousse cake and crème caramel. The look of this
second-floor restaurant, entered through a green lattice, is
a mix of garret (*grenier* means "loft" or "granary") and garden room. The exposed slats and beams of the slanted ceiling are painted light green, as are the walls; tables are
romantically set with green and pink linens, candles in hurricane globes, and flowers in cut-glass vases. In the popular
screened porch, painted vine tendrils climb posts to the roof.
The owners also operate the Patisserie Française downstairs, offering breakfast, lunch, and fresh pastry. *Upper
Main St., tel. 508/693–4906. Reservations strongly advised.
Dress: casual. AE, MC, V. BYOB. Dinner only. Closed Jan. and
Feb.*

Moderate–
Expensive
Black Dog Tavern. An island landmark, the harborside
Black Dog serves basic chowders, pastas, fish, and steak,
along with such dishes as grilled bluefish with avocado salsa,
sirloin tips with aïoli, or shrimp with Thai green curry sauce
(you may have more success with the basics). The Black Dog
Bakery on Water Street provides the little loaves served
with dinner and a large selection of desserts. The glassed-in
porch, lighted by ship's lanterns, overlooks the harbor; the
nautical theme is continued in rustic ship's-planking floors,
photographs of sailing ships, and quarterboards. The wait
for a table is often long; put your name on the list and walk

around the harbor area to pass the time. *Beach Rd. Ext., tel. 508/693–9223. No reservations. Dress: casual. BYOB. AE, D, MC, V.*

West Tisbury

Expensive **Lambert's Cove Country Inn.** The country-inn setting (*see*
★ Lodging, *below*), soft lighting and music, and fine Continental cuisine make this the coziest, most romantic dining spot on the island. The daily selection of entrées may include poached salmon with varied sauces, roast duck breast with cranberry-honey glaze, or herb-crusted veal scaloppine with sun-dried tomato and roast garlic butter. In summer, a lavish Sunday brunch is served on the deck overlooking the orchard. *Off Lambert's Cove Rd., tel. 508/693–2298. Reservations required. Dress: smart casual. AE, MC, V. BYOB. Dinner and Sun. brunch only. Closed weekdays in the off-season.*

Moderate– **Roadhouse.** Good barbecued ribs and chicken are still the
Expensive mainstays, but the menu has been expanded with several daily salads and lots of chargrilled and other seafood, such as smoky grilled lobster with lime butter. A beautiful mahogany counter, made by the owner's boat-builder brother, centers the otherwise simple, bright room with linoleum floor and shiny pine tables (whose wood, incidentally, once graced Fenway Park). Taped blues or jazz plays in the background. *State Rd., North Tisbury, tel. 508/693–9599. Reservations advised for 6 or more. Dress: casual. D, MC, V. BYOB. Closed Columbus Day–Mar.*

Lodging

You can reserve a room at many island establishments by a toll-free direct line at the Woods Hole ferry terminal waiting room year-round. The Chamber of Commerce maintains a listing of availability in the peak tourist season, from mid-June to mid-September. During these months, rates are at their highest and reservations are essential. In the winter, rates go down by as much as 50%.

Martha's Vineyard and Nantucket Reservations (Box 1322, Lagoon Pond Rd., Vineyard Haven 02568, tel. 508/693–7200 or 800/649–5671 in MA), **Accommodations Plus** (RFD 273, Edgartown 02539, tel. 508/627–7374), and **House Guests Cape Cod and the Islands** (Box 1881, Orleans 02653, tel. 800/666–HOST) book cottages, apartments, inns, hotels, and B&Bs. **DestINNations** (tel. 800/333–INNS) handles a limited number of Vineyard hotels and B&Bs but will arrange any and all details of a visit.

An 85-bed, dorm-style **AYH hostel** (Edgartown Rd., West Tisbury 02575, tel. 508/693–2665), near a bike path but 7 miles from the nearest beach, is open April–November.

Martha's Vineyard Family Campground (Box 1557, Edgartown Rd., Vineyard Haven 02568, tel. 508/693–3772), open mid-May–mid-October, has wooded sites, tent-trailer rentals, a rec room, and cable TV hookups. **Webb's Camping**

Area (Barnes Rd., Oak Bluffs [RFD 2, Box 100, Vineyard Haven 02568], tel. 508/693–0233), on 90 acres, is more woodsy and private, with some water-view sites and a store. It is open mid-May–Labor Day. Both take tents and RVs but no pets, and offer bathrooms, showers, laundry facilities, and playgrounds.

For cottages and summer homes, try one of the realtors listed in the chamber of commerce's guidebook, such as **SandcastleRealty** (Box 2488, 256 Edgartown Rd., Edgartown 02539, tel. 508/627–5665 or 800/537–3721) or **Martha's Vineyard Vacation Rentals** (51 Beach Rd., Box 1207, Vineyard Haven 02568, tel. 508/693–7711).

Category	Cost*
Very Expensive	over $200
Expensive	$150–$200
Moderate	$100–$150
Inexpensive	under $100

all prices are for a standard double room in high season, excluding 5.7% state tax and (Down-Island only) 4% local tax

Chilmark

Moderate **Breakfast at Tiasquam.** Set amid acres of peaceful farmland and forest of oak and beech is this B&B, built in 1987 in a contemporary design with 20 skylights, sliding glass doors, and private decks that connect the interior with the natural setting. This is a location for people who want to get away from it all, to bike on country roads, to walk in the woods, or just to lie in the hammocks and read. Lots of comfortable common areas invite mixing. The room decor is spare and soothing, emphasizing fine craftsmanship, as in the woodwork and the baths' hand-thrown ceramic sinks. A few pieces of art adorn the white walls; except for seafoam-green carpeting, earth tones dominate. The "master bedroom" has a two-person Jacuzzi and a wood stove. Breakfast is hearty and varied, served at a handcrafted dining room table. *Off Middle Rd., RR1, Box 296, 02535, tel. 508/645–3685. 8 rooms, 2 with private bath (6 share 3¹/2 baths). Facilities: full breakfast, bikes and car for rent, beach passes, 2 disabled-accessible rooms. No credit cards. No smoking.*

Edgartown

Very Expensive **Charlotte Inn.** From its original structure, the 1865 home of
★ a whaling company owner, the Charlotte (now a Relais & Châteaux member) has grown into a five-building complex of meticulously maintained accommodations and an excellent restaurant, L'étoile (*see* Dining, *above*). Gery Conover, owner for more than 20 years, and his wife, Paula, supervise every detail of the inn, which they have furnished through annual antiquing trips to England. Hallways are hung with original oil paintings and prints; in one, Gery's large collection of antique brass flashlights is displayed in a glass case.

Two rooms in the 18th-century Garden House, with its own fireplaced common room, have porches looking onto a flower-filled English garden. The Summer House has a veranda with wicker chairs and a very large room, No. 14, with a fireplace and a baby grand piano. All guest rooms have down pillows and comforters; some have working fireplaces, TVs, or phones. *27 S. Summer St., 02539, tel. 508/627–4751. 24 rooms, 2 suites. Facilities: Continental breakfast, afternoon tea in summer, restaurant, art gallery, pay phone, common TV. AE, MC, V.*

Mattakesett. This community of individually owned three- or four-bedroom homes and condominiums is within walking distance of South Beach. All units have been recently renovated, are spacious, sleep eight, and have phone, full kitchen with dishwasher, washer/dryer (cable TV available), and decks with or without bay and ocean views; some have whirlpools or wood-burning stoves. The staff provides plenty of service, and the children's program, pool, and barbecue grills add to the definite family atmosphere; some units are more removed from the action. Usually there's a one-week minimum; it's best to book by January 15. *Katama Rd., RFD 270, 02539, tel. 508/627–4432 (off-season, c/o Stanmar Corp., 130 Boston Post Rd., Sudbury, MA 01776, tel. 508/443–1733). 92 units. Facilities: private tennis club with 6 Har-Tru and 2 all-weather courts, heated outdoor pool, swimming lessons, bicycles, aerobics classes, children's program, ferry auto reservations. No credit cards. Closed Columbus Day–Memorial Day.*

Expensive– Very Expensive
Harbor View Hotel. A multimillion-dollar renovation of this historic hotel was completed in 1991, including all-new interiors, landscaping, a new pool, and an elegant water-view dining room with an airy Victorian flavor. The result is a beautiful property with luxurious accommodations, full services, and a great location. The original Victorian architecture of the 1891 gray-shingled main building was maintained, with the addition of a gazebo to the wraparound veranda that looks out across landscaped lawns to the harbor, the lighthouse, and the ocean beyond. Many rooms are spacious and have private decks; town houses have cathedral ceilings, decks, kitchens, and large living areas with sofa beds. All rooms have similar light, period-inspired decor — pastel carpeting and walls, painted wicker, pickled-wood armoires, floral drapes tied with gold braided cord — plus phones, air-conditioning, cable TV with remote control, minifridges, and a wall safe; room VCRs, fax machines, and rooms with kitchenettes or two phones are available. The location is in a residential neighborhood just minutes from town. A beach good for walking stretches ¾ mile from the jetty, from which there's good fishing for blues; children enjoy the sheltered bay. Packages and theme weekends are available. *131 N. Water St., 02539, tel. 508/627–7000 or 800/225–6005, fax 508/627–7845. 124 units. Facilities: 2 all-weather tennis courts, heated outdoor pool, privileges at Farm Neck Golf Club, volleyball, poolside food service, piano lounge, restaurant, gift shop, concierge, room service, no-smoking rooms,*

daily newspaper, laundry service, baby-sitting. Children under 12 stay free. AE, DC, MC, V.

Expensive **Kelley House.** The less pricey sister property of the Harbor View occupies an entire block at the center of town. Renovations completed in 1991 include all-new decor, an odd mix of Early American and country French, with Shaker-inspired furniture and duvets made with island wool. The new concept is to combine services and amenities with a country-inn feel, through complimentary Continental breakfasts, afternoon wine and cheese receptions, and evening cookies and milk. The 1742 white-clapboard main house, originally a tavern, and the Garden House, with most of the inn's rooms, are surrounded by pink roses. The five large suites in the Chappaquiddick House and the two spacious town houses with full kitchens in the Wheel House have porches (most with harbor views) and living rooms. All guest rooms have cable TVs, phones, and air-conditioning. The 1742 pub, with original handhewn timbers and ballast-brick walls restored in 1992, serves light lunches and sandwiches until 10:30 PM; ten beers are on tap. *23 Kelly St., 02539, tel. 508/627–7900 or 800/225–6005, fax 508/627–8142. 52 rooms, 7 suites. Facilities: heated outdoor pool, use of Harbor View's tennis courts, daily newspaper, concierge, no-smoking rooms, laundry service, baby-sitting. AE, DC, MC, V. Closed mid-Oct.–Apr.*

Moderate–Expensive **Harborside Inn.** Right on the harbor, with boat docks at the end of a nicely landscaped lawn, the inn offers a central town location, harborview decks, and lots of amenities. Seven two- or three-story buildings are ranged around a wide lawn with formal rose beds, brick walkways, a brick patio with gas grills and café tables, and a pool. The rooms have colonial-style furnishings (which could use some updating), brass beds and lamps, and light floral wallpapers; each has cable TV/HBO, phone, minifridge, and individual heat and air-conditioning. *3 S. Water St., Box 67, 02539, tel. 508/627–4321 or 800/627–4009. 86 rooms, 3 suites. Facilities: heated outdoor pool, sauna and whirlpool room, recreation room (ping-pong, pool, large color TV/VCR), gas grills, boat rentals, in-room VCR rentals, fax. AE, MC, V.*

Moderate **Colonial Inn.** Part of a busy downtown complex of shops, the inn is hardly a tranquil escape, but if you like your modern conveniences and being at the center of the action, this may be for you. The rooms, renovated in 1990, are pleasantly decorated in pale shades of either mauve and gray-blue or teal and peach, with new white pine furniture, wall-to-wall carpeting, and brass beds and lamps. Each has a good-size bath, cable TV in an armoire, a phone with computer modem port, and air-conditioning; suites have a sofa bed, two TVs, and a minifridge. One common fourth-floor deck (like some rooms) has a superb view of the harbor. *N. Water St., Box 68, 02539, tel. 508/627–4711 or 800/627–4701, fax 508/627–5904. 39 rooms, 2 suites, 1 efficiency. Facilities: restaurant, Continental breakfast, games, fax, beach towels, shops. Children under 16 stay free. AE, MC, V. Closed Jan.–mid-Apr.*

★ **Daggett House.** The flower-bordered lawn that separates the main house from the harbor makes a great retreat after a day of exploring town, a minute away. Breakfast and dinner are served in the 1750 tavern (*see* Dining, *above*), where raised-wood paneling hides a secret staircase (now a private entrance to an upstairs guest room, but the innkeeper may let you peek in if the room is unoccupied). This and two other buildings are decorated with fine wallpapers, antiques, and reproductions; a small new suite has a private roofwalk with a superb water view and a Jacuzzi. *59 N. Water St., Box 1333, 02539, tel. and fax 508/627–4600. 22 rooms, 4 suites with kitchen. Facilities: Continental breakfast, common TV and phones. AE, MC, V.*

Edgartown Commons. Just a block or two from town is this condominium complex of seven buildings, from an old house to motel units around a busy pool. The studios and one- or two-bedroom units all have full kitchens and cable TV/HBO, and some are very spacious. Each has been decorated by its owner, so the decor varies — some have an older look, some are new and bright (like pool units 29 and 30). Definitely family-oriented, the place has lots of kids to keep other kids company; units away from the pool are quieter. *Pease's Point Way, 02539, tel. 508/627–4671. 35 units. Facilities: outdoor pool, playground, shuffleboard, picnic areas with barbecue grills, laundry. AE, MC, V. Closed Nov.–Apr.*

The Victorian Inn. An 1820 whaling captain's home, listed on the National Register of Historic Places, the gingerbread-trimmed Victorian is an easygoing inn furnished with some fine antiques (and a teddy bear in every room). Several of the spacious third-floor rooms, many with comfortable sofas, have balconies with a view of the harbor. Some bathrooms are quite small. In season, the sumptuous gourmet breakfast is served in the garden courtyard. *24 S. Water St., Box 947, 02539, tel. 508/627–4784. 14 rooms. Facilities: full breakfast, central phone. AE, MC, V.*

Gay Head

Very Expensive **Outermost Inn.** In 1990, Hugh and Jeanne Taylor converted
★ the home they built 20 years ago by the Gay Head Cliffs into a bed-and-breakfast. Their design takes full advantage of the superb location: standing alone on acres of moorland, the house is wrapped with windows revealing breathtaking views of sea and sky in three directions. The romantic Lighthouse Suite has a separate entrance and French doors leading onto a private deck with a great view of the Gay Head Lighthouse, adjacent to the property. The decor is simple, with white walls and polished light-wood floors; each room has a phone, and one has a Jacuzzi. Dinners are served two to four nights a week spring through fall and are open to the public. The beach is a 10-minute walk away. Hugh has sailed area waters since childhood and charters out his 33-foot sailboat to guests for excursions to remote beaches or other destinations. *Lighthouse Rd., RR 1, Box 171, 02535, tel. 508/645–3511, fax 508/645–3514. 7 rooms. Facilities: full breakfast, afternoon setups and hors d'oeuvres, beach passes, TVs, box lunches available in season. AE, MC, V.*

Menemsha

Expensive– **Beach Plum Inn and Cottages.** The main draws of this 10-
Very Expensive acre retreat are the woodland setting, the panoramic view
of the ocean and the Menemsha harbor, and the romantic
gourmet restaurant offering spectacular sunsets. Cottages
(one with Jacuzzi) are decorated in casual beach style. Inn
rooms — some with private decks offering great views —
have modern furnishings and small new baths; some are
air-conditioned. MAP rates include breakfast, dinner, and
afternoon cocktails and hors d'oeuvres served on the terrace; EP rates are also available. *North Rd., 02552, tel.
508/645–9454. 5 inn rooms, 3 cottages. Facilities: restaurant,
tennis court, pond for fishing, passes to Chilmark beaches,
twice-daily maid service, baby-sitting, bike rentals. AE, D, MC,
V. Closed Nov.–Apr.*

Moderate **Menemsha Inn and Cottages.** For 40 years *Life* photographer Alfred Eisenstaedt has returned to his cottage on the
hill here for the panoramic view of Vineyard Sound and
Cuttyhunk beyond the trees below. Older cottages with '50s
motel furnishings and plaster and wood-paneled walls, as
well as several cottages newly remodeled in a modern style
with fireplaces and new full kitchens, are nicely spaced on
10 acres and vary in privacy and water views; all have
screened porches. Rooms in the 1989 inn building and suites
in the Carriage House have white walls, blond-wood trim,
plush blue or sea green carpeting, and Appalachian light
pine reproduction furniture. All rooms and suites have private decks, some with water and sunset views; suites have
sitting areas, desks, minifridges, and big tiled baths. *North
Rd., Box 38, 02552, tel. 508/645–2521. 9 rooms, 6 suites, 12 cottages. Facilities: Continental breakfast (inn only), all-weather
tennis court, passes to Chilmark beaches, common phones. No
credit cards. Closed Thanksgiving–Apr.*

Oak Bluffs

Moderate **Oak House.** The wraparound veranda of this pastel-front,
★ 1872 Victorian looks across a busy street to a wide strand of
beach. Several rooms have private terraces, and some have
air-conditioners or TVs; if you're bothered by noise, ask for
a room at the back. The decor centers on well-preserved
woods — some rooms have oak wainscoting from top to bottom — choice antique furniture, and nautical-theme accessories. An afternoon tea with fancy tea cakes baked by the
innkeeper, Betsi, a former pastry chef, is served in a
glassed-in sun porch, with lots of white wicker and plants.
*Sea View Ave., Box 299, 02557, tel. 508/693–4187. 8 rooms, 2
suites. Facilities: Continental breakfast, afternoon tea, pay
phone. D, MC, V. Closed mid-Oct.–mid-May.*

Inexpensive– **Admiral Benbow Inn.** Located on a busy highway between
Moderate Vineyard Haven and Oak Bluffs harbor, the Benbow is a
small, homey B&B. The house, built for a minister at the
turn of the century, features elaborate woodwork, a comfortable hodgepodge of antique furnishings, and a Victorian
parlor with a stunning carved-wood-and-tile fireplace. *520*

New York Ave., Box 2488, 02557, tel. 508/693–6825. 7 rooms. Facilities: full breakfast, afternoon tea, common TV, courtesy phone. No smoking. AE, MC, V.

Martha's Vineyard Surfside Motel. Right in the thick of things (it gets noisy in summer) are these two buildings, the newest built in 1989. Rooms are spacious, bright (corner rooms more so), and well maintained, each with typical motel furnishings, carpeting, table and chairs, individual air-conditioning and heat, color TV, and phone; deluxe rooms have minifridges, remote control, and water views, and two rooms are disabled-accessible. *Oak Bluffs Ave., Box 2507, 02557, tel. 508/693–2500 or 800/537–3007. 35 rooms. AE, D, MC, V.*

Inexpensive **Attleboro House.** This mom-and-pop guest house across from bustling Oak Bluffs harbor is a big 1874 gingerbread Victorian with wraparound verandas on two floors. It offers small, simple rooms, some with sinks, powder-blue walls, lacy white curtains, and a few antiques; singles have three-quarter beds. Linen exchange but no chambermaid service is provided during a stay. The shared baths are rustic and old but clean. *11 Lake Ave., Box 1564, 02557, tel. 508/693–4346. 9 rooms share 4 baths. Facilities: Continental breakfast, common TV and phone. MC, V. Closed Oct.–mid-May.*

★ **Sea Spray Inn.** In 1989, artist and art restorer Rayeanne King converted a porch-wrapped summer house into a B&B that feels like a summer house. It is a quiet spot, situated on a drive circling an open, grassy park; just a minute's walk away is a sandy ocean beach. The decor is simple and restful, highlighted by cheerful splashes of color, including painted furniture and floors. In the Honeymoon Suite (one room), an iron-and-brass bed is positioned for viewing the sunrise through bay windows draped in lacy curtains; the cedar-lined bath includes an extra-large shower. *2 Nashawena Park, Box 2125, 02557, tel. 508/693–9388. 7 rooms (2 with shared bath). Facilities: Continental breakfast, common phone, refrigerator, barbecue grill. MC, V. No smoking. Closed mid-Nov.–mid-Apr.*

Vineyard Haven

Moderate– **Thorncroft Inn.** Set on 3½ acres of woods about a mile from
Expensive the ferry, the main inn, a 1918 Craftsman bungalow, has
★ been renovated from top to bottom. Fine Colonial and richly carved Renaissance Revival antiques are combined with tasteful reproductions to create an environment that is somewhat formal but not fussy. All rooms have air-conditioning, phones, and wiring for computers; nine have working fireplaces. Deluxe rooms have cable TV and minifridge; some have whirlpools or canopy beds (the prize room also has a private screened porch with a hot tub). Gourmet breakfasts are served at seatings and are conducive to meeting and chatting with other guests. *278 Main St., Box 1022, 02568, tel. 508/693–3333 or 800/332–1236, fax 508/693–5419. 12 rooms, 1 suite. Facilities: full breakfast, afternoon tea, turn-down service, newspaper; 5-course dinners available. No smoking. AE, MC, V.*

Greenwood House. The Thorncroft's sister property features the same fine antiques, canopy beds, and attention to detail but trades some amenities for larger rooms and an easy walk from the ferry. Breakfast is served in the formal dining room. Each room has a phone and air-conditioning. *12–16 Greenwood Ave., Box 1022, 02568, tel. 508/693–6150 or 800/332–1236, fax 508/693–5419. 2 rooms, 4 suites. Facilities: full breakfast. No smoking. AE, MC, V.*

Moderate **Captain Dexter House.** Set in an 1843 sea captain's house at the edge of the shopping district, this B&B has an intimate, historic feeling about it. The small guest rooms are beautifully appointed, with period-style wallpapers, velvet wing chairs, and 18th-century antiques and reproductions, including several four-poster canopy beds with lace or fishnet canopies and hand-sewn quilts. The Captain Harding Room is larger, with original wood floor, fireplace, bay windows, canopy bed, sofa, desk, and large, bright bath with claw-foot tub. *100 Main St., Box 2457, 02568, tel. 508/693–6564. 7 rooms, 1 suite. Facilities: Continental breakfast, afternoon tea, common refrigerator, TV, phone. No smoking in common areas. AE, MC, V. Closed Dec.–Mar.*

Moderate **Tisbury Inn.** At the center of Vineyard Haven's shopping district is this hotel offering tiled bathrooms with tub showers, firm beds, and amenities, including a well-equipped health club, cable TV/HBO, room phones, and some air-conditioning. The once-sparse rooms have been softened with pastels, floral fabrics, a few ruffles, rocking chairs, and pleasant art. In summer, stay three nights and the fourth is free. *Main St., Box 428, 02568, tel. 508/693–2200 or 800/332–4112. 27 rooms, 2 suites. Facilities: Continental breakfast, health club (see Sports and Outdoor Activities, above), indoor pool, restaurant, pay phone. AE, D, MC, V.*

West Tisbury

Moderate **Lambert's Cove Country Inn.** This special place is what a ★ country inn should be. The 1790 farmhouse is secluded and peaceful, approached by a road through pine woods and set amid an apple orchard and a lovely English garden perfect for strolling. The inn is elegant with rich woodwork and floral displays yet makes you feel at home with good beds, electric blankets, and unpretentious furnishings. The many common areas include a large gentleman's library with fireplace. The romantic restaurant (*see* Dining, *above*) serves a popular Sunday brunch. *Lambert's Cove Rd., West Tisbury (RFD 422, Vineyard Haven 02568), tel. 508/693–2298, fax 508/693– 7890. 15 rooms. Facilities: restaurant, Continental breakfast, tennis court in woods, passes to Lambert's Cove Beach. AE, MC, V.*

The Arts and Nightlife

Both island newspapers, the *Martha's Vineyard Times* and the *Vineyard Gazette*, publish weekly calendars of events. Also see the *Best Read Guide*, free at shops and hotels.

The Arts

Throughout the year, lectures, classic films, concerts, plays, and other events are held at the **Old Whaling Church** in Edgartown; watch the papers.

Theater Plays can be seen year-round, thanks to the island's six theater groups. The **Vineyard Playhouse** (10 Church St., Vineyard Haven, tel. 508/693–6450 or 508/696–7333 in summer) offers a summer season (mid-June–early Sept.) of drama, classics, and comedies, performed by a mostly Equity troupe on the air-conditioned main stage; summer Shakespeare and other productions at the natural amphitheater at Tashmoo Overlook on State Road in Vineyard Haven (bring insect repellent and a pillow); children's programs (*see* What to See and Do with Children, *above*) and late-night cabaret (*see* Nightlife, *below*), also in season; and a full winter schedule of community-theater and Equity productions. Local art exhibitions are held throughout the year. One performance of each show is interpreted in American sign language. **Island Theater Workshop** (tel. 508/693–5290), the island's oldest year-round company, performs at various venues.

Music **The Tabernacle** in Oak Bluffs is the scene of a popular Wednesday-night community sing (*see* Tour 2: Oak Bluffs in Exploring, *above*), as well as other family-oriented entertainment. For a schedule, contact the Camp Meeting Association (Box 1176, Oak Bluffs 02557, tel. 508/693–0525).

The **Boston Chamber Music Society** (tel. 617/422–0086) gives two or three performances — called the Vineyard Concerts — at the Old Whaling Church in Edgartown in July and August.

Chilmark Chamber Players (tel. 508/645–9606 or 508/645–9771) perform eight summer concerts and three in winter at various venues.

A free **organ recital** by David Hewlett is given on a rebuilt 1840 organ at Federated Church (S. Summer St., Edgartown, tel. 508/627–4421) every Friday at 12:10.

The Sunday night (8 PM) **Vineyard Haven Town Band concerts** take place on alternate weeks in summer at Owen Park in Vineyard Haven and at the gazebo on Beach Road in Oak Bluffs.

Dance **The Yard** — a colony of dancers and choreographers, formed in 1973 — gives several performances throughout the summer at its 100-seat Barn Theater in a wooded setting (off Middle Rd., Chilmark, tel. 508/645–9662). Artists are selected each year from auditions that are held in New York. Dance classes are available to visitors. Special performances for children and senior citizens are sometimes offered.

Film A 24-hour hotline with schedules for all movie theaters on the Vineyard is 508/627–3788. The island has three first-run movie theaters: **Capawock** (Main St., Vineyard Haven), Oak Bluffs' **Island Theater** (Circuit Ave.) and **The Strand** (Oak

Bluffs Ave. Ext.). At least one stays open year-round. Films are shown at other locations from time to time; see newspaper listings.

Writing Workshop **Nancy Slonim Aronie,** a visiting writer at Trinity College and *McCall's* columnist, leads week-long summer workshops in Chilmark (tel. 508/645–9085 or 203/233–0030).

Nightlife

Dances and other events for different age groups are held throughout the summer at the **Chilmark Community Center;** watch for announcements in the papers.

Coffeehouse **Wintertide Coffeehouse** (Five Corners, Vineyard Haven, tel. 508/693–8830) offers live folk, blues, and other music featuring local and national talent, including open-mike nights, in a homey alcohol- and smoke-free environment. Light meals, desserts, and freshly ground coffees and cappuccino are served at candlelit tables year-round.

Cabaret The **Vineyard Playhouse** (*see* The Arts, *above*) has musical or comedy cabaret after the Friday and Saturday performances, from 10:45 to midnight, in season (BYOB).

Bars and Lounges At **David's Island House** (*see* Dining, *above*), renowned pianist David Crohan entertains with popular and classical music throughout dinner in season. Special musical guests perform in the lounge, where a light menu is served.

The **Ritz Café** (Circuit Ave., Oak Bluffs, tel. 508/693–9851), a popular bar with a pool table (off-season) and a jukebox, has live blues and jazz every weekend, more often in season.

The **Seafood Shanty** restaurant (Dock St., Edgartown, tel. 508/627–8622) has musical entertainment nightly in season.

Dance Clubs Two major clubs offer a mix of live rock and reggae and DJ-spun dance music. **Hot Tin Roof** (at the airport, tel. 508/693–1137 or 693–9320), open in summer, is larger and airier, has more live music, and features comedy nights.

A.C. The Island Nightclub (124 Circuit Ave., Oak Bluffs, tel. 508/693–7129), open year-round, offers fancy light and sound systems in the main room (including a strobe-lit dance floor topped by a glitter ball) and live R&B, blues, rock, and pop in the pub; a restaurant adjoins.

Miscellaneous **Victorian Suppers by the Sea** are given by Edgartown's Harbor View Hotel (*see* Lodging, *above*) on summer Sundays. Actors in Victorian garb stroll the lawn of the century-old hotel as diners enjoy roasts of whole pig, turkey, or lamb on tables or ground cloths, topped off by hand-cranked ice cream and warm berry pies.

5 Nantucket

At the height of its prosperity, in the early to mid-19th century, the little island of Nantucket was the foremost whaling port in the world. In the bustling harbor, ships set off for or returned from the whaling grounds of the Pacific while coastal merchant vessels put in for trade or outfitting. Along the wharves, a profusion of sail lofts, ropewalks, ship's chandleries, cooperages, and other such shops stood cheek by jowl. Barrels of whale oil were off-loaded from the ships onto wagons, then wheeled along the cobblestone streets to refineries and candle factories. On the strong sea breezes the smoke and smells of booming industry were carried through the town as its inhabitants eagerly took care of business.

The boom years didn't last long, but before they ended, some of the hard-won profits had gone into the building of grand homes that remain as eloquent testimony to Nantucket's glory days. The wharves still teem with shops of merchants and craftsmen who tend to the needs of incoming ships, though today those vessels are filled with tourists whose needs tend more toward T-shirts and chic handbags than to ropes and barrels.

Thanks in no small part to the island's isolation, 30 miles out in the open Atlantic (the name Nantucket is a corruption of the Indian word *Nanticut,* meaning "faraway land"), and to its frequently depressed economy, Nantucket has managed to retain much of its 17th- to 19th-century character. Indeed, the town — with its streets lit by old-fashioned street 198lamps and its hundreds of beautifully preserved houses — hardly seems changed since whaling days. But this remarkable preservation also owes much to the foresight and diligence of people working to ensure that what makes Nantucket special can be enjoyed by generations to come. In 1955, legislation to designate the island an official National Historic District was begun. Now any outwardly visible alterations to a structure — even the installation of air conditioners or a change in the color of paint — must conform to a rigid code.

The code's success is obvious in the restful harmony of the buildings, most covered in weathered-gray shingles, sometimes with a facade of clapboard painted white or gray (in early Nantucket a clapboard facade was a sign of wealth, because it would need painting; these practical people saw no need for more than one showy side). In town, which is more strictly regulated than the outskirts, virtually nothing jars. You'll find no neon, stoplights, billboards, or fast-food franchises. In spring and summer, when the many neat gardens are in bloom and the gray shingles are blanketed with cascading pink roses, it all seems perfect.

The desire to protect Nantucket from change extends to the land as well. When the 1960s tourism boom began, it was clear that something had to be done to preserve the breezy, wide-openness of the island — its miles of clean, white-sand beaches, the heath-covered moors — that is as much a part of its charm as the historic town. A third of the 12- by 3-mile island's 30,000 acres are now protected from development, thanks to the ongoing efforts of several public and private

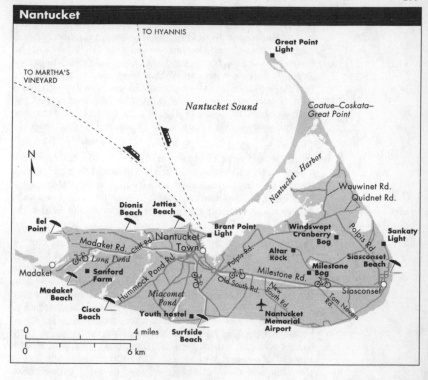

Nantucket

TO HYANNIS

TO MARTHA'S VINEYARD

Great Point Light

Nantucket Sound

Coatue–Coskata–Great Point

Nantucket Harbor

N

Wauwinet Rd.
Quidnet Rd.

Dionis Beach

Jetties Beach

Eel Point

Brant Point Light

Windswept Cranberry Bog

Polpis Rd.

Sankaty Light

Madaket Rd.

Cliff Rd.

Nantucket Town

Altar Rock

Siasconset Beach

Madaket

Long Pond

Sanford Farm

Polpis Rd.

Milestone Rd.

Milestone Bog

Hummock Pond Rd.

Old South Rd.

New South Rd.

Siasconset

Madaket Beach

Miacomet Pond

Tom Nevers Rd.

Cisco Beach

Youth hostel

Nantucket Memorial Airport

0   4 miles

Surfside Beach

0   6 km

organizations and the generosity of Nantucketers, who have donated thousands of acres to the cause. The Nantucket Conservation Foundation, established in 1963, has acquired through purchase or gift more than 8,200 acres, including working cranberry bogs and vast tracts of moorland. A land bank, funded by a 2% tax on real-estate transactions, was instituted in 1984 and has since acquired almost 1,000 acres. Most of these areas are open to the public and marked with signs on the roadside.

The first settlers came to the island to get away from repressive religious authorities on the mainland — having themselves fled to the New World to escape persecution in England, the Puritans of the Massachusetts Bay Colony proceeded to persecute Quakers and those who were friendly with them. In 1659, Thomas Mayhew, who had obtained Nantucket through royal grant and a deal with the resident Wampanoag tribe, sold most of the island to nine shareholders for £30 and two beaver-skin hats. These shareholders then sold half shares to people whose skills the new settlement would need. The names of these families — Macy, Coffin, Starbuck, Coleman, Swain, Gardner, Folger, and others — are inescapable in Nantucket, where three centuries later many descendants still live.

The first year, Thomas Macy and his family, along with Edward Starbuck and the 12-year-old Isaac Coleman, spent fall and winter at Madaket, managing with the assistance of the local natives. The following year, 1660, Tristram Coffin and others arrived, establishing a community — later named Sherburne — at Capaum Harbor, on the north shore. When storms closed the harbor early in the 18th century, the center of activity was moved to the present Nantucket Town. Relations with the Wampanoags seem to have been cordial, and many of the tribe would become expert whalemen. Numbering about 3,000 when the settlers arrived, the native population was greatly reduced by a 1763 plague; the last full-blooded Wampanoag on the island died in 1855.

The settlers first tried their hand at farming, though their crops never thrived in the sandy soil. In 1690 they sent for a Yarmouth whaleman to teach them to catch right whales from small boats just offshore. In 1712 a boat was blown farther out to sea and managed to capture a sperm whale, whose oil was much more highly prized; thus began the whaling era on Nantucket.

In the 18th century, whaling voyages never lasted much longer than a year; by the 19th century the usual whaling grounds had been so depleted that ships had to travel to the Pacific to find their quarry and could be gone for five years. (Some Nantucket captains have South Sea islands named for them — Swain's Reef, Gardner Pinnacles, and so forth.) The life of a whaler was hard, and many never returned home. An account by Owen Chase, first mate of the Nantucket whaling ship *Essex*, of "the mysterious and mortal attack" of a sperm whale, which in 1820 ended in the loss of the ship and most of the crew, fascinated a young sailor named Herman Melville and formed the basis of his 1851 novel, *Moby-Dick*.

The fortunes of Nantucket's whaling industry rose and fell with the tides of three wars and ceased altogether in the 1860s — a result of diminished whale populations, the replacement of whale oil by cheaper kerosene, and the emergence of a sandbar that prevented the large whaling ships from entering Nantucket harbor. By the next decade tourism was being pursued, and hotels began springing up at Surfside, on the south shore. Developments at Siasconset (called 'Sconset), to the east, followed, and in the 1920s the area was a fashionable resort for theater folk. The tourist trade waxed and waned until the 1960s and has since become the island's main industry.

Like the original settlers, most people who visit Nantucket today come to escape — from cities, from stress and hurry, and in some ways from the 20th century. Nantucket has a bit of nightlife, including two raucous year-round dance clubs, but that's not at all what the island is about. It's about people's pride in their heritage, and the chance to experience a piece of our country's past through the wonderfully preserved whaling town. It's about small gray-shingled cottages covered with pink roses in summer, about daffodil-lined roads in spring. It's about the moors, swept with brisk salt breezes and scented with bayberry, wild roses, and cranberries. Perhaps most of all, it's about rediscovering a quiet place within yourself and within the world, getting back in touch with the elemental and taking it home with you when you go.

Essential Information

Important Addresses and Numbers

Tourist
Information
The **Chamber of Commerce** (Pacific Club Bldg., Main St., tel. 508/228–1700) is open Labor Day–Memorial Day, weekdays 9–5; Memorial Day– Labor Day, weekdays 9–5, Saturday 11–5. The **Nantucket Information Bureau** (25 Federal St., tel. 508/228–0925) is open July–Labor Day, daily 9–6; Labor Day–June, Monday–Saturday 9–4. The **Helpline** (tel. 508/228–7227) has information on island health services, activities, and transportation.

Emergencies
Dial 911 for **police or fire emergency.** The **Nantucket Cottage Hospital** (S. Prospect St., tel. 508/228–1200) has a 24-hour emergency room.

Late-night
Pharmacies
Island Pharmacy (Finast Plaza, Sparks Ave., tel. 508/228–6400) is open daily until 8 or 9 year-round. Aside from normal business hours off-season, **Congdon's** (47 Main St., tel. 508/228–0020) is open nightly until 10 from mid-June to mid-September; **Nantucket Pharmacy** (45 Main St., tel. 508/228–0180), until 10 nightly from Memorial Day to Labor Day or Columbus Day.

Cash Machines
ATMs are at the **airport** (lobby), **Steamship Authority terminal** (Steamboat Wharf), **Nantucket Bank** (2 Orange St. or 104 Pleasant St., tel. 508/228–0580), **Pacific National Bank** (Main St., tel. 508/228–1917), **A&P** (Straight Wharf, tel. 508/228–9756), and **Finast** (Lower Pleasant St., tel. 508/228–2178).

Arriving and Departing by Plane

Airport and
Airlines
Nantucket Memorial Airport (tel. 508/325–5300) is about 3½ miles southeast of town via Old South Road.

Business Express/Delta Connection (tel. 800/345–3400) flies from Boston year-round, from New York (LAG) in season. **Cape Air** (tel. 508/771–6944 or 800/999– 1616) directly connects the island with Martha's Vineyard and New Bedford year-round; it also has joint fares with Continental, Delta, and USAir and ticketing-and-baggage agreements with American, Midwest Express, Northwest, and United. **Continental** (tel. 800/525–0280) has nonstops from Newark Memorial Day–Labor Day. **Island Airlines** (tel. 800/775–6606 or 800/698–1109 in MA) and **Nantucket Air** (tel. 508/790–0300, 508/228–6234, or 800/635–8787 in MA) fly from Hyannis year-round and offer charters. **Northwest Airlink** (tel. 800/225–2525) flies from Boston year-round, from Newark in season.

Ocean Wings (tel. 508/325–5548) and **Coastal Air** (tel. 508/228–3350) are year-round charter companies with island bases. **Westchester Air** (tel. 914/761–3000 or 800/759–2929) flies charters out of White Plains, New York.

Arriving and Departing by Ferry

From Hyannis The **Steamship Authority** runs car-and-passenger ferries to the island from Hyannis's South Street dock year-round. (For policies and restrictions, *see* Arriving and Departing by Ferry in Chapter 4, Martha's Vineyard.) The trip takes 2¼ hours. *Tel. 508/540–2022 for reservations; on Nantucket, 508/228–0262 or 508/228–3274 for reservations; TDD 508/540–1394. Cost, one way: $9.75 adults, $4.90 children 5–12; cars, $83 mid-May–mid-Oct., $65 mid-Oct.–mid-May; bicycles, $4.50.*

Hy-Line passenger ferries make the 1¾- to 2-hour trip from Hyannis from mid-May through October. The MV *Great Point* offers a first-class section with a private lounge, rest rooms, upholstered seats, carpeting, a bar, and a snack bar ($19.50 one way, adult or child). The "Around the Sound" cruise, a one-day round-trip from Hyannis with stops at Nantucket and Martha's Vineyard, is available June–mid-September ($31 adults, $15.50 children 5–12, $13.50 bicycles). *Ocean St. dock, tel. 508/778–2600 or 508/778–2602 for reservations; on Nantucket, 508/228–3949. Cost, one way: $10.50 adults, $5.25 children 5–12, $4.50 bicycles.*

From Martha's Vineyard **Hy-Line** makes 2¼-hour runs to and from Nantucket from mid-June to mid-September — the only interisland passenger service. (To get a car from the Vineyard to Nantucket, you must return to the mainland.) *Tel. 508/778–2600, 508/228–3949 on Nantucket, 508/693–0112 in Oak Bluffs. Cost, one way: $10.50 adults, $5.25 children 5–12, $4.50 bicycles.*

Arriving and Departing by Private Boat

Harbor facilities are available in town year-round at the **Boat Basin** (tel. 508/228–1333 or 800/626–2628), with shower and laundry facilities, electric power, cable TV, fuel dock, and summer concierge service.

Madaket Marine (tel. 508/228–9086) has moorings May–October and slips year-round for boats up to 32 feet in Hither Creek.

Getting Around

One of the attractions of a Nantucket vacation is escape from the fast lane. Most visitors find themselves walking a lot more than they're used to and taking advantage of the island's miles of scenic bike paths. Even so, in high season the main streets are clogged with traffic (and the parking spaces filled), and residents beg you to leave your car at home.

If your visit will be short and spent mostly in town and on the beaches, taxis and beach shuttles can supplement foot power adequately. If, on the other hand, your focus will be on the farther-out beaches and nature preserves, or if you'll be staying a week or longer, a car may make life simpler. Renting a car on the island for a day or two is cheaper and less troublesome than bringing one over on the ferry (but do reserve).

Some of the island's most beautiful and least touristed beaches and other areas are accessible only by over-sand, four-wheel-drive vehicles. Check with the Chamber of Commerce about regulations passed in 1992, making some areas off-limits to vehicles and designating hours and times of year when driving is allowed on others. Coatue–Coskata–Great Point is open to Jeeps but requires licenses (*see* Tour 2 in Exploring Nantucket, *below*).

By Car Cars and Jeeps are available at the airport desks of **Budget** (tel. 508/228–5666), **Hertz** (tel. 508/228–9421), **National** (tel. 508/228–0300), and **Nantucket Windmill** (tel. 508/228–1227 or 800/228–1227). **Nantucket Jeep Rental** (tel. 508/228–1618) rents Jeep Wranglers and delivers. In high season, you will pay up to $60 a day for cars, up to $150 for Jeeps (reserve well ahead for Jeeps; they disappear quickly).

By Bus From mid-June to Labor Day, **Barrett's Tours** (20 Federal St., tel. 508/228–0174), across from the Information Bureau, runs beach shuttles to 'Sconset ($5 round-trip, $3 one-way), Surfside ($3 round-trip, $2 one-way), and Jetties ($1 one-way) several times daily. Children pay half-fare to 'Sconset and Surfside.

By Taxi Taxis usually wait outside the airport or at the foot of Main Street by the ferry, or call **A-1 Taxi** (tel. 508/228–3330 or 508/228–4084), **Aardvark Cab** (tel. 508/228–2223), **All Points Taxi** (tel. 508/228–5779), or **Atlantic Cab** (tel. 508/228–1112). Rates are flat fees, based on one person with two bags: $3 within town (1½-mile radius), $6 to the airport, $10 to 'Sconset, $11 to Wauwinet.

By Bicycle and Moped Mountain bikes are best if you plan to explore the dirt roads. To drive a moped you must have a driver's license and helmet; you may not use the vehicle within the town historic district between 10 PM and 7 AM, and you may never drive it on the bike paths. Moped accidents happen often on the narrow or dirt roads — watch out for loose gravel.

Rentals are available at Steamboat Wharf from **Young's Bicycle Shop** (tel. 508/228–1151), which also rents cars and four-wheel-drive vehicles in season, and from **Nantucket Bike Shop** (tel. 508/228–1999; Apr.–Oct.). Both provide excellent touring maps. Daily rentals (shop around) cost $12–$18 for a bicycle, $30–$50 for a moped; half-, full-, and multiple-day rates are available.

By Horse-drawn Carriage **Carried Away** (tel. 508/228–0218) offers narrated carriage rides through the town historic district in season.

Guided Tours

Orientation **Barrett's Tours** (20 Federal St., tel. 508/228–0174) and **Nantucket Island Tours** (Straight Wharf, tel. 508/228–0334) give 1¼- to 1½-hour narrated bus tours of the island from spring through fall; buses meet the ferries.

Gail's Tours (tel. 508/257–6557; Apr.–Dec.) are lively 1¾-hour van tours narrated by sixth-generation Nantucketer Gail Johnson, who knows all the inside stories.

Walking Tours **Anita Stackpole Dougan** (tel. 508/228–1861), a 12th-generation Nantucketer, and her husband, Edward, lead 1½-hour walking tours of town focusing on the people who have lived in the historic homes seen along the walk.

Roger Young's historic walking tours (tel. 508/228–1062; in season) of the town center are entertaining and leisurely.

Special-Interest Cruises *Yachting* magazine named Nantucket's harbor one of the 10 most romantic in the world. Boats of all kinds leave from Straight Wharf for harbor sails throughout the summer; many are available for charter as well. The 31-foot Friendship sloop *Endeavor* (Slip 15, tel. 508/228–5585) offers harbor tours and sails to Coatue, where you are rowed ashore to spend a private morning beachcombing. The renovated lobster boat *Anna W II* (Slip 12, tel. 508/228–1444) offers sunset and moonlight cruises, as well as lobstering demonstrations and winter seal cruises. The 40-foot sailing yacht *Sparrow* (Slip 19, tel. 508/228–6029), with a teak, brass, and stained-glass interior, offers 1½-hour sails for six guests, plus charters.

Great Point **Beach Excursions Ltd.** tel. 508/228–5800) offers Jeep trips to Great Point, with views of the spit's beaches, eagle nesting grounds, clamming and oyster ponds, and lighthouse.

Nature **The Maria Mitchell Association** (Vestal St., tel. 508/228–9198) organizes wildflower and bird walks from June to Labor Day (*see also* What to See and Do with Children, *below*).

Whale-watching **Nantucket Whalewatch** offers naturalist-led excursions Tuesday through Thursday from July through September. *Hy-Line dock, Straight Wharf, tel. 508/283–0313, 800/942–5464, or 800/322–0013 in MA. Cost: $40 adults, $22 children under 12.*

Exploring Nantucket

The 12- by 3-mile island of Nantucket has one town, also called Nantucket; the village of 'Sconset, with a number of services, on the east coast; the village of Madaket, on the west, with a harbor, good sunsets, a restaurant, and bluefishing off the point; and a number of residential areas with no commercial or tourist facilities. Although major roads will take you to most of these areas, exploring them must often be done on dirt roads. Bike paths lead east to 'Sconset, south to Surfside Beach, and west to Madaket.

Nantucket Town has a small commercial area of a few square blocks leading up from the waterfront; beyond it, quiet residential roads fan out. As you wander you may notice a small round plaque by some doorways. Issued by the Nantucket Historical Association, the plaques certify that the house dates from the 17th century (silver), 1700–1775 (red bronze), 1776–1812 (brass), 1813–1846 (green), or 1847–1900 (black). Unfortunately, they all seem to turn coppery green or black with age.

Highlights for First-time Visitors

Altar Rock (*see* Tour 2: Town–'Sconset–Polpis Loop)
Eel Point (*see* Nature Areas, *below*)
First Congregational Church, for the view (*see* Tour 1:
Nantucket Town)
Museum of Nantucket History (*see* Tour 1:
Nantucket Town)
Siasconset (*see* Tour 2: Town–'Sconset–Polpis Loop)
"Three Bricks" (*see* Tour 1: Nantucket Town)
Whaling Museum (*see* Tour 1: Nantucket Town)

Tour 1: Nantucket Town

Numbers in the margin correspond to numbered points of interest on the Nantucket Town map.

❶ The geologic and historical overview given by the **Museum of Nantucket History** helps put into perspective the sights you will see when touring the island. The brick building in which the museum is set was built by Thomas Macy after the Great Fire of 1846 — which destroyed the wharves and 400 buildings, about a third of all those in the town — as a warehouse for the supplies needed to outfit whaling ships. It has been restored to be accurate historically, down to period doors, hatchways, and hoists. Inside, audio and visual displays include an early fire-fighting vehicle, ship models, blowups of old photographs, and a 13-foot diorama (with narration) showing the shops, ships, and activities of the bustling waterfront before the fire. Live demonstrations of such early island crafts as candle making are given daily from mid-June to Columbus Day; through 1993, a second-floor exhibit documents Nantucket's "Changing Landscapes" through dioramas, a wave machine, a slide show, and more. *Straight Wharf, tel. 508/228–3889. Admission: $2 adults, $1 children 5–14. Open late Apr.–Memorial Day, weekends 11–3; Memorial Day–mid-June, daily 11–3; mid-June–Labor Day, daily 10–5 and 7–10; Labor Day–Columbus Day, daily 11–3; Columbus Day–early Dec., weekends 11–3. Closed early Dec.–late Apr. The museum is run by the Nantucket Historical Association (tel. 508/228–1894), which oversees 14 properties. A Visitor Pass allowing a single visit to all 14 is available at any of the sites for $5 adults, $2.50 children 5–14.*

❷ Walking up Main Street, you'll come to the redbrick **Pacific Club** building, still housing the elite club of Pacific whaling masters for which it is named. Understandably, since the last whaling ship was seen here in 1870, the club now admits whalers' *descendants*, who gather for the odd cribbage game or a swapping of tales. The building began in 1772 as the counting house of William Rotch, owner of the *Dartmouth* and *Beaver*, two of the three ships that hosted a famous tea party in Boston. (According to the Historical Association, the plaque outside the Pacific Club identifying the third ship, the *Eleanor*, as Rotch's is incorrect.) Upstairs is the office of the **Chamber of Commerce** (*see* Important Addresses and Numbers in Essential Information, *above*),

Nantucket Town

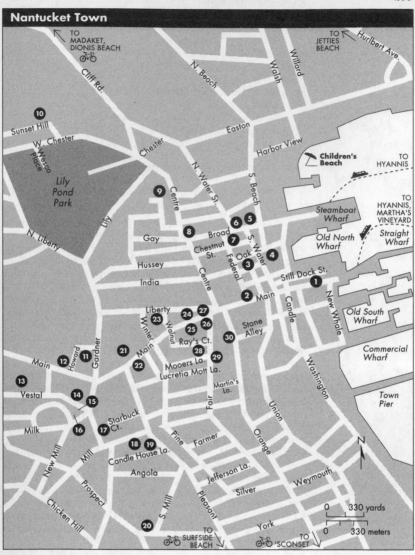

TO MADAKET, DIONIS BEACH

TO JETTIES BEACH

Hurlbert Ave.

Cliff Rd.

N. Beach

Walsh

Willard

Sunset Hill

W. Chester

Chester

Easton

Harbor View

Children's Beach

TO HYANNIS

Lily Pond Park

Lily

N. Liberty

N. Water St.

Centre

Gay

Broad

Chestnut St.

Oak

S. Beach

S. Water

Federal

Steamboat Wharf

Old North Wharf

TO HYANNIS, MARTHA'S VINEYARD

Straight Wharf

Hussey

India

Centre

Still Dock St.

Main

Candle

New Whale

Old South Wharf

Liberty

Walnut

Ray's Ct.

Stone Alley

Mooers La.

Lucretia Mott La.

Martin's La.

Commercial Wharf

Washington

Town Pier

Winter

Main

Gardner

Howard

Main

Vestal

Milk

Starbuck Ct.

Fair

Pine

Farmer

Union

Orange

New Mill

Mill

Candle House La.

Angola

Jefferson La.

Silver

Weymouth

Prospect

Chicken Hill

S. Mill

Pleasant

York

TO SURFSIDE BEACH

TO 'SCONSET

0   330 yards

0   330 meters

N

Atheneum, **3**

Charles G. Coffin House, **25**

Dreamland Theatre, **4**

1800 House, **18**

Fire Hose Cart House, **11**

First Congregational Church, **9**

Greater Light, **12**

Hadwen House, **22**

Henry Coffin House, **24**

Hinchman House, **16**

Jared Coffin House, **8**

John Wendell Barrett House, **26**

Macy-Christian House, **23**

Maria Mitchell Science Library, **15**

Mitchell House, **14**

Moors' End, **19**

Museum of Nantucket History, **1**

Nantucket Information Bureau, **7**

Old Gaol, **13**

Old Mill, **20**

Oldest House, **10**

Pacific Club/Chamber of Commerce, **2**

Pacific National Bank, **27**

Peter Foulger Museum/Nantucket Historical Association Research Center, **6**

Quaker Meeting House/Fair Street Museum, **28**

St. Paul's Episcopal Church, **29**

Starbuck refinery and candle works, **17**

"Three Bricks", **21**

Unitarian Universalist Church, **30**

Whaling Museum, **5**

where you might want to stop for maps and other information.

From here you get the most photographed view of Main Street. The cobblestone square has a harmonious symmetry; at the foot it is anchored by the Pacific Club, and at the head, by the Pacific National Bank, another redbrick building. The only broad thoroughfare in town, Main Street was widened after the Great Fire leveled all its buildings except those made of brick, to safeguard against flames hopping across the street in the event of another fire. The cobblestones — brought to the island as ballast in returning ships — were laid to prevent the wheels of carts heavily laden with whale oil from sinking into the dirt on their passage from the waterfront to the factories.

At the center of Lower Main is an old horse trough, today overflowing with flowers. From here the street gently rises; at the bank it narrows to its pre-fire width and leaves the commercial district for an area of mansions that escaped the blaze. The simple shop buildings that replaced those lost are a pleasing hodgepodge of sizes, colors, and styles. Elm trees — thousands of which were planted in the 1850s by Henry and Charles Coffin — once formed a canopy over Main Street, but Dutch elm disease took most of them; 1991's Hurricane Bob took two dozen more.

Time Out You can breakfast or lunch inexpensively at several soup-and-sandwich places, including **David's Soda Fountain** (Congdon's Pharmacy, 47 Main St., tel. 508/228–4549) and another at **Nantucket Pharmacy** (45 Main St., tel. 508/228–0180). At indoor café tables, **Espresso Cafe** (40 Main St., tel. 508/228–6930) serves excellent coffee, espresso, cappuccino (try it iced), and desserts, as well as quick and good lunches. **Off Centre Cafe** (29 Centre St., tel. 508/228–8470) serves such breakfasts as huevos rancheros or fruit popovers and pancakes, sandwiches made from its own breads, homemade desserts, and Mexican dinners in a small indoor space or outside.

Turning down Federal Street, you'll come to a huge white Greek Revival building with an odd windowless facade and fluted Ionic columns. This is the **Atheneum** (Lower India St., tel. 508/228–1110), Nantucket's town library, built in 1846 to replace a structure lost to the fire. The opening ceremonies featured a dedication by Ralph Waldo Emerson, who — along with Daniel Webster, Henry David Thoreau, John James Audubon, and other important men of the day — later delivered lectures in the library's second-floor Great Hall (open one afternoon a week). In the 19th century the hall was the center of island culture, also hosting public meetings, suffrage rallies, and county fairs.

A right turn onto Oak Street brings you to South Water Street. Across the way is the **Dreamland Theatre,** a good illustration of early Nantucketers' penchant for multiple use of dwellings as well as for moving houses around. Trees, and therefore lumber, were so scarce, Herman Melville joked in *Moby-Dick* "that pieces of wood in Nantucket are carried about like bits of the true cross in Rome." Currently a summer movie theater, the Dreamland was built on Main Street as a Quaker meeting house; became a straw factory, then an entertainment hall; was moved to Brant Point as part of the grand Nantucket Hotel in the late 19th century; and was floated across the harbor by barge about 1905 and installed in its present location.

From Oak Street, turn left on South Water; at the end is the ⑤ **Whaling Museum,** set in an 1846 factory built for refining spermaceti and making candles. (Spermaceti candles, incidentally, which you'll see for sale at various shops, give off a clean, steady light and only a slight fragrance, which is why they became such popular replacements for smelly tallow candles.) This museum immerses you in Nantucket's whaling past with exhibits that include a fully rigged whaleboat, harpoons and other implements, portraits of sea captains, a large scrimshaw collection, a full-size tryworks (used to process whale oil aboard ship), the skeleton of a 43-foot finback whale, replicas of cooper and blacksmith shops, and the original 16-foot-high glass prism from the Sankaty Light. The knowledgeable and enthusiastic staff gives a 20- to 30-minute introductory talk peppered with tales of a whaling man's life at sea (call for tour times). Don't miss the museum's gift shop next door (*see* Specialty Stores in Shopping, *below*). *Broad St., tel. 508/228–1736. Admission: $3 adults, $1.50 children 5–14; or NHA pass. Open late Apr.- mid- June, daily 11–3; mid-June–Labor Day, daily 10–5; Labor Day–Oct., daily 11–3; Nov.–early Dec., weekdays 2–3 for one tour; weekends 11–3; early Dec.–Christmas, sporadic openings. Closed Christmas–mid-Apr.*

⑥ The next building up on Broad Street houses the **Peter Foulger Museum** and the **Nantucket Historical Association Research Center.** The latter's extensive collection of manuscripts, books, photographs, ships' logs and charts, genealogical records, and audiovisual materials on Nantucket maritime and other history is open only to those doing research. The museum displays changing exhibits from the permanent collection, including portraits, lightship baskets, textiles, porcelains, silver, furniture, and more. *Tel. 508/228– 1655. Research permit: $5 (2 days). Library open weekdays 10–5. Museum admission: $2 adults, $1 children 5–14. Open Memorial Day–mid-June, daily 11–3; mid-June–Labor Day, daily 10–5; Labor Day–Columbus Day, daily 11–3. Closed Columbus Day–Memorial Day.*

Time Out   Across the street, the **Juice Bar** (12 Broad St., tel. 508/228-5799; Apr.–early Dec.) offers homemade ice cream (with lots of toppings), waffle cones, and baked goods, plus fresh-squeezed juices, frozen yogurt, specialty coffees, and always a long line.

⑦ Just around the corner on Federal Street is the **Nantucket Information Bureau** (*see* Tourist Information in Essential Information, *above*), with public phones, rest rooms, and a bulletin board posting events.

Most of the Greek Revival houses you will see as you continue up Broad Street were replacements for buildings lost in the Great Fire. Pause to admire the **Jared Coffin House,** which has operated as an inn since the mid-19th century. Coffin, a wealthy merchant, built this Georgian brick house with Ionic portico, parapet, hip roof, and cupola — then the only three-story structure on the island — for his wife, who wanted to live closer to town. They moved here in 1845 from their home on Pleasant Street, but (so the story goes) nothing would please the woman, and within two years they had left the island altogether for Boston.

❾ A right onto Centre Street takes you past the **First Congregational Church** (also known as the Old North Church), Nantucket's largest. Its tower — whose steeple is capped with a weathervane depicting a whale catch — rises 120 feet, providing the best view of Nantucket to be had. On a clear day the reward for climbing the 92 steps (many landings break the climb) is a panorama encompassing Great Point, Sankaty Light, Muskeget and Tuckernuck islands, moors, ponds, beaches, and the winding streets and rooftops of town. Peek in at the church's interior, with its old box pews, a chandelier seven feet in diameter, and a trompe-l'oeil ceiling done by an Italian painter in 1850 and since restored. The organ, installed in 1904, has 914 wood and metal pipes. (Organ aficionados may want to have a look at the 1831 Appleton organ — one of only four extant — at the United Methodist Church, next to the Pacific National Bank on Main Street.) The Old North Vestry in the rear, the oldest house of worship on the island, was built in 1725 about a mile north of its present site. The main church was built in 1834. *62 Centre St., no tel. Admission: $1.50 adults, 50¢ children under 15. Open mid-June–mid-Oct., Mon.–Sat. 10–4. Closed mid-Oct.–mid-June.*

❿ A short walk along Centre Street (past lovely Lily Street) and West Chester Street leads to the **Oldest House,** also called the Jethro Coffin House, built as a wedding gift for Jethro and Mary Gardner Coffin. The most striking feature of the 1686 saltbox — the oldest house on the island — is the massive central brick chimney with brick horseshoe adornment; other highlights are the enormous hearths and diamond-pane leaded-glass windows. Cutaway panels show 17th-century construction techniques. The interior's sparse furnishings include an antique loom. *Sunset Hill, tel. 508/228-1894. Admission: $2 adults, $1 children 5–14; or NHA pass. Open Memorial Day–mid-June, weekends 11–3; mid-June–Columbus Day, daily 10–5. Closed Columbus Day–Memorial Day.*

Turn left off West Chester Street onto North Liberty Street, where you'll see the entrance to **Lily Pond Park,** a 5-acre conservation area a few minutes from town. Its grassy lawn and wetlands (there is a trail, but it's muddy) foster abundant wildlife, including birds, ducks, and deer.

⓫ A bit farther on, you'll come to the **Fire Hose Cart House.** Built in 1886 as one of several neighborhood fire stations — Nantucketers had learned their lesson — the house displays a small collection of fire-fighting equipment used a century ago. *8 Gardner St., tel. 508/228–1894. Admission free. Open Memorial Day–mid-June, daily 11–3; mid-June–Labor Day, daily 10–5; Labor Day–Columbus Day, daily 11–3. Closed Columbus Day–Memorial Day.*

Turn into the little street just before the firehouse. At the end, on the right, is **Greater Light,** an example of the summer homes of the artists who flocked to Nantucket in its early resort days. In the 1930s two unusual Quaker sisters from Philadelphia — an actress and an artist — converted a barn into what looks like the lavish set for an old movie. The exotic decor includes Italian furniture, Native American artifacts and textiles, a wrought-iron balcony, bas reliefs, and a coat of arms. The sisters also remodeled the private house next door, called Lesser Light, for their parents. *8 Howard St., tel. 508/228–9591. Admission: $2 adults, $1 children 5–14; or NHA pass. Open Memorial Day–mid-June, daily 11–3; mid-June–Labor Day, daily 10–5; Labor Day–Columbus Day, daily 11–3. Closed Columbus Day–Memorial Day.*

Continue on Howard Street to the end; turn right, then left on Bloom, then right; a sign on the right points the way to the **Old Gaol,** an 1805 jailhouse in use until 1933. Shingles mask the building's construction of massive square timbers, plainly visible inside; walls, ceilings, and floors are bolted with iron. The furnishings consist of rough plank bunks and open privies, but you needn't feel too much sympathy for the prisoners: Most of them were allowed out at night to sleep in their own beds. *15R Vestal St., tel. 508/228–1894. Admission free. Open Memorial Day–mid-June, daily 11–3; mid-June–Labor Day, daily 10–5; Labor Day–Columbus Day, daily 11–3. Closed Columbus Day–Memorial Day.*

Head left when you come out of the jail; at the beginning of Vestal Street is the **Mitchell House,** birthplace of astronomer and Vassar professor Maria (pronounced "Mah-RYE-ah") Mitchell, who in 1847, at age 29, discovered a comet while surveying the sky from the top of the Pacific National Bank. (Her family had moved to quarters over the bank, where her father — also an astronomer — worked.) The restored 1790 house contains family possessions and Maria Mitchell memorabilia, including the telescope with which she spotted the comet. The kitchen, of authentic wide-board construction, retains the antique utensils, iron pump, and sink of the time. Tours of the house, the roof walk, and the wildflower garden are available; the adjacent observatory is used by researchers and is not open to the public. *1 Vestal St., tel. 508/228–2896. Admission: $3 adults, $1 children under 13. Open mid-June–Aug., Tues.–Sat. 10–4. Closed Sept.–mid-June.*

Across the street is the **Maria Mitchell Science Library,** which has natural-history books and periodicals, including field-identification guides and gardening books. *Tel. 508/228–9219. Admission free. Open mid-June–mid-Sept., Tues.–Sat. 10–4; mid-Sept.–mid-June, Mon.–Thurs. 2–5.*

⑯ Next door, at the corner, is the **Hinchman House** — a natural-science museum, with specimens of local birds, shells, insects, and plants. *7 Milk St., tel. 508/228–0898. Admission: $3 adults, $1 children under 13. Open mid-June–Aug., Tues.– Sat. 10–4. Closed Sept.–mid-June.*

The three previous properties — as well as the **Loines Observatory** (Milk St. Ext., tel. 508/228–9198), which offers Wednesday-night stargazing in July and August; and an aquarium near Commercial Wharf (*see* What to See and Do with Children, *below*) — are administered by the Maria Mitchell Association, established in 1902 by Vassar students and Maria's family. A combination admission ticket to all sites is $4.50.

One of 10 children of Quaker parents, Mitchell attained many firsts in her day — first woman astronomy professor in the United States, first woman to discover a comet — and world fame to boot. It is not surprising that a Nantucket woman would do so, given the history of women on the island. During the whaling days men would be gone for up to five years at a time; the women learned to keep the town going. They became leaders in every arena, from religion to business. Mary Coffin Starbuck helped establish Quakerism on the island and was a celebrated preacher. Lucretia Coffin Mott was a powerful advocate of the antislavery and women's-rights movements. During the post–Civil War depression, Centre Street near Main Street became known as Petticoat Row, a reflection of the large number of women shopkeepers.

Cross Milk Street and walk down New Dollar Lane; on your **⑰** left, down a long driveway, are the remains of the **Starbuck refinery and candle works,** now used as apartments and **⑱** garages. A left at the end of the street leads to the **1800 House,** typical of a Nantucket home — one not enriched by whaling money — of that time. Once the residence of the high sheriff, the house features locally made furniture and other household goods, a six-flue chimney with beehive oven, and a summer kitchen. *10 Mill St., tel. 508/228–1894. Admission: $2 adults, $1 children 5–14; or NHA pass. Open Memorial Day–mid-June, daily 11–3; mid-June–Labor Day, daily 10–5; Labor Day–Columbus Day, daily 11–3. Closed Columbus Day–Memorial Day.*

The massive brick structure at the corner, at 19 Pleasant **⑲** Street, is **Moors' End,** the handsome Federal brick house where Jared Coffin lived before building what is now the Jared Coffin House. It is a private home, but insiders tell of vast murals of the whaling era on the walls, and of scrawled notes about shipwreck sightings in the cupola. Behind high brick walls is a lavish garden.

Make a right onto Pleasant Street and another onto South **⑳** Mill Street for the **Old Mill,** a 1746 Dutch-style octagonal windmill built with lumber from shipwrecks. Several such windmills sat on hills in Nantucket in the 1700s, but only this one remains. The Douglas-fir pivot pole used to turn the cap and sails into the wind is a replacement of the originial pole, a ship's foremast. The mill is worked with wood gears and wind power (when the wind is strong enough) to grind corn into meal that is sold here. *South Mill St., tel. 508/228–1894. Admission: $2 adults, $1 children 5–14; or NHA pass. Open Memorial Day–mid-June, daily 11–3; mid-June–Labor Day, daily 10–5; Labor Day–Columbus Day, daily 11–3. Closed Columbus Day–Memorial Day.*

From here, return to town via Pleasant Street. At the end is Upper Main Street, where many of the mansions of the golden age of whaling were built. Facing you, at Nos. 93–97,

㉑ are the well-known **"Three Bricks,"** identical redbrick mansions with columned, Greek Revival porches at their front entrances. Similar in design to the Jared Coffin House but with only two stories, they were built between 1836 and 1838 by whaling merchant Joseph Starbuck for his three sons (one still belongs to a Starbuck descendant).

The two white, porticoed Greek Revival mansions across the street — referred to as the Two Greeks — were built in 1845 and 1846 by superrich factory owner William Hadwen, a Newport native, for himself and for the niece he and his wife had adopted. (Hadwen's wife, incidentally, was a sister of the three Starbuck brothers; another sister lived at 100

㉒ Main Street.) Number 96, called the **Hadwen House,** is now a museum. A guided tour points out the grand circular staircase, fine plasterwork, carved Italian-marble fireplace mantels, and other architectural details. Regency, Empire, and Victorian furnishings are accented with portraits, needlework, silver doorknobs, and other 19th-century decorative objects. Behind the house are period gardens. *96 Main St., tel. 508/228–1894. Admission: $2 adults, $1 children 5–14, or NHA pass. Open Memorial Day–mid-June, daily 11–3; mid-June–Labor Day, daily 10–5; Labor Day–Columbus Day, daily 11–3. Closed Columbus Day–Memorial Day.*

㉓ A turn down Walnut Lane leads to the **Macy-Christian House,** reopened to the public in 1992. The two-story lean-to, built c. 1740 for another Thomas Macy, features a great open hearth flanked by brick beehive ovens and old paneling. Part of the house reflects the late 19th-century Colonial Revival style of the 1934 renovation by the Christian family; the formal parlor and upstairs bedroom are in authentic Colonial style. *12 Liberty St., tel. 508/325–4015. Admission: $2 adults, $1 children 5–14; or NHA pass. Open Memorial Day–mid-June, daily 11–3; mid-June–Labor Day, daily 10–5; Labor Day–Columbus Day, daily 11–3. Closed Columbus Day–Memorial Day.*

Back on Main Street, facing each other, are two more attrac-
㉔ tive brick houses built for brothers: the **Henry Coffin House**
㉕ (at No. 75) and the **Charles G. Coffin House** (No. 78). Wealthy shipping agents and whale-oil merchants, the Coffins used for these 1830s houses the same mason who later built the Three Bricks.

㉖ The last of the grand Main Street homes is the **John Wendell Barrett House,** on the right at No. 72. Legend has it that Lydia Mitchell Barrett stood on the steps and refused to move when, during the Great Fire, men tried to evacuate her so they could blow up the house to stop the spread of the fire; luckily, a shift in the wind settled the showdown.

㉗ Across the street is the 1818 **Pacific National Bank.** Like the Pacific Club it faces, the bank is a monument to the far-flung voyages of the Nantucket whaling ships it financed. Inside, above old-style teller cages, are murals of street and port scenes from the whaling days. Near the bank, at 62 Main Street, is Murray's Toggery, the site of R. H. Macy's first retail store.

㉘ A right on Fair Street will bring you to the **Quaker Meeting House,** built around 1838 as a Friends school and now a Quaker place of worship in summer. A small room of quiet simplicity — white-and-gray walls, windows with 12-over-12 antique glass, and unadorned wood benches — it is in keeping with these peaceful people, who believe that the divine spirit is within each person and that one does not require an intermediary to worship God.

Attached to the meeting house is an unattractive 1904 concrete building that houses the **Fair Street Museum.** Exhibited inside are artworks from the collection of the Artists Association of Nantucket, including works done on the island or by island artists in the 20th century. Notable among them are *Life* photographer Louis Davidson's sepia-tone prints from the '40s. *1 Fair St., tel. 508/228–1894. Admission: $2 adults, $1 children 5–14; or NHA pass. Open July–Aug., weekends 11–3. Closed Sept.–June.*

㉙ Across the street is the 1901 **St. Paul's Episcopal Church,** a massive granite structure adorned at the front and back by beautiful Tiffany windows. The interior is cool and white, with dark exposed beams. From here, you might take a minute to wander down one of the pretty side streets, such as Lucretia Mott Lane or Mooers Lane.

Continue along Fair Street to Martin's Lane and make a left onto Orange Street. On the left, past the only **row houses** ever built on the island (1831), is the 1809 **Unitarian Univer-**
㉚ **salist Church,** also known as South Church, with the gold-domed spire that soars above the town as the First Congregational Church's slender white steeple does. Also like First Congregational, South Church features a trompe-l'oeil ceiling painting, this one a false, intricately detailed dome, executed in 1840 by another European painter. Here, however, illusion is taken to greater lengths: The curved chancel and paneled walls you see are also creations in paint. The 1831 mahogany-cased Goodrich organ in the loft is played at services and concerts. In the octagonal belfry of the tower, which houses the town clock, is a bell cast in Portugal that has been ringing out the noon hour since it was hung in 1815.

Across the street is **Stone Alley,** a byway that's as pleasant a way of returning to town as any. A left onto Union Street brings you back to the foot of Main Street. On the wall of the last building on the left on Washington Street, notice the sign listing distances from Nantucket to various points of the globe (it's 14,650 miles to Tahiti).

Tour 2: Town–'Sconset–Polpis Loop

Siasconset, 7 miles from town, is reached by road or by a mostly level bike path and makes a lovely day trip; off-season there's not a lot to see in the village, but the ride still has its attractions. From town, take Orange Street to the rotary, where Milestone Road and its bike path begin.

Time Out   The **Nantucket Bake Shop** (79 Orange St., tel. 508/228–2797; in season) is a great place to stop to fill a knapsack with Portuguese breads and pastries.

About 5½ miles east of the rotary (white stone mile-markers on your left tick out the distance to 'Sconset), signs on the left point to the **Milestone Bog,** more than 200 acres of working cranberry bog surrounded by conservation land. Cultivated since 1857, the bog was the world's largest contiguous natural cranberry bog until it was subdivided after 1959. The land was donated to the Nantucket Conservation Foundation in 1968; the bogs are leased to a grower, who harvests and sells the crops. (For a map of the foundation's properties, visit NCF headquarters at 118 Cliff Rd., tel. 508/228–2884, weekdays 8–5. The map costs $3, or $4 by mail.)

The harvest begins in late September and continues for six weeks, during which time harvesters work every day from sunup to sunset in the flooded bog. The sight of the bright red berries floating on the surface while the moors turn the rich colors of autumn is not to be missed. At other times the color of the dry bog may be green, rust-red, or, in June and early July, the pale pink of cranberry blossoms, but always the bog and the moors have a quiet beauty that's worth the effort to get there.

Another half-mile on Milestone Road brings you to an intersection that marks the center of **'Sconset,** a charming village of pretty streets with tiny rose-covered cottages and driveways of crushed white shells. A community of cod and halibut fishermen and shore whalers from the 17th century, Siasconset was already becoming a summer resort during whaling days, when people from Nantucket town would come here to get away from the smells of burning whale oil in the refineries. In 1884 the narrow-gauge railway — built three years earlier to take spiffily clad folk from the New Bedford steamers to the beach at Surfside for sea bathing, as well as hot-air balloon rides, concerts, and fireworks — came to 'Sconset, bringing ever more off-islanders. These included writers and artists from Boston in the 1890s, followed soon by Broadway actors and actresses on holiday during the theaters' summer hiatus. Attracted by the village's beauty, remoteness, sandy ocean beach, and cheap lodgings (converted one-room fishing shacks, and cottages built to look like them), they spread the word, and before long 'Sconset had become a thriving actors' colony.

Today the village is almost entirely a summer community — it is said that 200 or so families live here year-round, but you would never know it. At the central square are a post office, a liquor store, a bookstore, a market, a restaurant, and a box-lunch place. The town is so small that you really can't go wrong no matter what route you take, but here's a suggestion.

Head back the way you came and turn left onto Morey Lane. Three side streets here — Evelyn, Lily, and Pochick — remain much as they were in the 1890s, when a development of rental cottages in the fishing-shack style was built here. Turn left onto Evelyn Street, then right and your first left onto Pochick Avenue, which ends at Ocean Avenue, the shore road. To the left on Ocean is the **Summer House,** an upscale inn with a fine restaurant and a poolside café (*see* Dining and Lodging, *below*). Walk on and you'll return to the square, here, turn onto Gulley Road for **'Sconset Beach** (or Codfish Park Beach), signaled by a children's swing set. Head back up Gulley to return to town.

At the rotary, turn right and follow Broadway around; a left just before the sign to Quidnet leads to a plaza and the **'Sconset Pump,** a preserved well marked with a plaque proclaiming it "dug in 1776." Turn up New Street, which leads past an art gallery on the right and, farther on, the much-photographed entryway of the **Chanticleer** (*see* Dining, *below*): A trellis arch topped by a sculpted hedge frames a rose garden with a flower-bedecked carousel horse at its center. Opposite the restaurant is the **Siasconset Casino,** built in 1899 as a tennis club and bowling alley and used during the actors'-colony heyday as a venue for theater productions (never for gambling). Though some theater is still seen here, the casino is mostly a summer tennis club and cinema. Farther on the left is the **'Sconset Union Chapel,** the village's only church, which on summer Sundays holds a Roman Catholic mass at 8:45 AM and Protestant services at 10:30.

Return to the Quidnet sign, which leads you out of 'Sconset by a different route. Outside town, turn right onto Bayberry Lane, then left to reach the red-and-white-striped **Sankaty Light,** one of three Coast Guard–operated lighthouses on Nantucket. Situated on a 90-foot-high bluff that has lost as much as 200 feet of shoreline in the past 75 years, the 1849 lighthouse is in danger of being lost, as Great Point Light was in 1984, to further erosion. A fragile piece of land, Nantucket loses more of its shoreline every year, especially at Sankaty and on the south shore, where no shoals break the ocean waves as they do on the north shore. Several ocean-front houses at Cisco were lost after a winter storm in 1990 eroded the bluff.

The lighthouse is at a dead end; as you head back out, on your right are the Scottish-looking greens of the private **Sankaty Head Golf Club.** A right turn will bring you back to the Polpis Road, alongside which hundreds of thousands of daffodils bloom in spring. A million Dutch bulbs donated by an island resident were planted along Nantucket's main roads in 1974, and more have been planted every year since. A bike path is planned for the Polpis Road in the near future.

Turning right onto Polpis, you'll pass **Sesachacha Pond** (pronounced "Seh-SAH-kah-cha" or, more often here, where long words seem to be too much trouble, just "SAH-kah-cha"). At the intersection of Quidnet Road, take either a right (which will bring you to an Audubon wildlife area a mile down the road [go right at the stop sign], with a walking path around the pond and a good view of Sankaty Light high above) or a left, remaining on Polpis Road. The entrance to the 205-acre **Windswept Cranberry Bog** (part working bog, part conservation land), with a parking area, is a bit farther on Polpis on the left. (A map of the bog, as well as the 30-page *Handbook for Visitors to the Windswept Cranberry Bog*, is available for $4 [$5 by mail] from the NCF; *see above*.)

Continuing on Polpis, a right onto Wauwinet Road leads (after about 2 miles) to the gateway of **Coatue–Coskata–Great Point,** an unpopulated spit of sand comprising three cooperatively managed wildlife refuges. The area may be entered only on foot or by four-wheel-drive vehicle, for which a permit ($50 for a year; $10 a day for a rental vehicle; tel. 508/228–2884 for information) is required. Issued only for a vehicle that is properly registered and equipped — confirm this with the rental agent if you plan to enter the area — the permits are available at the gatehouse at Wauwinet (tel. 508/228–0006) June–September or, in the off-season, from a ranger patrolling the property. If you enter on foot, be aware that Great Point is a 5-mile walk from the entrance on soft, deep sand; Jeepless people often hitchhike here. Another alternative is a Jeep tour (*see* Guided Tours, *above*).

Coatue is open for many kinds of recreation — shellfishing for bay scallops, softshell clams, quahogs, and mussels (license required); surf casting for bluefish and striped bass (spring through fall); picnicking; or just enjoying the crowdless expanse. Its beaches, dunes, salt marshes, and stands of oak and cedar attract marsh hawks, oystercatchers, terns, herring gulls, and many other bird species.

Because of frequent dangerous currents and riptides and the lack of lifeguards, swimming is strongly discouraged, especially within 200 yards of the 70-foot stone tower that is the **Great Point Light.** A 1986 re-creation of one destroyed by a storm in 1984, the new light was built to withstand 20-foot waves and winds of up to 240 miles an hour.

Continue on Polpis for 1.7 miles, past large areas of open moorland technically called lowland heath, which is very rare in the United States. On the left, an unmarked dirt track leads to **Altar Rock,** a high spot in the midst of moor and bog land from which the view is spectacular. The entire area, of which the Milestone Bog is a part, is laced with trails leading in many directions, so if you want to find your way back to Polpis Road, watch how you come . . . or leave a trail of crumbs.

About half-mile farther along Polpis, on the right, is the **Nantucket Life Saving Museum,** housed in a re-creation of an 1874 Life Saving Service station. Exhibits include original rescue equipment and boats, as well as photos and accounts of daring rescues. *Polpis Rd., tel. 508/228–1885. Admission: $1. Open mid-June–mid-Oct., daily 9:30–4:30. Closed mid-Oct.–mid-June.*

After 2 more miles, Polpis meets the Milestone Road just before the rotary, where Orange Street leads back into town.

What to See and Do with Children

Actors Theatre of Nantucket (*see* The Arts and Nightlife, *below*) offers post-beach matinees for children in July and August.

The Atheneum (Lower India St., tel. 508/228–1110) has a morning story hour in its children's wing year-round, and a Saturday-morning children's film in the off-season.

J. J. Clammp's is an 18-hole minigolf course set in gardens, reached by a path connecting with the 'Sconset bike path. Other amusements include remote-control boats on two ponds and a splash-gun game with castle-and-dragon target shooting. There's also a restaurant and a free shuttle from downtown. *Nobadeer Farm and Sun Island Rds., off Milestone Rd., tel. 508/228–8977. Admission: $6 adults, $5 children 6–12. Open July–Aug., daily 10 AM–midnight; June and Sept., daily (hours vary widely). Closed Oct.–May.*

Maria Mitchell Aquarium displays local marine life in salt- and freshwater tanks. Family shell- and plant-collecting trips are given weekly in season. *28 Washington St., near Commercial Wharf, tel. 508/228–5387. Admission: $1. Open mid-June–Aug., Tues.–Sat. 10–4. Closed Sept.–mid-June.*

Maria Mitchell Association (tel. 508/228–9198), in July and August, offers nature classes and astronomy lectures for children, and separate astronomy lectures for adults.

Murray Camp of Nantucket (Box 3437, Nantucket 02584, tel. 508/325–4600) offers four- or eight-week day camps for children 5–12. Activities include French instruction, water and other sports, arts and crafts, drama and music, and environmental-awareness classes.

Nantucket Island School of Design and the Arts (*see* The Arts and Nightlife, *below*) offers a year-round program of classes, lectures, and slide shows for children.

Off the Beaten Track

At **Bartlett's Ocean View Farm & Greenhouses,** a 100-acre farm run by eighth-generation Bartletts, visitors are welcome to tour the high-tech facilities, which include computerized greenhouses. A farm stand is open in season; in June you can pick your own strawberries. *Bartlett Farm Rd., off Hummock Pond Rd., tel. 508/228–9403. Admission free. Open in season, daily 9–5; off-season, Mon.–Sat. 9–5, Sun. 11–5.*

Miacomet Pond. A right turn off Surfside Road onto Miacomet Road (which begins paved but turns to dirt) leads to a freshwater pond surrounded by grass and heath and separated from the ocean by a narrow strip of sand. The pond — in whose reedy fringes swans and snapping turtles are sometimes seen, along with the resident ducks — is a peaceful setting for a picnic or quiet time.

Nantucket Vineyard. Five varieties of vinifera grapes grow at this vineyard and winery 2½ miles south of town. Tastings of red, white, and blush wines are available year-round, as are bottles for purchase. *3 Bartlett Farm Rd., tel. 508/228–9235. Admission free. Open Mon.–Sat. 10–6 (call first in winter).*

Shopping

The island specialty is Nantucket lightship baskets, woven of oak or cane, with woven covers adorned with scrimshaw or rosewood. First made in the 19th century by crew members passing time between chores on a lightship that stood off Sankaty Head, the baskets are now used as chic purses by those who can afford them (prices from $400 to well over $1,000).

Miniature versions of the baskets are made by plaiting fine threads of gold or silver wire. Some have working hinges and latches; some are decorated with plain or painted scrimshaw or small gems. Prices start at around $300 for gold versions.

A signature island product is a pair of all-cotton pants called Nantucket Reds, which fade to pink with washing; they're sold only at Murray's Toggery Shop (*see* Clothing, *below*).

The majority of Nantucket's shops are seasonal, opening sometime after April and closing between Labor Day and November, though an active core stays open longer.

Shopping Districts Nantucket Town's commercial district — bounded approximately by the waterfront and Main, Broad, and Centre streets and continuing along South Beach Street — contains virtually all the island's shops.

Old South Wharf, built in 1770, hosts crafts, clothing, and antiques stores; a ship's chandlery; and art galleries in small, connected "shanties." Phones are at the end of the wharf.

Straight Wharf, where the Hy-Line ferry docks, is lined with T-shirt and other tourist-oriented shops, a gallery, a museum, and restaurants. Phones and rest rooms are at the end of the wharf; boats for sails and charters line up alongside.

Food Market Monday through Saturday in season, colorful farm stands are set up on Main Street to sell local produce and flowers.

Auctions Auctions of fine antiques are held by **Rafael Osona** (tel. 508/228–3942) from Memorial Day to early December in the American Legion Hall at 21 Washington Street. Items range from the 18th to the 20th century and include everything from furniture and art to Nantucket baskets and memorabilia. For a schedule, write to Box 2607, Nantucket 02584.

Specialty Stores The "Nantucket Guide to Antique Shops" is available at
Antiques many of the following shops. (*See also* Art and Crafts, *below.*)

Forager House Collection (20 Centre St., tel. 508/228–5977) specializes in folk art and Americana, including whirligigs, wood engravings, vintage postcards, Nantucket lightship baskets, and antique maps and charts.

Nina Hellman Antiques (48 Centre St., tel. 508/228–4677) carries scrimshaw, ship models, nautical instruments, and other marine antiques, plus folk art and Nantucket memorabilia.

19 Petticoat Row (19 Centre St., tel. 508/228–5900) carries French and English country china, needlework, lace, linens, pottery, and furniture.

Tonkin of Nantucket (33 Main St., tel. 508/228–9697) has two floors of fine English antiques, including furniture, china, art, silver, marine and scientific instruments, and Staffordshire miniatures; plus new sailors' valentines and lightship baskets.

Art **Janis Aldridge** (7 Centre St., tel. 508/228–6673) has beautifully framed antique engravings, including architectural and botanical prints, plus home furnishings.

Paul La Paglia (38 Centre St., tel. 508/228–8760) has moderately priced antique prints, including Nantucket and whaling scenes, botanicals, and game fish.

Robert Wilson Galleries (34 Main St., tel. 508/228–6246), a merger of the Sherburne Gallery and Gallery One, carries fine contemporary American art, most of it representational.

Sailor's Valentine Gallery (40 Centre St., tel. 508/228–2011) has contemporary fine and folk art and exquisite sailor's valentines.

William Welch Gallery (Easy St., tel. 508/228–0687) exhibits Welch's signature watercolors, pastels, and oils of Nantucket scenes, as well as the Nantucket oil paintings of Jack Brown.

Books **Mitchell's Book Corner** (54 Main St., tel. 508/228–1080) has a room full of books on Nantucket and whaling, many ocean-related children's books, plus the usual bookstore fare.

Nantucket Bookworks (25 Broad St., tel. 508/228–4000) carries hardcover and paperback books, with an emphasis on literary works, plus a children's-book room and unusual gift and stationery items.

Clothing **Cordillera Imports** (18 Broad St., tel. 508/228–6140) sells exotic clothing, jewelry, and crafts from Latin America, Asia, and elsewhere.

Murray's Toggery Shop (62–68 Main St., tel. 508/228–0437) is a provider of traditional clothing (much of it designer-label) and footwear for men, women, and children. An outlet store at 7 New Street (tel. 508/228–3584) offers discounts of up to 50%.

The Peanut Gallery (60 Main St., tel. 508/228–2010) has a discriminating collection of children's clothing, including Mousefeathers, Cottontail Originals, and island-made items.

Zero Main (0 Main St., tel. 508/228–4401) has stylishly classic women's clothing, shoes, and accessories.

Crafts **Artisans' Store at Nantucket** (18 Broad St., tel. 508/228–4631) sells fine American arts and crafts, featuring hand-stitched quilts, jewelry, ceramics, and much more.

Claire Murray (11 S. Water St., tel. 508/228–1913 or 800/252–4733) features the designer's Nantucket-theme hand-hooked rugs and kits, quilts, and knitting and needle-work supplies.

Four Winds Craft Guild (6 Straight Wharf, tel. 508/228–9623) carries a large selection of antique and new scrimshaw and lightship baskets, as well as ship models, duck decoys, and a kit for making your own lightship basket.

Scrimshander Gallery (19 Old South Wharf, tel. 508/228–1004) deals in new and antique scrimshaw.

The Spectrum (26 Main St., tel. 508/228–4606) sells distinctive art glass, wood boxes, jewelry, kaleidoscopes, and more.

Basketmakers include **Nantucket Basket Works** (14 Dave St., tel. 508/228–2518) and **Sayle's** (112 Washington St., tel. 508/228–9876).

Food **Chanticleer to Go** (15 S. Beach St., tel. 508/325–5625) offers prepared gourmet foods from the 'Sconset French restaurant (*see* Dining, *below*), with instructions for home use, as well as pastries, salads, wine, and espresso and cappuccino.

Gifts **Museum Shop** (Broad St., next to the Whaling Museum, tel. 508/228–5785) has island-related books, antique whaling tools, spermaceti candles, reproduction furniture, and toys.

Seven Seas Gifts (46 Centre St., tel. 508/228–0958) stocks all kinds of gift and souvenir items, including an exhaustive paper-doll collection, shells, baskets, and Nantucket jigsaw puzzles.

Jewelry **The Golden Basket** (44 Main St., tel. 508/228–4344) and its affiliated shop, **Golden Nugget** (Straight Wharf, tel. 508/228–1019), sell miniature gold and silver lightship baskets, pieces with starfish and shell motifs, and other fine jewelry.

Sports and the Outdoors

Bicycling The **Madaket Bike Path,** reached via Cliff Road, is a hilly but beautiful 6-mile route to the western tip of the island. There are picnic tables by Long Pond along the way. The 6-mile **'Sconset Bike Path** starts at the rotary east of town and parallels Milestone Road, ending at 'Sconset. It is mostly level, with some gentle hills (*see* Tour 2 in Exploring Nantucket, *above*). The easy 3-mile **Surfside Bike Path,** which begins on the Surfside Road (from Main Street take Pleasant Street, then turn right onto Atlantic Avenue), leads to the island's premier ocean beach. Benches and drinking fountains are placed at strategic locations along the paths.

Nantucket Cycling Club (tel. 508/228–1164) holds open races most of the year.

Fishing   Bluefish and bass are the main island catches. The bluefishing is best at Great Point. **Barry Thurston's Fishing Tackle** (Harbor Sq., tel. 508/228–9595) and **Bill Fisher Tackle** (14 New La., tel. 508/228–2261) rent equipment and have lots of information on good fishing spots and more.

Leaving out of Straight Wharf in season are several fishing-charter boats, including the *Herbert T* (Slip 14, tel. 508/228–6655). For guided surf-casting by four-wheel-drive, including gear, contact **Whitney Mitchell** (tel. 508/228–2331) or **Beach Excursions Ltd.** (tel. 508/228–5800).

Golf   **Miacomet Golf Club** (off Somerset Rd., tel. 508/228–8987), a public course owned by the Land Bank and abutting Miacomet Pond and coastal heathland, has nine holes on very flat terrain.

Sankaty Head Golf Club (Sankaty Rd., 'Sconset, tel. 508/257–6655), a private 18-hole course, is open to the public from late September to mid-June. This challenging Scottish-style links course cuts through the moors and offers spectacular views of the lighthouse and ocean from practically every hole.

Siasconset Golf Club (Milestone Rd., tel. 508/257–6596) is an easy-walking nine-hole public course with diverse terrains.

Health and   **Club N.E.W. (Nantucket Exercise and Wellness;** 10 Young's
Fitness Clubs   Way, tel. 508/228–4750) offers StairMasters, Lifecycles, treadmills, rowers, Airdyne bikes, New Generation Nautilus, and free weights; aerobics, dance, and yoga classes; plus a nutritionist, personal trainers, and baby-sitting.

Sailing and   **Indian Summer Sports** (Steamboat Wharf, tel. 508/228–
Water Sports   3632) rents Sunfish, Windsurfers, surfboards, body boards, kayaks, and wet suits. **Force 5 Watersports** (Jetties Beach, tel. 508/228–5358; 37 Main St., tel. 508/228–0700) rents Sunfish, Windsurfers, kayaks, surfboards, boogie boards, and other water gear. Both outfits provide instruction.

The Sunken Ship (Broad and S. Water Sts., tel. 508/228–9226) offers complete dive-shop services, including lessons, equipment rentals, and charters; it also rents water skis, tennis racquets, fishing poles, and other gear.

Shellfishing   The **shellfish warden** (38 Washington St., tel. 508/228–7260) issues permits for digging for littleneck and cherrystone clams, quahogs, and mussels.

Swimming Besides the beaches (*see* Beaches, *below*) and many ponds, the **Summer House** in 'Sconset (tel. 508/257–9976) offers its pool, on the bluff above the ocean beach, to diners at its poolside café in season. Year-round, the Olympic-size, indoor **Nantucket Community Pool** (Nantucket High School, Atlantic Ave., tel. 508/228–7262) is open for lap swimming and lessons.

Tennis There are six asphalt **town courts** at Jetties Beach; sign up for one hour (usually the limit) of court time, or for lessons or tennis clinics, at the Park and Recreation Commission building there. *Tel. 508/325–5334. Open mid-June–mid-Sept.*

Brant Point Racquet Club, a short walk from town, has nine fast-dry clay courts and a pro shop and offers lessons and rentals. *N. Beach St., tel. 508/228–3700. Open mid-May–mid-Oct.*

Siasconset Casino is a private club with seven clay courts and one poor hard court. Infrequently the club has openings at 1 or 2 PM; call ahead to check. *New St., tel. 508/257–6661. Open mid-June–mid-Sept.*

Beaches

The water around Nantucket is warm from mid-June sometimes into October. The south and east shores have strong surf and undertow; those on the north and west side are calmer and warmer. Some beaches are accessible by bike path (*see* Bicycling, *above*), others by shuttle bus (*see* Getting Around in Essential Information, *above*), and others by foot or four-wheel-drive only. A mobile food truck serves the Cisco, Dionis, and Madaket beaches.

Children's A calm area by the harbor, Children's Beach is an easy walk from town (along South Beach Street from Steamboat Wharf) and is good for small children. It offers a grassy park with benches, a playground, lifeguards, food service, picnic tables, and rest rooms.

Cisco From the top of Main Street turn onto Milk Street, which turns into Hummock Pond Road; at the end — a 4-mile ride — is a long, sandy south-shore beach with lifeguards and body or board surfing.

Dionis To get to this north-shore beach, take the Madaket bike path to Eel Point Road and look for the white rock pointing to Dionis Beach — about 3 miles from town. The narrow strip of beach at the entrance turns into a wider, more private strand with high dunes and fewer children. The beach has a rocky bottom and calm, rolling waters, lifeguards, and rest rooms.

Eel Point Six miles from town and accessible only by foot, Eel Point (*see* Nature Areas, *below*) boasts the island's most beautiful and interesting beaches for those who don't necessarily need to swim — a sandbar extends out 100 yards, keeping the water shallow, clear, and calm. There are no services, just lots of birds, wild berries and bushes, and solitude.

Jetties A short bike or shuttle-bus ride from town, Jetties is the most popular beach for families because of its calm surf, lifeguards, bathhouse, rest rooms, and snack bar. It's a lively scene, especially with ferries passing, Windsurfer rentals and a playground on the beach, and tennis courts adjacent.

Madaket Known for great sunsets, this west-end surf beach is reached by the Madaket bike path and offers lifeguards and rest rooms. The Westender restaurant (*see* Dining, *below*) a short walk away has a takeout window, a bar, and a deck for drinks.

'Sconset Follow the 'Sconset bike path (or take the shuttle) to the **(Codfish Park)** village, then take your first right to this golden-sand beach with moderate to heavy surf, a lifeguard, and a playground. Food is a short walk away.

Surfside Three miles from town by the Surfside bike path or by shuttle bus, this is the premier surf beach, with lifeguards, rest rooms, a snack bar, and a wide strand of sand. It attracts college students as well as families.

Nature Areas

Coatue–Coskata–Great Point (*see* Tour 2: Town–'Sconset–Polpis Loop, *above*).

Eel Point is an unspoiled conservation area covered in places with goldenrod, wild grapes, roses, bayberries, and other coastal plants. A spit of sand with harbor on one side and shoal-protected ocean on the other, the area is a nesting place for gulls and also attracts great numbers of other birds, which perch on small islands formed by a sandbar that extends out 100 yards or more. The water is shallow (*see* Beaches, *above*), and the surf fishing is good.

Take a right off the Madaket bike path onto Eel Point Road; cars will have to be left along the dirt road about a ½-mile before the beach, 6 miles from town. Nature guides on Eel Point are available from the Maria Mitchell Association (2 Vestal St., Nantucket 02554, tel. 508/228–9198; $4.50) or the Nantucket Conservation Foundation (118 Cliff Rd., Box 13, Nantucket 02554, tel. 508/228–2884; $4).

Long Pond is a 64-acre Land Bank property with a diversity of habitats and terrain that makes birding especially good. To reach a 1-mile walking path along the pond, past meadows and a natural cranberry bog, take a left off Madaket Road onto the dirt road across from the sign to Hither Creek (near Madaket); across the bridge is a parking area and the entrance to the trail.

Milestone Bog and **Windswept Cranberry Bog** (*see* Tour 2: Town–'Sconset–Polpis Loop, *above*).

Sanford Farm/Ram Pasture and The Woods are more than 900 contiguous acres of wetlands, grasslands, forest, and former farmland off Madaket Road. Maps are available through the NCF (*see* Eel Point, *above*), which owns 767

acres, or the Land Bank (18 Broad St., Nantucket 02554, tel.
508/228–7240), which owns 165. Interpretive markers border the 6½-mile (round-trip) walking trail that leads to the
shore and offers great ocean and heath views. It begins off
the parking area near the intersection of Cliff and Madaket
roads, as do a 1.7-mile loop and a 3.1-mile round-trip to a
barn on high ground with views of the south shore. In addition to these NCF trails, a ¾-mile Land Bank walking trail
begins at the picnic tables on Madaket Road, just beyond
the Eel Point Road intersection heading west. It wanders
upland to an overview of a swamp, along a hawthorn grove,
and across meadows.

Dining

Dining in Nantucket's excellent restaurants is one of the
island's greatest — and most expensive — pleasures. In the
face of complaints about the expense, many establishments
now offer lower-priced café menus in addition to their regular menus (the price categories below are based on the latter
only). All the eating places are in town or in 'Sconset, except
for Madaket's Westender (*see below*). **Nantucket Picnic Basket** (7 N. Beach St., tel. 508/228–5177), **Provisions** (Straight
Wharf, tel. 508/228–3258), **Something Natural** (50 Cliff Rd.,
tel. 508/228–0504), and **Claudette's** ('Sconset center, tel.
508/257–6622) put up box lunches in season.

Category	Cost*
Very Expensive	over $40
Expensive	$30–$40
Moderate	$20–$30
Inexpensive	under $20

**per person, excluding drinks, service, and 5% tax*

Very Expensive

*Reviews by
Malcolm Wilson*

Chanticleer. Within a rose-covered cottage in 'Sconset is
what many consider the island's finest restaurant and others deem overpriced and overly touted — you decide. For
two decades owner-chef Jean-Charles Berruet has created
classic French fare using fresh local ingredients and herbs.
Characteristic dishes include roast spring lamb with rosemary, grilled sea bass with roasted peppers and aïoli, and
escargot-filled ravioli in garlic broth. Desserts may include
a puff-pastry apple tart with Calvados custard or a chocolate marquis (fudgy cake) with espresso sauce. A four-
course prix-fixe menu ($55) and a $35 grill menu are offered
at dinner (à la carte also available). The downstairs dining
room is formal, with a low ceiling, pearl-gray and faux-marble walls, flickering candle-bulb sconces, a fireplace, and a
view of the gardens through small-pane windows. The upstairs dining room is smaller and more casual, in pale pink.
Lunch in the rose garden is the closest thing to heaven. The
Wine Spectator Grand Award–winning wine cellar offers

more than 900 selections from California and France. *9 New St., Siasconset, tel. 508/257–6231. Reservations strongly advised. Jacket required at dinner. AE, MC, V. Closed Wed. and Columbus Day–Mother's Day.*

★ **Topper's.** Far from town at the exclusive Wauwinet resort (complimentary jitney service is provided), Topper's serves "country inn cuisine" based on fresh regional products, including such dishes as sautéed lobster with citrus, wild mushrooms, and roasted peppers in a Chardonnay beurre blanc; and roast rack of lamb with Parma-ham-and-mashed-potato pie. The list of mainly California and French wines has received the *Wine Spectator* Award of Excellence. The interior, a sophisticated yet relaxed setting with woodburning fireplace, reflects the quality of workmanship that is apparent throughout the inn: hand-decorated floors, fine wood paneling, lovely oil paintings. The outdoor patio overlooking the water is a pleasant place for lunch or drinks, especially at sunset. Also offered are a Sunday brunch ($25) and a summer bar menu featuring light fare. Daily in July and August, Topper's offers a one-hour cruise from town to Wauwinet, where guests debark for cocktails and dinner before returning to town by jitney. *Wauwinet Rd., tel. 508/228–8768. Reservations required. Jacket advised at dinner. AE, DC, MC, V. Closed mid-Dec.–mid-May.*

Expensive

Club Car. The name comes from the railway car — one of those that ran from Steamboat Wharf to 'Sconset years ago — in which the piano bar is housed. The dining room, though rather noisy, is pleasantly decorated with hanging plants, cane-back chairs, soft lighting, and linen and silver. The Continental menu, which often features seafood, changes with the season and includes game in fall. Cream of chanterelle soup is tangy with onion and herbs; rack of lamb is glazed with honey mustard and herbs. *1 Main St., tel. 508/228–1101. Reservations advised. Dress: smart casual. AE, D, DC, MC, V. Closed early Dec.–mid-May; mid-May–June and mid-Sept.–early Dec., closed Tues. and Wed.*

★ **Company of the Cauldron.** The small-pane windows at the entrance of this romantic spot are framed with climbing ivy. Inside, a profusion of flowers and antique decorative items — hanging copper pans, ship paintings and models, a Colonial chandelier, pie-plate sconces and pierced-tin lanterns with candles — completes the mood. A single four-course prix-fixe menu ($34–$38) is offered at one or two seatings each evening. An example: medallions of duck breast in rich gravy, sliced peach cooked with mango-chutney stock, snow peas, nutty wild rice, diced green and red sweet peppers, and dessert of pound cake in raspberry coulis. Service is unhurried but impeccable. *7 India St., tel. 508/228–4016. Reservations advised. Dress: smart casual. MC, V. No lunch. Closed Mon. and mid-Oct.–Memorial Day.*

★ **Summer House.** A prime location — a bluff looking out to sea in 'Sconset — as well as fine food attract a stylish clientele to this bastion of easygoing classiness. The bar/lounge is an informal area with piano music nightly in season. The dining room carries on the '30s and '40s beach look, with white painted furniture, rose and light-green linens, lots of flowers and hanging plants, and paintings of Nantucket scenes. The menu centers on fresh fish, such as sautéed salmon on oven-roasted pumpkin, turnip, and onion ragout. The poolside café lunches include grilled fish and Black Angus burgers, sandwiches, and frozen drinks. *Ocean Ave., Siasconset, tel. 508/257–9976. Reservations advised. Dress: casual. AE, MC, V. No lunch weekdays in season in dining room. Closed Columbus Day–Memorial Day; some weekdays in shoulder seasons.*

Moderate–Expensive

American Seasons. From a menu broken into regions — New England, Deep South, Wild West, and Pacific Coast — come such creative entrées as grilled loin of pork with pepper jelly and blackbean succotash, and such appetizers as a pancake of hickory-smoked lobster and wild mushrooms with American golden caviar. Folk art and tables handpainted with decorative game boards are part of the relaxed decor. *80 Centre St., tel. 508/228–7111. Reservations advised. Dress: smart casual. AE, MC, V. No lunch. Sun. brunch served Sept.– Dec. Closed Jan.–Mar.*

Boarding House. Under new ownership in 1992 after years of enjoying the highest reputation, this local favorite will be carefully watched. Initial results are good. Graduates of the New England Culinary Institute and alumni of several island restaurants, the new owners spice their contemporary Continental cuisine with Mediterranean and Asian influences, as in such dishes as roast swordfish with piperade, basil oil, and black olive quenelles. The pink cavelike walls and ceiling are enlivened a bit with art, a wall mural, and candles and lovely bouquets on the tables. Outdoor café tables provide a view of the downtown activity. A late-nite bistro menu offers less expensive fare. *12 Federal St., tel. 508/228–9622. Reservations advised in season. Dress: casual. MC, V.*

DeMarco. A chic, formal restaurant in a refurbished old home in the historic district, DeMarco serves Northern Italian cuisine "with a healthy flair," including homemade pastas, breads, and desserts and local vegetables and fish. Among the imaginative dishes produced here are poached lobster with a saffron-tomato broth and ragout of leek and Vidalia onion; and linguine with littlenecks, bell and hot peppers, onions, and marinated garlic. The overall look is refined rustic: Downstairs there's dark wood, brick walls, and lacy white curtains, while the upstairs is more spacious and brighter, with white walls. *9 India St., tel. 508/228–1836. Reservations required. Dress: smart casual. AE, D, MC, V. Dinner only. Closed Oct.–late May; some weekdays in June and Sept.*

India House. This downtown inn, built as a private home in 1803, has two small dining rooms that reflect their origins, with low beamed ceilings, hardwood floors, and small-pane windows with white café curtains. In the blue room, walls are covered half in wainscoting and half in colonial-print wallpaper, with period paintings and petit-point lacework. The pink room has the original wide-board floors and fireplace. The cuisine is nouvelle American. Appetizers like Indonesian pasta, callaloo, or baby-back ribs are all available in dinner portions; entrées are a mix of meats and such seafood dishes as pecan-cashew-glazed swordfish with carmelized Bermuda onions, lime, and thyme beurre blanc. There's also outdoor dining in summer. The popular Sunday brunch includes such temptations as three-berry French toast and poached eggs with smoked salmon and caviar. *37 India St., tel. 508/228–9043. Reservations advised for dinner; no reservations for brunch. Dress: casual. AE, D, MC, V. No lunch. Closed Dec.–Mar.*

Jared's. The formal restaurant of the Jared Coffin House is the island's most elegant dining room, with a high ceiling, salmon-colored walls, pale-green swag drapes, Federal-period antique furnishings, and chandeliers with frosted-glass globes. The American fare is equally elegant, typified by such dishes as sautéed chicken medallions and morel mushrooms with a rosemary pinot noir sauce; or seared salmon with strawberries and cassis on warm greens. A four-course prix-fixe meal is offered nightly at under $30. Service is impressive and pleasant, and the wine list is large. *29 Broad St., tel. 508/228–2400. Reservations advised. Jacket advised. AE, D, DC, MC, V. No lunch; no dinner Jan.–Apr. (breakfast year-round).*

Le Languedoc. This delightful place in a refurbished building in the historic district consists of an upstairs dining room simply decorated in English pine and checked tablecloths, a bistro-style café downstairs, and the garden terrace. Favorites among the innovative menu of American and Continental cuisine are roast rack of lamb with a honey-mustard crust, softshell crabs, and offal. The café menu (Inexpensive–Moderate ★) features a daily risotto and simply cooked seafood, as well as some more elaborate dishes; smaller portions are available. *24 Broad St., tel. 508/228–2552. Reservations advised for dining room. Jacket advised in dining room. AE, MC, V. No lunch July–Aug. Closed Jan.–mid-Apr.; Mon. mid-Apr.–June and Oct.–Dec.*

Sconset Cafe. In 'Sconset center one of the finest cooks on the island serves an imaginative American cuisine in a beach-café setting: white ceiling, walls, and ceiling fans; chintz tablecloths; and rotating displays of Nantucket art. Inexpensive lunch offerings include sandwiches and salads, such as the Café chicken salad: a grilled, marinated breast on spinach with toasted walnuts, Stilton cheese, and a mustard vinaigrette. Save room for the homemade desserts. The evening menu, which changes daily, features fish and more elaborate dinners, such as confit of duck with sun-dried Bing cherries. *Post Office Sq., Siasconset, tel. 508/257–4008. No reservations. Dress: casual. No credit cards. BYOB (liquor store next door). Closed mid-Sept.–mid-May.*

★ **21 Federal Street.** The epitome of sophisticated island dining, this is a place to be seen, as well as to enjoy some of the best new and traditional American cuisine served north of

Manhattan. An informal dining room extends into the dark-paneled bar. Beyond are two other dining rooms, with gray wainscoting, black-suede banquettes, and damask-covered tables; a curving staircase leads to a similar second floor. Lunch is served on the patio. Entrées include roast tenderloin of pork with coriander and fresh tomatillos, and grilled leg and rack of lamb with roasted garlic. *21 Federal St., tel. 508/228–2121. Reservations advised. Dress: smart casual. AE, MC, V. Closed Jan.–Mar.; may close Mon. and/or Tues. in shoulder seasons.*

Woodbox. The three small dining rooms on the first floor of this inn a few blocks from town reflect their 1709 origins, with seasoned variable-width plank floors, exposed beams, and braided rugs. One room at the back looks like the kitchen it was in the inn's early days, with walls of aged brick and extra-wide "king's boards," antique kitchen implements, and Colonial-style furniture. Yankee, contemporary American, and Continental dishes — chowder, scampi with sherry-mustard sauce, beef Wellington with cabernet sauce — and wonderful popovers are served on English china and silverplate. *29 Fair St., tel. 508/228–0587. Reservations advised. Jacket requested. No credit cards. Breakfast and dinner only. Closed Mon. and mid-Oct.–May.*

Moderate

Beach Plum Cafe and Bakery. A casual place well outside town, with polished-wood floors and softly hued local artworks on white walls, this restaurant offers an eclectic mix of cuisines. Choices may include Jamaican tuna with pineapple relish, pasta specials, or Delmonico steak with various sauces. The bakery sells take-out sandwiches, breads, and desserts. *11 West Creek Rd., tel. 508/228–8893. Reservations required for 6 or more. Dress: casual. AE, MC, V. No lunch Memorial Day–Columbus Day (breakfast and dinner served year-round).*

★ **The Hearth at the Harbor House.** On an outdoor patio and in an attractive dining room with parquet floor, oversize steel-and-copper weathervane chandeliers, antique-red walls, and comfortable upholstered chairs, simply prepared New England fare is served. Surf-and-turf combinations (filet mignon, lamb chop, and baked stuffed shrimp, for example) are popular, as is crabmeat-stuffed baked flounder with parsley butter. A lavish Sunday brunch buffet includes a raw bar and a dessert table. The four-course early-bird ("sunset special") helps beat the high cost of eating — it's served 5–7 year-round, and children under 13 dine free with parents. *S. Beach St., tel. 508/228–1500. Reservations advised; required for Sun. brunch. Dress: casual. AE, DC, MC, V. No lunch.*

Westender. A 100-yard walk from Madaket Beach, this newly rebuilt restaurant offers take-out burgers, salads, sandwiches, and fried fish; a bar with fireplace and old fishing photos; an outdoor cocktail terrace; the main dining room, with natural wood wainscoting and local art on white walls; and a second floor with views of the water and great sunsets. The menu features American grilled seafood, with nightly specials based on the day's catch, and always a lobster plate. A light menu includes nachos, quesadillas, popcorn shrimp, steamers, and a raw bar. *Madaket Rd., tel. 508/228–5197. No reservations. Dress: casual. MC, V. Closed Columbus Day–Memorial Day.*

Inexpensive–Moderate

★ **Quaker House.** This storefront restaurant — two small, prettily decorated rooms whose small-pane windows framed in lace look out onto Centre Street — is one of the best bargains on the island. Prix-fixe four-course dinners ($15–$24) feature such entrées as Bombay chicken (a curry with apple, raisins, and coconut), swordfish with béarnaise sauce, and beef and pasta dishes. The owners take pride in the quality of their ingredients, which include meats and poultry raised humanely and free of chemicals, hormones, or additives. At breakfast try the baked-apple pancake, huge and sweet, with cinnamony apples and powdered sugar. *5 Chestnut St., tel. 508/228–9152. No reservations. Dress: casual. MC, V. Breakfast and dinner only. Closed Columbus Day–Memorial Day.*

Rose & Crown. A fun, lively place, the Rose & Crown is a barnlike room with beam ceiling, walls hung with old signs and musical instruments, a big bar, and a dance floor (there's live music most evenings in season). Choose from appetizers such as a zesty chowder, Buffalo chicken wings, and popcorn shrimp; for main courses, there are grilled pizzas, burgers, and more adventurous offerings such as seafood pasta, peppered filet mignon, and chicken teriyaki. *23 S. Water St., tel. 508/228–2595. No reservations. Dress: casual. MC, V. Closed early Dec.–mid-Apr.*

The Tap Room. The downstairs tavern restaurant of the Jared Coffin House is a dark, woody, cozy room decorated with ship prints and whale models. The dinner menu features hearty meat and fish dishes, such as prime rib, fried clams, and baked stuffed shrimp; at lunch choose from a light menu or more substantial dishes like fried or broiled fish, eaten on the outdoor patio, weather permitting. *29 Broad St., tel. 508/228–2400. No reservations. Dress: casual. AE, D, DC, MC, V.*

Inexpensive

Atlantic Cafe. This casual, sometimes noisy place at the center of town offers an active bar and a fun menu, with large portions at a good price. Finger foods include zucchini sticks that are golden and crispy on the outside, moist on the inside, sprinkled with grated cheese, and served with a hot sauce. Entrées are a mix of simply prepared fish, chicken, burgers, Mexican items, salads and sandwiches, and more. At the front of the restaurant, with half-wainscoting walls, high peaked ceilings, and nautical art, are tables topped with floral cloths and glass; at the back are booths. *15 S. Water St., tel. 508/228–0570. No reservations. Dress: casual. AE, D, DC, MC, V.*

★ **The Brotherhood of Thieves.** Long lines are a fixture outside this English-style pub restaurant. Inside, lit by flickering candles, is a dark room with low ceilings, exposed brick and beams, and a fireplace that is especially welcoming on cold or rainy evenings. When the place gets busy, strangers are seated together at long tables; a section at the back has more intimate seating. A convivial atmosphere prevails — thanks partly to the live folk music at night and to the hundreds of coffee drinks and other alcoholic beverages on the menu. Dine happily on good chowder and soups, fried fish and seafood, burgers, jumbo sandwiches, and shoestring fries (long curls with the skins on). *23 Broad St., no tel. No reservations. Dress: casual. No credit cards.*

Lodging

Other than cottages (which are scattered throughout the island) and a few inns and hotels, all of Nantucket's lodging places are in town. Those in the center are convenient, but houses are close together and right on the street; in season there may be street noise until midnight. Inns a five- or 10-minute walk from the center, as on Cliff Road or Fair Street, are quieter. 'Sconset is quieter still and has the rose-covered cottages and less crowded beach, but those looking for action may be frustrated by the 7-mile commute to town.

Nantucket Accommodations (Box 217, Nantucket 02554, tel. 508/228–9559) and **Martha's Vineyard and Nantucket Reservations** (Box 1322, Lagoon Pond Rd., Vineyard Haven 02568, tel. 508/693–7200 or 800/649–5671 in MA) book inns, hotels, bed-and-breakfasts, and cottages. **House Guests Cape Cod and the Islands** (Box 1881, Orleans 02653, tel. 508/896–7053 or 800/666–4678) books B&Bs, cottages, and efficiencies. **Heaven Can Wait** (Box 622, Siasconset 02564, tel. 508/257–4000) plans island honeymoons. **DestINNations** (tel. 800/333–4667) handles a limited number of Nantucket hotels and B&Bs but will arrange any and all details of a visit.

A number of realtors (complete lists are provided by the chamber and the Information Bureau) offer rentals ranging from in-town apartments in antique houses to new waterfront houses. **Congdon & Coleman** (57 Main St., Nantucket 02554, tel. 508/325–5000, fax 508/325–5025) has properties islandwide; **'Sconset Real Estate** (Box 122, Siasconset 02564, tel. 508/257–6335 summer, 508/228–1815 winter), in the 'Sconset and Tom Nevers areas.

The **Nantucket Information Bureau** (*see* Important Addresses and Numbers in Essential Information, *above*) maintains a list of room availability in season for last-minute bookings. In the off-season, places that remain open drop their prices dramatically, by as much as 50%. No camping is allowed on the island.

The **Star of the Sea AYH-Hostel,** a 64-bed facility in a former lifesaving station, is a 3-mile ride on a bike path from town, at Surfside Beach. Planned for 1993 are four "family rooms" sleeping four. Reservations are essential in July and August, recommended always. *Surfside, Nantucket 02554, tel. 508/228–0433. Open May–Columbus Day.*

Category	Cost*
Very Expensive	over $200
Expensive	$150–$200
Moderate	$110–$150
Inexpensive	under $110

all prices are for a standard double room in high season, excluding 5.7% state tax and 4% local tax

Very Expensive

Cliffside Beach Club. Although the cedar-shingle exterior, landscaped with climbing roses and hydrangeas, and the pavilion on the private sandy beach a mile from town reflect the club's 1920s origins, the interiors have been redesigned in summery contemporary style, with white walls, fine woodwork, white or natural wood furniture, cathedral ceilings, and local art. All rooms have refrigerators, cable TV/HBO, and phones; some have air conditioning, kitchenettes, fireplaces, wet bars, or private decks. Two big "townhouse suites" have full kitchens and decks overlooking dunes, moors, and Nantucket Sound. *Jefferson Ave., Box 449, Nantucket 02554, tel. 508/228–0618. 19 rooms, 8 apartments, 1 cottage. Facilities: Continental breakfast; restaurant; piano bar; beach; playground; exercise room with Nautilus, Stair-Master, treadmill, free weights; day sails available. AE. Closed mid-Oct.–late May.*

Summer House. Here, across from 'Sconset Beach and clustered around a flower-filled yard, are the rose-covered cottages we associate with Nantucket summers. Each one- or two-bedroom cottage is furnished in a blend of unfussy, breezy beach style and romantic English country — papered or trompe-l'oeil-bordered walls, white lace and eyelet curtains and spreads, Laura Ashley floral accents, and stripped English-pine antique furnishings. Some cottages have fireplaces or kitchens; all have new marble baths with whirlpools. *Ocean Ave., Box 313, Siasconset 02564, tel. 508/257–4148, fax 508/257–6510. 8 cottages. Facilities: large Continental breakfast, 2 restaurants, piano bar; oceanfront outdoor pool, water aerobics, poolside bar; private beach, concierge; golf and tennis arranged at private clubs. AE, MC, V. Closed Nov.–mid-May.*

★ **Wauwinet.** An exquisite location, impeccable furnishings, and extensive services and amenities make this historic inn, which was completely renovated in 1988, a most luxurious perch. A sweeping lawn with white chaise longues leads to a pebbly private harbor beach (where you can play with the new life-size wooden chess set). A minute's walk through dunes brings you to sandy Atlantic Ocean beach stretching for miles in relative isolation — there is little else here, at the gateway to Coatue. Jitney service to and from town 8 miles away and Steamship pickup make the location convenient for those without cars. Each guest room — individually decorated in country/beach style, with pine antiques — has a phone, air-conditioning, and color TV with VCR; the most expensive have spectacular views of the sunset over the water. *Wauwinet Rd., Box 2580, Nantucket 02584, tel. 508/228–0145 or 800/426–8718, fax 508/228–6712. 25 rooms, 5 cottages. Facilities: full breakfast, afternoon port or sherry and cheese, restaurant, bar, room service, 2 Har-Tru tennis courts, Sunfish and lessons, harbor sails, Mercedes four-wheel-drive trips to Great Point, mountain bikes, croquet, turn-down service, concierge, videocassette library, business services, massage. AE, DC, MC, V. Closed mid-Dec.–May.*

Wharf Cottages. These weathered-shingle cottages sit on a wharf in Nantucket harbor, with yachts tied up just steps away. Each unit is pretty snug but well fitted out, with a little garden and sitting area, a telephone, cable TV with VCR, a fully equipped kitchen, and attractive modern decor with a nautical flavor: white walls, navy-blue rugs, light-wood floors and furniture. Studios have a sofa bed for sleeping; other cottages have one to three bedrooms. Some have large water-view windows; all have water views. There's a three-night minimum in high season; monthly and seasonal rates are available. *New Whale St., Box 359, Nantucket 02554, tel. 508/228–4620; for reservations, 800/475–2637. 27 cottages. Facilities: daily maid service, docking facilities. AE, D, DC, MC, V. Closed mid-Oct.–Memorial Day.*

★ **White Elephant.** For many years a hallmark of service and style on the island, the White Elephant offers above all a choice location — right on Nantucket harbor, separated only by a wide lawn. The main hotel, wrapped by a deck with a fine view of the bobbing boats, has a formal restaurant with waterside outdoor café, a lounge with entertainment, and a large new harborfront pool and Jacuzzi, beautifully landscaped with pink roses on white wrought-iron fencing. Rooms have an English country look, with stenciled pine armoires, sponge-painted walls, and floral fabrics. The Breakers, a separate unit, offers more luxurious accommodations that include minibars and minifridges. Its rooms have a cool elegance, with sumptuous fabrics in shades of green and cream, dark woods, half-canopy beds, and window walls; in its top-price rooms, French doors open onto the lawn or a private deck with a great view. The several groupings of gray-shingled cottages (some with full kitchens) range from handsome waterfront units landscaped with big pink roses and done up in the English country style, to units in a pine grove modernized for 1992 and redone in a similar style. The entire property has been renovated since 1989, and everything is fresh and new. All rooms have phones and cable TV; some have VCRs and air-conditioning. *Easton St., Box 359, Nantucket 02554, tel. 508/228–2500; for reservations, tel. 800/475–2637. 48 rooms, 32 1- to 3-bedroom cottages. Facilities: Continental breakfast, restaurant, lounge with entertainment, room service, poolside food and bar service, concierge, heated outdoor pool (with lift for disabled), croquet court, putting green, reduced rate at local health and tennis clubs, minifridges, fully disabled- accessible rooms, meeting rooms,* *audiovisual equipment, fax, boat slips available. AE, D, DC, MC, V. Closed mid-Sept.–Memorial Day.*

Expensive

★ **Harbor House.** This family-oriented complex, like its more upscale sibling, the White Elephant, has been extensively renovated and prides itself on service. The 1886 main inn and several "town houses" are set on a flower-filled quadrangle steps from the town center. Standard rooms are done in English-country style, with bright floral fabrics and queen-size canopy beds; some have French doors that open onto decks. The generally larger town house rooms, in buildings grouped around the pool, have a more traditional look, with upscale pine and pastels; some have whirlpools, cathedral ceilings, sofa beds, and decks. All rooms have phones and TVs with VCR. The Garden Cottage has its own garden and a private-house feel, but its rooms (some with pressed-tin ceilings) are smaller. *S. Beach St., Box 359, Nantucket 02554, tel. 508/228–1500; for reservations, tel. 800/475–2637. 111 rooms. Facilities: restaurant, lounge with entertainment, poolside bar, room service, concierge, heated outdoor pool, putting green, business services, reduced rate at local health and tennis clubs. AE, D, DC, MC, V.*

★ **Westmoor Inn.** Built in 1917 as a Vanderbilt summer house, this yellow Federal-style mansion with widow's walk and portico matches the grandeur of its setting, amid open moorland less than a mile from town. The many common areas include the wide lawn, set with Adirondack chairs, and the garden patio, secluded behind 11-foot hedges. Beyond the entry hall and grand staircase is a large, gracious living room with piano and game table, where guests meet at a late-afternoon hospitality hour; and a wicker-filled sun room with the inn's only TV. A high point of a stay is breakfast in the glassed-in dining room, with views of the town, moors, and sky from walls and ceiling. Guest rooms are bright and white, with white eyelet comforters and pillows, old prints, and some very nice antiques; all have phones (for outgoing calls). One first-floor "suite" has a giant bath with extra-large Jacuzzi and French doors opening onto the lawn. Three apartments in a separate building were redone with new kitchens in 1991. An uncrowded ocean beach and the Madaket bike path are a short walk away. *Cliff Rd., Nantucket 02554, tel. 508/228–0877. 15 rooms. Facilities: Continental breakfast, bicycles, beach towels and chairs. AE, MC, V. Closed early Dec.–Apr.*

Moderate–Expensive

★ **Jared Coffin House.** This complex of six buildings is a longtime favorite of many visitors to Nantucket for its dependability and class. The main building, a three-story brick mansion built in 1845 by a wealthy shipowner and topped by a cupola, has a historic tone that the others don't. The public and guest rooms are furnished with period antiques (the other buildings, with reproductions), Oriental carpets, and lace curtains. The Harrison Gray House, an 1842 Greek Re-

vival mansion across the street, offers larger guest rooms
with large baths and some sofas, as well as less street noise.
All rooms have phones and, except in the main house, color
TV; some have minifridges. Small, inexpensive single rooms
are available. *29 Broad St., Box 1580, Nantucket 02554, tel.
508/228–2405, 508/228–2400, or 800/248–2405. 60 rooms. Facilities: full breakfast (off-season only), restaurant, tavern, outdoor café, concierge, some accommodation for pets. AE, D, DC,
MC, V.*

Nantucket Settlements. These attractively decorated properties consist of three apartment houses and a complex of
seven cottages, all with kitchens, TVs, phones, and access
to laundry facilities. Right in town are the Nantucket
Whaler (8 N. Water St.), an 1846 Greek Revival with pilas-
tered white clapboard facade and a large deck, and the 1822
Grey Goose (24 Hussey St.), with high ceilings, old moldings, and antique-looking furnishings. Within a half-mile of
town center is 95 Orange Street, a late 18th-century house
renovated in 1987 with all new kitchens and baths and a
brick patio with barbecue grill. Also a half-mile out are the
gray-shingled Brush Lane Cottages, in a quiet compound
with lots of flowers and greenery. The newest cottages are
spacious and bright, with cathedral ceilings, lots of white
and light wood, oak cabinets in big kitchens, and French
doors that open onto decks. *Office: 8 N. Water St., Box 1337,
Nantucket 02554, tel. 508/228–6597 or 800/462–6882, fax
508/228–6291. 24 units (studios to 3-bedroom cottages). MC, V.*

Wade Cottages. On a bluff overlooking the ocean, this complex of guest rooms, apartments, and cottages in 'Sconset
couldn't be better located for beach lovers. The buildings,
in the same family since the 1920s, are arranged around a
central lawn with a great ocean view; the prize catch is a
newer cottage nearer the water. Most inn rooms and cottages have sea views; phones were installed throughout in
1992. Furnishings are generally in somewhat worn beach
style, with some antique pieces. *Shell St., Box 211, Siasconset
02564, tel. 508/257–6308 or 508/257–6383; off-season, 212/989–
6423. 8 rooms, 3 with private bath; 5 apartments (1-wk min); 3
cottages (2-wk min). Facilities: Continental breakfast (inn
rooms only), ping-pong, badminton, swing set, common refrigerator, laundry, beach. MC, V. Closed mid-Oct.–late May.*

Moderate

Beachside Resort. Those who prefer rooms-around-a-pool
motels with all the creature comforts will find a very nice
one here, a bit of a walk from town center. Each unit in the
one- and two-story buildings is furnished in white wicker
and florals and has a queen-size or two double beds, tiled
bath, minifridge, cable TV/HBO, phone, and air-conditioning. All rooms have pool- view decks; some have French
doors opening onto them. Efficiencies are in a high-traffic
area but are inexpensive. *N. Beach St., Nantucket 02554, tel.
508/228–2241 or 800/322–4433. 87 rooms, 3 efficiencies. Facilities: Continental breakfast (in season), heated and disabled-accessible outdoor pool; tennis club adjacent. Children under 17*

stay free with parents. AE, DC, MC, V. Closed early Dec.–mid-Apr.

Centerboard Guest House. The look of this inn, a few blocks from the center of town, is different from any other. The white walls (some with murals of moors and sky in soft pastels), blond-wood floors, white or natural wood furniture, and natural woodwork with a light wash of mauve tint create a cool, spare, dreamy atmosphere. There is yet more white, in the lacy linens and puffy comforters on the feather beds. Touches of color are added by stained-glass lamps, antique quilts, and fresh flowers. The first-floor suite (right off the entry hall) is a stunner, with 11-foot ceilings, a Victorian living room with fireplace and wet bar, parquet floors, superb furnishings and decor, and a green-marble bath with Jacuzzi. Each room has a TV with VCR access (you rent tapes in town), a phone, and a minifridge. *8 Chester St., Box 456, Nantucket 02554, tel. 508/228–9696. 4 rooms, 1 suite, 1 studio. Facilities: Continental breakfast. AE, MC, V.*

Century House. This 1833 house, a few blocks from the town center, was built to serve guests, and innkeeper Jean Heron continues to do so with enthusiasm. The decor is casual: wallpapers and fabrics (including down comforters) in the Laura Ashley light-floral style, homey furnishings (some canopy beds) on spatter-painted wide-board floors. A breakfast buffet highlighted by homemade granola is served in the country kitchen or on the wide veranda. In the afternoon guests gather for tea or cocktails; setups and snacks are provided. The innkeepers also rent two cottages, one in 'Sconset across from the beach and one on Nantucket harbor. *10 Cliff Rd., Nantucket 02554, tel. 508/228–0530. 14 rooms, 12 with private bath. Facilities: Continental breakfast, common TV. No credit cards.*

★ **Cliff Lodge.** Guest rooms at this B&B are big, bright, and airy, with lots of sky blue and crisp white, pastel hooked rugs on spatter-painted floors, country curtains and furnishings, light floral wallpapers, white eyelet linens, and phones and small TVs. Built in 1771, the lodge preserves lots of old-house flavor, in moldings, wainscoting, and wide-board floors. Some baths are very small. The very pleasant apartment has a fireplaced living room, a private deck and entrance, and a large eat-in kitchen. In addition to the attractive common rooms, guests may take afternoon tea or cocktails (setups and snacks provided) in the wicker sun porch, on the garden terrace, or on the roofwalk patio, with a great view of the harbor. Also available are apartments on Old North Wharf, including a four-bedroom with fireplace and cathedral ceiling. *9 Cliff Rd., Nantucket 02554, tel. 508/228–9480. 11 rooms, 1 apt. Facilities: Continental breakfast, afternoon tea in season, common refrigerator and coffeemaker, barbecue grill, beach towels, parking. No smoking in rooms. AE, MC, V. Closed Jan.; weekdays in Feb.*

18 Gardner Street. Set in two antique buildings, including the 1835 main house with 9-foot ceilings, this B&B offers good-size rooms — 10 with working fireplaces — and a number of thoughtful amenities, like fresh-baked cookies always at the ready. Rooms are done in mauve and pale green, with satin wallcoverings, wide-board floors, mostly queen-size beds (some canopy or four-poster) with eyelet sheets and handmade quilts, some nice antique pieces, and brass lamps. Most have cable TV with remote. One common room has a TV, another a fireplace. Winter and holiday packages are available; summer holiday weekends feature a backyard barbecue. *18 Gardner St., Nantucket 02554, tel. 508/228–1155 or 800/435–1450. 14 rooms (2 share bath), 3 suites. Facilities: Continental breakfast (full in main house), common phone, guest fridges, beach towels, honor bar for sodas and snacks, bikes, parking; picnic baskets available. No smoking. MC, V.*

Parker Guest House. Clean and cheerful, with air-conditioning, a minifridge, color cable TV, and a coffee-maker in every room, this guest house is smack in the center of town. This makes it convenient, though it may be noisy at night. The decor is simple, with pine paneling and furnishings and country curtains. A common room was added in 1992. *4 E. Chestnut St., Nantucket 02554, tel. 508/228–4625 or 800/248–4625. 6 rooms (1 with detached private bath). No smoking. AE, MC, V.*

Seven Sea Street. This inn on a quiet side street in the center of town was built in 1987 by the owners, also publishers of *Nantucket Journal* magazine. Though the furnishings are in the Colonial style and colors, the place has a Scandinavian look, with tongue-in-groove light pine and red oak, exposed-beam ceilings, stenciled white walls with pine trim, and highly polished wide-board floors. Each room has a braided rug, a queen-size bed with fishnet canopy and quilt, a rocking chair, a modern bath with large fiberglass stall shower and brass fittings, a phone, cable TV, refrigerator, hairdryer, and desk area. Guests can relax in the garden patio or on the harbor-view widow's walk. *7 Sea St., Nantucket 02554, tel. 508/228–3577. 8 rooms. No smoking. Facilities: Continental breakfast, (group-size) Jacuzzi room, library of leather-bound classics. AE, MC, V.*

76 Main Street. Built in 1883 by a sea captain, just above the bustle of the shops, this B&B carefully blends antiques and reproductions, Oriental rugs, handmade quilts, and lots of fine woods. The Victorian entrance hall is of cherry and is dominated by a long, elaborately carved staircase. Room No. 3, originally the dining room, also has wonderful woodwork, a carved-wood armoire, and twin four-posters; spacious No. 1, once the front parlor, has three large windows, a high ceiling, massive redwood pocket doors, and a bed with eyelet spread and canopy. Both are on the first floor. The motel-like rooms in the 1955 annex out back have low ceilings and are a bit dark but are large and good for families: they have color TV and a refrigerator. *76 Main St., Nantucket 02554, tel. 508/228–2533. 18 rooms. No smoking. Facilities: Continental breakfast, common refrigerator. AE, MC, V.*

★ **Ten Lyon Street Inn.** A five-minute walk from the town center, this mostly new house has been rebuilt with historical architectural touches such as variable-width plank floors, salvaged Colonial mantels on the nonworking fireplaces, and hefty ceiling beams of antiqued red oak. The white walls and blond woodwork provide a clean stage for exquisite antique Oriental rugs in deep, rich colors; choice antiques, such as Room No. 1's French tester bed draped in white mosquito netting; and English floral fabrics, down comforters, and big pillows. Bathrooms are white and bright; several have separate shower and antique tub, and all have antique porcelain pedestal sinks and brass fixtures. *10 Lyon St., Nantucket 02554, tel. 508/228–5040. 7 rooms. Facilities: health-conscious Continental breakfast. MC, V. Closed mid-Dec.–mid-Apr.*

Inexpensive–Moderate

Carlisle House Inn. A block or two from the center of town is this 1765 Colonial. A deluxe first-floor guest room has an original wall of pine paneling with working fireplace, an Oriental carpet, a canopy bed, a marble-top dresser and side table, a TV, and a small bath. Most rooms have a casual, Grandma's-house feel, with wicker chairs, iron-and-brass or other antique beds, working fireplaces (five rooms), pumpkin-pine floors, country curtains and stenciled walls, and a claw-foot tub here and there. A complimentary Continental breakfast is served in a bright, glassed-in sun porch (with TV). Small single rooms are available. *26 N. Water St., Nantucket 02554, tel. 508/228–0720. 14 rooms, 8 with private bath (6 rooms share 2 baths). AE, MC, V.*

★ **Corner House.** Accommodations at this B&B a block or two from the town center range from small, rustic third-floor rooms with tiny baths in the main house (a 1790 gem with lots of old-house flavor) to spacious rooms with cathedral ceilings in a new building nearby. Some rooms have separate sitting or extra sleeping areas, TVs, or refrigerators; all have interesting beds (antiques, reproduction, canopy, brass, tall-post) on firm mattresses, topped with down pillows and comforters. The main house's original keeping room, where guests gather for tea, and a large living room with fireplace and TV both feature richly detailed Colonial woodwork, as do some rooms. There's also a wicker-filled screened porch and a garden terrace. Golf, tennis, and sailing packages are available. *49 Centre St., Nantucket 02554, tel. 508/228–1530. 14 rooms, 1 suite. Smoking discouraged. Facilities: Continental breakfast, afternoon tea, common TV, fax. MC, V. Closed early Jan.–mid-Feb.*

Inexpensive

Chestnut House. At this centrally located guest house, the innkeepers' hand-hooked rugs and paintings, along with their son's Tiffany-style lamps, are everywhere, creating homey guest rooms. All rooms have minifridges; each suite has a sitting room with sofa and TV. The guest parlor reflects the Arts and Crafts style, and some rooms have William Morris–theme wallpapers. The cottage sleeps four (queen-size bed and sofa bed) and has a full kitchen and bath and a small deck — a convenient option for a family here in the center of town. *3 Chestnut St., Nantucket 02554, tel.*

508/228–0049. 3 rooms, 3 suites, 1 cottage. Facilities: morning coffee, common TV. AE, MC, V.

Hawthorn House. Not only did innkeeper Mitch Carl continue the family business when he opened his guest house; he opened his inn just down the street from his folks' place, the Chestnut House (*see above*). Mitch and his wife, Diane, have filled their 1850 house with art, hooked rugs, and stained glass; each room has a minifridge. The small rooms are decorated with antiques, William Morris–style wallpapers, and Diane's handmade quilts. A dark but conveniently located cottage sleeps two and has air-conditioning and TV. *2 Chestnut St., Nantucket 02554, tel. 508/228–1468. 9 rooms, 7 with private bath; 1 cottage. Facilities: morning coffee, common TV, refrigerators. MC, V.*

★ **Martin's Guest House.** This casual and homey B&B in an 1803 house off the main drag offers mostly spacious rooms with country curtains, four-poster beds or canopies, pretty linens, and fresh flowers; several have queen-size beds and couches. Room No. 21, on the second floor, has a fireplace, a minifridge, and a private porch overlooking the backyard. The large, comfortable living room with a fireplace and a wide porch with hammock and rockers invite lingering. Third-floor rooms are sunny and bright, with a quirky under-eaves feel. *61 Centre St., Box 743, Nantucket 02554, tel. 508/228–0678. 13 rooms, 9 with private bath (4 rooms share 1 bath). Facilities: large Continental breakfast, sherry in rooms, common TV, piano. Smoking discouraged. AE, MC, V.*

Nesbitt Inn. This family-run guest house in the center of town offers comfortable, shared-bath rooms (including cheap singles) sweetly done in authentically Victorian style, with lace curtains, some marble-top and brass antiques, and a sink in each room. Some beds are not as firm as they should be, and the location (next door to a popular bar-restaurant) means it gets noisy (ask for a room on the quieter side), but the Nesbitt is still a very good buy, and the least expensive of listed inns. *21 Broad St., Nantucket 02554, tel. 508/228–0156 or 508/228–2446. 10 doubles and 3 singles share 3 baths. Pets allowed. Facilities: Continental breakfast, common refrigerator, swing set, backyard deck and grill, beach towels. MC, V. No smoking in rooms.*

The Arts and Nightlife

For listings of events, see the free seasonal weekly *Nantucket Map & Legend,* the ferry companion paper *Yesterday's Island,* and both island newspapers. All venues listed below are located in Nantucket Town, unless otherwise indicated.

The Arts

Nantucket Filmworks presents a different slide show on Nantucket each year, created by one of the island's best photographers, Cary Hazlegrove. Shows are given at the Methodist Church (Centre and Main Sts., tel. 508/228–3783) mid-June–mid-September.

Nantucket Island School of Design and the Arts (Wauwinet Rd., tel. 508/228–9248; for schedule, write to Box 958, Nantucket 02554) offers a year-round program of classes, lectures, and slide shows for adults and children.

Theater **Actors Theatre of Nantucket** (Methodist Church, Centre and Main Sts., tel. 508/228–6325) presents several plays each season (Memorial Day–Columbus Day), plus children's post-beach matinees, comedy nights, and readings.

Theatre Workshop of Nantucket (Bennett Hall, 62 Centre St., tel. 508/228–4305), a community theater since 1956, offers plays, musicals, and staged readings year-round.

Music **Nantucket Arts Council** (tel. 508/228–2227) sponsors a music series (jazz, country, classical) at the Methodist Church on Centre Street September– June.

Nantucket Chamber Music Center (Coffin School, Winter St., tel. 508/228–3352) offers year-round choral and instrumental concerts as well as instruction.

In July and August, **Nantucket Musical Arts Society** (Box 897, Nantucket 02554, tel. 508/228–3735) holds Tuesday-evening concerts featuring internationally acclaimed musicians (past participants include Virgil Thomson and Ned Rorem) at the First Congregational Church (62 Centre St.), and free informal "Meet the Artists" gatherings the previous evening.

Also in July and August, **Noonday Concerts** on an 1831 Goodrich organ are given Thursdays at noon at the Unitarian Church (11 Orange St., tel. 508/228–5466).

Band concerts (tel. 508/228–1700) are held on Sundays in July and August at 7 PM in Harbor Square.

Film **Dreamland Theatre** (19 S. Water St., tel. 508/228–5356) and **Gaslight** (N. Union St., tel. 508/228–4435) are the island's two first-run theaters. The **Siasconset Casino** (New St., Siasconset, tel. 508/257–6661) shows first-run films in season — bring a pillow for the metal folding chairs.

Nightlife

Tavern Restaurants **The Brotherhood of Thieves** (*see* Dining, *above*) has live folk music year-round. The well-stocked bar offers an interesting selection of beers and ales, plus dozens of cordials and liqueurs.

The Tap Room (*see* Dining, *above*) has live easy-listening piano or guitar, and sometimes Irish folk music, year-round.

Piano Lounges **The Hearth at the Harbor House** (*see* Dining, *above*) has dancing to live music (country to folk) in its attractive, fire-placed lounge on weekends year-round and to Top 40 tunes by a piano-and-vocal duo most nights in season. Also available are darts, backgammon, cribbage, sports on four large-screen TVs, and a fun light menu.

The Regatta at the White Elephant (Easton St., tel. 508/228–2500) has a formal, harbor-view lounge with a pianist playing show tunes most nights from Memorial Day to mid-September. Proper dress is suggested.

Dance Clubs Open daily year-round are **The Box** (aka Chicken Box; 6 Dave St., off Lower Orange St., tel. 508/228–9717) and **The Muse** (44 Atlantic Ave., tel. 508/228–6873 or 508/228–8801), where all ages dance to rock, reggae (especially popular on the island), and other music, live or recorded. The Muse also has a pizza shop.

The **Rose & Crown** (*see* Dining, *above*) is a friendly, noisy restaurant with a big bar and a small dance floor. Live bands perform six nights in season (with a DJ between sets), weekends off-season; plus there's some comedy.

Miscellaneous A series of winter concerts and children's events, along with a weekly auction of mid-range antiques year-round, are available separately or as part of early-dinner packages offered by the **Hearth at the Harbor House** (*see* Dining, *above*). Auctions with wine-reception previews are held two nights a week in winter, also available as dinner packages.

Hy-Line (tel. 508/228–3949) offers a weekly moonlight cruise with DJ and dancing in summer.

Index

Personal Itinerary

Departure *Date*

Time

Transportation

Arrival *Date* *Time*

Departure *Date* *Time*

Transportation

Accommodations

Arrival *Date* *Time*

Departure *Date* *Time*

Transportation

Accommodations

Arrival *Date* *Time*

Departure *Date* *Time*

Transportation

Accommodations

Personal Itinerary

Arrival *Date*   *Time*

Departure *Date*   *Time*

Transportation

Accommodations

Arrival *Date*   *Time*

Departure *Date*   *Time*

Transportation

Accommodations

Arrival *Date*   *Time*

Departure *Date*   *Time*

Transportation

Accommodations

Arrival *Date*   *Time*

Departure *Date*   *Time*

Transportation

Accommodations

Personal Itinerary

Arrival	*Date*	*Time*
Departure	*Date*	*Time*
Transportation		
Accommodations		

Arrival	*Date*	*Time*
Departure	*Date*	*Time*
Transportation		
Accommodations		

Arrival	*Date*	*Time*
Departure	*Date*	*Time*
Transportation		
Accommodations		

Arrival	*Date*	*Time*
Departure	*Date*	*Time*
Transportation		
Accommodations		

Personal Itinerary

Arrival   *Date*   *Time*

Departure   *Date*   *Time*

Transportation

Accommodations

Arrival   *Date*   *Time*

Departure   *Date*   *Time*

Transportation

Accommodations

Arrival   *Date*   *Time*

Departure   *Date*   *Time*

Transportation

Accommodations

Arrival   *Date*   *Time*

Departure   *Date*   *Time*

Transportation

Accommodations

Addresses

Name	*Name*
Address	*Address*
Telephone	*Telephone*
Name	*Name*
Address	*Address*
Telephone	*Telephone*
Name	*Name*
Address	*Address*
Telephone	*Telephone*
Name	*Name*
Address	*Address*
Telephone	*Telephone*
Name	*Name*
Address	*Address*
Telephone	*Telephone*
Name	*Name*
Address	*Address*
Telephone	*Telephone*
Name	*Name*
Address	*Address*
Telephone	*Telephone*

Addresses

Name	*Name*
Address	*Address*
Telephone	*Telephone*
Name	*Name*
Address	*Address*
Telephone	*Telephone*
Name	*Name*
Address	*Address*
Telephone	*Telephone*
Name	*Name*
Address	*Address*
Telephone	*Telephone*
Name	*Name*
Address	*Address*
Telephone	*Telephone*
Name	*Name*
Address	*Address*
Telephone	*Telephone*
Name	*Name*
Address	*Address*
Telephone	*Telephone*
Name	*Name*
Address	*Address*
Telephone	*Telephone*

Over 1500 Great Weekend Escapes...

in Six Fabulous Fodor's Guides to Bed & Breakfasts, Country Inns, Cottages, and Other Weekend Pleasures!

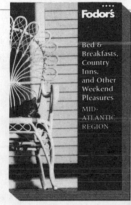

The Mid-Atlantic Region

The South

New England

The West Coast

England and Wales

Canada

Fodor's Travel Guides

U.S. Guides

Alaska

Arizona

Boston

California

Cape Cod, Martha's Vineyard, Nantucket

The Carolinas & the Georgia Coast

Chicago

Disney World & the Orlando Area

Florida

Hawaii

Las Vegas, Reno, Tahoe

Los Angeles

Maine, Vermont, New Hampshire

Maui

Miami & the Keys

New England

New Orleans

New York City

Pacific North Coast

Philadelphia & the Pennsylvania Dutch Country

San Diego

San Francisco

Santa Fe, Taos, Albuquerque

Seattle & Vancouver

The South

The U.S. & British Virgin Islands

The Upper Great Lakes Region

USA

Vacations in New York State

Vacations on the Jersey Shore

Virginia & Maryland

Waikiki

Washington, D.C.

Foreign Guides

Acapulco, Ixtapa, Zihuatanejo

Australia & New Zealand

Austria

The Bahamas

Baja & Mexico's Pacific Coast Resorts

Barbados

Berlin

Bermuda

Brazil

Budapest

Budget Europe

Canada

Cancun, Cozumel, Yucatan Peninsula

Caribbean

Central America

China

Costa Rica, Belize, Guatemala

Czechoslovakia

Eastern Europe

Egypt

Euro Disney

Europe

Europe's Great Cities

France

Germany

Great Britain

Greece

The Himalayan Countries

Hong Kong

India

Ireland

Israel

Italy

Italy's Great Cities

Japan

Kenya & Tanzania

Korea

London

Madrid & Barcelona

Mexico

Montreal & Quebec City

Morocco

The Netherlands Belgium & Luxembourg

New Zealand

Norway

Nova Scotia, Prince Edward Island & New Brunswick

Paris

Portugal

Rome

Russia & the Baltic Countries

Scandinavia

Scotland

Singapore

South America

Southeast Asia

South Pacific

Spain

Sweden

Switzerland

Thailand

Tokyo

Toronto

Turkey

Vienna & the Danube Valley

Yugoslavia

Special Series

Fodor's Affordables

Affordable Europe

Affordable France

Affordable Germany

Affordable Great
Britain

Affordable Italy

**Fodor's Bed &
Breakfast and
Country Inns Guides**

California

Mid-Atlantic Region

New England

The Pacific Northwest

The South

The West Coast

The Upper Great
Lakes Region

Canada's Great
Country Inns

Cottages, B&Bs and
Country Inns of
England and Wales

The Berkeley Guides

On the Loose in
California

On the Loose in
Eastern Europe

On the Loose in
Mexico

On the Loose in the
Pacific Northwest &
Alaska

**Fodor's Exploring
Guides**

Exploring California

Exploring Florida

Exploring France

Exploring Germany

Exploring Paris

Exploring Rome

Exploring Spain

Exploring Thailand

Fodor's Flashmaps

New York

Washington, D.C.

Fodor's Pocket Guides

Pocket Bahamas

Pocket Jamaica

Pocket London

Pocket New York
City

Pocket Paris

Pocket Puerto Rico

Pocket San Francisco

Pocket Washington,
D.C.

Fodor's Sports

Cycling

Hiking

Running

Sailing

The Insider's Guide
to the Best Canadian
Skiing

**Fodor's Three-In-Ones
(guidebook, language
cassette, and phrase
book)**

France

Germany

Italy

Mexico

Spain

**Fodor's
Special-Interest
Guides**

Cruises and Ports
of Call

Disney World & the
Orlando Area

Euro Disney

Healthy Escapes

London Companion

Skiing in the USA
& Canada

Sunday in New York

**Fodor's Touring
Guides**

Touring Europe

Touring USA:
Eastern Edition

Touring USA:
Western Edition

**Fodor's Vacation
Planners**

Great American
Vacations

National Parks of the
West

**The Wall Street
Journal Guides to
Business Travel**

Europe

International Cities

Pacific Rim

USA & Canada

WHEREVER YOU TRAVEL, *H*ELP IS NEVER FAR AWAY.

From planning your trip to providing travel assistance along the way, American Express® Travel Service Offices* are always there to help.

Boston/Cape Cod

American Express Travel Service
One Court Street
Boston
(617) 723-8400

**For the office nearest you, call
1-800-YES-AMEX**